InDesign

In Detail

D1514983

ISBN 0-13-016521-2

90000

9 780130 165213

To help you stay up-to-date with InDesign,
we have developed a companion web site to
accompany this book,
a sort of "living appendix":

The Site

*Your source for expert insight into
Adobe's breakthrough publishing package, InDesign!*

Sponsored by Prentice Hall PTR and...
InDesign InDetail
by
Frank Romano and David Broudy

InDesign is pretty inCredible...

...but, like any 1.0 software, it's also a "work in progress," with its share of improvements to come. You'll want some help with those, and that's our site's #1 goal: to give you the up-to-date tips and info you need to survive the transition from whatever you're using now.

...then, there are InDesign's powerful workflow and PDF features, which just might make you a whole lot more productive but call for some serious learning and a good deal of insight into the best ways to get stuff done — from idea through presswork. So that's our #2 goal: to share that real-world insight with you (and to learn from your experiences too).

...and, then comes our #3 goal: to deliver to you Adobe's fixes, enhancements, and updates to InDesign as they happen, to keep you up-to-date from here on out.

**So, go to http://www.phptr.com/indesign
and stay in touch with InDesign throughout the year...**

InDesign
InDetail

Frank Romano ▪ David Broudy

Prentice Hall
PTR

PRENTICE HALL PTR, UPPER SADDLE RIVER, NJ 07458
WWW.PHPTR.COM

Editorial/Production Supervision: *Patti Guerrieri*
Acquisitions Editor: *Tim Moore*
Editorial Assistant: *Julie Okulicz*
Buyer: *Maura Goldstaub*
Art Director: *Gail Cocker-Bogusz*
Interior Series Design: *Meg Van Arsdale*
Cover Design: *Anthony Gemmellaro*
Cover Design Direction: *Jerry Votta*

© 2000 Prentice Hall PTR
Prentice-Hall, Inc.
Upper Saddle River, NJ 07458

The publisher offers discounts on this book when ordered in bulk quantities.
For more information, contact

Corporate Sales Department,
Prentice Hall PTR
One Lake Street
Upper Saddle River, NJ 07458
Phone: 800-382-3419; FAX: 201-236-7141
E-mail (Internet): corpsales@prenhall.com

Printed in the United States of America

10 9 8 7 6 5 4 3 2 1

ISBN 0-13-016521-2

Prentice-Hall International (UK) Limited, *London*
Prentice-Hall of Australia Pty. Limited, *Sydney*
Prentice-Hall Canada Inc., *Toronto*
Prentice-Hall Hispanoamericana, S.A., *Mexico*
Prentice-Hall of India Private Limited, *New Delhi*
Prentice-Hall of Japan, Inc., *Tokyo*
Pearson Education Asia Pte. Ltd.
Editora Prentice-Hall do Brasil, Ltda., *Rio de Janeiro*

CONTENTS

FOREWORD

InDesign opens a new chapter in Adobe's publishing strategy. We have spent over five years crafting an architecture and implementing features that will take us and the design community into the next century.

Really great tools allow the designer to create anything that the imagination can conceive, and make the hopelessly complex task seem simple.

We believe that InDesign is a tool that does both.

John Warnock
Chairman of the Board & Chief Executive Officer
Adobe Systems, Inc.

ACKNOWLEDGMENTS

We would like to thank many people. First and foremost, Tim Cole of Adobe Systems, Inc. He was, and continues to be, an almost limitless resource about InDesign. Catch his demos at a Seybold conference or some other event if you can—it will be well worth the time.

Also from Adobe, Kevin McGrath and the Chairman of the Board who types his own e-mail, John Warnock.

At Prentice-Hall, thanks to Tim Moore, Patti Guerrieri, and our favorite copyeditor, Truly Donovan.

At RIT, Dave Clark and Ron Goldberg were there when we really needed the help.

Frank Romano
David Broudy

1

INTRODUCTION

What's InDesign?

Adobe InDesign was released August 30, 1999.

Well, let's start by clarifying what InDesign is *not*. It's not a word processor, though you could use it for that. It's not an illustration program, though you could also use it for that too. InDesign (and any other page layout application) is *intended* to be used to assemble documents from text, illustrations, and images generated in other applications, but it's certainly possible to create terrific pages and most of their elements without ever leaving InDesign. Here's a short list of what you can do with InDesign.

- Create books, magazines, newspapers, flyers, brochures, newsletters, posters, banners, billboards, and just about anything else, but then you've always been able to create these things in QuarkXPress and PageMaker. But you now have more precision and more control than ever before.

- Create pages that are up to 1,296 picas (18 feet or 5.48 meters) square, or as small as a single pica (0.16 inches or 0.421 centimeters) square, with up to ten pages in a spread—now *there* is a gatefold. QuarkXPress and PageMaker limit your document size to 48 inches in each direction. QuarkXPress offers an unlimited number of pages per spread, as long as the spread doesn't exceed 48 in. in width. PageMaker never supported spreads wider than two pages. You could, if you wanted, create a ten-page spread in InDesign with 18-foot pages, giving you a 180-square- foot document. This is just the thing for that custom linoleum printing project, assuming you have access to an 18-foot wide decorating gravure press. Actually, the growth of wide-format printing necessitates some of this.

- Draw and illustrate within the program. InDesign offers many of the same illustration tools that Adobe Illustrator does, such as Bézier curves and blends, and it also lets you create content frames that can be nested within other frames. QuarkXPress 4 offers similar tools, but it doesn't offer the frame-nesting capability. PageMaker doesn't offer any drawing tools other than the ability to draw circles and rectangles, and its frames are little more than an afterthought in reaction to the frames that QuarkXPress has had since version 1.0 in 1987. PageMaker was frame-less until version 6.5.

- Import existing PageMaker (version 6.5 only) and QuarkXPress (versions 3.3 and 4.0) files and templates from both Macintosh and Windows versions, within limits, of course. Don't expect translated InDesign documents to be exact replicas of the originals, but InDesign offers a simple means of incorporating "legacy" documents and templates into a new InDesign workflow. We estimate that you can convert 90 percent of the QuarkXpress files, with manual "noodling" to tweak them to 100 percent. If you have PageMaker files from versions older than 6.5, you'll have to convert them to version 6.5 format in PageMaker 6.5 in order to use them with InDesign.

- Switch to (within limits) the key commands and shortcuts used in QuarkXPress. Sorry, no key command sets for PageMaker are included. If these aren't what you want, you can assign a keystroke to nearly anything.

- Create layered documents that might contain, for example, different language versions of a particular project. You could create a sales sheet with the translated copy residing in multiple layers, then simply turn on each layer as needed for printing or display. Layers are also very handy for creating versions of documents based on the same format, such as product brochures, and they make it easy to separate a document's design elements for ease of selection and editing. Layers are available on document pages and on master pages. QuarkXpress has never had a layers feature, but PageMaker added it in version 6.5.

- Create new layouts automatically from a source document with the automatic layout adjustment feature. You can set many parameters to control how InDesign performs autolayout adjustment. You could change a document's page orientation from portrait to landscape, for example, with a minimum of cleanup work by using the autolayout adjustment function.

- Create Acrobat PDF (Portable Document Format) and HTML (Hypertext Markup Language, the lingua franca of the world wide web) versions of InDesign projects. QuarkXPress and Acrobat have not gotten along very well, and PageMaker simply adds an automated function to send a document to Acrobat Distiller. InDesign reads and writes Acrobat PDF without any extra software.

- Creating HTML web pages from a page layout application used to be a huge pain—QuarkXPress had no means of writing HTML without add-on XTensions, and PageMaker's HTML generation was poorly implemented and not really that useful. InDesign will export an entire document as a complete set of HTML documents, including the images. Don't expect the HTML versions to look exactly like the original InDesign document, though; HTML will display differently on nearly every computer used to view it. This is just the way it works—the only way to ensure that your document looks the same on every computer is to serve it up as a PDF file. However, InDesign does a pretty good job of preserving a document's layout when converting to HTML.

- Use contextual menus for help and as shortcuts. InDesign offers a contextual system where you can control+click (MacOS) or right-click (Windows) the mouse on an object or panel and invoke a menu that's specific to that object or control. Neither PageMaker nor QuarkXPress offers contextual menus.

- Create paragraph *and* character styles. QuarkXPress 4.0 introduced the sorely needed character style; PageMaker never offered it.

- Package files for sending to a printer or graphic arts service bureau. PageMaker has always had a lead over QuarkXPress in this capability; QuarkXPress has the simple "Collect for Output" function, which merely moves the document and all linked images into a designated folder, which is useful—but no font collection. There are QuarkXTensions that include this capability. PageMaker and InDesign will do that, and both will also collect all fonts used in a document and save them to a specified folder (after warning you to make sure that your font license allows this). Both will also create "packages," compressed archives of everything used in a layout document. InDesign also adds a "preflight" function, which searches the document and alerts you to any potential prepress problems.

- Use ICC (International Color Consortium) color management functions and device profiles to maintain consistent color throughout the production process. Current versions of the Macintosh operating system include Apple's ColorSync color management system; an analogous system (ICM) exists for Microsoft Windows. QuarkXPress 3.0 introduced the industry's first stab at device-independent color management, called EFIColor, which was a nice try, but it never worked (if you still use QuarkXPress 3.3 with EFIColor, get rid of the EFI extensions if you plan on getting consistent color output). InDesign uses the new Adobe Rainbow Bridge color management interface technology for ICC color management.

- Create multilingual documents, and hyphenate and spell words correctly in any of 21 languages supported by InDesign. QuarkXPress offers its very expensive Passport version of QuarkXPress that supports seven European languages, whereas PageMaker only exists in single-language versions. InDesign includes this capability for free. We like free. You might think it's no big deal, but if you use foreign words like "smörgåsbord" or whatever in your work, InDesign can hyphenate and spellcheck them correctly because you can specify a language for every word in a document. This is handy if you need to use foreign-language copy in your documents and don't know the language.

- InDesign supports many languages and specialty dictionaries standard with the program, as shown in Figure 1–1.

- In the past, these dictionaries were either not available in all countries or cost quite a bit of money to purchase. Unlike Quark's Passport, however, you can't change the operating language of InDesign without buying, for example, a French version of the program, but you can hyphenate and justify a paragraph in another language, which is more useful, especially if you have a bilingual document.

- Support the most extensive plug-in capabilty ever created, so that developers can extend InDesign functionality in almost any direction. Certain plug-ins will be required and InDesign will not open without them. But in every other case, InDesign will open a file even if a plug-in is missing. There will be gray boxes for missing plug-ins. Over 30 plug-in developers are at work. If you hold down the Command/Control key as you click "About InDesign" you will get the screen showing plug-ins installed, program version, and other useful information, as shown in Figure 1–2. This is similar to Quark's "Environment" screen.

- Create an object-oriented program with a modular architecture that will eventually allow Adobe to outdevelop virtually anyone. Look for more workflow functionality.

```
Catalan
Danish
Dutch
English: UK
✓ English: USA
English: USA Legal
English: USA Medical
Finnish
French
French: Canadian
German
German: Reformed
German: Swiss
Italian
Norwegian: Bokmal
Norwegian: Nynorsk
Portuguese
Portuguese: Brazilian
Spanish: Castilian
Swedish
```

Figure 1–1
Language support in InDesign.

Check the Adobe web site constantly for so-called dot upgrades. We expect a number of them.

Figure 1–2
InDesign plug-in capability.

- Open a file created in, for example, a Danish version of InDesign for additional design and production in an English version of the program without having all of the hyphenations go insane. You can't do this in QuarkXPress unless you have the Passport version, and you can't do it at all in PageMaker unless you have an optional dictionary installed for that specific language. If you're running a non-Roman operating system (for example, Chinese or Russian) or have a language kit installed, you can also enter, save, and edit non-Roman text in any Roman-language version of InDesign. No program before has ever offered these multiple language features as a standard component.

The first release of InDesign should be considered a work-in-progress. Future versions will include additional features that are missing in version 1.0, or plug-ins will be available to perform some functions that are missing in the first or other versions.

For example, you can't create a table of contents, or an index, without purchasing plug-ins. There's no simple imposition function like PageMaker's "build booklet" feature.

Trapping in version 1.0 only works with PostScript Level 3 RIPS which have the optional in-RIP trapping module. Object-level trapping and trapping support for older PostScript Level 2 RIPs may appear in future versions or may be provided by a third-party plug-in. Current trapping solutions like ScenicSoft (formerly Imation, formerly Luminous, formerly Aldus), TrapWise, or DK&A Trapper will, however, trap InDesign files in a traditional pre-RIP trapping workflow.

Expect the user interface to evolve as well. PageMaker and Quark-XPress didn't do it all either when they were first released. InDesign has been the largest single effort in Adobe's history; yet despite that, there's simply no way to cram every possible feature into the first release. But we think there is more than enough to create exceptional work.

Documents on the Adobe Systems web site cover many InDesign issues as well as the following special topics:

- Converting QuarkXPress and PageMaker documents, with details on preparing documents for conversion.
- Prepress applications and InDesign, with details on fitting InDesign into prepress workflows.

To view or download these documents, follow the links to the InDesign section of the Adobe Systems web site (www.adobe.com) and then to the sections devoted to conversion and prepress issues.

A Little History

A then-unknown company called Aldus Corporation in Seattle, Washington, delivered a primitive page layout program in 1985 called PageMaker. Its release coincided with that of Apple's revolutionary LaserWriter printer. PageMaker 1.0 was very limited, could only handle about ten pages, and its abilities would be laughed at mightily today, but this program and the LaserWriter started the revolution in desktop and digital publishing, a business that's now worth multiple billions of dollars annually. Soon other programs were released that also did the same thing, most of them long forgotten: MacPublisher, Ready!Set!Go! (that one deserved to die solely because of its name), and QuarkXPress, which came in 1987.

On the PC side, nothing was available that even came close to doing what PageMaker could do on the Mac, until an upstart company called Ventura Software released its Ventura Publisher application. This program ran circles around what was available on the Mac at the time, but it was difficult to use and ran under Digital Research's GEM system, an early and unsuccessful (though more advanced) graphical user interface that preceded the Microsoft Windows environment by a year or so. Xerox had it for a while but could not figure out what to do with it. Ventura Publisher succeeded in some high-end applications and is still around today as a product of Corel Software, although its market share is tiny.

Aldus realized that the PC market was critical to its success and devoted much time and effort to developing a Windows version of PageMaker. In doing so, the Mac version languished at the expense of the Windows version, and Quark's XPress program was released at a very receptive time in the Mac publishing market. It became very popular among graphic professionals because it offered high-end typographical and color printing features that PageMaker lacked and didn't offer until it was far too late to catch up. This is one reason why PageMaker never really caught on with Mac-based professionals, although it did and does remain the leader with Windows users.

The other applications eventually went away, except for Ventura Publisher, and Ready!Set!Go! hung on until a few years ago.

The page layout software market has been moribund for years—Quark is king and Adobe's PageMaker has been an also-ran. Quark took almost seven years from the time version 3.0 was released to deliver the underwhelming version 4.0 of XPress, yet many professionals still use version 3.3 for lots of reasons: it's fast, very stable, and very well supported by the vast majority of prepress shops, equipment vendors, and professional software applications that automate the printing process. QuarkXPress 3.3 is definitely beginning to show its age though—it does not run well on some of the newer Macintosh and Windows computers, and it doesn't run at all under Windows NT. It will run under Windows 98, but only in 16-bit emulation mode, which translates to "glacially slow." PageMaker was last revised in 1996 with version 6.5; further development of this program is unclear, so don't expect big changes to it other than maintenance fixes to support new computers or revised operating systems, since Adobe is planning to continue the product.

There's a number of reasons why PageMaker never really caught on in the generally Mac-based graphic arts industry, despite its popularity in Windows-based business environments. PageMaker's biggest flaw has always been its closed architecture. Quark early on adopted an open software model that allowed third-party companies to develop special software extensions, officially called XTensions by Quark, that add certain functions to the program.

These extensions range from free things that add a little bit of function, like the Bobzilla (whatever!) extension that came with QuarkXPress 3.3 and added the ability to quickly pop up a list of pages and then go right to a specific page, to huge, industrial-strength applications that costs thousands of dollars and range from newspaper publishing systems to database printing and variable-data printing systems (see *Personalized and Database Printing: The Complete Guide* [Salem, NH: GAMA Publishing, 1999] for more info on that).

When Quark introduced version 4.0 of QuarkXPress, many of the extensions for version 3.3 did not work at all or only worked partially. QuarkXPress 4.0 took liberties when converting version 3.3 files to version 4.0 without bothering to tell anyone, and users found themselves paying for useless film and separations from service bureaus. For example, QuarkXPress 4.0 would often create unwanted and badly formed clipping paths around all images present in a version 3.3 file, which most users didn't even notice until presented with a big fat bill for useless film.

The new version also "broke" most professional prepress applications that perform trapping and imposition, and it was some time before these expensive programs were updated to fix all of the problems caused by QuarkXPress 4.0. There are other reasons why the new

like PageMaker or QuarkXPress. That's why the hardware requirements for InDesign are so steep compared to those of the other two programs. Price of progress and all that. Improvements in computer hardware performance have historically outpaced the ability of software developers to take advantage of them. That paradigm may be changing soon, as we expect the modular application approach to become much more prevalent in the future.

PageMaker lives on as a down-market application targeted at home and office users in a version called PageMaker 6.5 Plus, which is really the same application delivered with an enormous number of pre-built templates and a large library of clip art and stock photos. Expect a flood of look-alike documents and publications to hit laser printers everywhere. Look ma, I'm a designer!

InDesign and Other Adobe Applications

In developing InDesign, Adobe leveraged its investment in its other graphic arts applications, namely Photoshop and Illustrator, and developed a central graphics software model, or engine, called Adobe Graphics Model. These applications now share a common user interface, a common imaging model, and even many common commands.

InDesign has very close ties to Photoshop 5, Illustrator 8, and Acrobat 4, and all of these programs are designed to work together without a lot of file exporting and format changes.

InDesign supports placement of native Photoshop and Illustrator files without having to save these as TIFF or EPS files. It also supports placement and export of Acrobat PDF files, and it is the lone page layout application designed to work in a PDF-based workflow.

Some technical features of InDesign and Photoshop 5, Illustrator 8, and Acrobat 4:

- They all use the Adobe Graphics Model (AGM) for the on-screen display of images and illustrations. AGM is Adobe's graphics display engine, loosely based on the Display PostScript technology first seen in the NeXT computer. It is designed to provide consistent image display from one Adobe application to another.

- InDesign incorporates the Adobe Rainbow Bridge and the Adobe CMS (color management system). The Rainbow Bridge acts as an interface for various color management systems (CMSs), such as Apple ColorSync, Microsoft ICM, Adobe's own CMS, Kodak's CMS, and others. An application like InDesign or Illustrator uses the Rainbow Bridge to communicate with an operating-system-level CMS (like ColorSync), or a third-party CMS (like that of Kodak or Adobe), which allows for platform- and CMS-independent color management.

- InDesign displays EPS files, using a modular parsing system, which in essence is a built-in PostScript interpreter that is used to render the on-screen appearance of imported EPS at high magnifications with the high-resolution display preference enabled. A similar system is used in Photoshop for rasterizing imported EPS images, and in Illustrator for parsing and converting EPS files from other applications. A nice benefit of InDesign's parsing system kicks in when you are placing EPS files: if PostScript errors are present in the file, you'll be alerted to this fact when placing the file, not when your job is at a print shop and causing the operator of a $350-per-hour computer-to-plate system to wish you grave bodily harm.

If you have enough memory, you can keep InDesign, Illustrator, and Photoshop all open at once, and either drag and drop or copy and paste illustrations from Illustrator right into an open InDesign document, where they will be interpreted and then treated as editable InDesign objects. You can't drag Photoshop images into InDesign or Illustrator; however, you can place native Photoshop files into InDesign, which will flatten any layers and convert the image to TIFF format. This saves you the extra step of flattening and saving a Photoshop image as a TIFF file. You can also drag or paste artwork from Macromedia Freehand 8 and Corel Draw into InDesign; the modular parsing system will convert this artwork to editable InDesign objects.

All objects dragged into an InDesign document from an illustration program are placed within a frame and can be further edited with the Direct Selection tool.

You can export an InDesign document as a PDF file directly, without having to first save the document as a PostScript file and then digest that through Acrobat Distiller. It's the first page layout application to do all this stuff right in the program; you don't need to constantly switch between programs in order to make a change, export the file again, then re-place the image or illustration back into the page layout program. This is a time-saver that graphics professionals will love.

Overall, InDesign is huge improvement in document assembly and layout. PageMaker barely tolerates other Adobe applications, cannot use native Illustrator and Photoshop files, does not support drag-and-drop technology from outside the application, can't directly export PDF, and uses an interface inconsistent with other Adobe programs. The same is true for QuarkXPress.

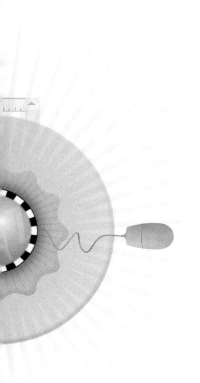

2

GETTING STARTED

We'll assume you've already installed InDesign according to the instructions in the InDesign manual.

System Requirements

Let's face it, InDesign has some pretty stiff hardware requirements for optimum performance. While Adobe says it'll run on a PowerPC 603e-equipped Power Macintosh with at least 32 MB of free memory, or a Pentium-equipped Windows computer with 48 MB of free memory, forget about running it on the bare minimum system. We don't recommend even bothering trying to run it unless you have a Power Macintosh with at least a 604e processor running at 200 MHz or faster, or a Pentium II running at least 300 MHz or faster; if you can swing it, go with the fastest G4 Mac or Pentium III system you can get your hands on. Stuff as much memory into the computer as you can afford because not only does InDesign like lots of free

For the absolute best performance:

- **PowerPC G3/G4.**

- **128 MB or more of physical RAM.**

- **24-bit display.**

- **Internet connection.**

For Mac Users Only:

InDesign is initially set to use 20 MB of RAM. You can reset the amount of memory allocated to InDesign. Select the InDesign application icon from the Finder (do not start InDesign), and choose File ➠ Get Info. In the dialog box that appears, choose *Memory* from the Show pop-up menu, and, depending on the amount of RAM in your system, type the following value in the Preferred field:

- **30 if you have 128 MB of RAM**

- **50 if you have 256 MB of RAM**

---

memory, you'll need it if you plan to run any other applications alongside it, like Photoshop or Illustrator. Disk space is cheap nowadays, so you might as well upgrade storage capacity at the same time. Lastly, an accelerated video card for either platform will make a huge difference in perceived performance because these can increase scrolling and panning speed several hundred percent.

InDesign requires the latest versions of the operating system—for Power Macs, you need MacOS 8.5.1 or higher (don't use 8.5; it's got a few problems), and Windows users need to be running Windows 98 or NT 4.0 with Service Pack 3 or higher. There are currently no plans to offer InDesign for Linux, BeOS, or DEC Alpha versions of Windows NT.

Recommended System Configuration for the Serious InDesign User

Macintosh

- A G3 processor, preferably 300 MHz or better. You can get G3 processor cards for older PCI Power Macs that, along with an accelerated video card, can bring these older systems up to the performance level of the wacky-looking blue and white G3 systems. Look for cards that offer at least 1 MB of "backside" cache, even though you wouldn't think your backside would ever need to be cached. Alternatively, a 333 MHz Revision D iMac with plenty of memory would make a decent system for running InDesign, although the built-in 15" display is a little puny. As we write this, the new G4 has been introduced. Apple says it is so fast, it is faster than itself.

- Upgraded video memory to 4 MB (built-in video for PCI Power Macs) or an accelerated PCI video card with at least 4 MB and preferably 8 MB of video memory.

- For older PCI Power Macs, invest in an Ultra Wide SCSI card and a nice fast Ultra Wide drive like the Seagate Barracuda. Newer G3 systems and iMacs use the IDE/ATA drive interface, but they can benefit from the newer UltraATA disk drive standard, which is faster and offers higher capacities than the older plain IDE/ATA standard.

Romano's Law: Data will expand to fill all available disk space. You might think an 18-GB drive will hold you for a few years, until you get comfortable with the idea of such enormous capacity.

Windows

- A Pentium II or III processor running at least 400 MHz. Older systems can sometimes be upgraded with a new processor, so check with your system vendor for upgrade information. The many variants of "Wintel" systems and processors can make this sort of thing into a major research project just trying to figure out what will work with what, especially since many of the Pentium-class processors are not made by Intel, or are cost-reduced versions such as the Celeron processor, which sounds like some sort of vegetable extract or kitchen appliance, and some of these aren't compatible with each other.
- An accelerated video card with at least 4 MB and preferably 8 MB of video memory.
- Since Windows and SCSI have never really gotten on all that well, the newer UltraATA hard disk drives are a good and relatively inexpensive way to upgrade your system storage. Mac users are often jealous of the 2X price differential between an ATA and a SCSI version of the same drive.

Both

- At least 128 MB of system memory, preferably 256 MB. Memory is so cheap these days that there's really no excuse for not having as much as you can cram into the machine. Some Power Macs and Pentium systems can take as much as 1 gigabyte of main memory, although in 1999 that's overkill. In 2002 it probably won't be so. InDesign lets you move between Illustrator and

On systems with less than 128 MB, there is not necessarily a noticeable improvement in performance when you adjust the Preferred setting.

To launch InDesign, the amount of RAM specified in the Preferred field must be available, plus an additional 1 MB of system heap memory (with Virtual Memory turned on), or an additional 20 MB of system heap memory (with Virtual Memory turned off). If InDesign reports that there is insufficient memory to start up, decrease the value in the Preferred field such that enough memory becomes available. If you have reset the Preferred field correctly and InDesign still reports that there is insufficient memory to start up, try restarting your Macintosh to reset system memory.

Apple just introduced an LCD display that is fit for Cinemascope. You can actually see a full spread plus all the InDesign palettes.

Photoshop so both programs will be open, and that is another reason to increase memory.

- Invest in the biggest monitor you can afford and that your desk can support without collapsing (19-in. to 21-in. monitors can weigh 75–100 lbs!). Like other layout programs, InDesign cries for more screen real estate. With all those palettes, you need a big monitor. Look for the brightest, sharpest display; often, monitors that use the Sony Trinitron picture tube deliver very bright, sharp pictures, although some of the monitors that use the Invar shadow-mask technology are just as bright and sharp. Avoid suspiciously cheap big-screen monitors because they're usually dim and blurry and will destroy your eyes within a few weeks. LCD monitors are going to be the Next Big Thing, but currently there's a bit of a standards battle going on, and the things are very expensive anyway. Wait.

- There's nothing more soul-destroying than a failed hard disk drive, a system crash, or a virus/trojan horse that wipes out all of your files and programs. This is why a data backup system like a tape drive can save your sanity if the unthinkable occurs. If it's never happened to you, wait. It will. Our last book was pushed back a few weeks because one of our computers was hit by a malicious program (a trojan horse) that corrupted the main drive, and the last backup was a few weeks old. If you don't want to bother with a tape drive—they're expensive, slow, and usually tie up your system for hours—at least buy something like a Zip or Jaz drive and regularly copy your work onto a removable disk or even two. For extra insurance, make extra copies and store one off-site somewhere in case of fire or other disaster. Virus protection programs are a good investment, but the bad guys always seem to be one step ahead.

When printing from InDesign, be sure to specify *PostScript 2 Only* or *PostScript 3 Only* in the printer driver's PostScript

- A PostScript printer is a must—many of the features of InDesign (and Illustrator, and Photoshop) don't work with non-PostScript printers such as most inexpensive inkjets or most laser printers designed for Windows systems. There are PostScript software drivers for many inkjets, such as BirmyRIP and Adobe's new PressReady (which works via Acrobat), that

its age though—it does not run well on some of the newer Macintosh and Windows computers, and it doesn't run at all under Windows NT. It will run under Windows 98, but only in 16-bit emulation mode, which translates to "glacially slow." PageMaker was last revised in 1996 with version 6.5; further development of this program is unclear, so don't expect big changes to it other than maintenance fixes to support new computers or revised operating systems, since Adobe is planning to continue the product.

There's a number of reasons why PageMaker never really caught on in the generally Mac-based graphic arts industry, despite its popularity in Windows-based business environments. PageMaker's biggest flaw has always been its closed architecture. Quark early on adopted an open software model that allowed third-party companies to develop special software extensions, officially called XTensions by Quark, that add certain functions to the program.

These extensions range from free things that add a little bit of function, like the Bobzilla (whatever!) extension that came with QuarkXPress 3.3 and added the ability to quickly pop up a list of pages and then go right to a specific page, to huge, industrial-strength applications that costs thousands of dollars and range from newspaper publishing systems to database printing and variable-data printing systems (see *Personalized and Database Printing: The Complete Guide* [Salem, NH: GAMA Publishing, 1999] for more info on that).

When Quark introduced version 4.0 of QuarkXPress, many of the extensions for version 3.3 did not work at all or only worked partially. QuarkXPress 4.0 took liberties when converting version 3.3 files to version 4.0 without bothering to tell anyone, and users found themselves paying for useless film and separations from service bureaus. For example, QuarkXPress 4.0 would often create unwanted and badly formed clipping paths around all images present in a version 3.3 file, which most users didn't even notice until presented with a big fat bill for useless film.

The new version also "broke" most professional prepress applications that perform trapping and imposition, and it was some time before these expensive programs were updated to fix all of the problems caused by QuarkXPress 4.0. There are other reasons why the new version was a resounding thud with the industry: the first releases were full of bugs, Quark refused to acknowledge that there were any bugs in the product at all (but quickly and quietly released updates to the program), and they charged owners of previous versions nearly the full price of the program for an upgrade.

PageMaker never supported this level of extensibility, and nobody much bothered trying to develop custom add-ons to PageMaker because of its low visibility in the graphic arts industry. PageMaker supports scripting and a minimal level of application interfaces for extensions, but it's nothing comparable to what QuarkXPress offers. PageMaker also has an image problem—Quark pros tend to sneer at it, and its users tend to be classified as amateurs who couldn't learn how to use a real program. Prepress people can be very catty, and some of the terms we've heard for PageMaker and its users really should not be printed here.

However, aside from the closed architecture, there wasn't anything really wrong with PageMaker; we've created a number of large color jobs with it that separated and printed beautifully. PageMaker now has better typographic controls than does QuarkXPress (though that's a matter of opinion), it's fast, and some people just prefer the way it works over QuarkXPress. PC users especially embraced the program over QuarkXPress, party because early Windows versions of Quark-XPress were really unstable and buggy and partly because the program is easier to learn and use than QuarkXPress. There are a lot more Windows computers than Macs, so the numbers make sense.

Aldus secretly began to work on the successor to PageMaker in the early '90s. They realized that the closed architecture of PageMaker was going to hurt them in the long run, and there was no way of opening it up without rewriting PageMaker from scratch. Instead of doing that, though, Aldus engineers began to specify and develop a completely new software model for PageMaker's successor. Code-named "Shuksan" after a mountain in the Cascade range in Washington state (Aldus was in Seattle), this model was completely modular and object-oriented. Any future software built on Shuksan would consist of a core application and a number of libraries, and would be completely open and accessible to anyone who wanted to develop extensions.

Adobe acquired Aldus Corporation in 1994 and quickly released several updates and eventually some major upgrades to PageMaker. Development on InDesign began in earnest in 1996, after Adobe and former Aldus engineers nailed down the specifications for Shuksan. The Shuksan architecture is expected to be incorporated in other future Adobe products. InDesign is the first.

Adobe had a big hole in its product line, which PageMaker filled nicely while Adobe worked furiously on InDesign. Code-named K2 (after the world's second-tallest mountain, also known as Mount Godwin Austen, in the Karakoram range of the western Himalayas), it has been in development for about four years. When Adobe representatives were asked why Adobe chose "K2" over "Everest," the reply was simply "more climbers have died trying to climb K2 than trying to climb Mount Everest."

InDesign is built very differently from any other desktop application. There's a small core program file; all additional required resources are stored separately in code libraries, and extensions to InDesign are installed by simply being dragged to the InDesign Plug-ins folders. It's an interesting and efficient means of program design, and it makes updating and upgrading a simple operation of replacing an old plug-in with a new one. The modularity means that a developer can create plug-ins that add to InDesign's functionality, that can completely replace an Adobe-written plug-in and that add enhanced functionality, or that modify and work with Adobe plug-ins. This goes beyond modular. It is extraordinary.

For developers, Shuksan gives unprecedented access to all of the application's APIs and internal routines; for end users, Shuksan means no more 20 MB downloads of updates—instead, Adobe will release updates as new plug-ins, and the Adobe Online system built into InDesign can be set up to check for newly updated program components and download them automatically. Make sure you register to have access to this feature.

However, there's a downside to all this modularity. All of the program components are constantly messaging each other, chatting up a storm and flinging huge amounts of data at each other, so the overall effect is a decrease in performance relative to a "monolithic" program like PageMaker or QuarkXPress. That's why the hardware requirements for InDesign are so steep compared to those of the other two programs. Price of progress and all that. Improvements in computer hardware performance have historically outpaced the ability of software developers to take advantage of them. That paradigm may be changing soon, as we expect the modular application approach to become much more prevalent in the future.

PageMaker lives on as a down-market application targeted at home and office users in a version called PageMaker 6.5 Plus, which is really the same application delivered with an enormous number of pre-built templates and a large library of clip art and stock photos. Expect a flood of look-alike documents and publications to hit laser printers everywhere. Look ma, I'm a designer!

InDesign and Other Adobe Applications

In developing InDesign, Adobe leveraged its investment in its other graphic arts applications, namely Photoshop and Illustrator, and developed a central graphics software model, or engine, called Adobe Graphics Model. These applications now share a common user interface, a common imaging model, and even many common commands.

InDesign has very close ties to Photoshop 5, Illustrator 8, and Acrobat 4, and all of these programs are designed to work together without a lot of file exporting and format changes.

InDesign supports placement of native Photoshop and Illustrator files without having to save these as TIFF or EPS files. It also supports placement and export of Acrobat PDF files, and it is the lone page layout application designed to work in a PDF-based workflow.

Some technical features of InDesign and Photoshop 5, Illustrator 8, and Acrobat 4:

- They all use the Adobe Graphics Model (AGM) for the on-screen display of images and illustrations. AGM is Adobe's graphics display engine, loosely based on the Display PostScript technology first seen in the NeXT computer. It is designed to provide excellent quality results on these types of printers. Ideally, though, your printer will have PostScript built into it, such as almost all high-end imagesetters and platesetters and digital color printers, Apple LaserWriters, many HP LaserJets, and all color laser printers, because software PostScript alternatives usually require two or three additional steps to produce printed pages.

- A scanner isn't a necessity, but when you need one, you need it bad. Don't bother with the $99 scanners you see at the CompuMegaMarts; they're barely adequate for text scanning and cannot offer the detail and density range you'll get with the better scanners. Scanners can be useful in some cases for scanning low-resolution FPO (for placement only) images that can later be replaced with professionally scanned, high-resolution images.

- Lastly, nobody can work for long at a station that is not ergonomically correct. Your chair and desk should be at the proper height, you should be using a wrist rest for typing, and your choice of pointing device should not cause your wrist or hand to ache after a few hours. We'll not make any specific recommendations, but after trying a variety of expensive trackballs and other mouse substitutes, one of us went back to the plain old Apple mouse when none of the replacements offered relief and indeed introduced new pains in the wrists.

You can avoid repetitive stress disorders like the notorious carpal tunnel syndrome by using ergonomic equipment, a well-configured desk and chair, and by taking frequent breaks from mousing and keyboarding.

Working Across Platforms

The ongoing battle between Macintosh and Windows users started in earnest around 1989 and shows no signs of letting up. Just visit some of the comp.sys.*.advocacy newsgroups and you'll see people flailing away at each other on-line for weeks about the superiority of one over the other. You have to wonder if these people have a life.

Settings dialog box. The driver's *PostScript 1, 2, and 3 Compatible* option amounts to support for Level 1, which does not meet InDesign's PostScript Level 2 requirement.

Anyway, while we feel it's a little short-sighted to yank Macs out from under users who are used to them and replace them with Windows computers in the name of cost reduction (haha!), fundamentally, there are very few differences in the way most common applications work on a Mac and on a Windows box.

Aside from differences in keystrokes, file-naming conventions, font technology, and printing, InDesign works the same way on both platforms. So do Photoshop, Illustrator, Freehand, QuarkXPress, PageMaker, Corel Draw, et cetera.

Personal preference, experience, and sometimes company policy will dictate which one you will use. Both of us are long-time Mac users, going back to the very first one in 1984, so we'll be the first to admit to some bias.

InDesign actually works more efficiently with a two-button mouse. Mac users can get such an animal and the special software they require.

The biggest obstacle to switching between platforms is the keys used to invoke certain commands.

Mac users have four modifier keys: Shift, Command, Option, and Control. Windows users have three: Shift, Alt (has anyone figured out what "Alt" means?), and Control.

Table 1–1 is the world's simplest guide to Mac <—> Windows key conversion.

There are a few other differences, as shown in Figure 2–1. The *del* key on a PC is really a foward-delete key on the Mac. That is, when pressed, the character to the *right* of the text cursor will be deleted. The *delete* key on a Mac keyboard is the same as the backspace key on a PC. The *return* key on a Mac keyboard is the same as the *enter* key on a PC, but the *enter* key on the far right of a Mac keyboard is different from the *return* key on the same keyboard.

Table 1–1

Key conversions.

Mac		Windows
Command	<—>	Control
Option	<—>	Alt
Control	<—>	Right-hand mouse button
Shift	<—>	Shift

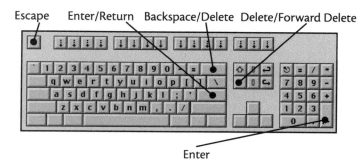

E Z Keys
Windows/Macintosh

Escape   Enter/Return   Backspace/Delete   Delete/Forward Delete

Enter

Figure 2–1
Mac/Windows keyboard comparison.

Another keyboard/mouse difference between the two concerns the rightmost mouse button on Windows computers. Mac mouse devices (usually) only have one button; to "right-click" with a Mac, you hold down the control key and click. On both systems, this action shows a *context-sensitive menu*, the contents of which will change according to where you are and what you're doing (context context context).

File-Naming Conventions

In the old days (before Windows 95), files on PCs were required to conform to the "8.3" file-naming convention, where the file could only have eight characters in the name, plus three in the extension (the part after the period) as in 12345678.123.

For example, IYKWIMAI.TXT is a legal DOS/Windows 3.1 file name, and the Mac could not have cared less about this file name either, and never has, but IYKWIMAITYD.text isn't a valid DOS/Windows 3.1 file name. Macs have always allowed 31 characters in the file name, and the MacOS uses its own internal system for keeping track of what file belongs to which application so it doesn't need extensions on the file names.

Windows 95 and higher allow 256 characters in the file name, but it still requires an extension to figure out what file goes with what program. It's a rather shaky system that persists today, but at least the extensions are now hidden from the user in most cases. If you change a file's extension from .QXD to .P65, for example, a Windows system will think that a QuarkXPress file is now a PageMaker 6.5 file and will launch PageMaker if you double-click the file's icon. It's screwy.

In order to maintain, well, order when moving files between Macs and PCs, it's important for Mac users to recognize this special need of Windows, and Windows users need to keep file names to 31 characters or fewer. Mac users can't put certain characters into file names destined for Windows systems because these have a number of characters that can't be used in file names, and a Windows computer will squawk and complain and fail to recognize the files if they contain "illegal" characters. Here they are: colon, quotes, question mark, asterisk, slash (virgule), backslash, greater-than, less-than (in other words, : " ? * / \ < >). The only character that's off-limits for Macs is the colon (:), which is analogous to the Windows/DOS backslash (\) as a directory delimiter. Table 2–2 summarizes the extensions used in Windows.

Table 2–2
Windows file extensions.

QuarkXPress 3.3/4.0:		
.QXD	(document file)	
.QXT	(template file)	
PageMaker 6:		
.PM6	(document file)	
.PT6	(template file)	
PageMaker 6.5:		
.P65	(document file)	
.T65	(template file)	
InDesign:		
.indd	(document file)	
.indt	(template file)	

(Note that file extensions longer than three characters are only supported in Windows 98 and Windows NT4; these can have mixed cases.)

New Font Technologies

InDesign is the first major application to support the upcoming Adobe/Microsoft OpenType specification. This is a new initiative designed to end the so-called font wars once and for all. A bit of history is in order here: Adobe and Apple worked closely together to develop the PostScript Type 1 font format, which was how the first outline fonts were shipped with the Apple LaserWriter, the first PostScript printer. Adobe kept the Type 1 format a closely guarded secret, and other font vendors had to use the less sophisticated Type 3 format.

Eventually, Apple decided to develop its own font technology, called TrueType, because at the time Apple and Adobe weren't on the best of terms and Apple did not want to rely on another company for such a key technology. Apple stumbled and forgot that many users already had a significant investment in Adobe typefaces and they weren't particularly pleased with this new format, which was incompatible with the Type 1 format and which received little support from typeface vendors (and certainly not from Adobe).

Well, ironically, Apple licensed the Truetype technology to Microsoft, which incorporated it into Windows 3.0, and the rest is history. The majority of Windows computers use only Truetype fonts, and additional software in the form of Adobe Type Manager (ATM) is required for the use of Type 1 fonts on a Windows computer.

There's been some contention that Type 1 technology is superior to that of TrueType. That's not quite true, but what is true is this: few vendors of professional-quality typefaces ever supported the Truetype format, and most of the so-called junk type is released in Truetype format for Windows. So, there's much more garbage floating around in TrueType format than there is in Type 1 format. There's no reason that TrueType typefaces can't contain the same level of quality that Type 1 faces do, but the publishing industry has long used Type 1, and many graphics shops still refuse to accept jobs that contain TrueType fonts. It's more than a bias, though, because some types of imaging equipment have trouble processing Truetype fonts. This isn't the format's fault, though.

Enter OpenType. First, it's cross-platform. The same physical file can be used on either a Mac or Windows computer. The current version of MacOS, 8.6, provides limited support for OpenType. MacOS 9.0 and OS X, which are not that far away, are alleged to include more extensive support of OpenType. The next major release of Windows will also natively support OpenType because OpenType is an extension of TrueType, which Windows has supported for years. Presently, OpenType fonts are only supported directly in InDesign on both platforms.

Even with OpenType supported by the operating system, application support is required to take advantage of the character substitution features of OpenType. This feature, called *glyph substitution*, lets a program automatically substitute ligatures, old-style figures, true or "cut" small caps, and other advanced typographical entities. For example, the most common ligatures are those for the letter pairs "fi" and "fl."

These are built into nearly all Macintosh Type 1 and TrueType fonts, although until now only QuarkXPress has offered automatic substitution of fi and fl ligatures for these letter pairs, and only on the Macintosh. Ligatures are not supported with Windows fonts; you'll need an expert version of a typeface to use them. InDesign will ultimately offer the most extensive glyph substitution ever, so that typography can truly be automated.

What in the World Are You Talking About?   Here are a few examples of ligatures, old-style figures, and cut small caps. It's a lot simpler to show them than it is to explain just what they are. Use of these typographical entities is the mark of a professional designer who cares about typography.

Ligatures are single-glyph replacements for certain pairs of letters (plain pairs on the left, ligatures on the right).

fi fl ff ffi ffl   fi fl ff ffi ffl

Notice the difference between the ligatures and the plain letter pairs. Ligatures are sometimes created for other letter pairs like ct and st, typically for use in decorative or historical typesetting. InDesign 1.0 will only substitute the ff, ffl, and ffi ligatures automatically when the text is set in an OpenType font, and then only if the font contains them. Not all OpenType fonts will offer a full set of ligatures. InDesign will break automatic ligatures if manual kerning is applied.

Lining numerals vs. *old-style figures* (on the right):

1 2 3 4 5 6   1 2 3 4 5 6

Old-style (sometimes called nonlining) figures are frequently used in book typesetting. They're much easier to read in passages of text than the modern (lining) figures that end up being used by default in most cases. Few typefaces use these by default, and it's always been a huge pain to swap out lining figures from the standard version of a typeface with nonlining figures from an expert version of the typeface.

Unfortunately, InDesign 1.0 will only support this feature with OpenType fonts, and the same caveats apply here as with ligatures.

Cut small caps:

AA BB CC DD   AA BB CC DD

Cut small caps look a lot more like full caps because the character weight is preserved. Notice how the artificially generated small caps on the left look a little spindly in comparison to the full caps—they are simply squashed versions of the full caps, and the stroke weights suffer in the squashing process. InDesign *will* properly substitute Type 1 Expert small caps if there is a matching expert font loaded with the base font.

Currently and in the past, using these typographical entities involved buying an "expert" version of a typeface, and it also involves a lot of work on the designer's part to manually search and replace the plain entities with the expert versions. OpenType will eliminate this tedious business, and the advanced entities can be turned on or off with a simple preference setting in the application.

InDesign is the first program that will support automatic glyph substitution, although currently the feature only works with OpenType fonts. InDesign doesn't support ligature and old-style figure substitution with Type 1 fonts, even with the expert version installed, which is a real shame since nobody even has any OpenType fonts yet. The program ships with an OpenType version of the Tekton typeface, which if you like that sort of thing, will be a nice benefit.

We sure hope Adobe offers this ability with Type 1 fonts, since it doesn't actually require an OpenType font to implement this feature, Adobe's expert sets all have the same encoding, and many people and businesses have a fortune invested in large Type 1 type libraries. It's also incredibly more efficient for typesetting than the old way of having to switch fonts or search and replace.

OpenType will be a huge bonus for languages, such as Arabic, Japanese, Hebrew, Thai, and many others, that use non-Roman alphabets and glyphs. It also supports positional glyph substitution, important in Arabic because the particular symbol used for a character depends on its position within a word. In addition, a single OpenType font file can contain numerous versions of a typeface, for example, both Roman and Cyrillic versions of a particular typeface can be stored within the same file. This simplifies multilingual typesetting significantly.

What's in the InDesign Folder?

Plenty. Figure 2–2 and Figure 2–3 show what you should see in the program folder after you install InDesign. Note that some of the items shown may or may not be present in the final version of the software, but, in general, the folder organization should remain the same.

Inside the InDesign Folder   The files starting with *AGM* are the code libraries that provide support for the Adobe Graphics Model.

Fonts folder—this is where OpenType fonts supplied with the program are stored. In the future, when Mac and Windows operating systems support OpenType, this folder may no longer be needed, but for now, it is. Any fonts located in this folder will be available to InDesign, but they won't be available to any other applications.

Help folder—The InDesign help databases are stored here.

InDesign Defaults—Here's where all of the settings and adjustments you make to InDesign's preferences, which you invoke from File ➡ Preferences, are saved. If you want to reset the preferences to the just-installed state or if you suspect that a corrupted preferences file is causing some problems, just delete this file. InDesign will create a new one the next time you start it up. Preferences are discussed in detail in Chapter 3.

InDesign Libraries—This is a set of code modules that InDesign loads as needed.

Figure 2–2
The InDesign folder on a Macintosh.

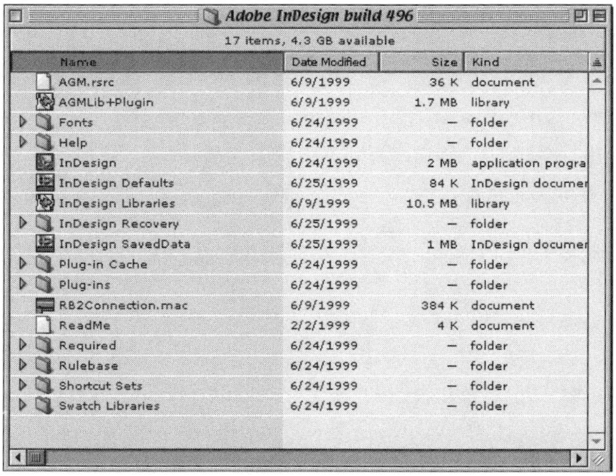

Name	Date Modified	Size	Kind
AGM.rsrc	6/9/1999	36 K	document
AGMLib+Plugin	6/9/1999	1.7 MB	library
▷ Fonts	6/24/1999	—	folder
▷ Help	6/24/1999	—	folder
InDesign	6/24/1999	2 MB	application progra
InDesign Defaults	6/25/1999	84 K	InDesign documer
InDesign Libraries	6/9/1999	10.5 MB	library
▷ InDesign Recovery	6/25/1999	—	folder
InDesign SavedData	6/25/1999	1 MB	InDesign documer
▷ Plug-in Cache	6/24/1999	—	folder
▷ Plug-ins	6/24/1999	—	folder
RB2Connection.mac	6/9/1999	384 K	document
ReadMe	2/2/1999	4 K	document
▷ Required	6/24/1999	—	folder
▷ Rulebase	6/24/1999	—	folder
▷ Shortcut Sets	6/24/1999	—	folder
▷ Swatch Libraries	6/24/1999	—	folder

Adobe InDesign build 496
17 items, 4.3 GB available

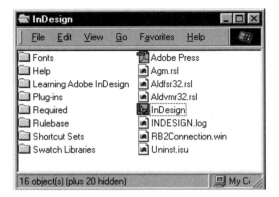

Figure 2–3
The InDesign folder on Windows 98.

InDesign Recovery folder—when you work on an InDesign document, a temporary copy is stored here automatically and the program
saves your document here every few minutes. When you invoke the
Save or *Save as* commands, all changes made to the file since the last
Save operation are written from the automatic recovery file to the
saved file. This also occurs when you quit the program.

If your computer crashes, the power goes out, or a small child
yanks the plug out of the wall, chances are good that you'll be able to
recover most of your work once you get the thing back up and running. When you open the document you last had open, InDesign will
display an alert asking if you want the changes saved in the recovery
file added to the document. You can choose to accept the changes or
discard them. If you accept the changes, immediately invoke the *Save
as* command and save a copy of the file.

There might be a time when the crash or whatever was so serious
that the data contained in the recovery file might have become corrupted. If InDesign crashes when attempting to recover a document,
then the recovery data has probably become corrupted. Restart the
computer, and when asked if you want to recover the document,
choose *No*; the document will be opened at the state it was in the last
time you explicitly saved it. It's always a good idea to frequently save

any documents while you work; never rely on this feature to protect against data loss.

InDesign SavedData—this file contains state-maintenance information for InDesign, such as a catalog of the current plug-ins, the locations of palettes and panels, and general housekeeping data.

Plug-in Cache folder—when you start InDesign for the first time or add a new plug-in, plug-ins that allow themselves to be cached are mapped into a quick-access file that is faster to load than each individual plug-in.

Plug-Ins folder—Since InDesign is a very modular program, it's easy to add functionality to it by adding plug-ins to this folder. Plug-ins are little software programs that you can't run by themselves, but they do "plug in" to whatever application they're designed for. Photoshop and Illustrator users have had the ability to use plug-ins for a long time. The analogous feature in QuarkXPress has been the XTension.

To install a plug-in, quit the InDesign application and simply drag the plug-in into this folder, then restart InDesign. InDesign ships with a number of plug-ins that add various features to the program. You can move a plug-in out of the Plug-ins folder and into an unused Plug-ins folder if you don't need it. Don't trash it, though, since you might need it later. You could create a new folder *outside* of the Plug-ins folder called "disabled plug-ins" if you like and store unused plug-ins there. Any folders within the Plug-ins folder that contain plug-ins will be used by InDesign. You can put plug-ins into any subfolder within the Plug-ins folder, or you can leave them loose in the Plug-ins folder. The default folder hierarchy inside the Plug-ins folder isn't required, but it's there for organizational purposes.

InDesign lacks a plug-in manager along the lines of the XTension Manager in QuarkXPress 4.0, but this feature is expected to be addressed either in a future revision or by a third-party plug-in manager plug-in. Ouch.

Users of QuarkXPress may fondly (or not) remember the Pasteboard XTension, if only because any documents edited with that XTension loaded could not be opened at all by users who did not have

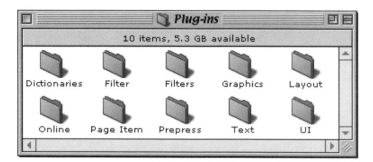

Figure 2–4
Inside the Plug-ins folder.

that XTension. InDesign will allow you to open documents that were modified in some way with a plug-in, even if you don't have it. In most cases, you won't need the missing plug-in unless you need a particular function that it provides. Plug-ins that are used to create or modify artwork in an InDesign document may cause images in that document to be grayed-out or tagged as missing if the document is opened without the plug-in's presence. Figure 2–4 shows the content of the Plug-ins folder.

RB2Connection.mac or *RB2connection.win*—This file provides the Adobe Rainbow Bridge function to InDesign.

Required folder—This folder contains plug-ins and code modules that are required for InDesign to function properly. Do not remove anything from this folder.

Rulebase folder—This folder contains the default layout adjustment rules file. Other layout adjustment files may be installed here depending on whether you are using a non-Roman language version of InDesign. Don't add anything to or remove anything from this folder.

Shortcut Sets folder—InDesign includes a set of keyboard commands here that mimic those found in QuarkXPress 4. These are stored within the *Shortcut Sets* folder. If you create additional keyboard shortcuts, they will be stored here automatically. If you receive a shortcut file from another InDesign user, copy it to this folder and restart the program to use it.

Swatch Libraries folder—this is where InDesign color swatch files are stored. InDesign includes swatch libraries for most of the color matching systems used around the world, such as those from Pantone, TruMatch, and Toyo, and it also includes swatch sets optimized for computer screen usage and for creating documents for the World Wide Web.

You can add other swatch libraries for color matching systems, such as PANTONE Hexachrome (a 6-color process), if they become available, by copying the swatch file to this folder and restarting InDesign. You can also copy InDesign and Illustrator files to this folder to use any colors within them as a swatch library.

3

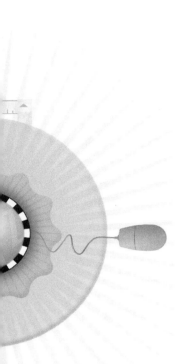

InDesign Tour

InDesign's Tools

If you've used recent versions of other Adobe applications like Illustrator or Photoshop, InDesign's toolbox should look very familiar—in fact, it's almost identical to the one in Illustrator. Adobe is working very hard to have a consistent user interface across their many products.

If you're migrating to InDesign from QuarkXPress or PageMaker, we'll point out the analogous tools (where they exist) between InDesign and those applications. At the end of this section we'll compare the construction of a document between InDesign, QuarkXPress, and PageMaker to help users of the programs visualize the differences.

Your use of InDesign comes down to using the modifier keys.

Modifier Keys?

These are keys you press along with a letter or number key to either type a character, like pressing Shift + 2 to get the "@" sign, or to perform a command, like pressing Command/Control + O to show the Open File dialog. On the Mac, the modifier keys are Shift, Command (the one with the "splat" symbol on it), Option, and Control.

On Windows machines, the modifiers are Shift, Control, and Alt. Since there's no agreed-upon symbology for representing these keys, we'll separate the keystrokes needed for a paricular operation, for example, "press Command/Control + P to open the Page Setup dialog." The first key is on the Mac keyboard, and the second is on the Windows keyboard.

Moving the mouse pointer over each tool will, after a short delay, display a little reminder (or tool tip) of what the tool is and what the keyboard shortcut is to invoke the tool, like the one in Figure 3–1.

Adobe has no space on both sides of the plus sign, but we will use the space to better present the keyboard functions. Adobe has tried to make all of its program interfaces consistent, but naturally the different functions of InDesign, Illustrator, and Photoshop call for variation in the tools. Their toolboxes are shown in Figure 3–2.

Figure 3–3 is an annotated diagram of the tools in the InDesign toolbox. Where applicable, the letter following the tool's description is the keyboard shortcut you press to select that tool. Some tools have more than one function—these can be chosen by pressing the Shift key plus the indicated letter. It's the same tool selection method used in Photoshop 5.0 and Illustrator 8.0. You don't need to press any modifier keys to swap tools.

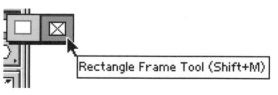

Figure 3–1
Tool descriptions.

Click and hold on a tool marked with a
small triangle to select hidden tools

InDesign Toolbox   Illustrator 8 Toolbox   Photoshop 5 Toolbox

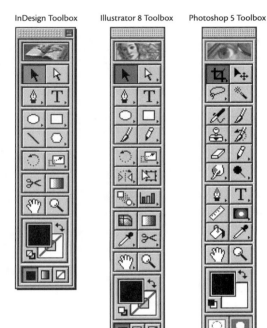

Figure 3–2
Comparison of InDesign, Illustrator, and
Photoshop tools.

Figure 3–3
Annotated InDesign toolbox.

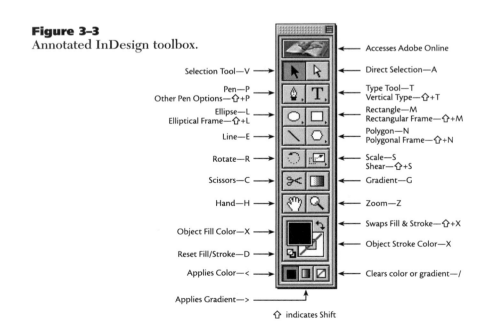

Accesses Adobe Online

Selection Tool—V
Direct Selection—A

Pen—P
Other Pen Options—⇧+P
Type Tool—T
Vertical Type—⇧+T

Ellipse—L
Elliptical Frame—⇧+L
Rectangle—M
Rectangular Frame—⇧+M

Line—E
Polygon—N
Polygonal Frame—⇧+N

Rotate—R
Scale—S
Shear—⇧+S

Scissors—C
Gradient—G

Hand—H
Zoom—Z

Object Fill Color—X
Swaps Fill & Stroke—⇧+X

Object Stroke Color—X

Reset Fill/Stroke—D

Applies Color—<
Clears color or gradient—/

Applies Gradient—>

⇧ indicates Shift

If you haven't used Illustrator before, the presence of two selection pointers can be a little confusing. In both Illustrator and InDesign, the solid pointer (Selection tool) is used to move things around and to resize objects.

The Selection tool is analogous to the Item tool in QuarkXPress and the Selection tool in PageMaker. The white pointer (Direct Selection tool) is used to edit paths or frames, to select frame content, or to move an anchor point on a path. It's analogous to the Content tool in QuarkXPress, and there's no analog in PageMaker. If you're a QuarkXPress user, recall that the Content tool modified a frame's content whether it was text or an image. InDesign treats text as a distinct entity, and you'll need to get used to using the Text tool for modifying textual content within a frame, since the Direct Selection tool only operates on an object, not text. This will be the first area you must master. With experience, you will get the hang of it.

Hints for PageMaker Users

Figure 3–4 compares the InDesign and PageMaker toolboxes.

- The Selection tool ![selection tool icon] works the same in InDesign as it does in PageMaker—you use it to drag elements around and to resize frames or other page objects.
- The Direct Selection tool ![direct selection tool icon] is analogous to the functions of PageMaker's cropping tool ![cropping tool icon]. With it, you can resize a frame or move the contents of a picture frame, without resizing the content like PageMaker's Selection tool does. This tool does a lot more than just crop images, however.
- The Text tool ![text tool icon] also works the same; you can click and drag to create a text frame, and you use this tool for direct text editing. In InDesign, clicking the Text tool on a frame drawn with the frame tools converts it to a text frame.
- The frame ![frame tool icon] and object-drawing tools ![object-drawing tool icon] work the same. In InDesign, you have to click and hold on a drawing-object's toolbox icon to select the frame version of the object, or you can press Shift + the tool's keystroke to select different tool versions. You can always convert a drawn object to a frame later.

Figure 3–4
InDesign and PageMaker toolbox comparison.

- The line-drawing tool ▨ in InDesign consolidates PageMaker's constrained ▨ and free-form ▨ line-drawing tools into one tool. Holding down the Shift key while drawing will constrain the line to 45° increments.
- The Hand ▨ (scrolling) tool works the same in both programs, but to access the Hand without choosing it in the toolbox, you press and hold the space bar in InDesign instead of the Option/Alt key in PageMaker. If you have the Text tool selected and there's an insertion point active, you need to hold down Option/Alt to enable the Hand tool, just like you'd do in PageMaker.
- In PageMaker and InDesign, you use Command/Control + 1, 2, 4 or Command/Control + the plus or minus sign to zoom in and out for page magnification. In InDesign, you can choose the Zoom tool by pressing the Z key or by pressing Command/Control + space bar to temporarily switch to the Zoom tool. Adding the Option/Alt key to this command changes the tool from Zoom In to Zoom Out.

- The Rotate tool ⟳ works the same in both programs—you can also type numeric rotation values into the Measurements palette. In InDesign, you can use the tool to establish a center-of-rotation point, where in PageMaker it always rotates the object with reference to wherever you first click with the tool selected.

Hints for QuarkXPress 3.3 and 4.0 Users   Figure 3–5 compares the InDesign and QuarkXPress toolboxes.

- The Selection tool ▶ in InDesign works the same as the Item tool ✥ (lovingly known as the throwing star) does in QuarkXPress—you use it to drag elements around and to resize frames or other page objects. In both, selecting an object with this tool and then choosing Copy or Cut from the Edit menu will copy or cut the object or frame, including any content within a frame.
- The Direct Selection tool ▶ works like the Content tool ☞ in QuarkXPress, but only with objects and pictorial content within frames. The QuarkXPress Content tool is context sensitive—for instance, if you use it on a text frame, you can edit text and resize a text frame; if you apply it to a picture frame, you can move the picture around within the frame and you can also resize the frame. In both programs, selecting frame content with this tool, and then choosing Copy or Cut from the Edit menu will copy or cut the picture or any selected text, but not the enclosing frame.
- The Hand ☞ (scrolling) tool in QuarkXPress is always accessible when the Option/Alt key is held down. To access the InDesign Hand without choosing it in the toolbox, press and hold the space bar instead of the Option/Alt key. If you have the Text tool selected and there's an insertion point active, you need to hold down Option/Alt to enable the Hand tool, just like you'd do in QuarkXPress.
- You don't need to draw a frame before importing text or images into an InDesign document, unlike QuarkXPress and similar to

InDesign   **QuarkXPress 3.3**   **QuarkXPress 4**

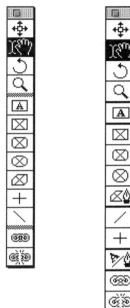

Figure 3–5
InDesign,
QuarkXPress 3.3, and
QuarkXPress 4.0
toolbox comparison.

PageMaker. But you can certainly create the frame first if that's how you prefer to work. InDesign will automatically set the frame content type depending on whether you place text or an image in the frame.

- In QuarkXPress 3.3, frames must be created as either text or picture from the start. In QuarkXPress 4.0, frames can be changed from text to picture, and vice versa, at any time (but you lose the content when you change the frame's type). In InDesign, you can only change a frame's content type after deleting all content; the program won't let you change the content type if the frame contains anything.

- The line-drawing tool  in InDesign merges QuarkXPress 3.3's constrained □ and free-form □ line-drawing tools into one tool. Holding down the Shift key while drawing will constrain the line to 45° increments.

- The Text Linking and Unlinking tools in QuarkXPress don't have direct analogs in InDesign, which uses in and out "ports" on text frames to control text flow from one frame to another.

Issues Specific to InDesign and QuarkXPress 4.0

- InDesign's Pen tool 🖊 puts the functions of QuarkXPress 4.0's scattered pen tools in one place. You can use it to perform the same functions as the Bézier Text Box tool ⬚, the Bézier Picture Box tool ⬚, and the Bézier Line-drawing tool 🖊. InDesign 1.0 does not support text on a Bézier path; this function is provided in QuarkXPress 4.0 by the Bézier Text on a Path tool ⬚. Text on a Bézier path may be supported in a future release of InDesign.

- Clipping paths weren't handled well in QuarkXPress 4.0, showing up where they weren't wanted and based upon a low-resolution screen preview of an image. You could end up with a clipping path around an image that never had one in the first place, which was a big surprise to people who opened older QuarkXPress 3.3 files with the new version. Quark has fixed a number of problems with this feature, but it's still something to be used with care. InDesign gives you the option of creating a frame from an image's embedded clipping path, and it won't sneak in a clipping path on images that don't have them embedded. If you want to use an embedded clipping path, you'll need to select InDesign's "create frame from clipping path" option, which we'll cover in Chapter 6. You can try to have InDesign create a clipping path in an image that doesn't have one, by detecting edges in the image, but this is risky, and if you want to create a clipping path in an image, do it the right way: draw it in Photoshop.

More About InDesign's Selection Tools

First we need to talk about *bounding boxes*. There are two kinds of InDesign bounding boxes:

- those created when you draw something
- those placed around images and vector art

Let's say you draw a round frame in InDesign, then place an image into it. The frame itself has a bounding box, shown here after being selected with the Selection tool. Note that even though the image is round, the bounding box has a rectangular shape.

Switching to the Direct Selection tool with this object selected shows the actual frame's construction.

Clicking on the image with the Direct Selection tool displays the actual bounds of the image, only a part of which shows in the object's round frame.

This capability shows how far the image extends past the edge of the frame, which is actually cropping the image in this example.

The two tools are context sensitive and can work very differently, depending on the contents of the frame you are modifying.

- Text frames—With the Selection tool, you can move and resize text frames. With the Direct Selection tool, you can select and modify points on the frame's path; for example, you can select and drag corner points on a rectangular text frame and turn it into a trapezoid or whatever you like. See Figure 3–6.
- Frames containing InDesign objects (artwork, for example, or frames that contain items you've drawn in InDesign, or items you've dragged or pasted in from an illustration program)— With the Selection tool, you can move or resize the frame; however, if you resize the frame, the contents will be resized as well. With the Direct Selection tool, you can directly edit the contents of the frame or the frame's shape. Note that each object drawn in InDesign will generate its own frame—dragged

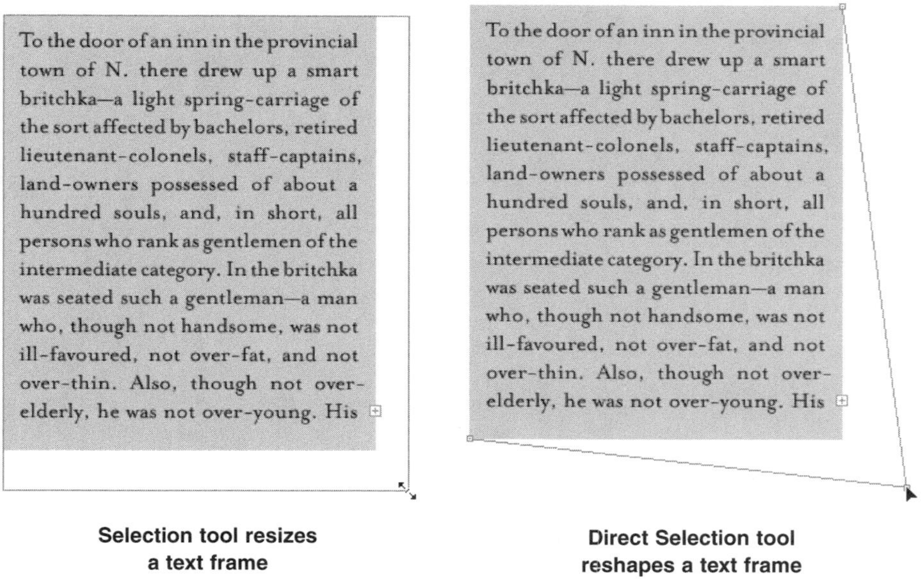

To the door of an inn in the provincial town of N. there drew up a smart britchka—a light spring-carriage of the sort affected by bachelors, retired lieutenant-colonels, staff-captains, land-owners possessed of about a hundred souls, and, in short, all persons who rank as gentlemen of the intermediate category. In the britchka was seated such a gentleman—a man who, though not handsome, was not ill-favoured, not over-fat, and not over-thin. Also, though not over-elderly, he was not over-young. His

To the door of an inn in the provincial town of N. there drew up a smart britchka—a light spring-carriage of the sort affected by bachelors, retired lieutenant-colonels, staff-captains, land-owners possessed of about a hundred souls, and, in short, all persons who rank as gentlemen of the intermediate category. In the britchka was seated such a gentleman—a man who, though not handsome, was not ill-favoured, not over-fat, and not over-thin. Also, though not over-elderly, he was not over-young. His

**Selection tool resizes
a text frame**

**Direct Selection tool
reshapes a text frame**

Figure 3–6
Comparison of the Selection tools used with a text frame.

**Selection tool *resizes* an object frame
and the contents**

Figure 3–7
Comparison of the Selection
tools used with an object.

**Direct Selection tool *modifies* objects in
an object frame**

or pasted objects from an illustration program will be grouped
into a single frame, which can be ungrouped if you like.
Grouped objects are treated as groups with the Selection tool;
they are individually accessible with the Direct Selection tool.
See Figure 3–7.

- Frames containing *placed* artwork (EPS or native Illustrator)—
The content of these frames is not editable, unlike the content
of frames containing pasted or dragged artwork. Resizing the
frame with the Selection tool only changes the size of the frame
and works the same as the Content tool in QuarkXPress.
Resizing the frame will not scale the artwork within the frame,
unless you hold down the Command/Control key while scaling
the frame.
You can also add the Shift key to constrain the scaling proportionally, or you can use the scaling functions in the Transform
panel, described below; holding the Shift key will *not* force the
frame to a square as it does in QuarkXPress.

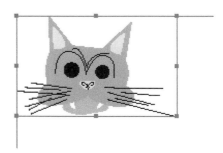

Selection tool *resizes* a frame
with placed content

Direct Selection tool
***modifies* placed content**

Figure 3-8
Comparison of the Selection tools used with placed content.

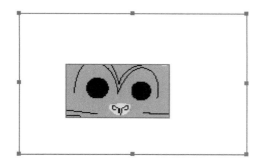

Figure 3-9
Results of resizing the frame with the Selection tool and moving the frame content with the Direct Selection tool.
Note that the outline of the placed content is visible when selected with the Direct Selection tool.

You can resize the *contents* of the frame with the Direct Selection tool; you can also modify the shape of the frame; and you can move the frame's content within the frame to reposition it or to crop the image by using the frame's edges to hide portions of it. These uses of the Selection tools are shown in Figures 3–8 and 3–9.

- Frames containing placed TIFF, bitmapped EPS, or converted Photoshop images—Resizing the frame with the Selection tool works the same way as for placed EPS or Illustrator artwork. You can also resize image content with the direct selection tool. However, if you place images that contain a clipping path (silhouette) and use the clipping path option upon import, then try to scale the frame, the frame and the clipping path will scale, but not the content. What's more, if you try to scale the image content with the Direct Selection tool, you'll reduce or enlarge

Frame, clipping path, and con-tents proportionally scaled with Shift + Command/Control and Selection tool

Frame and clipping path only, scaled with Selection tool

Figure 3–10
Using the Selection tool with images.

the image, but the clipping path will remain unchanged. Be very careful here! If you want to scale the frame, the clipping path, and the image, you must also hold the Command/Control key (with or without Shift) while scaling the frame with the Selection tool, or use the Transform panel to make your changes.

Figure 3–10 illustrates the use of the Selection tools with images.

You can also edit the imported clipping path with the Direct Selection tool. InDesign imports Photoshop clipping paths from TIFF and EPS images intact, and you can edit the path later. You cannot import clipping paths or masks created in Illustrator or Freehand; only those created in Photoshop can be turned into an editable clipping path. Clipping paths created in Illustrator or Freehand are honored when printing, but you can't edit them in InDesign.

InDesign Panels and Palettes

Palettes are small tool or control boxes that house one or more con-trol panels. Composite (grouped) palettes really don't have names, since they are freely customizable by the user, except for the toolbox palette. We'll show you how to customize and organize panels and palettes.

The Default Palettes Default palettes appear when you start InDesign for the first time or after you delete the InDesign Defaults and InDesign SavedData files.

Toolbox The toolbox, discussed above, contains all of the elementary drawing, text, and object creation and manipulation tools you'll use frequently. If you could only have one palette open, this would have to be it as you can't do much in InDesign without it, unless you've mastered all the keyboard shortcuts needed to access the tools you want to use.

Transform Panel The Transform panel, shown in Figure 3–11, is analogous to the Measurements panel in both QuarkXPress and PageMaker. Here you can specify X and Y coordinates, width and height, horizontal and vertical scale, rotation angle, and shear angle. A *proxy* representation of an object lets you set the point of origin for transformations.

The Transform panel is only active if you have one or more objects selected. If you select more than one object, the values displayed represent all of the objects as if they were a group.

The Transform panel will always be selected and ready if you double-click either the Rotate, Shear, or Scale tools in the toolbox, and

Figure 3–11
The Transform panel's controls.

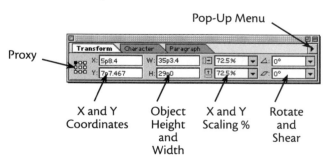

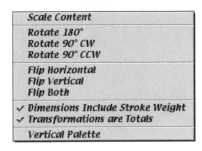

Figure 3–12
The Transform panel's pop-up menu.

the panel option relevant to the tool selected will be selected and ready for a value.

The proxy in the Transform panel specifies the point of origin for a number of measurements and transformations, including those performed with tools from the toolbox. The proxy is a little diagram that represents a selected object. You can click on any of the nine points on the proxy to specify a point of origin, including the center of the object. The proxy is a new concept to QuarkXPress users, but PageMaker users will find that their old friend is still there. Using the proxy is beyond easy: select an object with either the Selection tool or the Direct Selection tool, then click on any of the nine points on the proxy to set the point of origin for further movement, scaling, or transformation.

The pop-up menu of the Transform panel (Figure 3–12) enables further manipulations.

You can choose to scale a frame's content by selecting *Scale Content* from the panel's pop-up menu. This option is off by default, and you can choose to scale frame content by holding down Command/Control while scaling with the Selection tool. Turning the option on lets you scale frame content via the Transfom panel, but not by dragging a corner of the frame with the Selection tool, which will only scale the frame and not the content.

By default, the menu choice that affects nested objects, *Transformations are Totals*, is selected. You can tell because there's a checkmark next to it. This option lets you determine if displayed measurements of nested objects are relative to the document pasteboard (the default) or to the parent object. Deselect this option if you want nested object measurements displayed relative to the parent object.

The menu choice *Dimensions Include Stroke Weight* is also selected by default. This choice tells InDesign to take a frame's stroke weight into account when displaying measurements in the Transform panel. When checked, the measurements displayed will represent the outer edge of an object's stroke. In InDesign, stroke weights always grow from the center of the stroke, and this option tells InDesign to treat the outside of the stroke as the object's outside boundary.

If you want the stroke weight disregarded in the measurements, deselect this option. PageMaker and QuarkXPress do not draw strokes from the centerline of a frame or other stroked object; Illustrator and Freehand draw strokes from the center of a path, and so does InDesign, although you can only see this when selecting a stroked object with the Direct Selection tool. Strokes drawn on InDesign frames appear to be inside the frame when selected with the Selection tool.

QuarkXPress lets you specify whether strokes are drawn inside or outside a frame, and strokes drawn on the outside of the frame are taken into account in the QuarkXPress measurements palette. PageMaker strokes are always drawn on the inside of the frame or container.

Character Panel The Transform, Paragraph, and Character panels, as shown in Figure 3–13, appear in a grouped palette by default when you are starting InDesign for the first time or after resetting defaults.

The Character panel, shown in Figure 3–14, is used for stylizing and setting selected text. You can apply typefaces, sizing, kerning, scaling, and also tag text with a specific spelling dictionary.

InDesign displays typefaces a little differently from most other programs. The typeface *name* is displayed separately—for example, Cronos MM. The style variant will display the available variations in

Figure 3–13
Transform, Paragraph, and Character panels in a grouped palette.

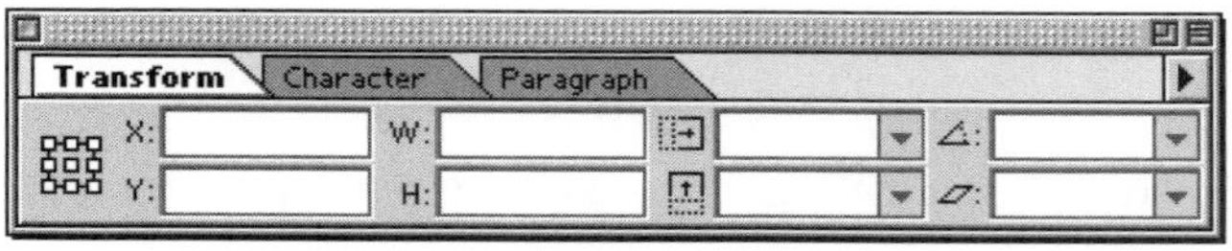

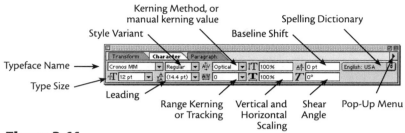

Figure 3–14
The Character panel's controls.

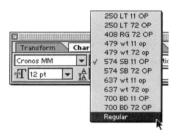

Figure 3–15
A multiple-master typeface and its style variants.

the typeface, such as plain, roman (Times Roman roman), bold, demi, italic, oblique, and a host of other variant names. Adobe Multiple Master typefaces will display style variants as the available instances contained within that typeface—the base instance will display as "Regular."

The Character panel displays typefaces differently from the Type Font menu, where the available style variants are listed in a sub-menu, as shown in Figure 3–15.

If you select a typeface, for example, Times, and select the bold variant, then later change the typeface to something else, for example, Minion, InDesign will attempt to maintain the style variant previously chosen, in the new typeface. If the new typeface does not contain the chosen variant or if the variant is named differently—for example, if the bold variant of the new typeface is actually called "demi," InDesign will mark the variant as a missing font.

Type size and leading values can be entered manually in the Character panel. Type sizes can range from 0.1 to 1296 points in increments of 0.001 points, and leading can range from 0 to 5000 points in increments of 0.001 points.

The kerning controls let you specify either an automatic kerning method or a manually entered kerning amount in units of 1/1000 of an em space when the insertion point is between a pair of letters to be kerned. InDesign offers the expected automatic kerning based on metrics built into a typeface, and it also features an optical kerning method that bases kerning values on the appearance of letters, for typefaces that lack kerning metrics for some or all of the possible letter pairs. In general, choosing Metrics in the kerning control box will produce the best results as long as your installed typefaces include complete kerning pairs.

Most professional typefaces include thousands of kerning pairs, but many low-cost (or "junk" types, depending on who is asked) do not include any kerning pairs or include only a few. InDesign will take full advantage of the former when *Metrics* is chosen and will attempt to provide optimum kerning for the latter when *Optical* is chosen in the kerning control box. With either automatic kerning method, selecting a range of text will display the chosen kerning method in the panel; placing the insertion point between a pair of letters will display the actual kerning value as an integer in parentheses.

Of course, you can always override InDesign's automatic kerning by entering kerning values in the control box. You can also use keyboard shortcuts to apply kerning. Pressing Option/Alt + left arrow or + right arrow will decrease or increase the kerning. The default kerning unit used with the keyboard method is 1/50 em. Holding the Control key while applying kerning with the keyboard method increases the kerning unit to 1/10 em. You can adjust the default keyboard kerning unit in the InDesign preferences.

Tracking operates on a range of selected text. If any manual kerning has been applied to the range, it will be maintained. Tracking is also applied in units of 1/1000 of an em, and you can either choose from the values in the pop-up menu in the tracking control box, or you can enter a value manually. You can also select Optical, Metrics, or none (0) in the kerning control box to specify an automatic tracking method for a range of text. Selecting none (0) turns off InDesign's automatic tracking function for that range of text.

The width of an em space will vary according to the definition of an em space within a given typeface, and will also vary as the type's point size is reduced or enlarged. Kerning values remain proportional to the specified type size. In QuarkXPress you can specify a "flex" space as a percentage of the width of an en space. InDesign does not offer this function.

You can scale type vertically and/or horizontally, although this can lead to serious distortion of the type and can even destroy the character and color of the type. Use these features sparingly, if at all. Expanding or condensing a typeface is tolerable in small amounts, but nobody likes seeing **big fat type** or spindly scrunched type. You can easily see the distortion introduced into the type by such brute-force methods of copyfitting or attempts at stylization.

InDesign allows you to specify a range of horizontal type scaling as an aid in justification and copyfitting. By specifying a rather narrow range (and we mean narrow, like less than 5 percent), you can enhance justification without causing noticeable type distortion. See the discussion on glyph scaling in Chapter 7, Type and Typography, for more information.

Paragraph Panel A paragraph is defined as a block of text terminated in a hard return. The Paragraph panel, illustrated in Figure 3–16, allows setting of justification method, indents, baseline locking, space before and after, and drop cap specifications. The pop-up menu gives you the option of adjusting the justification parameters, hyphenation settings, keeps options, rules, and the composition method.

Figure 3–16
The Paragraph panel.

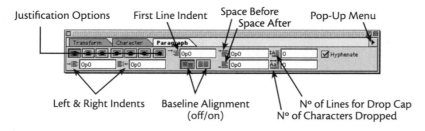

These options are explained in Chapter 7, (type) and Chapter 8 (text).

To apply paragraph options, you need to either select some or all of the text in a paragraph or just have an insertion point in the paragraph. Triple-click in the paragraph to select all of it quickly.

Justification options are the usual left, center, right, and justified methods. When choosing justified, you can opt to have the last line set left, centered, right, or you can force-justify the last line. Adding a flush space character before a special end-of-story character like an ornament will force the ornament all the way to the right, filling in the balance of the line with white space, a nice effect.

You can quickly modify left and right indents simply by entering a measurement into the fields. First-line indents will reflect the amount of indent space specified. A negative value here will create a hanging indent. Changes in the indents here will be reflected in the Tabs panel.

Space Before and *Space After* specify how much white space to insert before or after a paragraph. This is a nice professional way of visually separating paragraphs without adding additional returns.

Drop caps are a snap in InDesign. Simply specify the number of lines that the drop cap is to use and the number of characters to be dropped.

Checking the Hypenation checkbox enables hyphenation for the selected paragraph. If you don't want to hyphenate a particular paragraph, uncheck the box.

The pop-up menu, illustrated in Figure 3–17, gives you a number of options, including the choice of composition method. The default is the Adobe Multi-line Composer, described in detail in Chapter 7. The alternative Adobe Single-line Composer is faster but does not provide the precision spacing and justification of the Multi-line

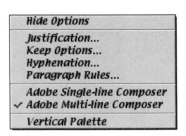

Figure 3-17
The Paragraph submenu.

Composer. Other options include Justification, Keep Options, Hyphenation, and Paragraph Rules. These topics are also discussed in Chapter 7.

> **Tip:**
>
> In QuarkXPress, the *Enter* key on the keypad is used to force a new page, or to insert a "next column" character or a "next text box" character, when pressed with *Shift*. With InDesign, the same function is performed by assigning a Keep Options attribute to the paragraph from the pop-up menu.

The Swatch, Paragraph Style, and Character Style Panels

Swatches

The Swatches panel, illustrated in Figure 3–18, holds the default Black, Paper (white, of course), None, and Registration colors. New colors can be added at any time with the Swatches pop-up menu or from an open swatch library, such as the PANTONE Coated library supplied with InDesign, along with others.

The options in the Swatches panel are described in detail in Chapter 9. InDesign does not support the HLS/HSB color model.

Figure 3–18
The Swatches panel.

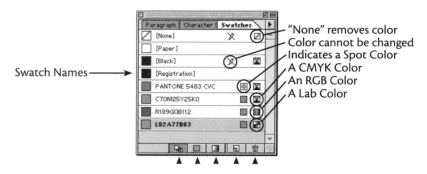

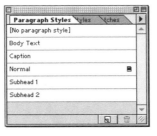

Figure 3–19
Sample Paragraph Styles panel.

Styles Panels   Paragraph styles and character styles live in their respective panels. *Styles* are simply a predefined set of typographical specifications that can be quickly applied to selected text.

A paragraph style sets the specifications for the entire paragraph, whether the insertion point is clicked in the paragraph, a few words or letters are selected, or the entire paragraph is selected. See Figure 3–19.

Character styles allow modification of words or letters independently of the chosen paragraph style, which is handy for instances when you need to set a word or two in a different typeface or font; for example, you could set up a character style that applied an old-style figure font to text set in a particular typeface, such as Adobe Minion.

The old-style figures are actually in a different font, Minion Regular Small Caps, and InDesign will only do automatic old-style figure replacement with OpenType fonts, which Minion is not (it will probably be released, along with a few others, when this book is published). Creating a character style is an easy way to apply this font to any selected text. Paragraph styles include a character style as well, but any character style applied to selected text will override the type specifications present in a paragraph style.

You can apply type attributes within an empty text frame (make sure the insertion point is active in the text frame). However, if you copy and paste the empty text frame, the pasted copy loses the type attributes you applied and instead uses your defaults for type.

When defining or editing a character or paragraph style or when defining *Find/Change* formatting, the *Language* setting lists only those languages that have been applied to characters within the document you are working on.

If you apply a character style that specifies a font family style variant (such as bold or italic) to text formatted with a Multiple Master font, the *Character* palette may lose track of the available instances of the Multiple Master font. The instances are still listed, however, in the Type ➠ Font menu.

The Pages, Layers, and Navigation Panels

Navigation Panel   If you've used Adobe Photoshop 5 or Illustrator 8, the navigator, illustrated in Figure 3–20, will be a familiar tool. It provides a thumbnail view of the currently selected page or spread at the chosen magnification. You can use the triangular slider at the bottom of the Navigator panel to quickly zoom in or out on a layout.

A red box on the thumbnail shows you the view relative to the entire page or spread. You can also "grab" the red box and move it within the Navigator panel to change the current view to another location on the page or spread.

More on Navigation   Not "morons on navigation" please. Of course, there are other ways of zooming and scrolling in InDesign. Use the scroll bars, the panning (Hand) tool for live scrolling, and the Zoom tool. There are other tools available for navigating around your document.

You can type a magnification value into the little box at the extreme lower–left corner of the InDesign document window or choose a

Figure 3-20
Navigator panel controls.

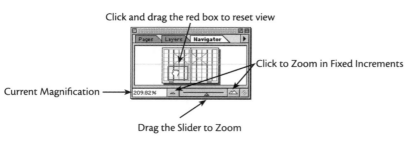

Figure 3–21
Magnification pop-up menu.

Figure 3–22
Page forward/backward tool.

magnification value from the pop-up menu located there, as illustrated in Figure 3–21.

For getting around to specific pages, you can use the page forward/backward tool, illustrated in Figure 3–22 and located next to the magnification pop-up.

The two buttons on each end take you to the first or last page in the document. The other two move back or forward one page. The current page number is displayed in the middle, which is really an entry field. You can press Command/Control + J to "jump" to this field, where you can type in the number of the page that you want to see, or you can double-click on the number to select it and then enter a new one.

Pressing Page Up or Page Down rolls the view up or down—it doesn't actually go to a specific page, similar to how these keys work in QuarkXPress. In PageMaker, these keys always go to the next page or spread. To really go to the next or previous page, add Shift when pressing these keys. Add Option/Alt to go to the last or first page in the document, or add Command/Control to go to the last page you looked at (Page Up) or the one after that (Page Down), which seems a bit like using a web browser.

The View menu (Figure 3–23) lists other ways of viewing pages or spreads.

Figure 3-23
View dialog box.

Pages and Layers Panels   InDesign's Pages panel gives you an at-a-glance picture of your entire document layout. You can also add, delete, and move pages, and use it to create additional master pages. This is a pretty powerful device, so we'll cover it in-depth in Chapter 4, along with the Layers panel.

Other panels can be invoked from the File, Type, Object, and View menus. We'll cover these in the appropriate sections.

Working with Panels

Many InDesign panels have side pop-up menus that are specific to that panel and that appear when you click and hold on the little triangle at the upper-right corner of the panel.

What's really great about Adobe's palette and panel system (it's the same in Illustrator, InDesign, and Photoshop) is that you can drag a panel's tab and combine it with another panel, creating a new composite palette, or you can make the panel a standalone palette. Don't you like having some of the type controls separated?

You can easily make a palette that contains all of the typographic controls by dragging panel tabs. For example, one of the default palettes contains the Transform, Character, and Paragraph panels. You could drag the transform panel out, then open others from one of several menus that are more directly related to typesetting, as illustrated in Figure 3–24.

Most panels within palettes are invoked from the Window menu, though some are in other locations. The Paragraph, Character, Tabs, Character Styles, Paragraph Styles, and Story panels can be invoked from the Type menu. The Links panel is found under the File menu. The Text Wrap panel is under the Object menu. The last two will

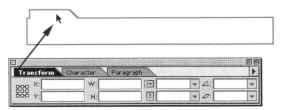

**The same palette after dragging in Character,
Paragraph, Text Wrap, and Tabs panels**

Drag out the unwanted panel by its tab

Figure 3–24
Customizing palettes.

open as a single-panel palette, but you can change that easily. Most panels have corresponding keystrokes that will either open them or bring them to the foreground in a multipanel palette. Sometimes it becomes hard to see a panel's name in a multipanel palette; pressing the panel's activation keystroke will always bring it to the front.

The Transform and Character/Paragraph panels will activate automatically depending on what you're doing. If you select the Text tool and click an insertion point, the Character or Paragraph panel will come to the foreground if in a multipanel palette such as the default one, or it will become the active panel if several palettes and panels are already open.

To quickly hide all palettes, just press the Tab key. Be sure that you don't have any text insertion point active, because this will just type a tab character.

To hide all the palettes except the toolbox, press Shift + Tab.

Selecting a specific panel will almost always resize the palette to accommodate it. Some panels have extra controls in them that you might not need, so you can make the panel smaller by double-clicking its tab.

Double-clicking the tab again will minimize the entire palette to show just the panel tabs. See Figure 3–25.

Character panel—full size

Character panel—small size   **Character panel—minimized**

Figure 3–25
Panel manipulation.

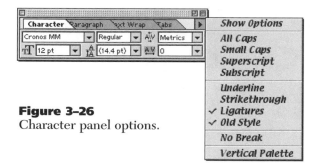

Figure 3–26
Character panel options.

You can also use the zoom, windowshade (Mac only), and close boxes on the palette's title bar to close or minimize it.

Panel options are available in the pop-up menu that appears when you click the small black triangle at the right side of the panel. The options for the Character panel are shown in Figure 3–26.

You can specify panel contents by choosing *Show/Hide Options* (which does the same thing as double-clicking on the panel's tab), or change the orientation of the palette from horizontal to vertical, as shown in Figure 3–27.

All Adobe products feature a "docking" system for palettes. As you work, you're bound to move palettes all over the place. As shown in Figure 3–28, palettes will automatically snap to the top or bottom closest neighboring palette when moved, as if they were magnetized. You can almost hear the "kachunk" as they snap.

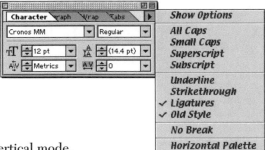

Figure 3–27
The Character panel in vertical mode.

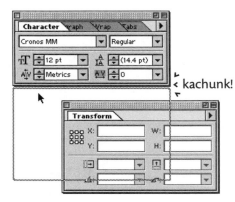

Figure 3–28
Snapping palettes.

Palettes are an essential element in program use, but they take up a lot of screen real estate. A 21-inch monitor is almost essential, and the advent of LCDs means even larger screens are coming.

Moving Objects by the Numbers   You can do basic math in the palettes to modify existing values. For example, to move something up 6.5 units (inches, picas, or whatever you've chosen), you could just type "–6p6" (for picas) after the current Y axis measurement in the Transform panel and press *Enter*; see Figure 3–29.

You can also temporarily override the current measurement system you've chosen by using the notation in Table 3–1. Just type your math operator, the number of units, and then the specified letter(s) to denote the measurement system you want the number to represent.

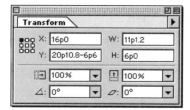

Figure 3-29
Shifting an object's vertical location up 6p6.

This is very helpful when there is a last-minute change and you need to modify existing values.

For example, let's say a comp comes back with a note saying "move this thing up 3/4 inch!" As shown in Figure 3–30, with picas chosen as the default measurement system, you can just type "–0.75i" after the Y value in the Transform palette, instead of trying to convert 3/4 inch to picas and points.

Or use "/2" to divide the value in half, or "*2" to double it.

QuarkXPress does this as well but uses the inch mark instead of the letter "i."

Table 3-1

Unit Conversion Notation.

Units	Notation	Example
Ciceros	c	8c
Inches	i, in, inch	3.125in
Millimeters	mm	12.5mm
Picas	p	6p
Points	p	p8
Picas and Points	p	6p8

Notice the position of the "p" when specifying picas and points.

Today most graphic designers use inches, but many continue to use picas and points, which are easier to deal with when small increments are required (try figuring out what three-eighths is on a ruler).

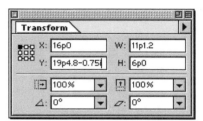

Figure 3–30
Moving an object up 3/4 in. with a pica measurement system chosen.

InDesign Shortcuts

InDesign includes a lot of keyboard shortcuts, but the best thing is that you can define your own, or, if you're coming out of Quark-XPress, you can choose a set of keyboard shortcuts that mimics, to the extent possible, the keyboard shortcuts of QuarkXPress. There are limitations here as some InDesign functions have no direct analog in QuarkXPress. See the appendix for a complete list of InDesign and QuarkXPress keyboard shortcuts.

To edit keyboard shortcuts, choose File ➡ Edit Shortcuts (Command/Control + Option/Alt + Shift + K) to display the Shortcut Editor, as shown in Figure 3–31.

Figure 3–31
The Shortcut editor.

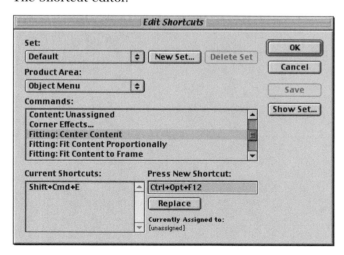

The Shortcut Editor is also a quick-and-easy keyboard shortcut reference—if you want to look up a command's shortcut, just locate it in the editor and the shortcut will be displayed. To switch to the QuarkXPress set or another customized set, choose it from the Set list and close the editor. To edit a shortcut, first choose the relevant "Product Area," select it from the list, then type the shortcut you'd like in its place.

If the shortcut is already in use, a reminder will appear in the lower right of the editor window. If you go ahead and assign the keystroke to the selected function, the function whose keystroke you just usurped will have its keystroke deleted and unassigned. You can't edit the default Shortcut Set or the QuarkXPress 4.0 set; a prompt to create a new set appears if you try this. Pressing Option/Alt in the Editor changes the Cancel button to Reset—you can use this to completely clear all of your edits in case you change your mind.

You can use any character and function key, and any modifier key, to create a shortcut. You should probably avoid using the ESC key, as it would be easy to create a shortcut that will force-quit InDesign on a Mac (pressing Option + Command + ESC on a Mac causes any program to forcibly quit, with possibly unpleasant consequences) or cause the Task Manager to pop up in Windows. The ESC key is really intended for operating-system-level commands.

InDesign, like QuarkXPress, differentiates between keystrokes that use the row of number keys at the top of the keyboard and those that use the numbers on the keypad. Pressing Command/Control + 1 (top row) resets the view to actual size; pressing the same keystroke combination, but using the "1" on the numeric keypad doesn't do anything—these keypad shortcuts are quick and handy for changing paragraph or character styles but not for shortcuts. You can also create shortcuts for styles in the Style editor.

These shortcuts shouldn't be misinterpreted as macros, actions, or any other sort of scripted command. InDesign supports scripting through AppleScript (Mac) or Visual Basic (Windows). See the *Scripting Guide* included with InDesign for information about scripting, which is really a topic for an entire book.

Scripts can automate many InDesign functions, and you can even create additional functions if you're feeling really ambitious. However, writing scripts requires a lot of patience, and some programming experience certainly won't hinder your efforts. An "actions" feature like that in Photoshop 5 would be a nice addition to future versions of InDesign.

For a complete list of the keyboard shortcuts in any set, click the Show Set button. A list of all shortcuts will be created and opened for you in SimpleText (Mac) or Notepad (Windows). You can then format it and print it out for quick reference.

Opening, Placing, Saving, and Autorecovering

InDesign can open files created in QuarkXPress 3.3 and 4.0 and PageMaker 6.5; it can also open an InDesign file from another platform without making you save it as another file. For instance, in PageMaker 6.5, you can open a PageMaker for Windows file with PageMaker for the Mac, but the file will open as "untitled" and you'll have to save it as something else. InDesign will always work with the original file regardless of the platform from which it originated, which is really handy for cross-platform networks.

To open a file, choose File ➡ Open or press Command/Control + O (the letter "O", not zero) to display the Open File dialog box. Navigate to the file's location, select it, then click Open. InDesign will display all of the file types that it can open or import.

The Open File dialog gives a number of options, as shown in Figure 3–32. Note that InDesign supports the new, improved (some

Figure 3–32
The Open File dialog (Macintosh).

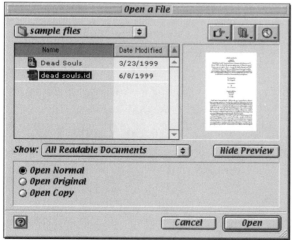

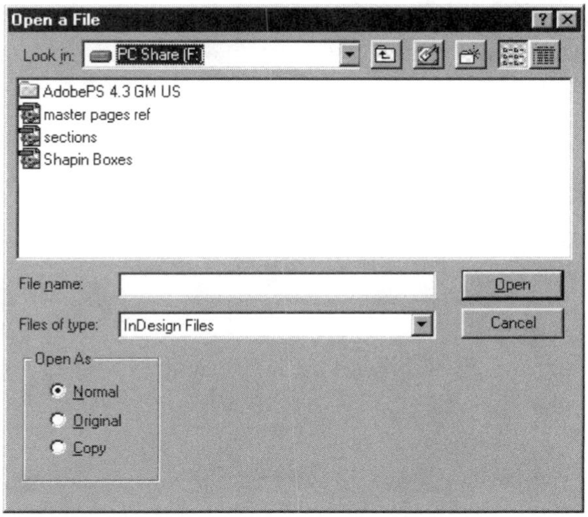

Figure 3–33
The Open File dialog (Windows).

of you may have a different opinion on that) file dialogs introduced with MacOS 8.5.

You can toggle the Preview on or off: preview is only available for InDesign files and shows only the first page of a document.

The three icons at the upper right are new to MacOS 8.5—the left icon provides a list of volumes currently on-line and lets you open a network connection; the middle offers a shortcut to a "favorites" folder that you can also define with the menu, and the right icon displays a list of the last 10 documents that you opened in InDesign. Clicking the question mark at the lower left launches Apple's new Help system, where you can get more details about this possibly unfamiliar file dialog.

Figure 3–33 shows the Windows version of the Open File dialog.

Both platforms—The *Open Normal* and *Open Original* options let you open a template as a new untitled document, or open the original template. *Open Copy* creates a new untitled copy of a document, as if it were a template. The Show (Mac) or Files of Type (Windows) pop-up menu lets you choose between showing only InDesign documents, files that InDesign can open or convert, or all files within a particular folder. However, you can't open anything except InDesign, QuarkXPress, or PageMaker files.

Windows Note: QuarkXPress and PageMaker document and template files must have the correct file extension appended to them—.QXD/.QXT for QuarkXPress and .P65/.T65 for PageMaker 6.5—for InDesign to recognize them correctly. This is especially important in the case of files moved over from a Macintosh, which does not use filename extensions. You also must choose the appropriate file type from the Files of Type pop-up menu.

Converting QuarkXPress and PageMaker Files

It's simple: open them with the *Open File* dialog.

OK, there's more to it. Because of the way all three programs work, there will be things that InDesign can and cannot convert, and the resulting document will almost always require additional hand-tuning before it looks like the original. You can convert QuarkXPress 3.3 and 4.0x files and PageMaker 6.5 files.

If you have files in the formats used by older versions of these programs, you'll have to first open then with the current version of the program, then save them.

For example, to get PageMaker 4.0, 5.0, or 6.0 files into InDesign, you need to open them in PageMaker 6.5 and save them as PageMaker 6.5 files first. For QuarkXPress 3.3 and 4.x documents, open them and make sure all graphics and fonts are updated and resaved. If you are using XTensions like QX-Tools, you may need to turn them off in the XTensions Manager and resave the document.

A note about converting QuarkXPress and PageMaker files. While InDesign tries its best to preserve the original layout, things will move when a document is converted. This feature is best applied when converting existing templates from QuarkXPress and PageMaker to InDesign. It should only be used when converting completed documents if you plan to rework the content or start a new version using the old layout, columns, guides, etc., as a template. Don't convert documents in the middle of production—that's just a really bad idea.

Testing indicates that this conversion, on the average, gets you about 90 percent of the way to the original file. There will be rewrap and reflow, and you should plan for this.

Here's what happens when PageMaker 6.5 files are converted.

- Any ICC profiles are preserved.
- Linked images and text files are preserved, as are the links.

Unlinked or embedded images are ignored (meaning they will appear as gray placeholder boxes in the converted document) and will need to be replaced. Pasted images are ignored. Images linked through Microsoft OLE are ignored.

- All "stories" (basically, any PageMaker text container, whether it was created as a frame or a text block) are converted to InDesign text frames.
- Image frames are converted to InDesign image frames.
- Drawn lines and strokes and object colors are converted to the corresponding InDesign objects.
- Styles are preserved.
- Layers are preserved, but master objects in layers now appear behind other objects on page layers instead of behind all page objects, as they appeared in PageMaker.
- Guides from PageMaker are placed on a new Guides layer.
- Master pages and all master page items are preserved.
- Colors are placed in the Swatches panel. Colors created in PageMaker with HLS values are converted to RGB colors. Process (CMYK) colors are reinterpreted according to the CMYK values they contain. Verify all colors.
- Trapping parameters are discarded.

Here's what happens when QuarkXPress 3.3 and 4.0 files are converted.

- ICC profiles are preserved. EFI Color profiles are discarded, and you'll need to reapply ICC profiles.
- Any images linked through Microsoft OLE are ignored—this is only an issue on Windows computers. Images pasted into a document are ignored and must be replaced.
- Objects created with Quark XTensions are ignored.
- All text and image frames and their contents are preserved and converted to InDesign frames.
- Drawn lines and strokes and object colors are converted to the corresponding InDesign objects.
- Paragraph and Character (QuarkXPress 4.0 only) styles are preserved.

- Master pages and all master page items are preserved. Guides on master pages are also preserved, but they are not placed on a separate layer.
- Colors are placed in the Swatches panel. Colors created in QuarkXPress 3.3 with HSB values are converted to RGB colors, as are HSB and Lab colors created in QuarkXPress 4.0. Process (CMYK) colors are reinterpreted according to the CMYK values they contain.
  Verify all colors after conversion.
- Trapping parameters and object-level traps are discarded.

Save any converted files immediately, which leads us to...

Saving Files

This one's easy. You should already be familiar with how to save a file on your computer. The only option when saving an InDesign file is to decide whether to save it as a regular document or as a template.

Choose InDesign Template from the Save as Type menu (Windows), or choose Stationery Option from the Format menu, then choose Stationery (MacOS).

InDesign saves automatically. It is very much like Filemaker in this regard. A temp file is created during a session and that file is saved as you go along.

Autorecovery

InDesign keeps a scratch copy of any open documents in the recovery folder on your hard disk drive. As you work, all changes are saved to this scratch file and are written to the document file when you Save, Save As, or Quit InDesign.

All computers crash: the MacOS "bomb" with its many nuances ("The application Bumblewrite has unexpectedly quit." So if it was expected to quit, you could have prepared for it?) and Windows' GPF errors and the heart-stopping Blue Screen of Death are probably familiar experiences to many of you.

If your computer crashes or if the power fails or if any number of small or large disasters occur, the scratch file should contain all of the revisions to the document that you'd made since the last explicit Save. However, because system crashes can garble data and a shaky system can write garbage to open files immediately before a crash, the Autorecovery feature is no guarantee that your document will magically open up exactly where you were before the crash.

If your system crashes or loses power, restart it as usual, then start InDesign. Don't launch InDesign by double-clicking a document file, however. InDesign will know that something was temporarily rotten in your Denmark and will automatically recover any documents that were open at the time of the crash. You can tell when a document has been recovered because the document's name will have "[Recovered]" added to it in the title bar.

This document isn't really the same one that you originally were working on; it's a resurrection made from the hidden scratch files. If you want to save this as a regular document, go ahead, but don't save over the original document—make a copy instead. There may be things missing in the recovered document that could not be recreated from the recovery data.

If you are fed up with the whole thing, simply close the recovered document without saving and open the original, which will only be current up to the last time you explicitly saved it before the crash occurred.

If InDesign crashes during or after an autorecovery, chances are the autorecovery data was corrupted in the initial crash. If it keeps crashing whenever you try to start it up, open the InDesign folder and trash the InDesign Recovery folder within. Sorry, but you won't be able to use Autorecovery if this happens.

Placing Files

You can place the following types of files into an InDesign document through the Place dialog (Command/Control + D).

When a file uses missing fonts, the missing font names are listed in a special "Missing" section of the InDesign font menus (such as in the Type ➠ Font menu, and in the Character palette). There may be cases where one or more font menus may not be updated in response to font changes in the document, such as after pasting or placing text with missing fonts. To make sure these menus are up-to-date, press Command/Control + Option + Shift + /.

Bitmapped images—TIFF, EPS, JPEG, native Photoshop files, Windows BMP (both platforms), DCS EPS, GIF, Macintosh bitmap PICT (both platforms), PCX, PNG, Scitex CT.

Vector artwork—EPS, native Illustrator, Windows WMF. Vector Macintosh PICTs are not supported.

Text files—ASCII, tagged QuarkXPress ASCII, tagged PageMaker ASCII, RTF, Microsoft Word 2000, Word 98 (Mac), Word 97, Word 4.0–7.0, Microsoft Excel 98, Excel 97, WordPerfect PC 6.1–8.0.

Acrobat PDF files—from any version. We think that someday PDF could replace EPS.

The ability of InDesign to parse QuarkXPress and PageMaker tags is an outstanding feature, and it is a very good means of getting text out of legacy QuarkXPress and PageMaker documents and into InDesign without the hassle of opening and converting document files. Inline images in tagged text will generate an error message in the text where they appear in the original document; however, if you consider these to be placeholders for image placement, they're quite handy.

Support for tagged text is especially beneficial for automatic text generation systems and database publishing—there's no need to wait for an InDesign-specific version of these systems as long as they can create and export text tagged with QuarkXPress or PageMaker formatting tags.

InDesign Preferences

Choose File ➠ Preferences or press Command/Control + K to display the preferences. Like QuarkXPress and PageMaker, InDesign has both document and application preferences. Document preferences are only in effect while a specific document is open. Application preferences are in effect all the time, unless a document preference overrides an application preference.

For example, with no document open, you can add some frequently used colors to the Swatches panel. These will then always be present whenever you create a new document or import a QuarkXPress or PageMaker document, but they won't appear in the

Swatches panel if you open an InDesign file that was created without those swatches in the panel at the time.

You can set a number of preferences as application preferences, which will carry through in all new and converted documents you create. The most common use is the Measurements setting, so if you prefer to work in inches instead of picas, you can make this preference change with no documents open, and all new documents created after that will default to inches. You'll probably find many other preferences to change for your own set of defaults.

General Preferences   Figure 3–34 shows the general options.

Images gives you three options: Gray Out, Proxy Images, and Full Resolution Images. Gray Out is analogous to the "Greek Pictures" option in QuarkXPress and works the same as the Gray Out option in PageMaker: in any case, you won't see placed images at all because they'll be represented by a gray box. This is handy for working with long, image-loaded documents when the images are already placed and you just want to make some textual changes. It really speeds up the screen display.

Figure 3–34
The Preferences dialog, general preferences.

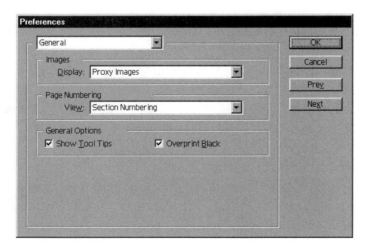

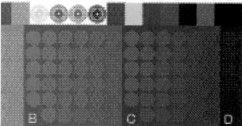

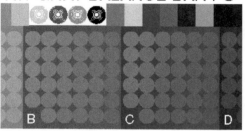

**EPS image with Full Resolution Images
unselected (proxies used)**

**EPS image with Full Resolution Images
selected**

Figure 3–35
Result of image display options.

Proxy Images presents a low-resolution preview of all TIFF and EPS images that does not get any better with enlargement. Use the Adobe Modular Parsing System to display EPS images "live," that is, without relying on the built-in EPS preview; InDesign will parse and render EPS images at full resolution when you choose Full Resolution Images.

TIFF images will also benefit from this option. However, choosing this option will significantly slow down the screen refresh when scrolling or zooming. Figure 3–35 illustrates the difference between proxy images and full-resolution images. InDesign will only adjust the screen display of color-managed images if Full Resolution Images is selected in the Display setting.

Page Numbering View lets you see and specify page numbers as Section Numbering or Absolute Numbering. You can use absolute page numbers when, for example, printing out selected pages. If you have Absolute Numbering selected, then you can just enter "1-12" in the Print dialog instead of "*1-*12" or "i-xii" in the Print dialog.

Page Numbering View makes tracking actual pages in a document with numerous section breaks a little easier. It also allows you to keep a running page count so you can make sure it is a multiple of 4, or 8, or 16, for signature printing. If you prefer to work with Section Numbering, leave it set at the default.

General Options, which should be called something else, gives just two options: Show Tool Tips and Overprint Black. The former isn't very important; it allows the presentation of the little on-screen hints that appear if you hold the mouse pointer over a tool for a few seconds. The latter is a bit more important. In general, you will want to leave Overprint Black set to the default "on" setting.

In some printing processes, such as newspaper printing, you may not want black to overprint but rather to knock out anything below it.

The black ink used for newspaper printing is pretty low in density and it does a bad job of hiding anything printed underneath it. Some toner-based printing stystems will also benefit from knocking out anything under heavy areas of black coverage. It all depends on the printing process you intend to use.

For large areas of black, you might want to knock out black no matter what process you use. However, if you turn off Overprint Black, you'll have to be careful about setting your trapping options. Overprinting black is an easy way to avoid having to trap a number of things, but if you turn it off, you'll have to trap black as you would any other color. See "Trapping" in Chapter 9 for more information about knockouts and overprints.

Text Preferences   Figure 3–36 shows the Text options.

In the *Character Settings* section, where you specify how much a character is reduced, and where it is positioned relative to the baseline, when you choose superscript or subscript formatting. You can also specify how much an uppercase character is reduced in size to create an artificial small cap. It is always preferable to use a true small cap and superior characters if they are available, but this trick will work in a pinch.

Most expert typefaces include cut small caps and cut superiors that will always look a lot better than the artificially created ones invoked by choosing Small Caps, Superscript, or Subscript in text formatting.

Type Options sets a few parameters about type display and text entry. Anti-Alias Type softens the hard black and white edge of characters by creating a tiny gray-scale ramp between the white and black

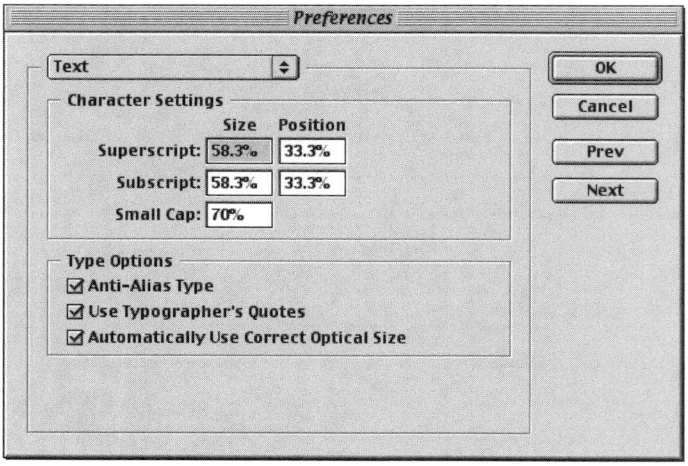

Figure 3–36
The Preferences dialog, text preferences.

transitions. This greatly improves the appearance of type on-screen, but it does exact a performance penalty and can impair readability of small type on-screen. The images in Figure 3–37 are enlarged a bit to show the differences.

Use Typographer's Quotes tells InDesign to automatically replace typed quote marks with typographer's quotes. If you specify a language other than English for a particular passage, typed quotes will be entered as appropriate for that language; for example—if you select French and then type a quote mark, it will display as a guillemet.

Without Typographer's Quotes   With Typographer's Quotes
        "The Cheese"   "The Cheese"

Examples of various language quotes:

French: «Allons-y!»
German: „Schnell!"
Finnish: "Voi Luoja!"
British English: 'Let's go'

ANTI-ALIAS

Anti-Aliasing turned off

ANTI-ALIAS

Anti-Aliasing turned on

Figure 3–37
Effect of anti-aliasing.

Automatically Use Correct Optical Size lets you use the built-in optically correct font sizes present in some Adobe Multiple Master typefaces. Optical sizing means that a character with correct optical sizing will at six points looks a little heavier than the same character with correct optical sizing at 72 points—in fact, setting both optical sizes manually to the same point size will show that the smaller optical-size version is noticeably different. This harkens back to the days of hand-cut and hot-metal type, where the type and mold cutters would account for the differences in size in the interests of readability by making slight changes to the character weight for each size.

Optical sizing is an attribute in some Multiple Master typefaces that adjusts the weight of the type when it is set in different sizes. Using this preference will automatically substitute the closest optically correct instance of a Multiple Master typeface. To get better optical scaling of a particular size, you should create new instances of the typeface with the optical scaling set to the size you plan to use.

You can create new instances of optical sizes with any of a number of Multiple Master typeface creation tools, including the one built into Adobe Type Manager Deluxe. Most of these typefaces are shipped with optical sizing for small (10–12 pt) and large (72 pt) sizes, but you can create new ones to suit sizes you might want to use, such as 24 or 36 pt. You can use the Multiple Master Creator tools in Adobe Type Manager Deluxe, as shown in Figure 3–38.

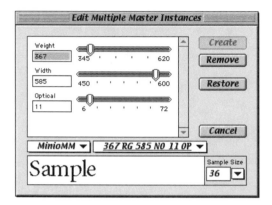

Figure 3–38
Creating a new Multiple Master instance.

All Multiple Master typefaces have at least one scalable axis; most have two, and some have three, as in the example of Adobe Minion Multiple Master shown. Not all of them include optical scaling.

Composition Preferences   This area lets you choose the primary text composition method and also has a number of display options to alert you to the presence of composition problems. Figure 3–39 shows the composition options.

The options for the Multi-line Composer let you choose how many lines ahead the composer will use when setting a paragraph, and the number of breakpoint alternatives to consider when setting the type. Setting a higher number for the Look ahead option can improve composition, but it can seriously slow down composition speed. This is why newer, higher-speed computers are a must.

Turning on *Highlight* for Keep Violations, Substituted Fonts, and H&J Violations will show you that there's a problem with your type by highlighting the ill-behaved type with a colored tint over the offending material. Keep violations are situations where the widow, orphan, and other paragraph break controls you set are nonconforming. Substituted fonts can be highlighted for easy identification: They will display as shaded pink lines. This is a very good feature for those who are fastidious in their typography.

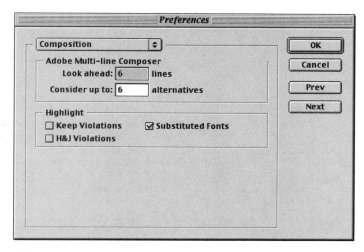

Figure 3–39
The Preferences dialog, composition preferences.

This really helps when you have a single character accidentally set in another font, especially if it's a space character, and you can't seem to find out where it's used. H&J violations are nonconformances in your word and letter spacing specifications.

Although InDesign's Multi-line Composer is the greatest composition tool to ever hit desktop computers, it can't fix everything. Lines that don't conform are highlighted in various shades of yellow. The darkest shade of yellow means that the line has a serious problem with spacing; lighter shades indicate less severe problems.

Units and Increments Preferences   Figure 3–40 shows the options for Units and Increments.

Ruler Units lets you specify your preferred measurement system in points, picas, inches, decimal inches, millimeters, centimeters, ciceros, and there's also a custom option that lets you specify the ruler increments in points.

Keyboard Increments lets you define the amount of movement when you invoke a keyboard shortcut or move a selected object with the arrow keys.

Settings in the Preferences ⇒ Unit and Increments dialog box determine the increments InDesign uses for changing type size and leading, baseline shift, and kerning. The QuarkXPress set lets you use the QuarkXPress key combinations to increase and decrease these attributes, but you'll need to use the Preferences feature if you want those short-cuts to use the exact increments Quark uses.

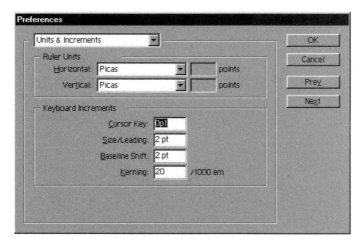

Figure 3–40
The Preferences dialog, units and increments preferences.

Cursor Key specifies the distance moved when you press an arrow key once.

Size/Leading and *Baseline Shift* specify the increments by which point size, character leading, and baseline shifting are increased or decreased with a keyboard shortcut. *Kerning* lets you define the increment of one kerning keystroke in 1/1000 em increments.

Grids Preferences   Figure 3–41 shows the options for grids.

Baseline Grid options let you define the grid color, the origin (usually a few picas below the upper edge of the page), and the grid's increments, which will usually be the same leading value (or a multiple thereof) as used in your body copy. The *View Threshold* is the magnification at which the guides will appear, below which they will not be displayed.

The *Document Grid* settings let you choose the grid color, the gridline increments, and the subincrements. You choose the number of grid subdivisions by entering an integer value in the *Subdivisions* box. The default, 8, will display eight small squares between each gridline.

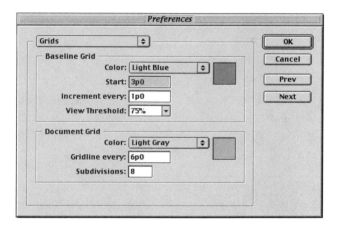

Figure 3–41
The Preferences dialog, grids preferences.

Guides Preferences   Figure 3–42 shows the Guides options.

The only Guides options are color choices, guides front or back, and the snap distance. Choosing *Guides in Back* will display all guides behind everything on a page. The snap distance is defined as a pixel value, so it will remain constant no matter what the chosen magnification is.

If you don't like the preset color choices and want to make your own, double-clicking any grid or guide color patch will display the system color picker.

Figure 3–42
The Preferences dialog, guides preferences.

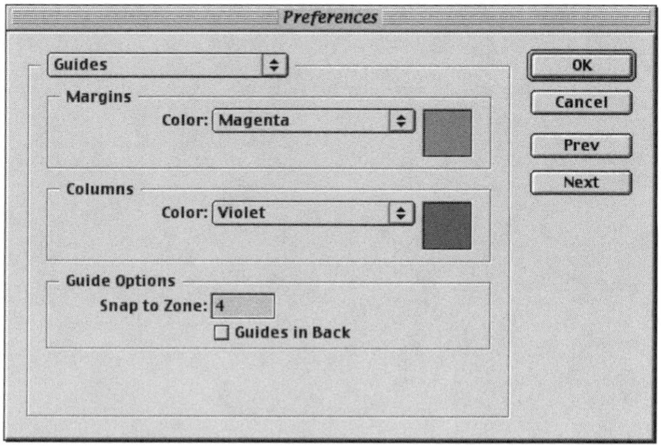

Most cursor icons in InDesign, like the drawing tool cursors and the "loaded" cursors that appear when you place text or graphic files, change appearance to indicate when InDesign's "snap to" features will determine the exact positioning of objects.

These snap-to icons remove the guesswork of knowing when the cursor is within the snap-to zone relative to a guide or grid increment. The snap-to zone distance is specified in the File ➡ Preferences ➡ Guides dialog box.

Dictionary Preferences   Figure 3–43 shows the Dictionary options.

Dictionary Preferences allow you to select the hyphenation and spelling dictionary to use for the dominant language or specialty. You can always tag selected text with a different dictionary as you work.

The Hyphenation Vendor and Spelling Vendor selections, for now, are limited to Proximity. You may be able to add other dictionary vendors as options in the future.

We expect plug-ins by the time this book is out.

After you've set all your preferences, just click OK. If you ever want to reset all preferences back to the defaults, quit the program, delete the InDesign Defaults file within the InDesign folder, then restart InDesign. A new InDesign Defaults file will be created for you.

Figure 3–43
The Preferences dialog, dictionary preferences.

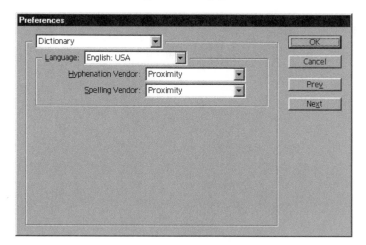

We herewith provide our usual caution about relying entirely on a spelling checker to check your work. Some of us think it is a substitute for proofreading. No matter how good the spellchecker is, it is no substitute for a human being.

Last Note   InDesign always verifies that a specified amount of disk space is available before carrying out particular transactions such as saving or exporting a document and will warn you if there is not enough disk space to proceed with the transaction.

If InDesign thinks that it has the minimal amount of disk space available but runs out of disk space while performing the transaction (in other words, it thought wrongly), a message appears which says "Adobe InDesign is shutting down. A serious error was detected."

Although other conditions can result in the same error message appearing, it is possible that you can simply make more disk space available by deleting some files, restart InDesign, and complete the transaction.

4

PAGE SETUP AND LAYOUT

This chapter details the process of creation and setup of documents and provides some information about document layout management with master pages, layers, and the available guides and grids. This is the very heart and soul of document assembly.

InDesign uses the frame metaphor of QuarkXPress: frames or boxes for text, images, or even frames or boxes about nothing (like the Seinfeld show). This approach goes way beyond PageMaker and improves upon QuarkXPress.

What is different about the InDesign approach is the way you interface with these objects. It is just different enough from QuarkXPress that it will take a little getting used to if you are making the transition. If you are coming to InDesign cold turkey, you have less baggage and should "get it" pretty fast. We did it in about a week (after over a decade of dealing with QuarkXPress).

Creating a New InDesign Document

Choose File ➤ New. The New Document dialog (Figure 4–1) appears.

The settings in the New Document dialog mirror those found in File ➤ Document Setup and Layout ➤ Margins and Columns. Remember that you can enter units for any value in the measurement system of your choice.

Page Size and Orientation   As an example, you might specify a custom 6 in. by 9 in. page by typing "6i" and "9i" in the width and height fields, when the chosen measurement system is in inches. The page size pop-up menu gives you a number of predefined page sizes, though you can't add additional predefined sizes. Page orientation is either portrait (tall) or landscape (wide). You can change a document's orientation with the Automatic Layout Adjustment feature. For most documents that will be printed, you will want to make the page size the trim size of the final document.

More on that to follow. Switching between portrait and landscape automatically adjusts the values in the height and width fields.

Figure 4–1
The New Document dialog.

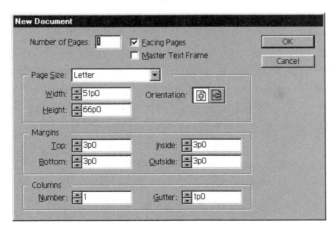

Document Settings

Margins and Column Guides Specifying margins in InDesign works exactly the same way it does in QuarkXPress and PageMaker. If you choose to include a master text frame and you specify more than one column, the frame is created with that number of columns, just as it is in QuarkXPress. If you don't choose a master frame, column guides are created instead, as in QuarkXPress. In PageMaker, you cannot specify the number of columns or a master text frame when creating a new document.

You have to create the document, then set column guides on the master page with Layout ➠ Column Guides. By default, newly created multiple columns have equal widths. To create uneven-width columns, create the number of columns needed, then click and drag one of the column guides on either side of the gutter to change the relative width.

Facing Pages Creating a document with 2-page spreads in InDesign is simply a matter of choosing Facing Pages in the New Document dialog, which is the same way you do it in QuarkXPress and in PageMaker. However, in PageMaker you have the option of choosing "double-sided" with or without facing pages. You don't have this option in InDesign, and frankly it wasn't all that useful in PageMaker unless you preferred not to view facing pages in spreads.

The options found in File ➠ Document Setup let you change the page size of an open document, and change it from facing pages (2-page reader spreads) to single pages. However, if you convert an open document from facing pages to single pages, then any masters with facing pages will retain the 2-page spreads and new pages based on a facing-pages master will be created as island spreads. You need to manually convert master page spreads to single pages, and vice versa. We'll talk more about the various types of InDesign spreads in a bit.

Master Text Frame   Specifying a master text frame is useful for creating long documents that have uniform pages, such as a book or journal. A master text frame in both InDesign and QuarkXPress allows you to create a single-page document into which you import a text file; with a master text frame, as many additional pages as needed are created to contain the imported text. However, in InDesign, you don't need to create a master text frame in order to autoflow imported text, as you must do in QuarkXPress (which is what you do when you check "Automatic Text Box" in the New Document dialog). You cannot autoflow text at all in QuarkXPress unless you specify a master text frame at the time you create the document. Manually linking multiple text boxes does not count.

InDesign's autoflow function works very much like that in PageMaker—you can use the Autoflow function to automatically create additional needed pages. You can either autoflow the entire text file, flow it onto a single page, or semiautomatically flow it from one page to another. The last is handy if you have multiple page layouts set up in master pages.

There's no way to semiautomatically flow text in QuarkXPress because the add pages feature is set to various levels of "on" or simply "off" in the QuarkXPress general preferences. InDesign will usually honor column guides when autoflowing text, even if a master text frame is not used.

InDesign will not add pages automatically as you create content. In QuarkXPress, if you create a master text frame and then type your content rather than import it from a text file, QuarkXPress will add pages automatically to accommodate the growth of your prose. InDesign will not do this, which is a shame. For those who compose in their page layout program, having new pages generated as text is accumulated is quite useful. However, many authors use a word processor to create their prose and then import text into the page layout application.

If you do write in InDesign, you'll have to stop, add one or more pages, link the text frames, then resume typing—just as in

PageMaker, and at least in PageMaker you could always bang away into the Story Editor even if you'd run out of room and flow the new content later. We hope this shortcoming will be addressed in a future release. We also hope someone will add a word count as QuarkXPress has when you spellcheck. This is useful for authors who must write to a specific article or chapter word amount.

There's no such thing as a master text frame in PageMaker; you can certainly create a text frame on a master page in PageMaker, but it will not have the autoflow capabilities of those in InDesign and QuarkXPress.

Autoflow in InDesign works without a master text frame, but the automatically created frames will default to the size of the document's margins. If you want to autoflow text into a frame that's different from the margin sizes, you'll need to create the frame on a master page and then autoflow the text.

Creating Customized New Document Defaults   If you alter the settings in File ➠ Document Setup and/or Layout ➠ Margins and Columns with no documents open, then all new documents created afterwards will use those settings—a global function, if you will. This is handy if you frequently use one particular page size and layout and provides a workaround for the inability to add a user-defined page to the Page Size pop-up menu in the New Document dialog.

You can also specify a master text frame in Document Setup, as long as there aren't any documents open. Once a master text frame is specified (or not), you cannot add or remove a master text frame in the Document Setup dialog. If you want to add or remove a master text frame, you'll need to manually add or remove it from the appropriate master page.

Spreads and Pages

Obviously, all page layout programs use the page as the underlying basis for construction of a document, but each program treats them differently.

Figure 4–2
Masters in PageMaker 6.5 can be
managed in the Master Pages panel.

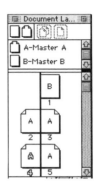

Figure 4–3
QuarkXPress Document Layout panel.

Pages in PageMaker   There's no central document layout panel in
PageMaker like the one in QuarkXPress and in InDesign—you see all
of your master and document pages as a row of icons at the bottom
left of the screen, as illustrated in Figure 4–2.

Pages in QuarkXPress   QuarkXPress 3.3 and 4.0 use the Document
Layout panel, shown in Figure 4–3, to manage both document and
master pages. You can add and rearrange pages by dragging page
proxy icons around, and you can delete selected masters and document pages.
    Both programs show you at a glance the basic document layout—
facing or nonfacing pages.

InDesign Pages   InDesign groups all pages, masters and document,
into one panel, shown in Figure 4–4. Choose View ➠ Pages or press
F12 to show the pages panel.

Pages in General   First, we'll look at the document pages portion of
the panel. Some of the basic page arrangement functions also work
with masters. Master pages are discussed later in this chapter.
    The most basic distinction between types of document layouts is
the choice of facing or nonfacing pages. Nonfacing pages are single
pages that are displayed sequentially. Facing pages are two pages that
are displayed side by side on the monitor. Pretty basic stuff.

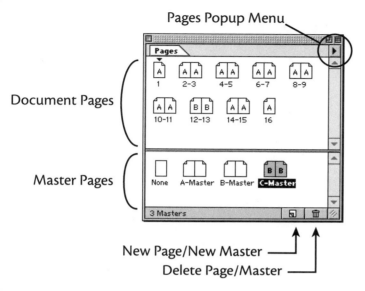

Pages Popup Menu

Document Pages

Master Pages

New Page/New Master

Delete Page/Master

Figure 4–4
InDesign Pages panel.

The choice of facing or nonfacing pages in many cases is a matter of personal preference—for publications, the final arrangement, or *imposition*, of document pages is performed without regard to the status of facing pages in the document. Some people prefer not to work with facing pages as working with two pages on the screen can be a big pain unless you have an enormous monitor. However, it is the only way to see the relationship of text and objects on the spread.

Figures 4–5 through 4–7 show a few examples of layouts in InDesign. The views have been reduced to 8% to show the full layout of the document.

Here, we should point out that InDesign considers even a single page to be a spread, as evidenced in the lower left-hand corner of this sample pages panel.

Spreads and Facing Pages   What's the difference? Not much—a set of two facing pages is the most basic form of a spread. A spread is two or more pages set side by side. As in QuarkXPress, InDesign spreads can contain more than two pages; in fact, a spread can have

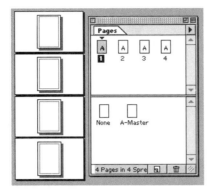

Figure 4–5
An InDesign document with
nonfacing pages.

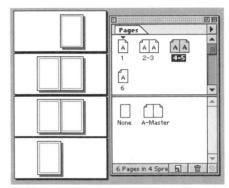

Figure 4–6
An InDesign document with facing pages.

up to ten pages in it for those extra-long accordion foldouts.
PageMaker does not support more than two pages in a spread.

You can change a PageMaker document from facing to nonfacing
pages quite easily. In QuarkXPress, you cannot change a document
from facing pages to nonfacing pages, nor vice versa. This causes all
sorts of problems if you want to manually create an inposition (printer's spreads) from a document that was set up as facing pages—you
can't do it at all.

Spreads in all three programs refer to *reader's spreads*. They're
called that because the story flows from one side of the spread to the
other, just as in a book. *Printer's Spreads* are completely different and
represent the layout of the pages in strange-looking arrangements to
accommodate the nature of the printing and binding processes. The
arrangement is called an *imposition*.

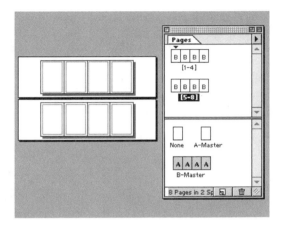

Figure 4–7
An InDesign document set up as two 4-page spreads.

If you aren't familiar with the idea of printer's spreads, just grab a weekly news magazine like TIME and remove the staples (in printer's language, "stitches"). Then, take the thing apart and observe how the flat sheets are laid out in relation to the actual page order. These are printer's spreads at their simplest.

The stitched binding is the easiest to impose for; other impositions for bindings like perfect and case binding can become quite complicated.

Actually, magazines like TIME aren't really printed in printer's spreads, but you can see how a simple 16-page newsletter might be put together from this example. Most magazines and books are printed on large rolls or sheets of paper at very high speeds, and as many as 64 document pages might be printed on each sheet or section of a paper roll.

These large sections might even contain the entire set of pages for a magazine. The sections are then cut into sheets if roll-fed, then folded by powerful machines into *signatures.*

A signature usually contains a multiple of four document pages, and after it is folded, the signature is bound either singly or with others, then the edges are trimmed to create the final magazine or whatever the finished document is. Books are usually made from many signatures; most weekly magazines are usually made from one or two signatures.

The example of the four-page spread can be used for a four-panel brochure that is to be printed on both sides then accordion-folded. You can also have spreads in a catalog or booklet—everyone's seen catalogs with one sheet that folds out of the main document—like this layout with a three-page spread that will be printed and bound into a catalog and used as a foldout. We need two such spreads because the foldout is printed on both sides—the far-right page of the first spread is the front of the foldout, and the far-left page of the second spread is the back of the foldout, as shown in Figure 4–8.

PageMaker users should pay extra attention here. In PageMaker, you can't have more than two pages in a spread, as PageMaker never really "got" the concept of spreads in the first place. Sure, you could make one long giant page and chop it up manually into page-sized bits, but who wants to do that? So, if you've been doing your 3+ panel spreads that way in PageMaker, you don't have to do that anymore.

Figure 4–8
Three-page foldouts.

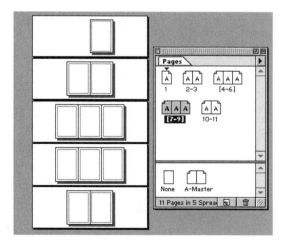

Figure 4–9
Pages panel options.

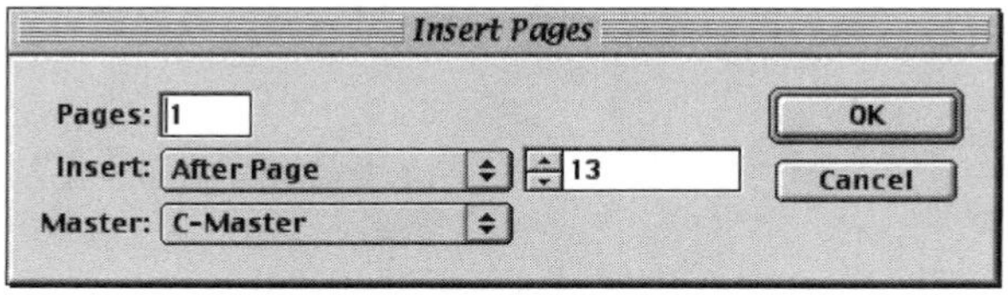

Figure 4–10
Insert Pages dialog.

"Okay, Mister Smarty, how do these magic spreads account for the margin changes needed to accommodate folds?" Easy. Make a folding dummy, using the sheet size you plan to use for the print job, usually a signature that will have multiple pages printed on it. Measure the distance required to inset the contents of a page panel to clear the fold. Then don't put anything in that clearance area!

The pop-up menu on the Pages panel has several options, as shown in Figure 4–9.

Some of these options refer to master pages, which we'll get to shortly.

Choosing *Insert Pages* lets you specify the number of new pages, the master page upon which they are based, and the location in the document where they are to be inserted, as shown in Figure 4–10.

Choosing *Duplicate Spread* creates a copy of the currently selected spread at the end of the document.

Choosing *Delete Spread* lets you remove any selected spreads.

Section Options lets you start and specify section markers in a document and also change the page numbering. We'll talk about sections later in this chapter.

To create and maintain spreads with more than two pages in them, you use the *Set as Island Spread* menu item. *Island spreads* are InDesign-ese for spreads with more than two pages, and the *Island* part probably refers to the fact that once set, an island spread cannot be broken up until you choose to do so.

Brackets appear around the spread's page numbers in the pages panel when it is set as an island. You can insert document pages into a spread at any time, and you can move pages out of a spread just by dragging them in or out.

Select and Target   Before we get into the nuances of shuffling pages around, it's important to note two contexts within which you work with InDesign page and spreads. You target a page or spread by double-clicking its page number(s) under the icon of the pages. By doing so, you make that spread or page "active," and it appears in the document window.

A spread (and let's just call a page a spread for now) needs to be targeted before you can work with anything on it, or add or delete objects. You can also target a spread in a reduced view by just clicking on it or on its pasteboard (the area to the left and right of your page on the screen that acts as a storage area for page items).

To make changes in the document's layout—for example, adding, moving, or deleting spreads, or changing margins and columns—you need to *select* a spread. Yes, this is confusing. For instance, to delete three consecutive pages contained in two spreads of two pages, shift-click on the three page icons in the pages panel, *not* on the page numbers displayed below the icons, then drag them to the little trash can on the pages panel. Selecting spreads/pages tells InDesign that you are doing something with the pages themselves, and not their contents.

Simply put, double-clicking on a spread's *page numbers* will target it and also bring it into view. Single-clicking on a page icon will select it. Single-clicking on a spread's page numbers will also select all pages within the spread. Shift + Click can select more than one page, even if the pages are in different spreads. Double-clicking on a page icon targets that page as well as the spread in which it resides.

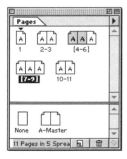

Figure 4–11
Targeting and selecting.

In the example in Figure 4–11, the spread with pages 7, 8, and 9 is targeted and is visible in the document window. Pages 4 and 5 in the first three-page spread are selected.

Adding, Deleting, and Moving Pages   In QuarkXPress, you can move pages around in the document directly while in the Thumbnails view, or you can do this from the Document Layout palette. In PageMaker, you can't move pages at all without the Sort Pages add-in (add-ins are PageMaker's response to Quark XTensions, but they never really worked at the same level).

Without this add-in, first you'd have to insert new blank pages where you want the originals to go, copy and paste all of the contents to the new pages, then delete the old ones, which is really a rather silly way to do it. Even with the Sort Pages add-in, moving pages around in PageMaker was never interactive—you couldn't see the results of a move until after you closed the Sort Pages dialog.

You can move any InDesign spread (remember: a spread is a page, and a page is a spread) wherever you want.

To move an entire spread, drag it by its numbers and move it to the destination, either between two other spreads or within another spread. The document layout will automatically readjust, as will any automatic page numbers you've specified. This works the same whether the spread being moved contains just one page or up to ten pages.

An example document, shown in Figures 4–12 through 4–14, shows the results. We've put some page numbers on the pages at 250 point to help.

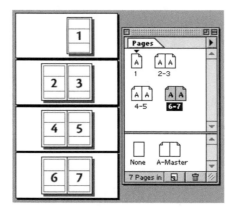

Figure 4–12
Moving spreads: Base order.

Here we're moving spread 6–7 between spread 1 and spread 2–3.

Figure 4–13
Moving spreads: First move.

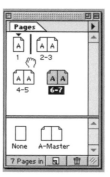

And here's the result in Figure 4–14.

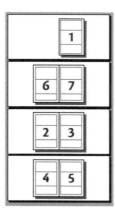

Figure 4–14
Moving spreads: Result
of first move.

In Figure 4–15, we're moving the same spread *into* spread 2–3, splitting it apart. You can insert the spread between the pages of the other one, or insert it just before the first page, or just after the second page.

The vertical insertion point shows you where the pages will be inserted.

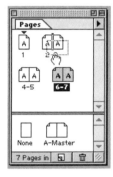

Figure 4–15
Moving spreads: Another move.

Here's the result in Figure 4–16.

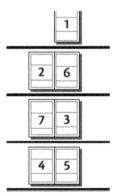

Figure 4-16
Moving spreads: Final result.

Page Numbering and Running Heads

InDesign page numbering is like that in PageMaker and QuarkXPress: You go to a master page, draw a text frame, and insert a page number marker. In InDesign, you can insert it from the Layout menu (Layout ➧ Insert Page Number). You can also insert a page number marker with the contextual menu—Control/Right-click in the text frame and choose Insert Special Character ➧ Auto Page Numbering. Or, press Command + Option/Control + Alt + N.

You can also add whatever text you want to the frame with the page number for running headers. Automatic page number markers display on master pages as A, B, C, etc., depending on the master page they're on.

The neat thing that InDesign does that the other two don't is allow you to stick an automatic page number on a document page using the same method you'd use on a master page. The document page number automatically adjusts to any layout changes. InDesign also supports section markers—these are labels you can put on a master or document page that change according to the settings you've made in the Section Start options. As with page numbers, section markers can appear on master pages or on document pages.

Sections and Section Starts

Sections are pages in a document that use different page numbers, running heads/footers, or numbering systems, such as the front matter of a book that uses lowercase Roman numerals.

PageMaker does not support section starts; it only lets you choose the numeral style for automatic page numbers, so you have to break sections into discrete documents. QuarkXPress lets you set a section start along with a choice of numeral styles, and a section prefix.

InDesign offers basically the same section start features that QuarkXPress does. To designate a page as a section start, select the page in the pages panel, then choose *Section Options* from the pages

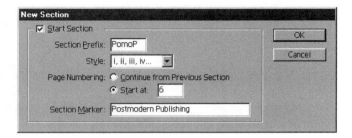

Figure 4–17
New Section dialog.

panel pop-up menu, to display the Section Options dialog, shown in Figure 4–17.

These settings produce a running footer on the bottom of each page that's included within the section, shown in Figure 4-18. This page number differs from the master page for this section, which will only display an automatic page number.

Figure 4–19 shows the available numeral styles in InDesign.

To enable section markers—that is, the automatic placement of the text entered into the Section Marker field—insert a section marker character into a text frame on the appropriate master or document page.

Figure 4–18
Section running footer.

Figure 4–19
Numeral styles.

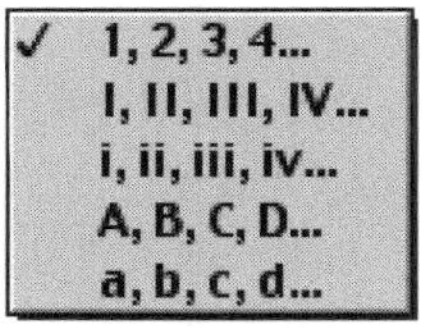

Figure 4–20
Section prefix.

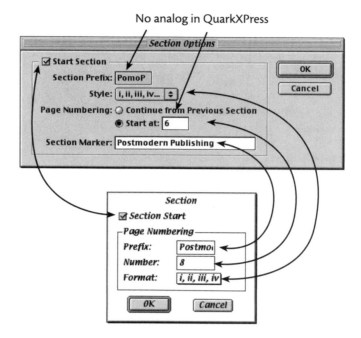

Figure 4–21
Comparison of Section options in QuarkXPress and InDesign.

The section marker character can be found on the contextual text pop-up menu. (Control/Right-click with Text tool insertion point active in a text box to invoke this menu.)

Usually, a section marker will go with an automatic page number, but it's also handy for running heads or footers. As you apply them, keep in mind that many books start new chapters on right-hand pages and you may need to generate a blank left-hand page to accomplish this.

A section prefix in InDesign refers to the name you enter into the Section Prefix field of the Section options dialog. The prefix will appear in the lower left-hand corner of the screen in the page locator, as shown in Figure 4–20.

Section prefixes are limited to five characters. A section prefix in QuarkXPress is really the same thing as a section marker in InDesign. Figure 4–21 compares of the section options in both programs.

Figure 4–22
Example of a Roman-numeral section followed by an
Arabic-numeral section.

You can easily identify a section start in the pages panel by the small triangular mark that appears over the page's icon. By default, the first page in a document is already a section start, which is why all first pages display the section mark. To start a document with Roman numerals, simply set this in the first page's section options, then create a new section start wherever you want Arabic numerals to appear. Figure 4–22 illustrates the resulting page layout.

Master Pages

As an experienced user of QuarkXPress or PageMaker, you already know how master pages work and how valuable they are. InDesign's master pages are similar in concept to those in QuarkXPress and PageMaker, with a few differences. Here's a summary of each program's method of handling master pages.

PageMaker Master Pages   PageMaker has a Master Pages panel from which you can apply a master page to a selected (visible) document page and also to a range of pages that you specify. Clicking on a different master page will apply that master to the current page or spread. You can insert pages (Layout ➡ Insert pages) and specify a master page for the new pages. You can duplicate master pages, but you cannot edit or move master page items; you can only choose to show them or not.

PageMaker does not display any visual cues about which master page is applied to a document page unless you have the master pages panel open. Since you can't change master page items on a document page, applying a new master to a page preserves all content that was added to that page. You can set up both single and facing master pages, but only if you created the document with facing pages. PageMaker lets you specify different master pages for the left and right sides of a spread when inserting pages.

QuarkXPress Master Pages   You can directly add or insert new pages in a document by dragging a master page icon to the document layout panel. You apply master pages to document pages by dragging the master page's icon to the document page's icon in the Document Layout panel.

Each document page in the layout panel displays a small letter that indicates which master page is applied to it. Items on QuarkXPress master pages appear as editable objects on document pages, and you can change them at will. However, what happens when you apply a new master or reapply the existing master depends on the setting you've made in:

Edit ➡ Preferences ➡ General (QuarkXPress 3.3)
Edit ➡ Preferences ➡ Document ➡ General (QuarkXPress 4.0)

If you have "keep changes" selected, all local overrides to master page items on a document page will be preserved and the original master page items are *added* to the document page.

If you have "delete changes" selected, all local overrides are *discarded* and *replaced* by the original master page items.

You can set up both single and facing master pages, but only if you created the document with facing pages. You can also insert pages with Page ➡ Insert and specify a blank page, that is, one with no master at all applied to it. These pages will display in the document layout panel without an identifying letter.

You cannot specify different left and right pages when inserting pages with Page ➡ Insert; you can apply only one master to both sides of a spread this way.

You can replace one master with another in QuarkXPress, but this action is pretty drastic and replaces all content, guides, margins, and master text frames. You can change the name of a master page, but not its identifying letter, which will always reappear, even if you delete it from the master's name.

Master pages created by duplicating an existing master retain no ties to the original master—a change to the original master will not be reflected in the duplicated master.

InDesign Master Pages   Master pages in InDesign work a little like the ones in PageMaker, a little like the ones in QuarkXPress, and quite unlike either overall. No, really.

The biggest difference, for QuarkXPress users at least, is the fact that although master page items on document pages are editable, you can't select them just by clicking on them with the selection tool— you have to hold down Command/Control + Shift while clicking on the object to select it. The reasoning behind this to prevent accidental selection and alteration of master page items. Putting in this little barrier ensures that you *really* want to change a master page item on a document page (are you sure about that?).

It's a little overprotective, but we can see the virtue of it. Of course, if you're a PageMaker user, you'd never notice since master page items to you are inviolate and can only be changed on the master page.

You can create a series of master pages from one original, then modify each as you please. InDesign creates a parent/child relationship with duplicated master pages—if you create, say, five masters from one original, you can modify the heck out of of them, but if you add an object to the parent master, it will appear on all of its kids. Neither QuarkXPress nor PageMaker provides this function.

To avoid inadvertently creating a parent/child master page relation, create a new master rather than making a duplicate of an existing one. You must give this process some thought as you go through it and think about all master page relationships.

You can create *local overrides* to master page objects on document pages, and if you reapply the same master or a different one to the page, the overrides are preserved. You can apply a master to another master—this replaces all margins and guides but preserves any objects on the receiving master.

Pages Popup Menu

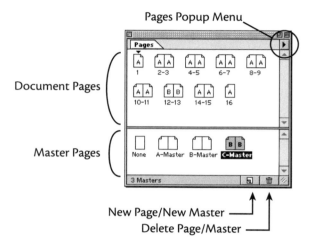

Document Pages

Master Pages

New Page/New Master
Delete Page/Master

Figure 4–23
Pages panel.

Figure 4–23 illustrates the Pages panel. In the upper portion are the document pages, which display their masters. Masters are in the lower portion. Applying a master to a page or spread is as simple as dragging the master's icon over that of the page or spread. In this example, you can see that the master spread C is based upon master spread B, because the little letter B appears in it, and you can see that spread 12–13 is based on master B.

You can slide the divider of the pages panel up and down by clicking on the divider. The cursor will change to the double-ended arrow, as shown in Figure 4–24. If you miss the tall skinny Document Layout panel in QuarkXPress, just resize the InDesign pages panel.

The pop-up menu on the Pages panel has several options for master pages; we've already covered the options that don't pertain to masters, shown in Figure 4–25.

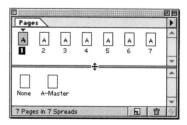

Figure 4–24
Resizing parts of the Pages panel.

```
Insert Pages...
New Master...
Duplicate Spread
Delete Spread

Master Options...
Section Options...

Apply Master to Pages...
Remove All Local Overrides

Save as Master
Set as Island Spread
```

Figure 4–25
Pages panel pop-up.

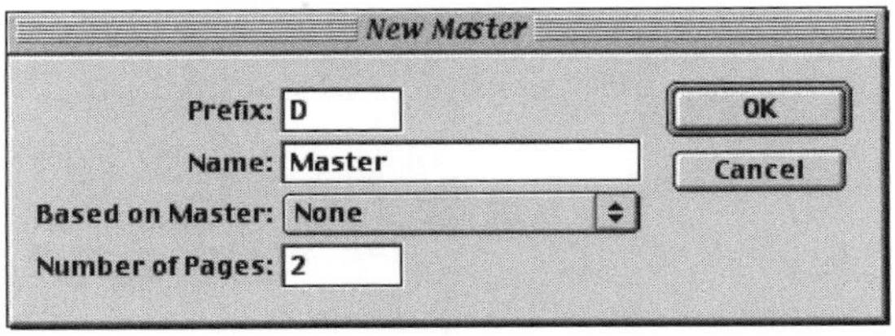

```
New Master
Prefix: D
Name: Master
Based on Master: None
Number of Pages: 2
                           OK
                           Cancel
```

Figure 4–26
New Master dialog.

Choosing *New Master* lets you base a new master on an old one or create a fresh one. As Figure 4–26 illustrates, you can also choose a name and a prefix (the identifying letter) here as well as the number of pages a master spread will contain. Master spreads with more than two pages are created as *island spreads*. More about those in a bit.

You can also hold Command + Option/Control + Alt and click on the New Page button to do the same thing. Remember that basing a new master on an existing one will create a "child" master that's linked to the parent master.

The *Master Options* item is enabled when you have a master spread selected and gives you the same options as *New Master*, meaning you can redefine a master anytime as based upon another master.

To apply a master to a spread or a single page, you can do a number of different things. You could use the *Apply Masters* to Pages item on the Pages menu, which lets you choose a master to apply to a range of pages. We'll show you other ways of applying masters when we cover the rest of the menu items.

Remove All Local Overrides removes all changes made to master page items on a document page. Remember that you can select master page items by pressing Command/Control + Shift + Click and then locally override anything about that item. Use this one with care.

Save as Master lets you make any document page or spread into a master spread. The new master will be based on the document page's master page but will include any local overrides and additional content and changes. A master created in this fashion becomes the child of the master upon which the document page is based.

You can create master spreads as island spreads. Choose the master spread, then select *Set as Island Spread* from the pop-up menu.

Adding and Applying Masters   In addition to applying masters with the pop-up menu, you can use the page panel to do it quickly. To just add some more pages, er, spreads to the document, drag the desired master to the location you want in the document pages area, as shown in Figure 4–27 and Figure 4–28.

To *apply* a master to an existing document page or spread, drag the master's icon over that of the target page or spread. If your document

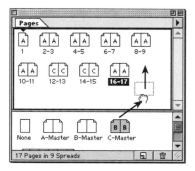

Figure 4–27
Adding a spread to the end.

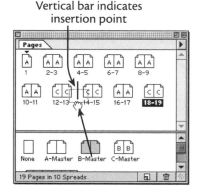

Vertical bar indicates insertion point

Figure 4–28
Inserting a new spread between two other spreads.

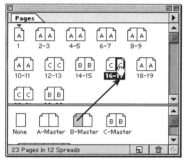

Applying a master page to a document page

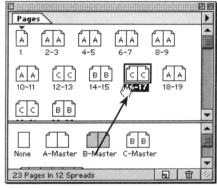

Applying a master spread to a document spread

Figure 4–29
Applying master page or spread to a document.

is composed of nonfacing pages, you just apply one master page to one document page (yes, yes, we know it's a spread, but it's not!).

If you do have facing pages or island spreads, you can either apply a single page from a master spread to a single document page or apply an entire master spread to a document spread.

Consider the examples in Figures 4–29.

Note carefully the appearance of the little box around the destination page. Applying a master spread is pretty easy, but applying a single master page can be a little tricky.

Island Spreads As mentioned already, island spreads are groups of pages arranged horizontally that contain two or more pages. If your document is set up as facing pages and you later change it to nonfacing pages with File ➡ Document Setup, all two-page spreads convert to island spreads that you'll have to break manually.

Island spreads carry their pages throughout a document no matter how much you move or add or arrange pages.

An island spread is denoted in the pages panel by the presence of brackets around the spread's page number range.

To mark pages as an island spread, select them, then choose *Set as Island Spread* in the Pages panel pop-up menu. The pages will then appear in the panel as a grouped spread. This is illustrated in Figures 4–30 and 4–31.

To remove pages from an island spread, just select one or more and drag them out, or delete them.

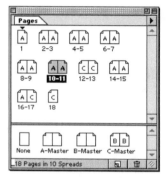

A facing-pages document after creating an island spread across pages 10-11

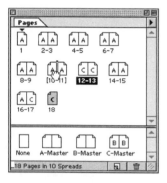

Dragging page 18 into the middle of the new spread

Figure 4–30
Creating a 3-page spread.

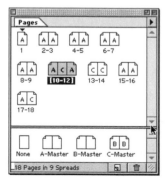

Figure 4–31
The new 3-page spread.

Choose *Clear Island Spread* to break the spread into regular spread that will conform to the settings you've made in File ➧ Document Setup.

Stacking Order   Objects on master pages appear behind objects on document pages. To force a master page object to appear above (or in front of) a document page object, you can do one of two things:

- Create a new, higher layer, then move the master page object to that layer (see Layers later in this chapter).
- You can also change the stacking order of a master page object on a document page by pressing Command/Control + Shift + Click, then choosing Object ➧ Arrange ➧ Send to Front. This will create a local override on the document page of the master object.

The Pasteboard   InDesign uses a fixed-size pasteboard for each spread. You can store objects on the pasteboard for future use. The pasteboard is similar to the metaphor used in QuarkXPress—each pasteboard is tied to a spread, unlike PageMaker where the pasteboard is global—for instance, an object on the pasteboard in PageMaker can be accessed from any page or spread.

QuarkXPress lets you change the size of the pasteboard in relation to the document page size, but InDesign does not. InDesign does let you rotate objects that overlap the pasteboard and not generate that annoying QuarkXPress error message: "This item can't be positioned off the pasteboard."

Rulers, Guides, and Grids

You can set preferences for guides and grids by choosing File ➧ Preferences ➧ Guides/Grids. Preferences are reviewed in Chapter 3, "InDesign Tour."

Zero Point   The zero point is the point where the vertical and horizontal rulers intersect, in the upper left-hand corner of the document window. To reset the zero point, just drag it to wherever you like. To reset the zero point back to 0,0, just double-click on it. To lock the zero point, Control/Right-click on it and choose the lock option.

Guides   There are two types of InDesign guides:

- page guides
- spread guides

Page guides only appear within a page boundary; spread guides appear across the entire spread and on the spread's pasteboard. To make a page guide, drag a guide from either ruler starting within the page boundaries. To make a spread guide, drag a ruler starting outside of the page boundary, on the pasteboard.

If the pasteboard isn't visible for some reason, hold Command/Control and drag a guide out to create a spread guide. You can also create a spread guide by double-clicking the specific position for the guide on one of the rulers. You can create a set of vertical and horizontal guides at the same time by Command/Control + Clicking on the zero point and dragging the result to the desired location. Guides are local to the layer in which they were created. You can make a layer just for guides if you like (see Layers later in this chapter). To create precision, by-the-numbers guides, choose Layout ➠ Create Guides (Figure 4–32).

"Columns" created here are not the same as the columns created by the settings in Document Setup. Columns made with Create Guides columns are simply guides and do not influence text flow.

Figure 4–32
Create Guides dialog.

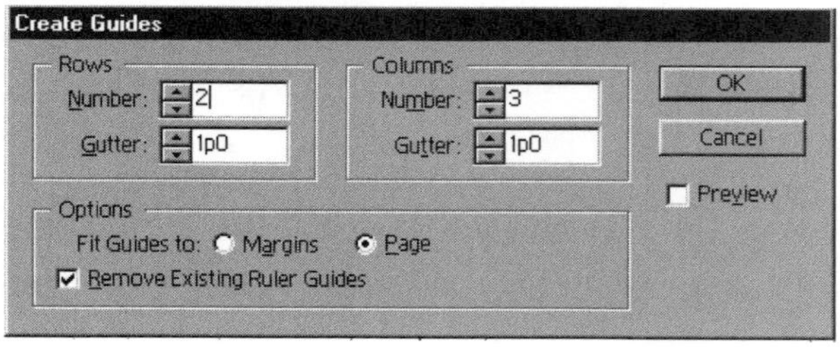

Rows are simply horizontal sets of guides. Both can have a "gutter" specification. *Fit Guides to* lets you choose whether the divisions are made with reference to the page margins or to the page dimensions. It probably isn't necessary to further expand upon *Remove Existing Ruler Guides*.

You can move, copy, cut, and paste guides anywhere throughout the document. To select a guide, just click on it. Shift + Click to select multiple guides. Press Command + Option/Control + Alt + G to select all of the guides present on a spread. If you can't seem to select any guides, check the status of View ➠ Lock Guides.

To move guides, just drag them. Hold Shift while dragging to snap guide movement to ruler tick marks. Move spread guides by dragging the part of the guide that's on the pasteboard. You can copy and paste guides to other spreads and pages. To remove guides, select them and press Delete. To enable object snapping, choose View ➠ Snap to Guides or press Command/Control + Shift + ;. Set the snap distance in the Guides Preferences.

You can choose to have guides displayed at the front or the back of a page or spread. Putting guides on different layers doesn't visually change their relation to page objects—guides will always adhere to the Guides in Back setting in Guides Preferences.

Grids   There really aren't very many options for grids—most of the pertinent settings for grids are in the Grid Preferences described in Chapter 3. Grids are uneditable, cannot be moved, and are either on or off—you can't have just a few pages with grids displayed. It's all or nothing. Baseline grids only appear within page boundaries; document grids cover the entire spread and pasteboard. Grids appear below everything else on a page and can't be assigned to layers.

Layers

A nifty feature that QuarkXPress still lacks (although it's rumored for Version 5), layers are a versatile means of organizing a document, especially for managing multiple versions of a document.

For example, if you're creating a brochure to be printed in English, French, and Swedish, you can just create one document file and create layers for each language version plus one for any graphics. By turning one language layer on and the other languages off, you can print each version easily while retaining all common graphics.

InDesign does not have the "suppress printout" function of PageMaker and QuarkXPress; items on hidden layers will not print, so this is how you can control what will and won't print in an InDesign document. You can create a new layer called "nonprinting" or whatever and place objects on it to effect the same results as "suppress printout."

Layers are documentwide and don't distinguish between document pages and master pages, oops, spreads. If you turn off a layer, it vanishes throughout the document, even on master pages. New InDesign documents always contain one default layer. Anything on a master page displays under anything on a document page, within the same layer. As you might expect, master page objects honor layer stacking order.

Figure 4–33 shows a sample Layers panel with a multilingual document.

You will see "eyeballs," which indicate visibility, and "little pencils with the slash through them" to indicate that the layer is locked. Click each symbol to toggle visibility or locked status.

The "little pen" icon on the English Text layer indicates that it is the active layer. The new layer and delete layer buttons at the bottom work the same as their analogs in other panels.

Figure 4–33
Layers panel.

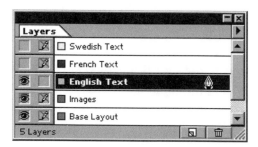

Similarly to how you target and select spreads, you do the same when working with layers.

- Targeting a layer makes it active, which lets you add, delete, or otherwise modify its content. To target it, just click on it once. It can be pretty easy to forget that a layer is targeted and to accidentally create or place something on the wrong layer. When you select an object, a little dot appears next to the layer name in the layers panel to tell you where the object currently resides, as shown in Figure 4–36 later in this chapter.
- Selecting one or more layers (Shift + Click to select more than one) lets you perform operations on the layer from the Layers panel pop-up menu.

To create a new layer, click the new layer button at the bottom of the panel or choose *New Layer* from the pop-up menu as seen in Figure 4–34. Double-clicking on an existing layer produces the Layer Options dialog (Figure 4–35), which presents the same options as choosing New Layer or clicking on the new layer button.

You can give unique names to layers, choose the color of the little square in the layers panel (which can help identify them), and select options for showing and locking layers and layer guides, though you can always do this directly in the panel. Layer guides display in the selected layer color only while you are dragging them and only when

Figure 4–34
The layers panel pop-up menu.

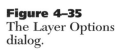

Figure 4–35
The Layer Options dialog.

they are selected. Once set, guides will always display in light blue—you can't change the color of ruler guides in the Preferences. It'd be nice if guides could be displayed according to the color of the layer in which they reside. Maybe in version 1.5?

To add objects to a layer, just target it. If the layer is locked, the current tool may show as the same small crossed-out pencil icon used in the Layers panel to indicate a locked layer. Unlock the layer to work with it.

Selecting objects on layers is pretty straightforward. Anytime you select an object on a spread, the object's layer becomes targeted. To select everything on a layer, press Option/Alt and click on the layer's name in the panel. When an object on a layer is selected, a little dot appears to the right of the layer's name.

To move things between layers, select them, then click and hold on the little dot and move it to the desired layer, as shown in Figure 4–36. Hold Command/Control while dragging to move objects to a locked layer.

Hold option/alt while dragging to copy the objects to another layer. It would seem to follow that holding Command + Option/Control + Alt lets you copy objects to a locked layer, and in fact that is how you do it.

To rearrange layers, select one or more and just drag them to the new position you want, as shown in Figure 4–37.

The state of the *Paste Remembers Layers* option in the Layers panel pop-up menu affects how objects copied and pasted within a document and into other documents are handled with respect to their layer assignments. If this option is selected (checked), objects pasted within a document retain their layer assignments. Since you can select objects on multiple layers, assuming none of them are locked, this makes it easy to keep track of where things are.

If the option is deselected, the pasted objects are placed into the target layer. When multilayer objects are pasted into another document that doesn't have the same layers as the source document, the layers from the source are created in the destination document. If this option is turned off, the objects are pasted into the targeted layer in the destination document.

Figure 4–36
Moving objects from one layer
to another.

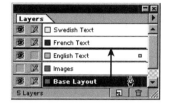

Figure 4–37
Rearranging layers.

Deleting a layer is simple—drag it to the trash icon at the bottom of the panel or use the pop-up menu. Shift + Click to select multiple layers for trashing.

If you're familiar with layers in Photoshop, then you know you must *flatten* the image before you can, for example, export it as a TIFF file. InDesign offers a flatten feature as well, on the panel pop-up menu, though there's no need to use it for exporting an InDesign document to another format since only visible layers are exported or printed.

You can also merge a layer with another—objects on the source layer end up on the target layer, and the source layer is deleted. Select the source layers, make sure the target layer is, er, targeted, then choose Merge Layers from the pop-up menu.

Caution: flattening all layers will throw everything onto a single default layer and could end up creating a messy disaster of a document. Use this option with care.

See Chapter 3 for information about what happens when you open a PageMaker file that contains layers in InDesign.

Autolayout Adjustment

This is one of the coolest things InDesign has to offer. If you've ever worked long and hard on a layout only to have an art director tell you that the layout is now to be landscape US Letter-half instead of portrait US Letter, you know what a hair-tearing experience it can be to basically start from scratch again and rebuild the document.

InDesign's automatic layout adjustment function will save you hours of work because, as the name implies, much of the work is done for you automatically. It's not perfect, nor can it ever be perfect, but it sure beats the alternative. Figure 4–38 illustrates the function.

Automatic layout adjustment works according to some rules you can set in the Layout Adjustment dialog. Adjustment attempts to maintain the same general proportions in the new layout as in the old, although this isn't always foolproof.

- It moves margin guides to accommodate the new layout if the page size changes.
- It moves column and ruler guides to maintain proportional distances from new changes to margins, page edges, and column guides.
- It adds or removes column guides if the new layout uses a different number of column guides.
- It moves objects that are snapped to guides in proportion to the placement changes of the guides after adjustment.
- It resizes objects that are aligned to two parallel guides.

Document as US Letter (8.5"x11"), portrait (tall)

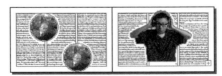

Document as US Letter half (5.5"x8.5"), landscape (wide), after automatic layout adjustment

Figure 4–38
Automatic layout adjustment.

Layout adjustment works best if the document is constructed with a well-designed set of guides, and doesn't work well at all with a document with no guides. Document grids have no effect on layout adjustment.

Text frame columns are not the same as column guides, and text columns will not change in number after adjustment. They will change in proportion only. To enable column number adjustment, select the relevant frames or the master frame, then choose Object ➠ Text Frame Options (Command/Control + B), and check the Fixed Column Width checkbox. This will cause layout adjustment to add or remove columns as necessary to maintain the same column width.

You enable automatic layout adjustment by choosing Layout ➠ Layout Adjustment and checking the Enable box. Layout adjustment occurs if you've enabled it, and then only if you make a change to File ➠ Document Setup or Layout ➠ Margins and Columns. See Figure 4–39.

Snap Zone tells InDesign how close an object must be to a margin or column guide or to the edge of a page, in order for it to align with the guide during adjustment.

Allow Graphics and Groups to Resize pretty much does just that. If it's off, objects will move, but they won't be resized.

Allow Ruler Guides to Move is also pretty basic.

Ignore Ruler Guide Alignments should be off if you've set up a guide system, but if you were lazy and didn't, you might want to turn this option on. Objects will realign relative to column and margin guides and to page edges.

Figure 4–39
The Layout Adjustment dialog.

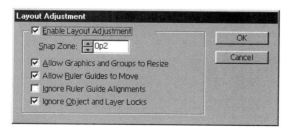

Ignore Object and Layer Locks should be on, else locked objects and layers will not be adjusted, which sort of negates the purpose.

After doing a layout adjustment, go through the entire document carefully and check the position of all objects that were affected by the adjustment. Margin-to-margin text frames should adjust well, but objects loose on a page might end up in some odd positions, along with loose text frames.

And, of course, make a backup copy of the document before you perform an automatic layout adjustment. Please. You'll be glad you did, someday.

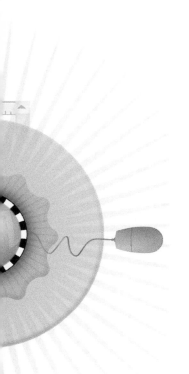

5

ILLUSTRATING AND DRAWING

InDesign contains drawing and illustration tools similar to those found in PageMaker, QuarkXPress, Illustrator, and Freehand. While InDesign's drawing tools are a lot more advanced than those in PageMaker and QuarkXPress 3.3, and somewhat more friendly than those in QuarkXPress 4.0, you're still better off doing complex illustrations in Illustrator or Freehand. It's easier and less error-prone to separate illustrations from other content by using them in a page layout as placed EPS files.

For instance, unless you lock everthing after drawing it, there's a chance that inadvertent changes could be introduced if you send files out to a printer or service bureau for imaging. It's also better for tracking version changes to an illustration. In most production workflows, illustration and page layout are two separate activities: a layout artist places things created by an illustrator. But, it is helpful to have the ability to create a last-minute piece of art in the layout program. However, if you're a real do-it-yourselfer and don't own an illustration program, then chances are that the tools in InDesign will be quite useful to you. And even if you're artistically challenged, you'll still need to know how to draw basic shapes and frames in InDesign to get the most out of it.

Properties of Drawn Objects   Anything you draw has the following attributes that you can change:

- page coordinates (X and Y location)
- width and height
- stroke color and width
- fill color, tint, or gradient (closed paths only)
- corner effects (corner points only)
- content type (if a frame)

Basic Concepts

Path   A path is any two or more points on a line or curve. Paths are open or closed and can exist as simple paths or compound paths, where there are two or more subpaths that make up the main path. Paths can be drawn by hand, created with the basic frame tools, or created by converting type to paths.

Converted type is a good example of a compound path—letters like O and A are really made of two paths: an outer one defining the letter's shape, and an inner one that describes the middle of the O and the A. The inner path always has a transparent fill so anything behind it will show through.

Stroke   Stroke is the outline of a path, which can have a number of attributes, such as stroke weight, stroke color, a dash pattern, and addition of end pieces like arrowheads. InDesign will also let you alter the stroke of characters even if they haven't been converted to paths.

Fill   Fill is the area inside a path, which doesn't have to be closed. As shown in Figures 5–1 and 5–2, InDesign will apply the fill, based on a closing segment between the path's starting and ending points.

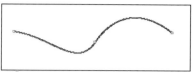

Figure 5–1
Open path with no fill assigned.

Figure 5–2
The same path with a solid fill assigned.

Fills can be colored, set to transparent, or made of a multicolor gradient. You can also apply fills to type.

Frame Any path in InDesign can be a container, or frame, for text or images, even if it's not closed. Frame content is distinct from a path's fill; you can always change a frame path's fill color without affecting the contents of a frame. Type converted to paths can also be used as a frame (at large point sizes, of course). Selecting any path and then placing content through either the Place command or the Paste Into command will turn any path into a frame, like the one shown in Figure 5–3.

Figure 5–3
A path turned into a frame.

Figure 5–4
The bounding box.

When you draw things in InDesign with the Pen tool, a bounding box is automatically created around the bounds of the drawn object. While the bounding box looks like a frame, it's not. It only shows you the object's outer dimensions.

Figure 5–4 shows the bounding box (the square) enclosing the frame (the circle, here with a text wrap offset applied to show the frame), which in turn contains an imported image.

Bézier curve   InDesign offers Bézier curves, a mathematical system for describing a curve with a minimum of two anchor points, named for the French mathematician Pierre Bézier. Additional points between the end points can be added to create complex shapes, or the handles of the end points can be adjusted to produce simple curves.

Anchors and Handles   An anchor is a point in a Bézier curve that, depending on your manipulation of the point's handles, defines the shape of the curve.

- Curve ("smooth") anchor point—a point with smooth transitions on each side. You make a curve point by clicking and dragging with the Pen tool.
- Corner anchor point—a point with an abrupt transition. Paths extending from a corner point can be curved or straight. You make a corner point by clicking (and not dragging) the Pen tool.
- Direction lines—these indicate the direction of the curve orginating from the anchor point. Length and angle of the direction line determines the shape of the curve.
- Handles—the little knobs at the ends of direction lines that let you grab and manipulate them.

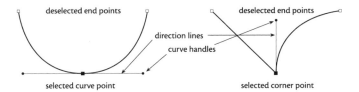

Figure 5–5
Anchors and handles.

Anchors and handles are shown in Figure 5–5.

Stroke Attributes   Stroke weight is the most basic stroke attribute. It is measured from the center of the path outwards—a six-point stroke is three points wide on each side of the stroke. Stroke weight for characters that have not been converted to paths is applied only to the outside path of the character to prevent the insides from plugging up.

Strokes applied to compound paths, like those created from the letter "O," are applied to the outside of the outer path and to the inside of the inner path.

Other stroke attributes include color, gradients, dash patterns, and end objects like arrowheads. You control all of these attributes from the Stroke panel (Window ➠ Stroke, or press F10). Stroke controls in PageMaker are located in Element ➠ Stroke menu, shown in Figure 5–6; they are accessed through the Modify dialog in QuarkXPress.

Figure 5–6
The Stroke panel (maximized).

InDesign allows customized dash patterns; PageMaker has a very limited "custom" option in the Stroke menu, but you can only change the weight of the predefined patterns. Stroke dash patterns in Quark-XPress 3.3 also aren't editable for pattern, only weight.

QuarkXPress 4.0 does let you create some cool custom strokes, including ones with mutiple colors in a dashed-line pattern, but you can't adjust the width of a dash gap, and you can't create new patterns either. Color dash gaps is not something to brag about but there are designers who say they need it.

InDesign lets you make an infinite number of customized dash patterns, though these can only contain one color per stroke. You can create multicolored and just plain wacky dash effects by layering differently colored paths exactly over each other and alternating the gaps, stroke colors, and stroke weights. In other words, you can achieve virtually any dash effect you can dream up.

Stroke Panel Controls

- Weight is fairly self-explanatory and is always specified in points, even if you have your default measurement system set to something else.
- Cap defines how the end of an open path appears. There's the butt cap ⊑, the round cap ⊑, and the projecting cap ⊑. The end caps have different effects, shown in Figure 5–7. Round and projecting caps extend past the end of the path by half of the specified stroke weight.

Figure 5–7
Butt, round, and projecting end caps.

Figure 5–8
Miter, round, and beveled joins.

- Miter Limit tells InDesign what to do with the stroke at corner points. If the miter (the pointy part of a corner) extends more than X times the stroke weight from the path, the miter will change from a pointy one to a beveled one. You control X with the value in the Miter Limit field. This only works with miter joins (below).
- Join defines how a stroked path appears at a corner. A miter join ⓕ creates pointy corners, a round join ⓕ makes nice smooth rounded corners, and a bevel join ⓕ lops off the pointy part that would otherwise appear in a miter join, as shown in Figure 5–8. Joins only have an effect on corner points.
- Choose Dashed from the Type pop-up menu to display the dash options. Enter at least two dash and gap sizes; if you create more you'll end up with alternating dash and gap widths. End cap settings do affect dashes, so if you choose round or projecting caps, make sure that the gaps are wide enough to accommodate them, or reduce the stroke weight; otherwise the gaps could close up.
- End shapes are added with the Start and End pop-up menus. You can choose from a wide array of arrowheads, and there are some other simple shapes you can stick on the ends of paths. End shapes will add to the length of a path, and they follow the direction line, if any, of the last point on a path.
  If you want to swap the ends of a path, select it and choose Object ➠ Reverse Path. See Figure 5–9.

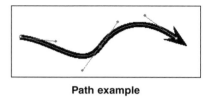

Path example

Figure 5–9
Path reversals.

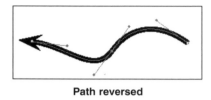

Path reversed

Press Option/Alt while selecting an end shape to apply it to both ends of a selected path. End shapes aren't editable, another good opportunity for a plug-in.

- You can specify whether stroke weight affects a path's bounding box and dimensions. Choose Weight Changes Bounding Box (whew) option in the Stroke panel's pop-up menu, as shown in Figure 5–10.

Character stroke weight always grows outward from character outline when the text has a fill. If the text doesn't have a fill, the stroke is centered as it is with other objects.

Checking this option causes the path or frame's bounding box to grow or reduce if you increase or decrease the path or frame's stroke weight. Why on earth you want to do that is a bit of a mystery, but you can if you want. Neither PageMaker nor QuarkXPress has a similar feature; both treat a frame's stroke as if it is drawn on the inside of the frame, which is also what happens if you don't use this option in InDesign. Figure 5–11 illustrates what happens with a 2–point stroke (left) that's been changed to 4 point with this option off (middle) and on (right).

Figure 5–10
Weight Changes Bounding Box option in Stroke panel.

Figure 5–11
Effect of Weight Changes Bounding Box option.

Figure 5–12
"Fancy" corner effect.

You can see that this is something you might not want to use for documents that have strict dimensional placement requirements for page objects.

Corner Effects for Strokes   InDesign gives you a few options for the corners of strokes. Frames and paths don't need to be closed in order to have effects added to them, but the object must have at least one corner point for added effects to work. Select a path or frame, then choose Object ➧ Corner Effects. There are a few basic effects you can apply, and as with end objects, you can't edit them or add new ones.

Paths with applied corner effects aren't altered; rather, the path is preserved and the effect is drawn independently of the path. The example in Figure 5–12 shows how the effect doesn't alter the path.

Elementary Shapes

The simplest shapes, rectangles, and ellipses, really don't need much explanation. To draw either, select the Rectangle (M) or the Ellipse (L) tool in the toolbox, then click and drag to draw the basic shape. Hold Shift to constrain the shape equally to draw a square or circle that is proportional.

This works the same in InDesign, PageMaker, and QuarkXPress. Select the Line (E) tool to draw lines; hold Shift to constrain lines to 45° increments. For multisided polygons, use the Polygon (N) tool. Double-click on it to specify the number of sides and the inset value. It really doesn't matter whether you choose the frame-drawing version of each tool or not, since you can turn any of these into a frame later. Shapes drawn with the nonframe tools simply become frames with unassigned content.

If drawn with the frame tools, the content by default is graphic, though this will change according to what you place in the frame. It's really nothing to be too concerned about.

Editing Basic Shapes   To change the shape of something drawn with one of the "insta-object" tools, click on it with the Direct Selection tool (A). You can move a single point on the object's path with the Direct Selection tool, as shown in Figure 5–13.

Unfortunately, you can't select more than one point on an object's path like you can in QuarkXPress 4, Illustrator, and Freehand.

You can manipulate direction lines with the Direct Selection tool after you draw ellipses and circles with the Ellipse (L) tool. These always have editable direction lines which you can change with the Direct Selection tool. You don't always have to use the Pen tool for basic manipulation of ellipses.

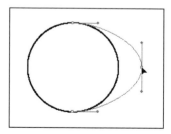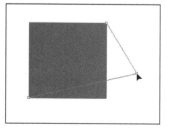

Figure 5–13
Clicking and dragging an anchor point on various paths with the Direct Selection tool.

Complex Shapes   The basic tools are fine and dandy for most work, but there will probably be times when you want something a little more fancy than you can get with the basic shape tools. That's when you need InDesign's Pen (P) tool. It's exactly like Illustrator's pen tool, which isn't very surprising—both pens let you place and convert points as you draw. Freehand's pen does too, but you just do it differently.

The pen tool in QuarkXpress 4.0 works a lot differently from, well, just about anything else, and we all know PageMaker never had a pen tool.

Let's say you want a scalloped edge on a heavy page border. You could draw and color such an object in Freehand or Illustrator, but it's a simple shape and it's not really worth firing up either program and doing the Save ➟ Save as EPS ➟ import shuffle. Instead, you could turn on the document grid in InDesign and very easily create a wavy-edged border with the Pen tool, as in this example:

1. With the document grid and "snap to grid" enabled, select the Pen tool and click the start point for the border, then the next one on the lower right, then move up two grid squares and click a third time (Figure 5–14). These are all corner points since no dragging is involved.

2. To give the third point a direction handle for the following curve, move the Pen tool over the point until the Pen tool changes to a change-direction icon ✎. Then, click on the point and drag a direction line out two squares (Figure 5–15).

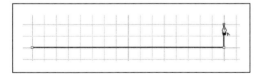

Figure 5–14
Creating a wavy border: Step 1.

Figure 5–15
Creating a wavy border: Step 2.

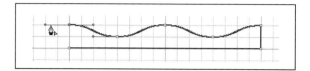

Figure 5–16
Creating a wavy border: Step 3.

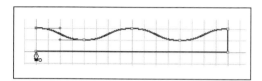

Figure 5–17
The wavy border: Ta-dah.

This step defines the point as a mixed straight/curve corner point. If we didn't do this step, the resulting wavy edge wouldn't look very uniform.

3. Click and drag to set the next point—drag direction lines out two grid squares to make the waves (Figure 5–16). Repeat four times.

4. Click and drag two squares to set the last curve point. Hold the pen tool over the point until the change-direction icon appears, then click once on the point. This tells InDesign that the next part of the path is going to be a straight line. Since it was drawn initially as a curve point, clicking once on it with the change-direction pen tells InDesign that you've changed it to a corner point with one curved segment.

5. Move the pen over the very first point drawn. The Pen tool changes to the close-path icon ♣ . Click once to close the path and finish the job (Figure 5–17).

A Plethora of Pens   The Pen tool in the toolbox pops out if you click and hold on it, displaying the alternative Pen tool options, shown in Figure 5–18.

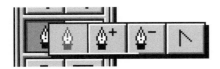

Figure 5–18
Pen tool options.

From left to right, these are the pen, the add-a-point pen, the remove-a-point pen, and the change-direction tool, which isn't really a pen, but there's probably no better place to put it. We're unsure if these are official Adobe names for these pens, but they work for us and they will work for you.

Most of the time, a pen's appearance will change according to what you are doing, or you can change the pen's behavior by holding the Option/Alt key, so you don't have to keep mousing over to the toolbox to change pen types.

When you are drawing, the pen icon will change a bit—the little symbol at the lower right of the pen's icon always displays the current status of the tool.

To start drawing a path, choose the Pen tool and click to set a corner point, or click and drag to set a curve point. The first point you set can really be either, but if you set the direction of the following curve initially by clicking and dragging to set the direction lines, it can make further edits a bit easier.

To finish a path, either close it as in step 5 on the previous page, or hold Command/Control, which changes to the Selection tool as long as you hold the key down. Click anywhere on the page to deselect the path. This tells InDesign that you're done with it.

While working on a path, you'll see these different pen icons.

- If the symbol is a triangle ◬ , it indicates that you and InDesign are ready to draw a new path or to continue with one in progress. Click to place the first or next corner point; drag to define a curve point.

- The change-direction symbol ✒ appears when you move the Pen tool over the last point drawn. As shown in the simple example above, this lets you set the direction of the curve that is to follow. You can also use it to convert a point from curve to corner, and vice versa.

  To change direction of a new point, click and drag to set the direction of the curve—you'll see one or two direction lines appear, depending on the type of point, and you can change the direction by moving the mouse around. Release the mouse button, then set your next point. To change a curve point to a corner point, move the Pen tool over the point until it changes to the change-direction symbol, then click the point once. Only one direction line appears when you've changed the point to a corner point. Release the mouse and continue drawing. If you alter the point any further, it'll change back into a curve point.

  Note: To set a corner point with two curved segments, set a curve point, but then press Option/Alt as soon as the direction lines appear. The direction lines will split and you'll be able to move them independently of each other.

- When you move the Pen tool over a path, the add-a-point symbol ✒ appears. You can add a point to a path any time this pen icon appears.

- If you move the Pen tool over any point in a path except for the last point drawn, the remove-a-point symbol ✒ appears. Clicking with this pen variant removes any point you touch with it. The change-direction symbol appears only over the last point drawn in a path, as long as the path is still selected and you haven't finished it.

- The continue-a-path symbol ✒ appears when you move the pen over the first or last point of a selected path that you've finished. To extend a path, click once on either end point with this icon visible, then continue drawing. To connect two open paths, click on the end point of the first path with this icon visible, then position the pen over the start of the second path until the join symbol ⚲ appears, then click once to complete the merger.

Editing Points and Paths   To edit points on an existing path, you can do it the tedious way or the easy way. There's no point in talking about the tedious way, so here's the easy way: choose the pen in the toolbox (P), then hold Command/Control to temporarily change to the selection tool. Click on the path you want to change and release the key. Now you can edit points without having to zip up to the tool-box and change to a different type of pen tool, but if you like, you can cycle between the various pen tools by typing Shift + P.

The pen icons will change according to the context of what InDesign will let you do with the pen when it's in a certain location over the path or a point on the path. The pen will appear as add-a-point ⚲ , remove-a-point ⚲ , or continue-a-path ⚲ . To convert a point from one type to the other, hold down the Option/Alt key and the pen will change to the convert-point tool ⌐ . Click once on a point with this tool to make it into a corner point; click and then drag out some direction lines to convert it to a curve point.

To adjust direction lines, either temporarily switch to the direct selection tool or just pick it in the toolbox (A). Grab the little knobs at the ends of direction lines to move them.

Note: You must delete points by using the remove-a-point pen. You can't use the Delete key, or else the entire path will disappear.

To move points on a path, either choose the Direct Selection tool (A) or temporarily hold down Command/Control to switch to the Direct Selection tool, then click on the path to select it. Now you can move points with the Direct Selection tool. To move the entire path without messing up its shape, click and hold the Direct Selection tool on a segment between two points.

To duplicate a path, hold Option/Alt—the Direct Selection tool will display a little plus sign—then click and drag a copy of the path. The tool changes to a double-arrow while you drag the path. Set the new path down wherever you like. This duplication feature works with the regular Selection tool too, and lets you duplicate any object on the page, though the Selection tool won't display the little plus sign like the Direct Selection tool does.

To split a path or frame into two or more separate paths, use the Scissors (C) tool. Frames can be split even if they have content. Select the path to be slashed apart with the Direct Selection tool (A) or just press Command/Control to switch to it temporarily, then select the Scissors tool.

To make two paths out of a closed one, you have to cut it twice or else you just end up with an open path, which will still look closed until you move one of the new end points.

The crosshair scissors cursor will show a tiny little circle in the middle ✦ when it's over a path. Just click once to cut the path, then you can move the new end points anywhere you like with the Direct Selection tool.

Text to Paths   Why on earth would you ever want to do this? Once you convert selected text to paths, it's no longer text; instead it's an object composed of one or more paths. You can't edit the text anymore, but the neat thing is this: you can now put stuff inside the outline of the character(s), or you can change the shape of a character. This is really only practical for huge point sizes—you certainly would never want to convert a body text paragraph to outlines.

This trick has been an old favorite in prepress when used in programs like Illustrator and Freehand because it eliminates the need to provide fonts. For example, if one giant letter was used in a Freehand illustration for something, the artist could just convert it to paths and do away with the need to provide a copy of the font to the printer or service bureau.

In a pinch, you could also do this with every text character in the file, but it's not really recommended unless you can't provide the font to someone else.

The lack of text editability once type is converted to paths is also a pretty big drawback, and unless you make a copy of the file with the text intact, changing a word or letter can be a supreme pain in the neck. QuarkXPress 4.0 allows you to convert selected text to a frame, but PageMaker and QuarkXPress 3.3 do not.

To convert text to paths (or outlines, as InDesign refers to them), you need to select it first. There are a few different ways to do this.

- You can select a frame that already contains text, which will result in every character within the frame being converted to a gazillion paths, but as long as the frame only has a few characters in it, this is manageable.
- You can select one of the characters within a frame with the text tool, which will be converted to inline objects. Inline objects behave like characters, even when they aren't, and always stay with the text—if the paragraph reflows, the objects move with it.

Once you've made your selection, choose Type ➟ Convert to Outlines, or press Command + Option/Control + Alt + O. The original text disappears after conversion, so if you want to retain it, choose Type ➟ Convert to Outlines while holding down Option/Alt. The outlines are created above the original type, and you can move them wherever you like.

After conversion, a character can be treated like any other frame or path. You can put images or text inside of it, you can apply a variety of strokes and fills, or you can edit the heck out of the shape with the Direct Selection tool (A). Be sure to select the final point size and kerning options before conversion; type that's scaled after conversion won't have any hinting or optical kerning applied to it.

Here's a giant "S" that's been converted to paths.

You can see the points created on a single outer path. The default stroke and fill color of the new path will be whatever was assigned to the letter before conversion. Remember that character strokes appear only on the sides of paths opposite the fill. Stroked characters will have the stroke applied to both sides of the path after conversion, so these strokes will appear to get fatter.

Compound paths are created from any character that contains more than one path, like the letter "O" shown here.

This is an example of a compound path, which we'll talk about next.

The inside path has a fill of none, and anything behind it will be visible through the path.

To put stuff (text or images) into a character path, select it, then choose File ➠ Place. To use a character outline as a mask for a pasted image, copy or cut the image to the clipboard, then choose Edit ➠ Paste Into. Anything placed into a compound path will only be visible between the inner and outer paths.

Compound Paths   As you've seen with converted type, compound paths let you create objects with transparent holes in them. You can also combine existing paths, even multiple, closed ones, into one compound path. This is helpful when you want multiple paths to act as frames for a single imported graphic or for a gradient; the contents of all paths joined as compounds spans across them.

Figure 5–19 is an example of an effect of compound paths.

The "P" and the "o" were set in separate frames, then converted to paths and moved into the desired position. The paths, plus that of the circle, were selected and made into a compound path. The rest of the text was set in one frame and moved into position.

Figure 5–19
Compound paths.

Some attributes of compound paths:

- Paths with differing strokes and fills, when compounded, will adopt the stroke and fill of the path that was created first.
- Paths inherit the contents, when compounded, of the back-most path with content. If more than one path contains anything, the contents of the frontmost paths will be replaced by the contents of the backmost path with content.
- Released subpaths retain the fill and stroke attributes of the compound path and also retain any image content; the placed image is duplicated and placed within released subpaths relative to the position of the image within the compound path.
- A path containing text can be compounded with other paths, and the text in the first path will flow into the other paths, but you cannot release such a compounded path and InDesign will forever more treat it as a single text frame. This can be useful in some design problems, but in general, it's better to use the text flow tools for flowing text.
- Changes to stroke and fill affect all subpaths in a compound path.
- The contents of compound paths are always positioned relative to the bounding box of the entire path.
- Expected transparency of subpaths might not be what you want, so you might need to reverse the direction of a subpath to get the transparency effect you want. If there are subpaths that cross each other more than once, you might not be able to set the desired transparency.

To create a compound path, select two or more paths or frames, then choose Object ⟹ Compound Paths ⟹ Make, or press Command/ Control + 8.

To separate a compound path back into individual ones, choose Object ⟹ Compound Paths ⟹ Release, or press Command/Control + Option/Alt + 8.

To change the transparency of a subpath, select a single point on the path with the Direct Selection tool (A), then choose Object ⟹ Reverse Path. Don't select the whole compound path.

6

WORKING WITH OBJECTS

Transforming Objects

Transformation refers to changing the size, shape, angle, and visual orientation of an object, which can be any InDesign frame or path. We showed you in Chapter 5 how to edit the shape of a frame or path with the Direct Selection tool, and in Chapter 3 how the choice of the Selection tool or the Direct Selection tool can make a drastic difference in the results. This section extends modification of objects.

Cautions About Tranformations

All transformations, especially of images, have the potential to significantly slow printing and final imaging and could result in some rather ugly output if not used judiciously. Before getting into these, we need to remind you of something important with reference to the Selection and Direct Selection tools: *when switching from the Direct Selection tool to the Selection tool, any content bounding box selected and made visible with the Direct Select tool remains selected by that tool even if you switch to the other.* To ensure that you really have the whole object and not just content selected after such a switch, always click off the object somewhere to deselect it, then click on it with the Selection tool, or press Command/Control + Shift + A to deselect everything on the page. If you accidentally mess something up, undo it and then deselect everything and try again with the right selection tool.

You can select an object with the transformation tools, but you can't select another object with one if there's an active selection. It's easier to select the frame or object with the Selection or Direct Selection tool and then to choose a transformation tool.

Double-clicking on a transformation tool in the toolbox automatically activates the relevant field in the Transform panel, where you can enter values directly.

If you need to rotate images, it's really a better idea to rotate them in a program like Photoshop before placing them into any page layout program. Printing will be a lot faster if the layout program doesn't have to spend extra time calculating rotations, which can be especially time-consuming for large, high-resolution images.

Scaling images is probably the most destructive transformation one can perform. Within a range of ±10%, you can usually get away with scaling an image in InDesign (or any other page layout program). If you start scaling up too much, the image becomes pixelated; that is, when you enlarge an image beyond a certain point, the individual pixels of the image start to become visible.

Scaling down is less visually destructive, but major reduction can result in fuzzy images. Always try to produce images in their final placement size when scanning or creating them. This only applies to bitmapped images like TIFF and bitmap EPS files; vector EPS artwork can be scaled up and down as much as you like. Shearing or distorting really only works well with type and vector objects. You can shear an image, but chances are it will look terrible when printed and will probably take a long time to print.

Reflection doesn't alter content, it just changes the visual orientation. Reflecting an image causes the same processing slowdowns as rotation does, though it's not a destructive transformation.

InDesign Objects: Anything created with InDesign's drawing tools or artwork from Illustrator or Freehand that was dragged and dropped or pasted in as an editable object becomes an InDesign object. Placed images and EPS art are not InDesign objects, though the frames containing them are.

Getting Things in and out of Frames   Anything you draw or place automatically gets a frame. There are a few different ways to move an object into another frame, depending on what it is you want to move.

- Usually, simply copying or cutting an object and then choosing File ➠ Paste Into (Command/Control + Option/Alt + V) will place copied objects inside a selected *empty* frame. The Paste Into function is unavailable if a target frame contains anything.
- To get multiple objects into a frame, group them first (see "Grouping and Ungrouping" later in this chapter). Grouped objects are considered to be a single object after grouping.
- A frame can contain only one object. You can nest a frame within another, and you can have multiple levels of nesting, but only one frame at a time.
- To copy text into another frame, select the characters to be copied with the Text tool, then paste them into the new frame.
- To copy an entire text frame into a new frame, select the frame and not the characters.
- Objects pasted into a frame inherit any transformations applied to that frame. For example, if you paste a text frame into another frame that has been scaled to 25%, the text frame and its contents will also be scaled to 25%.
- Selecting content with the Direct Selection tool (or Text tool) lets you delete the selected content by pressing Delete or Backspace. To delete an entire frame, select it with the Selection tool and press delete or backspace.
- If you select anything in a frame, whether text or graphic, and then copy/cut and paste it, a new frame is created for the content more or less randomly on the current spread, rather than the content being pasted into another frame.

Adjusting Frames and Content   You can adjust a frame to fit an object's bounding box or scale the content to fit the frame. Select the frame in question, then choose Object ➠ Fitting to see the available options, shown in Figure 6–1.

Text Frame Options...	⌘B	
Fitting	▶	Fit Content to Frame ⌥⌘E
Content	▶	Fit Frame to Content ⌥⇧⌘V
Text Wrap...	⌥⌘W	Center Content ⇧⌘E
Corner Effects...	⌥⌘R	Fit Content Proportionally ⌥⇧⌘E

Figure 6–1
Fitting options.

Frame adjustment does not affect any textual content; to change text alignment, use the Paragraph panel to access functions. To change text frame options, choose Object ➠ Text Frame Options or press Command/Control + B.

QuarkXPress and PageMaker users will recognize these options, although Fit Frame to Content was not available in QuarkXPress, and it's a handy option for fixing a frame that was accidentally resized.

Setting a Point of Origin As mentioned in Chapter 3, InDesign uses an object proxy in the Transform panel, which works just like the proxy in PageMaker—there is no proxy in QuarkXPress. Selecting one of the nine little squares in the proxy (Figure 6–2) sets the point of origin for any transformation that follows. The proxy resets itself after each transformation to the upper-left square.

Notice in these two views of the Transform panel how the X and Y coordinates reflect the current point of origin, which is always tied to the proxy setting.

Figure 6–2
Object proxy.

Figure 6–3
Moving the point of origin manually.

Setting Point of Origin with the Proxy

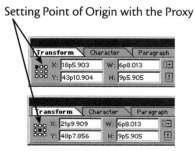

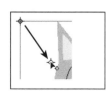

You can also set the point of origin in a free-form fashion when using one of the transformation tools. When you choose one of these tools and select an object with it, a movable point of origin appears. Once an object is selected for transformation, you can either move the point of origin by clicking and dragging it (Figure 6–3), or you can select an origin point in the proxy to set it.

Your selection context will affect what gets transformed. If you select the object with the Selection tool, the entire thing is transformed.

If you select content with the Direct Selection tool, the content is transformed within the frame, but the frame remains unaffected.

Frames with multiple objects in them require careful attention to the selection context when transforming anything.

If the frame contains a single object that was created within InDesign, like a path drawn with the Pen tool, the entire frame is transformed even if you select the object with the Direct Selection tool.

Frames containing multiple objects drawn in InDesign will not transform; only the selected object will transform, and the frame bounding box is adjusted accordingly.

These phenomena are illustrated in Figures 6–4 through 6–6.

Figure 6–4
Placed EPS after rotating the entire frame.

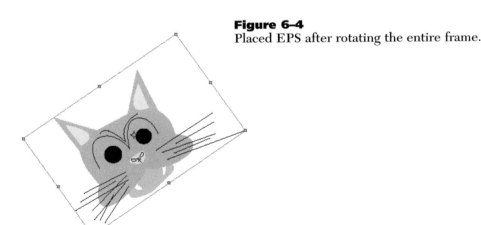

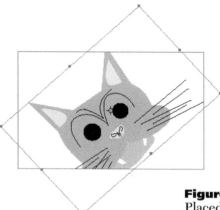

Figure 6–5
Placed EPS after rotating the content.

Figure 6–6
The same art pasted in from
Illustrator, after rotating one
element within the frame (ouch!).

The Transformation Tools

Scaling   There are a few different ways of scaling a frame in
InDesign, and the basic difference is in scaling a frame, scaling a
frame's content, and scaling both. Content scales, or doesn't, according to what's in the frame.

A brief refresher from Chapter 3:

- To scale a frame, grab one of its bounding box handles with the
  Selection tool.
- To alter a frame's shape, use the Direct Selection tool to modi-
  fy or move one of the points that make up the frame.

- Dragged-and-dropped items, art pasted in from other programs, grouped objects, or objects drawn in InDesign will scale along with a frame. Placed items and text within frames will not scale. To scale placed art or images along with the frame, hold Command/Control while scaling the frame with the Selection tool. Add the Shift key to maintain proportions.
- Images with clipping paths must be scaled carefully—always use the Command/Control key when scaling frames that contain images with clipping paths; otherwise, the frame and the clipping path are scaled, but the image isn't. Add the Shift key to maintain proportion when scaling with this method.

A few other points about scaling:

- It is extremely important before scaling anything to be aware of whether you have selected a frame or have selected content. This might sound a little obvious, but it's really easy to mix up the two selection contexts.
- Using the Transform panel to scale a frame by percentages results in everything—frame, content *including* text, and any clipping paths—being scaled as set by you, as long as you've selected the frame with the Selection tool. If you select content with the Direct Selection tool and then scale it with the Transform panel, only the content is scaled.
- The width and height functions in the Transform panel produce results similar to those of the percentage scaling functions in the same panel, except that if a frame is selected, content is not altered; if content is selected, the frame is not altered. Using the width and height functions prevents alteration of stroke widths.
- Type does not scale if you scale a text frame with the Selection tool or with the Scale tool (S).
- Type does scale if you use the transform panel to scale a text frame, but the character panel doesn't reflect scaling. There's no way to reflect the fact that the type has been scaled, for

example, 50% vertically and 75% horizontally, since the point size has not changed. If you rescale the frame back to 100%, the original point size of the type is still intact.

- Strokes *always* scale if you scale stroked objects with the Scale tool or by specifying a scale percentage in the Transform panel. Strokes *do not* scale if you instead change the width and the height of the object in the Transform panel or scale the object with the Selection tool. This behavior can be really confusing to users of Illustrator and Freehand, where strokes do not scale unless you specifically set that option. After scaling, the stroke weight in the Stroke panel will remain unchanged even though the stroke weight might be blatantly different from what's reported in the Stroke panel.

- InDesign "remembers" the scaling percentage of objects but only if you use the Scale tool or the scaling functions in the Transform panel. If you use the Selection tool for scaling, InDesign shows its scale at 100%, unless the object is a frame containing InDesign-created artwork or pasted-in art from Illustrator or Freehand. There is not a whole lot of consistency when scaling with the Selection tool.

There are a number of ways of scaling things in InDesign: with either of the selection tools, with the Scale tool, with the Transform panel, and by using the frame options in the Object menu. Using the selection tools is quick and dirty but does not preserve scaling "memory," for example, if you use a selection tool to scale something and change your mind a day later (long after multiple undo is able to help you), you can't reset the object back to 100%.

We've blathered on long enough about the perils of scaling with the selection tools, so now we'll cover the other two methods.

Scaling with the Scale tool   Select the object or content with one of the selection tools, choose the Scale tool (S), then set your point of origin however you like. Drag in the direction you wish to scale the object (Figure 6–7); add the Shift key to scale proportionally.

Figure 6-7
Scaling with the Scale tool.

Figure 6-8
Scaling with the Transform panel.

Scaling with the Transform panel   Select the object or content and apply either width/height changes or percentage scaling changes. You can select some predetermined percentages with the two pop-ups, or you can double-click the value in the percentage field and enter your own scaling value (Figure 6–8).

To preserve proportions without entering the same percentage in both fields, just enter one value and press Command/Control + Return/Enter—this trick also works if you hold Command/Control while selecting a percentage from the pop-ups.

When scaling with the Transform panel, you can choose whether or not to scale content by choosing the Scale Content option in the Transform panel's pop-up menu.

Rotating   Luckily, there are a lot fewer perils with the rotate function than there are with the scale function. The most important thing to remember is the usual distinction (nag, nag, nag) between selecting a frame and selecting content or individual objects in a frame.

Figure 6–9
Rotating with the Rotate tool.

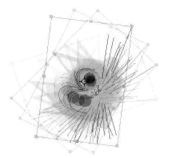

Rotating with the Rotate tool Select the frame or object to be rotated, then choose the Rotate tool (R). Set your point of origin, then drag the tool in the direction you want the object to rotate (Figure 6–9). Hold Shift to constrain rotation to 45° increments. With a center point of origin, the object will spin in place as you move the Rotate tool, resulting in one dizzy cat. Drag the tool further away from the point of origin for more precise control. The rotation angle in the transform panel changes to reflect the current rotation angle while you rotate something with the tool.

Rotating with the Transform panel Select the frame or object to be rotated, then double-click the Rotate tool in the toolbox to highlight the angle value in the rotate field of the Transform panel.

Type a new value or choose one from the pop-up menu (Figure 6–10).

Figure 6–10
Rotating with the Transform panel.

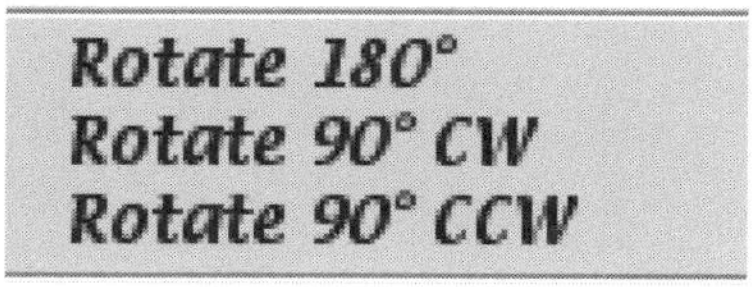

Figure 6–11
Rotate options in the Transform panel pop-up.

Figure 6–12
Shear/skew with the Transform panel.

Negative rotation angles turn things clockwise; positive values make them rotate counterclockwise.

You can also rotate an object in a limited fashion by selecting it, then choosing one of the Rotate options in the Transform panel's pop-up menu (Figure 6–11).

Shear/Skew   Shearing or skewing an object distorts it along the horizontal axis (Transform panel only—Figure 6–12), or along both axes if you use the Shear tool, Figure 6–13. It's sort of an ugly effect, but that's your call.

Figure 6–13
Shearing and skewing.

Shearing with the Shear tool

Select the object and then the Shear tool (Shift + S), set your point of origin, and skew away. The Shear tool distorts the object all over the place, as the tool is very sensitive and both shears and rotates the object at the same time (watch the Transform panel), so it'll take some experimentation to find the right mouse movement to get the effect you want.

Shearing with the Transform panel

Select the frame or object to be sheared, then double-click the Shear tool in the toolbox to highlight the angle value in the Shear field of the Transform panel (or just click the cursor into the field). Type a new value or choose one from the pop-up menu. This only shears an object along the horizontal axis.

Reflecting   There's no tool for this action—to reflect an object horizontally or vertically, select it, then choose one of the options from the Transform panel's pop-up menu (Figure 6–14).

To reflect a copy of the object, make a copy of it exactly on top of the original (see "Step and Repeat," coming up soon), then flip the copy. You can make some interesting effects with this feature (Figure 6–15).

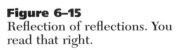

Figure 6–14
Reflecting pop-up.

Figure 6–15
Reflection of reflections. You read that right.

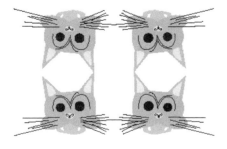

You can also reflect an object with the Selection tool by yanking one side of the bounding box across the other side or by entering negative values into the scaling fields of the Transform panel.

Reflecting with the Selection tool is arbitrary because the results can't be made proportional and you won't end up with a mirror image of the object.

Moving and Arranging Objects

The basic move tool is either of the selection tools: click, drag, finish. Specify exact moves in X and Y distances by using the Transform panel. To move items to other pages, select them, then either copy/cut and paste to another targeted spread. Or, drag items up to the very edge of the document window to force InDesign to scroll to the new destination, where you can drop them.

To move with the cursor keys, select objects and use the keys as desired. To increase the movement factor 10 times, hold shift while pressing any of the arrow keys. You set the movement factor in the *Units and Increments* preferences.

Stroked frames can be referenced in two different ways. By default, strokes are not included in the meaurements and positions reported in the Transform panel. Choosing *Dimensions Include Stroke Weight* from the Transform panel's pop-up menu (Figure 6–16) incorporates stroke width in all reported measurements.

Figure 6–16
Transform panel pop-up.

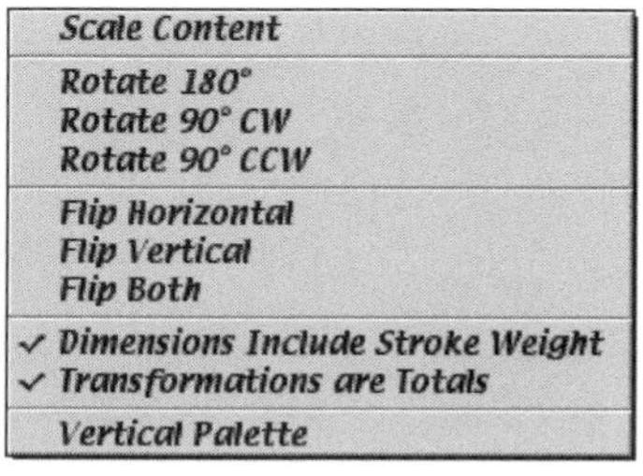

Scale Content
Rotate 180°
Rotate 90° CW
Rotate 90° CCW
Flip Horizontal
Flip Vertical
Flip Both
✓ Dimensions Include Stroke Weight
✓ Transformations are Totals
Vertical Palette

Duplicating Objects You can duplicate objects quickly without having to use cut, copy, and paste. Select one or more objects, then press Command/ Control + Option/Alt + D. The duplicated objects are placed above the originals and slightly offset to the right and down. To clone an object, that is, to create a copy of it exactly above the original object, you can use the step and repeat function (below). To duplicate objects as you transform them, add Option/Alt while using a transformation tool on an object. To duplicate while using the Transform panel, press Option/Alt + Return/Enter after typing a transformation value in the appropriate field.

To duplicate while moving an object, whether you use the mouse or the arrow keys, hold Option/Alt while moving the object—release the modifier key if using the arrow keys immediately after the first press of an arrow key, or else you'll end up with a duplicate for every press of the arrow key.

Step and Repeat The step and repeat function is really handy for creating precisely spaced duplicates of an object across or down a page. InDesign's step and repeat function works exactly the same as the one in QuarkXPress and in PageMaker (where it's called Paste Multiple; you need to copy an object to the clipboard before using this one).

For example, to build a 9" x 12" press sheet of U.S. standard (3" x 2") business cards, you need only create one card, then you can use the step and repeat function to create the sheet.

In Figure 6–17, we've created a business card for an obviously fictitious business (we hope) with a reference frame around it for sizing.

To duplicate the cards horizontally, group the entire card then choose Edit ➡ Step and Repeat (Command/Control + Shift + V)—Figure 6–18.

To finish the sheet, select all (Command/Control + A) and apply step and repeat again, resetting the repeat count, clearing the horizontal offset, and setting a vertical offset (Figure 6–19).

The finished sheet is ready. You can further use step and repeat to add cut and registration marks if you resize the sheet and give it about a half-inch of space all around.

Figure 6–17
Sample business card.

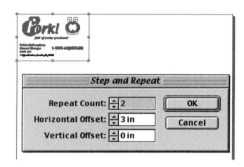

Figure 6–18
Duplication with step and repeat.

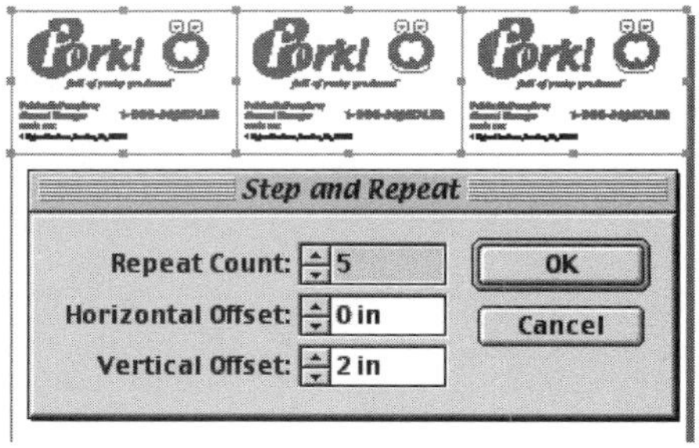

Figure 6–19
Vertical offset to fill out page.

To clone an object, select it, then specify a repeat count of 1 with no horizontal and vertical offset.

Stacking Order

Objects created or placed on a page observe a stacking order, even within the same layer. New objects always appear in front of existing objects. If the objects overlap and are not transparent, you might end up with things overlapping where they shouldn't. Remember that master objects always reside under everything else on a page, unless you specifically select and rearrange them. Use Object ➡ Arrange to change the stacking order of one or more selected objects.

It's tough to select an object if it's overlapped by another. In QuarkXPress, you had to hold three keys down and click on stacked objects to select through the stack. InDesign lets you cycle selection through a stack of objects by holding Command + Option or Control + Alt and clicking on the stacked objects. If you just hold Command or Control while clicking, only the object behind the currently selected object will be selected. This doesn't work if you've temporarily enabled the Selection tool by pressing Command/Control while another tool is active.

You can also select objects in a stack without even clicking the mouse. Move a tool, any tool, over the stack, then press Command/ Control + Option/Alt + [to progressively select from top to bottom in the stack. Use] to progressively select from bottom to top in a stack. Release the keys when the object you want is selected.

When the frontmost or rearmost object is selected by this method, you'll know it's at the top or bottom because the selection won't change. Add Shift to this hand-mangling set of keystrokes to automatically select the rearmost or frontmost object. Doing this with the Direct Selection tool active can produce some odd selections, especially if an object is a frame containing multiple objects such as pasted-in art from Illustrator. Once the target object is selected, choose from the four Arrange options to move its stacking order. If the object is already at the back or front of the stack, Send to Back/Bring to Front will be disabled.

Align and Distribute

Use the Align panel (Figure 6–20) to align and/or distribute objects with reference to each other. When selecting right, left, top, or bottom alignment, alignment will be in reference to the object that is furthest right, left, top, or bottom. Center alignment finds the exact center of each object and aligns with reference to that center point. Distribution of objects works in reference to object edges or centers and maintains an equal amount of space between these points. InDesign offers a distribute by object spacing feature, which helps to evenly distribute differently shaped or sized objects.

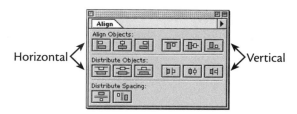

Horizontal / Vertical

Figure 6–20
Align panel.

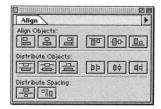

Figure 6–21
Unaligned objects.

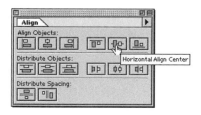

Figure 6–22
Objects aligned across centers.

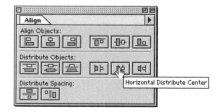

Figure 6–23
Objects evenly distributed across centers.

To use these functions, select the desired objects and open the Align panel (Object ➡ Align or press F8), then choose the desired alignment or distribution method. For example, someone put a bunch of spots all over this page, and they need to be aligned and distributed horizontally (Figure 6–21).

First, we'll align these horizontally across their centers (Figure 6–22).

Then, we'll distribute them, also across the centers (Figure 6–23).

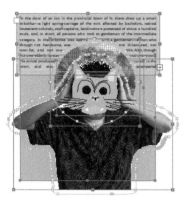

Figure 6–24.
Before grouping.

Figure 6–25.
After grouping. (Hey, nobody ever
claimed we were artists.)

Grouping and Ungrouping   Multiple objects (Figure 6–24) can be
grouped into one large object. It doesn't matter whether the objects
are of mixed types, like several text frames grouped with some image
frames. Grouped objects retain their stacking order, though the
entire group itself has its own stacking order relative to any other
page objects. Objects on different layers can be grouped, though the
resulting group will end up on the topmost layer that contained one
of the grouped objects. Groups themselves can further be grouped,
resulting in nested groups. The new bounding box of a group frame
will change to accommodate all of the objects (Figure 6–25).

   You can still select and modify individual objects in a group with
the Direct Selection tool, although stacking order within the group
cannot be changed, and the methods for selecting stacked objects
don't work within groups either. To group objects, select them, then
choose Object ➠ Group or press Command/Control + G. To ungroup a group, add Shift to the keystroke or choose Object ➠
Ungroup.

Nesting   There are two types of nested objects in InDesign: multiple groups of objects that are further grouped into one object, and frames that exist within other frames. See "Getting Things in and out of Frames" earlier in this chapter for instructions on putting frames within other frames. You can only have one frame inside another, but that frame can contain another, and another, and so on, to infinity or until your brain seizes up.

Nesting frames is useful for creating some types of artwork within InDesign. Nested frames (Figure 6–26) are not the same as inline objects, which are set within text (Figure 6–27). You can have an unlimited number of inline objects within text, but you can only have one frame inside another, and the outer frame can't contain anything else, though it can have a fill and stroke assigned to it.

Once a frame is nested within another, you can only select it with the Direct Selection tool. If you scale or rotate the outer frame, the nested frame(s) scale and rotate too. You can, however, transform nested objects independently of their containing frames by selecting them with the Direct Selection tool. Transforms are Totals is the default setting in the Transform panel's pop-up menu, which means that the rotation angles of a nested frame will always be displayed relative to the parent (outside) frame and the pasteboard. The sum of the nested frame's angle and the parent frame's angle will equal 360°.

Figure 6–26
A small text frame nested within another.

Figure 6–27.
The same frame pasted as an inline object within text.

Deselecting this option displays the rotation of a nested frame relative only to the parent frame, but the total of both frames' angles will still be 360°. We're still not quite sure why this is valuable information to anyone, but there's probably a good reason for it.

Selection Within Groups and Nested Objects This can get pretty complicated and requires a deft combination of the Direct Selection tool, the Selection tool, and something new called the Group Selection tool, which is invoked when the Direct Selection tool is active over a grouped or nested object and the Option/Alt key is held down. The Direct Selection pointer displays a little plus sign next to it, just like the one shown when Option/Alt is down for drag-duplicating an object.

To select a specific object within a group or nest, use the Direct Selection tool and, while holding Option/Alt, click repeatedly until the object you want is selected. To select multiple objects within a group, add Shift to Option/Alt and select the objects.

To move a nested frame or grouped object within its parent frame or group, you must select both the nested frame's bounding box and the content's bounding box with the Group Selection tool.

Usually, you can click on the object with the Direct Selection tool, then switch to the Selection tool to see its frame's bounding box. If you don't see any difference when switching tools, then the frame bounding box and object bounding box are the same size. Uh oh.

It can be really difficult to select a nested or grouped object if the frame's bounding box and the object's bounding box are the same size. In Figure 6–28, we've nested our favorite cat within another frame.

To move the cat's frame within the outer frame, we must select both the cat's frame bounding box and the cat's bounding box, which happen to be the same size. Selecting only the frame bounding box and moving it will crop the cat; selecting the content bounding box and moving it will also crop the cat, though differently. So, to select both, we must enlarge the frame's bounding box a little with the Direct Selection tool. Clicking on a nested frame

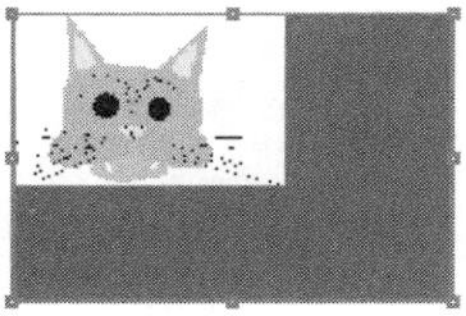

Figure 6–28
Nested frames.

Figure 6–29
Enlarged bounding box.

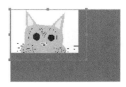

Figure 6–30
Frame and content bounding boxes moved.

with the Direct Selection tool automatically selects its frame bounding box. In Figure 6–29, we've dragged the frame bounding box out a little bit.

With the frame's bounding box selected, press and hold Option/Alt + Shift, then select the content's bounding box by clicking on the very edge of it. It won't be easy to see, though, and it might take a little trial and error. Once they are selected, you can see both and drag them to a new position within the parent frame (Figure 6–30). Later, you can select the frame bounding box and resize it back.

Image Cropping and Clipping Paths

A frame can act as a crop for placed images and artwork. If you draw a frame before placing an image, the image might be cropped anyway, and you can just drag the handles on the frame with the Selection tool to adjust its size, or you can use the frame adjustment functions to fit the frame to the image, or the image to the frame.

When you place an image with no frame selected or targeted, InDesign creates a new frame for it that matches the image's boundaries. Once it is placed, you can then adjust the frame to crop the images to your tastes.

Crop vs. Clipping Path   In traditional prepress, images were photographed with a graphic arts camera and cropped or masked mechanically by cutting holes in sheets of rubylith (a transparent red material) and shooting the image through the holes.

The film used in these cameras was highly sensitive to red, so the rubylith blocked anything that was underneath it. Digital cropping and masking accomplish the same thing: both block a part of the image.

The distinction between a crop and a clipping path becomes blurred in InDesign, but the most basic difference is this: you crop an image by adjusting its frame, and anything within the frame will be visible, as in Figure 6–31.

If you import or create a clipping path, the path defines what will be visible or not, not the frame.

Adjusting the frame of an image with a clipping path won't affect what's defined as visible by that path, unless you cover up part of it with the edge of the frame.

Figure 6–31
Resizing or reshaping the frame crops the image.

Figure 6–32
Clipping path import off (left) and on (right).

A clipping path is drawn with Bézier curves and follows the edge of an image. Anything on the outside of the path is masked; anything on the inside is preserved.

Multiple subpaths are possible in a clipping path; the image on the right in Figure 6–32 has three: an outer path, and two inner paths that mask the area created by the screaming guy's arms.

You can draw a clipping path in InDesign, you can have InDesign create one for you, or you can draw the path in Photoshop and have InDesign create an editable frame from an image's embedded clipping path.

You can also create clipping paths in Illustrator (where they're called masks) and Freehand (anything pasted inside a path, which then acts as a mask), but InDesign won't convert these to frames. Instead, these paths are honored when displaying and printing, but you can't edit them in InDesign.

An editable clipping path appears as a light blue border that hugs the edge of the image. You can use the Direct Selection tool to edit a clipping path, since it's really been transformed into an ordinary InDesign path.

Warnings About Clipping Paths   In general, if you already know how to create clipping paths in Photoshop, there's no real reason to stop making them there. The ability to edit clipping paths in

Figure 6–33
An image with a clipping path nested in a frame.

InDesign can recognize a clipping path in a native Photoshop file, so saving in TIFF or EPS format is unnecessary.

The Object ➠ Clipping Path command can generate a clipping path from vector graphics (such as a placed PDF file, for example) as well as from bitmap images.

InDesign is a mixed advantage; it allows for last-minute touchups without the need to reopen the image in Photoshop, but it also opens up the possibility of the clipping path being modified accidentally elsewhere in a workflow.

It's very easy to shift a clipping path independently of its image with the selection tools, which is a drawback. Clipping paths and their masked images should always move together.

InDesign treats images with clipping paths as nested objects within their frames. Remember this well: it can cause all sorts of grief later if you try to move things around (which you *will* be doing), because if you place a clipped image inside an existing frame, InDesign places it at the upper left of the targeted frame and it's very likely that that's not where you want it to be.

The examples in Figure 6–33 show the default location after placement (left), the results of moving just the image with the Direct Selection tool (middle), and the results of moving the image and its clipping path (right). The last is probably what most people want to achieve.

There are three ways to move images and their paths as a unit.

1. Click on an area just outside the clipping path with the Direct Selection tool—the image's bounding box is selected. Press Option/Alt + Shift, and click on the clipping path. Release the two keys, and now you can move the image and its clipping path freely within the parent frame.

2. Click on the edge of the clipping path with the Direct Selection tool. Switch to the Selection tool, which will select the image's bounding box. Hold Command/Control and drag the image and its path within the parent frame.

3. Select the image with the Selection tool, then choose Object ➡ Fitting ➡ Center Content (Command/Control + Shift + E).

When you import a Photoshop image that contains a clipping path, you can opt to have InDesign create a frame from the path by checking Show Import Options when placing the image.

If you choose not to have InDesign make a frame from it, the path is ignored and the image is imported without it. Remember that this so-called frame created from the clipping path is really a nested frame within the object frame.

Creating Clipping Paths   To create your own clipping path for an image that doesn't have one, first place the image. Choose the pen and draw your clipping path, using the edge of the image as a guide.

For inner paths, draw them next, then select all of the paths with the Direct Selection tool and make them into compound paths (Command/Control + 8). Figure 6–34 illustrates a clipping path.

Switch to the Selection tool, select and copy/cut the image, then select the clipping path and paste the image into it. Figure 6–35 illustrates the result.

Figure 6–34
A view of the clipping path.

Figure 6–35
The image with clipping path applied.

After, you can zoom way in and fine-tune the clipping path. You 'll probably want to change your image preview from Proxy to Full Resolution in the InDesign Preferences for this kind of detail work. InDesign can create clipping paths automatically for images that did not have them. A few points about this feature:

- Images are poor candidates for automatic clipping path generation if they don't have nice hard edges in them. InDesign looks for abrupt transitions in light and dark areas on which to base the created path. You're better off clipping these types of images by hand in Photoshop or by drawing a path in InDesign and pasting the image into that path.
  The picture on the left in Figure 6–36 has transitions that are too ill-defined for InDesign to create any sort of usable clipping path automatically. The one on the right is a good candidate for an automatic clipping path because there's already a white background.
- InDesign *replaces* a clipping path in an image that already has one if you apply automatic clipping path generation to the image.

Figure 6–36
Assessing candidates for automatic generation of clipping paths.

To use InDesign's automatic clipping path generation features, place and select the image, then choose Object ➡ Clipping Path, shown in Figure 6–37.

The default settings do a good job, but you can make adjustments to suit the particulars of your image. For these examples, we've placed the image over a gray box so you can see the results.

Figure 6–37
Automatic clipping path generation.

Options in the Clipping Path dialog:

- Threshold—This specifies the area of relative lightness or darkness in the image where the clipping path should start. Generally, the default of 25 is a good compromise, but you can adjust this up if the background isn't very light or if there's a slightly darker item in the background that you want masked. See Figure 6–38.

Figure 6–38
Threshold too high; the range of light to dark is too broad.

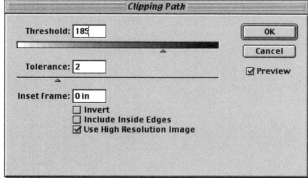

- Tolerance—This specifies how closely a pixel in the image has to match the threshold value. If tolerance is low, the match will be very tight, and you might end up with a very jagged clipping path with thousands of anchor points, which can really cause problems when trying to print. If it's too high, the clipping path will be sloppy and ill-formed, Figure 6–39. The default setting is fine unless there are a few stray specks in the background that are slipping through the threshold level. If this happens, either increase the threshold a small amount or increase the tolerance, until the preview shows that the specks are masked.

Figure 6–39
Tolerance too high; the path is sloppy.

- Inset Frame—Once you're happy with the threshold and tolerance values, you can change the inset up or down. This tells InDesign to adjust the entire path closer or farther away from the image by the amount of space you set here. A positive value makes the path tighter; a negative one makes it looser. Be careful not to overdo it—it's easy to lose a lot of edge detail if the path is too tight to the image (Figure 6–40).

Figure 6–40
Inset Frame—a bit too tight here, image is overclipped.

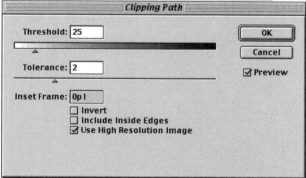

- Invert—This swaps the visible/invisible parts of the mask. It's like the Inverse Selection function in Photoshop, and instead of masking the outer parts of an image, it'll create a path that masks the inside parts of the image.
- Include Inside Edges—If checked, this will scan for areas inside the image that match the areas being masked outside the image and will create a compound clipping path with multiple areas of transparency.
- Use High Resolution Image—This should *always* be turned on. A clipping path created from a low-resolution proxy is more or less useless and will look terrible.

7

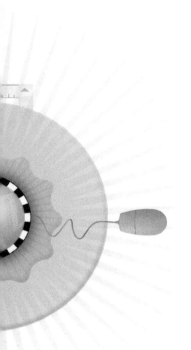

TYPE AND TYPOGRAPHY

InDesign provides comprehensive typographic controls for traditional typographers (and most are old, like one of the co-authors), as well as text formatting for professional page layout applications.

Let's start a job and set some type. Command or Control + N for New Document (see Figure 7–1) is faster than going to the File menu and clicking around.

Figure 7-1
New Document dialog box.

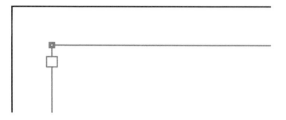

Figure 7–2
An active text frame.

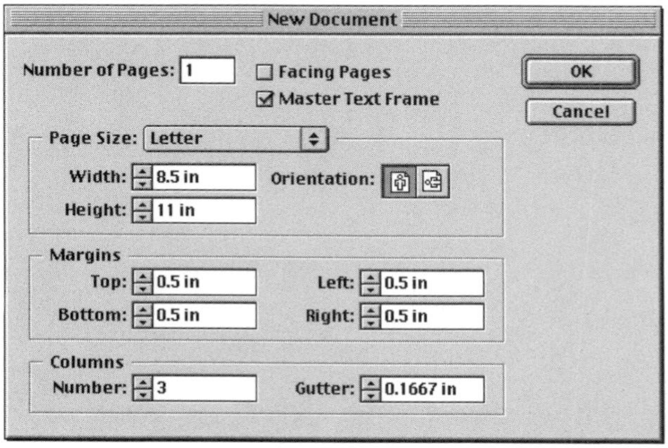

New Document

Number of Pages: 1   ☐ Facing Pages   OK
                            ☑ Master Text Frame   Cancel

Page Size: Letter

Width: 8.5 in   Orientation:
Height: 11 in

Margins
Top: 0.5 in   Left: 0.5 in
Bottom: 0.5 in   Right: 0.5 in

Columns
Number: 3   Gutter: 0.1667 in

Figure 7–3
Setting "3" in Columns box.

Facing Pages is the default and Master Text frame is not on. Let's change that and create an automatic text box and do single pages. Unlike those of QuarkXPress, the settings in the New Document dialog box are not sticky—that is, the settings are not repeated the next time you open the dialog box. It always reverts to its defaults.

Master Text Frame gives us an automatic text box. Hold down Command/Control + Shift and click in the frame on the page. You then see the little tick marks and in and out boxes to tell you the frame is active (Figure 7–2).

We want three columns, and the best way to get text to flow through muliple columns is to set this format in the New Document dialog (Figure 7–3). You can override this setting or change columns on a page later.

You can also set the number of columns by going to *Text Frame*, which is under the Object menu (Figures 7–4 and 7–5).

Don't use the column setting in the Margins and Guides dialog box, which is under the Layout menu. We want the text to flow automatically. You can also set up a Master Page.

You will need a text file. Import a file or key some text. Use real words (not the fake Latin of some sample files). See Figure 7–6.

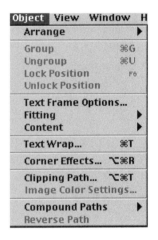

Figure 7–4
Object menu list.

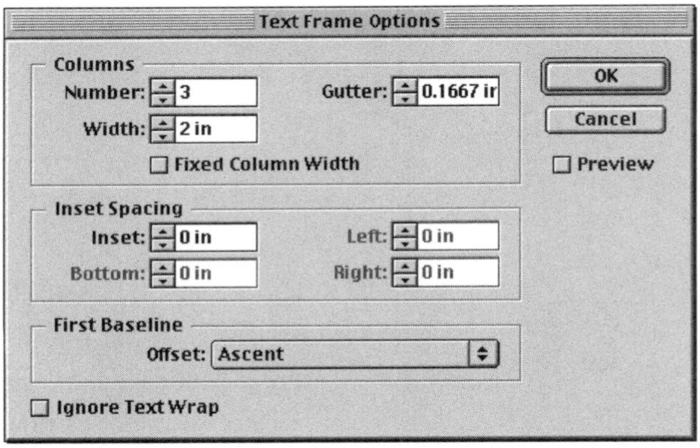

Figure 7–5
Setting "3" in Text Frames dialog box.

Figure 7–6
Text preview in Place dialog box.

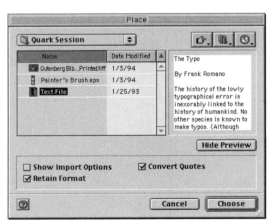

Note that you get a preview of the text. This is a very nice feature that confirms the file you are selecting.

We want to jump right to hyphenation and justification, one of the most important areas of type and typography.

Hyphenation and Justification (H&J)

One of the main goals of typography is to achieve the most elegant line breaks you can without fine-tuning every line manually. This means setting the typographical controls in the page layout program and then letting the program's built-in composition engine handle the rest. The "rest" depends on how good that engine is.

InDesign has two composition engines—the Single-line Composer and the Multi-line Composer—and you choose which to use for the typographic result you want. Both composers work by applying the type settings you specify to determine how much text fits on any line and how many lines fit in any text frame. The Single-line Composer—like traditional software composition engines—looks at one line at a time. Adobe's innovative new Multi-line Composer does something unique—it considers multiple lines at once (in fact, you specify how many). Both composers follow built-in rules that determine how they make trade-offs in your settings to achieve the best-looking lines with optimal line breaks.

For example, the Multi-line Composer favors even spacing, avoids hyphenation whenever possible, and assigns penalties to good and bad breakpoints to help rank them. Unlike traditional typesetters—in the past, considered superior to desktop typography—the Multi-line Composer is capable of looking both forward and backward in a paragraph to produce extraordinary results.

We will get to the composers in a minute. We now have a page of text to H&J (the shorthand for hyphenation and justification), Figure 7–7.

The Typo

By Frank Romano

The history of the lowly typographical error is inexorably linked to the history of humankind. No other species is known to make typos. (Although hippopotami are known to make hippos.) A typo must involve type. Without type, there cannot be a typo. Pictures with errors are pictos. Thus the typo was born with the invention of typographic communication.

The ancient Koreans developed the process of block printing. It is said that a queen was near death and the high priests ordered the writing of a prayer on small sheets of rice paper, probably printed with soy ink — the first edible printing. Technology came to the rescue and reproduced thousands of them — the first printed correspondence with a deity. The queen died anyway.

The Koreans were renowned for the quality of their work. There were even manuals for novices and journeymen. For instance, if a novice made one typo they lost a finger. The second typo caused the loss of a hand. This explains their reputation for quality . . . and the difficulty in recruiting new printers.

Later, monks who spent their lives in scriptoria scribbling their way to Heaven also made mistakes. One wonders what profanity they uttered as they lost control of their quill pen. To correct the error they could scrape away the ink from the vellum, which was the hide of a calf. Another method was to cover the error with a white paste and then write over it — the invention of White-Out, or in this case, Vellum-Out. In some cases, given the value of vellum, entire sheets were covered with medieval White-Out and used again. These are called palimpscests and archeologists often find that what was covered was more historically significant. I wonder if that will be true for modern memos. Or class notes.

Charlemagne standardized all writing throughout the Holy Roman Empire with an uncial writing style that would eventually be known as lowercase, designed by Alcuin of York, a British consultant. He could not standardize typographical errors, however, and individuality still prevailed, accounting for the breakup of the Empire into nationalistic states.

Gutenberg's secrecy was a marketing strategy. He wanted to sell mass-produced books at custom-produced prices. The Gutenbergian system of printing divided language into its basic building blocks — letters. Yet, the first work to be printed by moveable type was not a Bible, but rather an Indulgence, a sort of passport to Heaven, or more accurately, a form. Technologies may change, but bureaucracy endures.

After production of the first batch of Bibles, Johann Fust took several to Paris to sell. Since Bibles did not come on the market very often, their purchasers compared them. They found the same errors on the same pages. This had to be the work of the devil. Johann Fust died in Paris during that trip.

Now the opportunity for error was fully formed. A new profession was born — the corrector of the press, today known as the proofreader. Their sole duty was to find mistakes before they got into print. Finding them afterward, did not count. Aldus Manutius, who almost single-handed created the Renaissance, used the philosopher Erasmus as a proofreader, as the great Greek texts were put into print for the first time.

The Gutenbergian font of 292 letters and letter combinations was reduced over the centuries. But humankind had no problem adapting — they just increased the number of errors per character.

It was an act of graphic vandalism that almost destroyed Mark Twain. The first edition of "Huck Finn" had been printed and the handset type re-distributed. On one of the engravings someone had scratched an image that made it obscene. The pages had not only been printed, they were partially bound. The entire run had to be discarded and production re-started. Combined with his investment in the failed Paige "typesetting machine" he was virtually wiped out financially.

Handset type yielded to linecasting. And a new error crept in — the wrong font. We could now mechanize our errors.

Linecaster operators could not abort a line of type once started in the assembling elevator. Sensing an error, they would run their fingers down the first two rows of keys to produce ETAOIN SHRDLU which would be identified as a line to be discarded. However, the history of the newspaper industry reports that these lines often made their way into print and a generation of readers often asked "Who" or "What" was ETAOIN SHRDLU?

Paper tape and the TeleTypeSetter system allowed us to telecommunicate our typos to multiple sites at the same time. You no longer had to be present to see your errors in print.

Photographic typesetting was combined with computer automation. Ah, the computer. Now we

Figure 7–7
Placed text in the text frame.

The text is now ragged. Click the Type tool (the "T") and then select all the text and click the justify icon in the Paragraph palette (4th from left).

Hyphenation Overview

Hyphenation is the breaking of words at the end of lines of type according to rules. Line-end hyphenation is okay for text material, but should be avoided for headlines, subheads, and most display

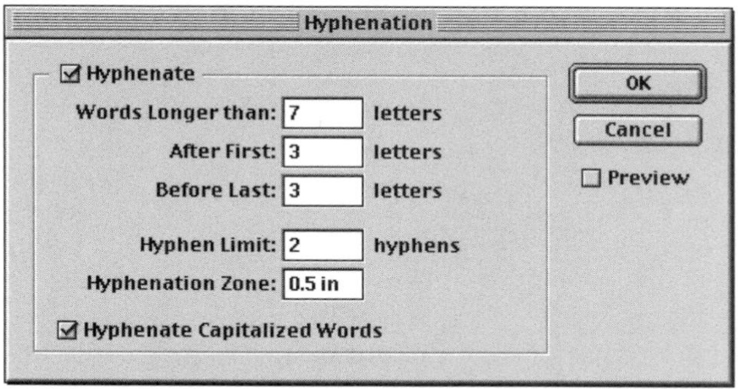

Figure 7–8
Hyphenation options dialog box.

(large) type. A user in most applications can set preferences that control the number of hyphens in a row, and the hyphenation zone, which will control the lining up of the ends of lines. Some rules:

• No more than three hyphens should be used in a row.
• There should always be a minimum of two letters before the hyphen and a minimum of three on the next line.
• Hyphenate where the break seems logical and the word is not confusing to read.
• Always hyphenate a compound word between the two words. An example is the word dragonfly, the hyphen going between the words dragon and fly.

InDesign lets you set hyphenation options. Figure 7–8 shows the options dialog box with the defaults that come with the program. Some situations where hyphenation should be avoided:

• Words with six or fewer letters.
• One-syllable words.
• Instances where only one syllable of two characters or fewer will be carried over. If the syllable is staying at the end of the line and the rest is carried over, hyphenation is okay.
• Quantities, figures, amounts, etc.

- Proper nouns.
- Abbreviations.
- Within a person's first, middle, or last name.
- Next to or after an abbreviated title.
- The name of a company product.

When hyphenating, make sure that the meaning of the word follows where it is being broken. Homographs are words that are spelled the same but have a different meaning and are often pronounced differently.

```
The pres-ent was a new shiny red bike.
When you pre-sent the gift, nod your head.
```

With InDesign, hyphenation is controlled a few ways. Words can be added to the exception dictionary indicating specific hyphenation. Suggested hyphenation can also be tested by using the *Suggested Hyphenation* under the Utilities menu. Another way to control hyphenation is by using the *H&J* function under the Preferences menu, which lets you specify the maximum hyphens in a row. Characters before and after the hyphen and word space values are also controlled there.

Finally, consult a dictionary to determine the accepted hyphenation of a word.

Justification Overview

Justified means that the lines line up on the right margin just as they do on the left margin. The opposite of justified is ragged.

Text is set so the left and right side of the column are aligned. Early books were not justified, but later books were, mostly for aesthetic purposes. Gutenberg wanted his books to look like handwritten books and used ligatures and contractions to achieve justification. Later, metal type required even copy blocks to allow for lockup into page form. This is accomplished by placing as much text as possible on a line and then dividing the remaining white space among the word spaces.

Think of word spaces as expandable wedges. That is why you should not use word spaces to space over or position text. Now, in ragged composition they are all the same width, but in justified composition their width depends on the need of the line for justification.

Justification is used most often in bookmaking and not used as much in advertising. With shorter lines, justification can become a problem, since the white space increases to a point where it is highly visible. Evenly adjusting word spacing, character spacing, or both may help solve awkward uneven spacing.

In unjustified composition, word spaces are fixed. Word spacing must always be larger than letter spacing and can be varied to adjust line length without affecting readability. Word spacing should be kept thin so that the text flows smoothly and the reader does not have to make large jumps between words.

Word spaces are usually within certain ranges—minimum, optimum, and maximum—and in many cases can be tailored by users to their own taste. Some type buyers prefer very tight spacing, and some old-timers like a hot metal look—somewhat wider spacing. In QuarkXPress, this is found in the H&J dialog box under Style. Figure 7–9 shows the InDesign Justification dialog box options, showing the minimum, desired (optimum), and maximum options for word spacing used for justification.

The minimum word space is the smallest value below which the space will not go. This would reduce the likelihood that a line would be set completely tight with no discernible word space. The maximum

Figure 7–9
Justification options dialog box.

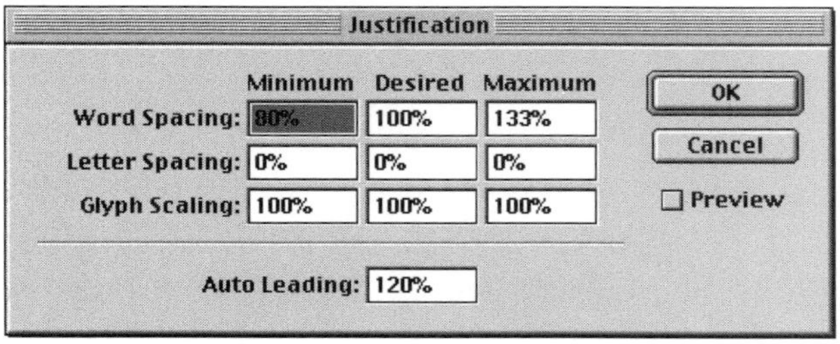

Table 7–1

Values to eliminate letter spacing.

	Minimum	Desired	Maximum
Word Spacing	85–90	100–110	130–170
Letter Spacing	0	0	0

is the widest value you would allow, and usually this is the threshold point where automatic letter spacing might be employed. The optimum is the value you would like most often for good, even spacing. In QuarkXPress, the value is a percentage of the standard word space as defined by the font.

Smaller word spaces, or kerned word spaces, often look better after commas, periods, apostrophes, or quotes. Word spaces work as variable wedges between words, expanding or contracting as needed to space the line out to its justification width.

The following values are a good place to start when working with spacing. Make sure the number in the space for flush zone is 0. That justifies the last line in a paragraph if it falls within the specified distance from the right margin. Generally, this is a bad idea.

Table 7–1 shows some values that try to eliminate letter spacing.

Setting Hyphenation

Hyphenation settings in InDesign are paragraph-level attributes, but hyphenation languages are specified at the character level to facilitate multilingual publishing. You can check the *Hyphenate* option in the palette to turn hyphenation on for a paragraph, then choose *Hyphenation* from the palette's menu to specify more options. Like hyphenation, the word spacing, letter spacing, and glyph scaling values you specify determine the overall composition of your text.

You can specify hyphenation parameters as part of a paragraph style, or you can use the Paragraph palette's *Hyphenate* checkbox and the *Hyphenation* command on the palette's menu.

Hyphenation can be on or off for any given paragraph.

- If hyphenation is off, only hard hyphens (as in compound words like mother-in-law) will cause words to break.
- If hyphenation is on and a word begins on a line but can't squeeze entirely onto it, hyphenation is activated.
- First, any manually inserted, discretionary hyphens are used. A discrectionary hyphen is inserted by a person. It is entered by—are you ready?—Command/Control + Hyphen. You can also right-click (Windows) or Control-Click (MacOS) to get a pop-up list. Place your discretionary hyphens in a word in one or more locations and only those locations will be used to break the word. Place one at the beginning of the word and it will never break.
- If no discretionary hyphens have been entered, the hyphenation dictionary for the language assigned to that word, and the supplemental dictionary associated with that language, are used for breaks. If neither dictionary contains the word, hyphenation rules apply.

You can edit words in the InDesign user dictionary by choosing Edit ➠ Dictionary, then selecting a language (Figure 7–10). You can also

Figure 7–10
Edit Dictionary dialog box.

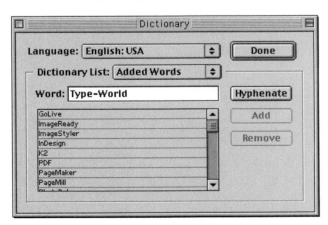

remove words from the dictionary or change hyphenation breakpoints. To summarize, when hyphenation is turned on, you can:

- Apply the *No Break* option to prevent a range of text, such as a web address, from hyphenating.
- Specify that words shorter than a certain number of letters cannot be hyphenated. Since hyphenating short words is a typographical faux pas, increasing the value from the default of seven letters to even nine can minimize the number of hyphens in a row by allowing fewer possible breakpoints.
- Set limits for how many letters precede or follow a hyphen. Short word fragments on either side of a hyphen are considered by many to impair readability. If you feel that two letters preceding a hyphen is an acceptable compromise but that at least three characters must always follow one, you can specify that preference.
- Limit the number of consecutive hyphens. The Ladder Limit controls how many consecutive hyphens are acceptable; the term "ladder" refers to the visual effect of stacked hyphens on the right edge of a paragraph.
- Prevent capitalized words from hyphenating by unchecking the *Hyphenate Capitalized Words* option.

When you're setting ragged text with the Single-line Composer, the *Hyphenation Zone* setting controls the raggedness of the unjustified edge of the text frame. If the first character of an overset word falls outside the hyphenation zone, InDesign will attempt to hyphenate the word (if *Hyphenation* is on). The narrower the zone, the more likely hyphenation becomes—a wider hyphenation zone results in a more ragged margin and fewer hyphens. Since many typographers feel that ragged right text should be hyphenated sparingly, increasing the hyphenation zone is a reasonable way to minimize hyphenation without turning it off, which results in even worse looking type.

Setting Justification (or Not)

Paragraph alignment—and specifically the choice between ragged and justified text—is one of the first design decisions you'll make when developing a document. InDesign offers seven options:

- Left ragged
- Center ragged
- Right ragged
- Left justify
- Center justify
- Right justify
- Full (or force) justify

The justified options are accessed from the Paragraph palette or specified as part of a paragraph style. The *Justification* dialog box (choose *Justification* from the Paragraph palette menu) contains options for word spacing, letter spacing, and glyph scaling (see Figure 7–11).

The *Word Spacing* and *Letter Spacing* options allow you to control how much the text composition engines can deviate from the spacing designed into the font. The *Glyph Scaling* option adjusts the shapes of the letters to lengthen or shorten a line of justified text. You can fine-tune the behavior of the composition engine by adjusting these values in the Justification dialog box. It is essentially horizontal scale brought to an automated level.

Figure 7–11
Glyph Scaling is expressed as a percentage of the font's width.

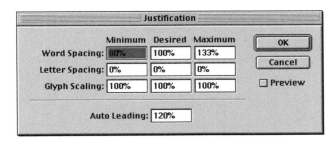

The *Word Spacing*, *Letter Spacing*, and *Glyph Scaling* options each offer settings for:

- Desired (or Optimum)
- Minimum
- Maximum

Desired allows you to specify the optimum word spacing value, which is what the program will try for most often, while *Minimum* and *Maximum* define a range of acceptable values. For the *Word Spacing* option, the default value for *Desired* is 100%, which means that InDesign will try to use the font's full word space without shrinking or expanding it. Because other characters have different widths, letter spacing is expressed as a percentage of change. In keeping with traditional typographic preferences, both of the composition engines will adjust the word spaces in a line of text to their minimum or maximum values before attempting to alter the letter spacing values.

While setting a highly restrictive range for either value might appear as a method to ensure even spacing, the different InDesign composition engines use these values in slightly different ways. For the Single-line Composer, setting smaller ranges makes sense, especially for justified text where the full range is used. Because the Multi-line Composer strives to achieve the desired spacing regardless of the paragraph's alignment, it yields better results when moderate ranges are defined.

Adjusting word spacing (within reason) is a fairly safe bet typographically. Glyph scaling and letter spacing offer alternative approaches to the next level of compositional tweaking. Unlike letter spacing, which crunches characters together or spreads them apart without changing the actual letterforms (and is anathema to typographic purists), glyph scaling alters the shape of the character slightly, leaving the spaces between letters intact. Glyph scaling functions like context-sensitive horizontal character scaling. If a line contains a word that doesn't fit, glyph scaling can shrink the widths of the characters on the line, within the range you specify, to make them fit.

Figure 7–12
Side pop-out menu.

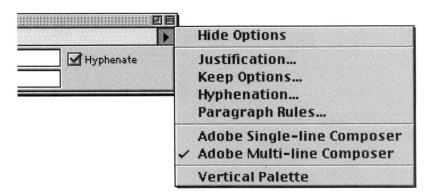

Figure 7–13
Side pop-out menu close-up.

Characters in a line can also expand slightly to move a word down to the following line. If the glyph scaling values you enter define a narrow enough range—say 97% for *Minimum* and 103% for *Maximum*—the differences in the letter shapes will be noticeable only to true typographic experts. Larger ranges should be avoided unless you want something really weird.

Justification options, like the Hyphenation options, are located in the side-pop-out menu of the Paragraph palette (Figures 7–12 and 7–13).

Get used to these side pop-out menus. InDesign uses many of them.

Note: The Character and Paragraph palette is an important palette (Figure 7–14) and should be kept open when you are working on a job.

A line with narrow spacing is called a *close* line, and one with wide spacing is an *open* line. Without good hyphenation, word spacing in justified lines can be quite erratic and inconsistent. Thus, many designers opt for ragged right and eliminate the problem altogether. With InDesign H&J we would expect that they will use more justified text because it it better.

Our text job is now justified (Figure 7–15).

Figure 7–14
Character and Paragraph palette.

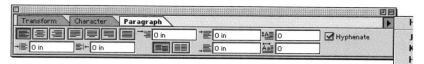

Figure 7–15
A page of justified text.

The Typo
By Frank Romano

The history of the lowly typographical error is inexorably linked to the history of humankind. No other species is known to make typos. (Although hippopotami are known to make hippos.) A typo must involve type. Without type, there cannot be a typo. Pictures with errors are pictos. Thus the typo was born with the invention of typographic communication.

The ancient Koreans developed the process of block printing. It is said that a queen was near death and the high priests ordered the writing of a prayer on small sheets of rice paper, probably printed with soy ink — the first edible printing. Technology came to the rescue and reproduced thousands of them — the first printed correspondence with a deity. The queen died anyway.

The Koreans were renowned for the quality of their work. There were even manuals for novices and journeymen. For instance, if a novice made one typo they lost a finger. The second typo caused the loss of a hand. This explains their reputation for quality . . . and the difficulty in recruiting new printers.

Later, monks who spent their lives in scriptoria scribbling their way to Heaven also made mistakes. One wonders what profanity they uttered as they lost control of their quill pen. To correct the error they could scrape away the ink from the vellum, which was the hide of a calf. Another method was to cover the error with a white paste and then write over it — the invention of White-Out, or in this case, Vellum-Out. In some cases, given the value of vellum, entire sheets were covered with medieval White-Out and used again. These are called palimp-

scests and archeologists often find that what was covered was more historically significant. I wonder if that will be true for modern memos. Or class notes.

Charlemagne standardized all writing throughout the Holy Roman Empire with an uncial writing style that would eventually be known as lowercase, designed by Alcuin of York, a British consultant. He could not standardize typographical errors, however, and individuality still prevailed, accounting for the breakup of the Empire into nationalistic states.

Gutenberg's secrecy was a marketing strategy. He wanted to sell mass-produced books at custom-produced prices. The Gutenbergian system of printing divided language into its basic building blocks — letters. Yet, the first work to be printed by moveable type was not a Bible, but rather an Indulgence, a sort of passport to Heaven, or more accurately, a form. Technologies may change, but bureaucracy endures.

After production of the first batch of Bibles, Johann Fust took several to Paris to sell. Since Bibles did not come on the market very often, their purchasers compared them. They found the same errors on the same pages. This had to be the work of the devil. Johann Fust died in Paris during that trip.

Now the opportunity for error was fully formed. A new profession was born — the corrector of the press, today known as the proofreader. Their sole duty was to find mistakes before they got into print. Finding them afterward, did not count. Aldus Manutius, who almost single-handed created the Renaissance, used the philosopher Erasmus as a proofreader, as the great Greek texts were put into print for the first time.

The Gutenbergian font of 292

letters and letter combinations was reduced over the centuries. But humankind had no problem adapting — they just increased the number of errors per character.

It was an act of graphic vandalism that almost destroyed Mark Twain. The first edition of "Huck Finn" had been printed and the handset type re-distributed. On one of the engravings someone had scratched an image that made it obscene. The pages had not only been printed, they were partially bound. The entire run had to be discarded and production re-started. Combined with his investment in the failed Paige "typesetting machine" he was virtually wiped out financially.

Handset type yielded to linecasting. And a new error crept in — the wrong font. We could now mechanize our errors.

Linecaster operators could not abort a line of type once started in the assembling elevator. Sensing an error, they would run their fingers down the first two rows of keys to produce ETAOIN SHRDLU which would be identified as a line to be discarded. However, the history of the newspaper industry reports that these lines often made their way into print and a generation of readers often asked "Who" or "What" was ETAOIN SHRDLU?

Paper tape and the TeleTypeSetter system allowed us to telecommunicate our typos to multiple sites at the same time. You no longer had to be present to see your errors in print.

Photographic typesetting was combined with computer automation. Ah, the computer. Now we could automate our typos.

Text processing entered the business office and changed forever the traditional typing process. A typist would begin typing on their Royal Remington or IBM Selectric. Al

InDesign Automates Typography   InDesign gives you choices for justification. To review those choices, let us look at composition engines. Some old-timers will recall the computer typesetting systems of the 1970s and 1980s—like CCI, Penta, and Quadex—that automated the process of typographic composition. Desktop programs placed more of the burden of typography on the user. InDesign brings back some of the automation of yesteryear while still allowing complete individual interaction with the page and with the document. It is the integration of the desktop and traditional typographic worlds.

Composition

The Multi-line Composer is based on the work of Donald E. Knuth,[1] a computer scientist and Stanford University professor who created a public-domain typesetting application, TeX, in the 1980s. Knuth and his co-author Michael F. Plass set out to improve upon the line-by-line approach used by most hyphenation routines. Knuth also needed an application that could provide high-quality type and was capable of setting difficult mathematical composition properly. The result was the line-breaking algorithm at the heart of TeX. Knuth made TeX available as a freeware program, and it is still used by the scientific, mathematical, and academic communities.

In 1984 John W. Seybold wrote that it was possible to have the best justification system on earth and still get results inferior to those achievable by a human, so long as the end-of-line decision was made in the vacuum of a single line of text. What makes the human operator's result better, in many cases, is the rejection of the line already composed. The operator then goes back and resets the preceding line, bringing a word down or up, or breaking the words in a different place, to get better results in the line that follows.

Many people think a computer routine should have the same capability and should be able to "look at" five or six lines at the same

---

[1] *The TEX Series*, Addison-Wesley Publishers, 1990.

time. If it can succeed in doing this and if it used a dictionary (word break list) with preferred hyphenation points, no human would be able to obtain comparable results as consistently. The Multi-line Composer in Adobe InDesign fulfills both Knuth's and Seybold's visions.

The settings you choose for the two composers play a vital role in determining how the composition engine will arrange text. Hyphenation controls determine whether words can be hyphenated, and if they can, what breaks are allowable. InDesign offers hyphenation controls that are customizable, even for multilingual text. With InDesign, justification is a term for the alignment of text in a frame and is controlled by the alignment option you choose, the word and letter spacing you specify, and whether you've used glyph scaling or not. Hyphenation and justification are two separate processes. What's more, you can define settings and apply them on-the-fly to individual paragraphs without having to define and save settings and then apply them through a cumbersome dialog box. And, of course, you can define both as part of a paragraph style sheet.

The Single-line Composer   The Single-line Composer is a traditional approach to composing text, and it is typical of the majority of page layout applications. It picks the best breakpoint for one line at a time, providing a fast approach and follows three principles when searching for a hyhenation point.

- Compressed or expanded *word* spacing is preferable to hyphenation.
- Hyphenation is preferable to compressed or expanded *letter* spacing.
- It is better to compress than to expand.

If the last word on a text line won't fit, InDesign first tries to compress the space between words in order to make room for that last word. If that doesn't work, the space between words is expanded. If that doesn't force the word onto the next line, hyphenation is considered. Finally, both letter and word spacing are compressed, and if that fails to pull the word up, then both word spacing and letter spacing are expanded in order to force the word to the next line. When an acceptable breakpoint is finally found, the program moves on to the next line. The Single-line Composer only considers one line at a time and does not consider multiple lines. With the Single-line Composer, it's not uncommon to have lines with poor spacing in the midst of well-spaced paragraphs—a problem that is time-consuming to correct manually by using the discretionary hyphen. This is what the Multi-line Composer eliminates.

The Multi-line Composer   The Multi-line Composer considers the effects of hyphenation points across a range of lines that you specify for more consistent word spacing and is not limited to finding the breakpoint for a single line of text, which could result in randomly spaced lines. The Multi-line Composer considers a series of breakpoints for a range of lines. Because the downstream (the following lines) implications of a line break can be evaluated, this approach can optimize earlier lines in a paragraph to eliminate especially unattractive breaks in later lines.

The overall result is more consistent spacing and fewer hyphens. The Multi-line Composer uses the *composition preferences* you set (File ➠ Preferences ➠ Composition to open the dialog box)—Figure 7–16.

The *Look ahead_lines* option establishes the number of lines the composer will analyze, and *Consider up to_alternatives* specifies the maximum number of possible breakpoints considered for each line. For both of these settings, higher values increase the complexity of the operation and improve the overall quality of the typographic results, but result in slower performance. The heart of the Multi-line Composer's approach to composition involves identifying possible breakpoints, evaluating them, and assigning a weighted penalty. You will like it.

To determine how heavily to weight a possible breakpoint, the engine uses several principles.

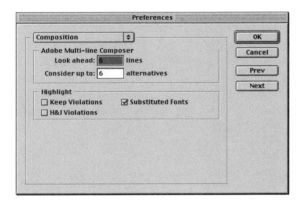

Figure 7–16
Composition Preferences dialog box.

- Evenness of letter and word spacing is considered the most important. Possible breakpoints are evaluated in terms of how much they deviate from the desired (optimum) spacing and are assigned a penalty accordingly.
- Hyphenation is avoided whenever possible. In addition to the spacing penalty, breakpoints requiring hyphenation are penalized even more.
- After breakpoints for a range of lines are identified and assigned a penalty by the Multi-line Composer, that penalty value is squared to magnify the evilness of bad breaks. Once identified, the potential breakpoints for each line—up to the number of alternatives you specify—are connected to the possible breakpoints they suggest for the following line, creating a treelike branching network of possible options. Once the options are established, the Multi-line Composer reviews the penalties for each possible path across the range of lines. The first line in the range is composed based on the path with the lowest penalty, and the sequence begins again for the second line. The first lines in a paragraph are more likely to be

problematic, because there are fewer allowable options to consider. Later lines in a paragraph, because they can be adjusted by changing preceding ones, have more consistent spacing.

Your hyphenation settings affect the Multi-line Composer's results. Possible hyphenation points that violate your hyphenation settings are automatically disqualified as breakpoints, so the more restrictive your hyphenation parameters, the more likely you are to see text with uneven spacing. You are at the mercy of line length, point size, and the text itself. If you set a ladder limit (number of hyphens in a row) of two in a narrow column, you will limit the number of stacked hyphens but will absolutely compromise spacing.

Composition Engines—The Choice   The two InDesign composition engines offer alternative approaches to getting your text on a page. How do you choose? The Multi-line Composer has the best balance between high-quality results and performance, especially for large amounts of text such as the body copy in a multicolumn magazine article. Because the Multi-line Composer can weigh the effects of composition choices across a range of lines, it can optimize the balance between spacing and hyphenation, and it usually results in text that is more even in color and that contains fewer hyphens.

If you're dealing with smaller amounts of text, such as captions and headlines, the differences are minimal. The line-by-line approach taken by the Single-line Composer may yield more user control.

If you're using the Multi-line Composer and you edit a line near the end of a paragraph, the Multi-line Composer will begin recomposing the text six lines above the edit, or more if you've increased the *Look ahead_lines* setting. It's possible that line breaks before the edit—as well as lines following it—may change as a result, and that may prove disconcerting.

You may prefer to have manual control over how lines break, and the Single-line Composer may be a better choice. Its functions are less computationally intensive and may offer better performance.

Those performance differences may not be significant for some tasks, but the Multi-line Composer may take longer to set the same text—while providing better results. It really depends on the computer you use.

We expect great debate about this composition choice. Adobe could have opted to provide only the higher-capability Multi-line Composer, but we think they did the right thing in providing users with composition alternatives. Users and their customers will ultimately decide for themselves which approach provides the acceptable level of composition. As faster computers come into use, and performance is no longer an issue, multi-line composition will prevail.

Our text was justified in our continuing example. The illustration in Figure 7–17 shows the last set of lines from that example that fit on the page.

Figure 7–18 shows the last lines that fit on the page after we applied the Multi-line Composer.

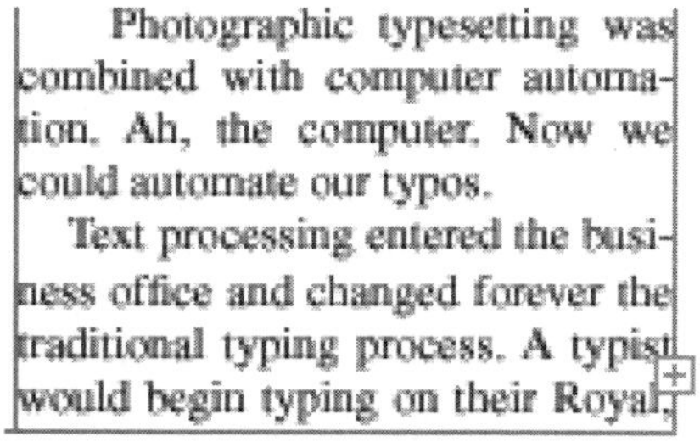

Photographic typesetting was combined with computer automation. Ah, the computer. Now we could automate our typos.

Text processing entered the business office and changed forever the traditional typing process. A typist would begin typing on their Royal.

Figure 7–17
Single-line Composer at work.

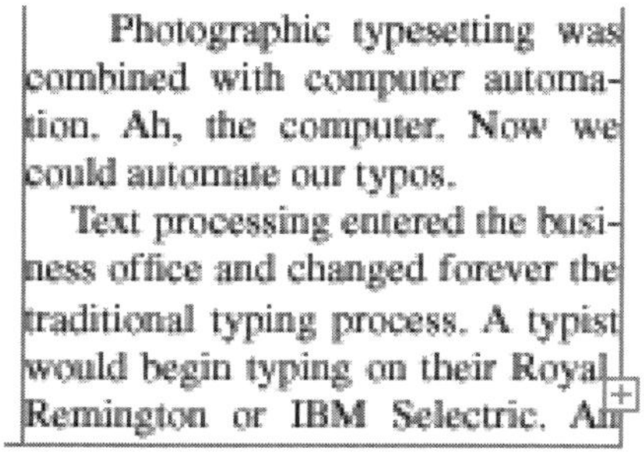

Photographic typesetting was combined with computer automation. Ah, the computer. Now we could automate our typos.

Text processing entered the business office and changed forever the traditional typing process. A typist would begin typing on their Royal Remington or IBM Selectric. An

Figure 7–18
Multi-line Composer at work.

The Multi-line Composer allowed us to gain one line. Overall, it gained a few more hyphens than the Single-line Composer and looked slightly better to our typographic eye. With a new Macintosh G3 or a Pentium chip on steroids, the computational overhead of the Multi-line Composer did not appear to be a factor (although on a 200-page book it might, but then we could get a G4). If you have a slower processor, it could cause a slight delay.

In either case, Adobe has worked hard to provide more justification efficacy than has yet been available in a desktop program.

Optical Margin Alignment and Hanging Punctuation   Optical margin alignment is a story-level attribute. It can adjust the position of characters at either end of a line in order to make the margins of a text frame appear straighter by optically adjusting the character alignment to appear more even. The effect is most pronounced for punctuation marks, such as quotes and hyphens, but the positions of other characters are subtly adjusted as well. The amount that characters adjacent to the frame edge move depends on the point size you enter in the *Optical Margin Alignment* area of the Story palette (Figure 7–19). This attribute applies to an entire story and best results occur if the value you enter matches the point size of the body text.

With optical alignment on the left and hanging punctuation on both sides (Figure 7–20), the result is, well, magic.

Figure 7–19
Optical Margin Alignment in Story panel.

Gutenberg's secrecy was a marketing strategy. He wanted to sell mass-produced books at custom-produced prices. The Gutenbergian system of printing divided language into its basic building blocks — letters. Yet, the first work to be printed by moveable type was not a Bible, but rather an Indulgence, a sort of passport to Heaven, or more accurately, a form. Technologies may change, but bureaucracy endures.

Figure 7–20
Optical alignment/hanging punctuation off (above); on (right).

Gutenberg's secrecy was a marketing strategy. He wanted to sell mass-produced books at custom-produced prices. The Gutenbergian system of printing divided language into its basic building blocks — letters. Yet, the first work to be printed by moveable type was not a Bible, but rather an Indulgence, a sort of passport to Heaven, or more accurately, a form. Technologies may change, but bureaucracy endures.

Multilingual Publishing

The language specified determines where words can be hyphenated. You specify a language from the Character palette (Figure 7–21) or as part of a character or paragraph style, so words from different languages can be hyphenated correctly.

For example, the German word "zucker" should become "zukker" when hyphenated according to traditional German rules of grammar. That's what happens—automatically—with InDesign. Using both the hyphenation dictionary assigned to each language, and rule-based algorithm (rules) hyphenation, InDesign handles most special cases.

InDesign includes 21 hyphenation-and-spelling dictionaries for different languages and dialects; each dictionary includes tens of thousands of words with standard syllable breaks. Each syllable break in the dictionaries is assigned a desirability rating, and more optimal breakpoints are strongly favored by the single-line and multi-line composers.

Figure 7–21
Selecting language in the
Character palette.

In addition to the dictionaries included with InDesign, you can use dictionaries developed by third parties (that's another area where the extensive plug-ins capability comes in). In the Dictionary Preferences dialog box (File ➠ Preferences ➠ Dictionary), you can specify separate spelling and hyphenation dictionaries for each language (Figure 7–22).

Every document is unique in its use of words and the resulting word breaks necessary for hyphenation and justification. The InDesign user-editable hyphenation dictionary allows you to select a language to ensure that words you use frequently hyphenate correctly.

Thus, words are stored by language and then activated when you select the language in the Character palette pop-up list. This allows mixed language composition with InDesign.

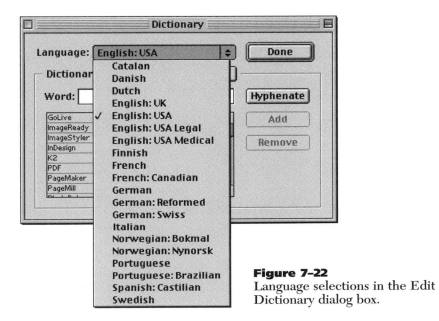

Figure 7–22
Language selections in the Edit Dictionary dialog box.

Character Formatting

The Character palette (Figure 7–23) contains the basic options for typographic formatting. You can also specify kerning, tracking, horizontal or vertical scaling, baseline shift, a skew value, and a language to be used for spelling and hyphenation. You can also define paragraph- or character-level styles.

Across the top line: Palatino is the font. Regular is the style. Metrics is the kerning. 100% is the vertical scale. 0 is the baseline shift. English is the language.

Across the botton line: 12 pt is the point size. 14.4 is the leading value. 0 is the tracking. 100% is the horizontal scale. 0 is the character tilt in degrees.

Typeface and Font   When you specify a font, you can select the typeface family and its specific style (such as bold or italic) independently. Choose Minion as the body font for a document and use Minion Bold for emphasis. Later, change the body font to Palatino.

Figure 7–23
Character palette.

Because the typeface style is assigned independently of the typeface family, the Minion Bold text automatically maps to Palatino Bold. Typeface options on the palette are limited to preserve the font designer's intentions. For example, Trajan is an uppercase roman face in a single weight designed as a titling face. InDesign doesn't list style options that would approximate a bold typeface.

You can also apply special formatting, such as underlining, strikethrough, all caps, small caps, and superscript or subscript, using the Character palette menu. In the Text Preferences dialog box, you can specify how large superscript, subscript, and small caps text is relative to the regular font, as well as the position of superscripts and subscripts relative to the baseline.

Character Scaling   InDesign also lets you distort the shapes of characters, but that does not mean you should. Using the Character palette, you can stretch characters vertically or horizontally, and you can skew them as well. Adjusting the widths of characters (horizontal scale) slightly can be a great aid when copyfitting—but knowing what "slightly" means is part of the problem. Adjusting the height of all characters (vertical scale) provides a creative capability. Combined, they let you fit display type to a specific layout (Figure 7–24).

You can scale all of the characters in a text frame both horizontally and vertically at the same time using the Scale tool (Figure 7–25).

The *Skew* option makes it easy to create fake italics by skewing selected text a specific number of degrees (Figure 7–26). There are few applications for this, but someone will find a use for it.

Text remains fully editable no matter how you torture it.

Tortured Type

Figure 7–24
Vertical scale 40% and Horizontal scale 90%.

Figure 7–25
Scale tool in the Tools palette.

Figure 7–26
Skew tool in the Character palette.

Leading   The leading value is the distance between lines of type, as measured from baseline to baseline. You can specify fixed leading amounts or use automatic leading (Figure 7–27).

Fixed leading gives you precise control over vertical spacing of lines, and lines will be evenly spaced regardless of the size of the characters. Automatic leading is specified as a percentage of the largest character on any given line, using a paragraph-level value you specify in the Justification dialog box—accessed as the side pop-out from the Paragraph palette. You would not think to look here. The default is autoleading and the value is 120% of the point size.

Figure 7–27
Auto Leading default is
120% of the point size.

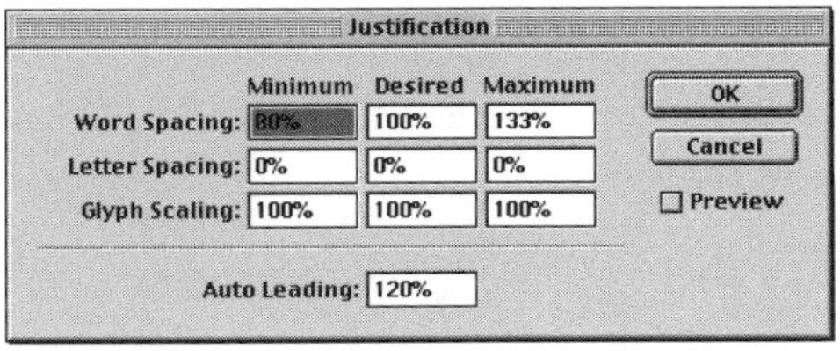

	Minimum	Desired	Maximum	
Word Spacing:	80%	100%	133%	OK
Letter Spacing:	0%	0%	0%	Cancel
Glyph Scaling:	100%	100%	100%	☐ Preview
Auto Leading:	120%			

Baseline Shift   If you want to adjust the vertical position of specific characters or an entire line of text, use the *Baseline Shift* option on the Character palette (Figure 7–28). You can specify how far above or below the baseline the selected characters rest. This is helpful when positioning subscript and superscript characters or just tweaking lines that do not align properly. If you use a keyboard shortcut, the increment is set in the Units Preferences under the File menu. We still use the QuarkXPress shortcut of Command/Control + Option/Alt + Plus (+) or Minus (-).

Language   The language specified for any word or words determines how those words are spellchecked and hyphenated. Character-level language attributes mean you can combine different languages in a paragraph and those words will be spellchecked and hyphenated correctly.

You can also specify a *No Break* option for a range of characters, like a web address, to prevent them from being split (Figure 7–29).

Paragraph Formatting The Paragraph palette (Figure 7–30) lets you select how you want your text to be aligned; whether it is indented or not; how much space precedes or follows the paragraph (space before and after); whether drop caps are used, and how they appear based on lines deep and characters used; and whether the text aligns to a baseline grid or not.

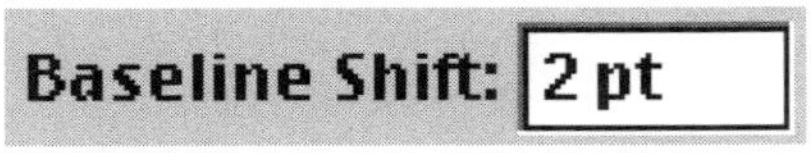

Baseline Shift: `2 pt`

Figure 7–28
Setting baseline shift increment in
Units Preferences.

Figure 7–29
Paragraph palette side pop-out
with *No Break*.

Figure 7–30
Paragraph palette.

Figure 7–31
Drop caps functions in Paragraph palette.

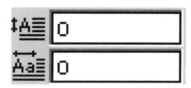

Using the Paragraph palette's menu, you can specify *Keep Options* for eliminating widows and orphans, paragraph rules, hyphenation settings, word and letter spacing, and glyph scaling. You can choose which composition engine you want to use for that paragraph. We will cover the specifics of this palette in areas where they apply, as in drop caps, coming up next. Stay tuned.

Drop Caps

To make typographic work look more elegant, drop caps are added. Drop caps were originally used to signal the start of a chapter or segment and were done by hand. Today's drop caps are not as fancy or as large as they used to be.

Drop cap functions are set in the Paragraph palette (Figure 7–31). Top sets number of lines and bottom sets number of characters.

A drop cap is sometimes also known as a sunken initial and in this version has an initial letter set so that the top of the initial is more or less even with the top of the first line of type. The initial is made larger than the rest of the text, but is the first letter of the paragraph.

Two letters that do not work well with this type of drop cap are the A and L, since the space between the letter and the text is not visually pleasing. With the letters I and T, the space is so small that it causes the same problem.

Another type of drop cap is a raised initial, in which the initial rests on the baseline of the first line of text and rises above the first line of text. With raised initials, more white space is required, which is why newspapers usually stick to the sunken initial.

The space around the dropped initial should be visually the same on the right side and bottom of the letter. A raised initial should always be on the baseline, and kerning should be applied as necessary.

Traditionally, the first word following the initial should be set in small caps. The lines adjacent to the cap should be contoured to flow around the curves or strokes of the letter to enhance the appearance.

"This is why you need to specify the number of characters to be dropped. Otherwise you get this:

"This is an example of what happens when only the first character is specified.

This is an example of what a sunken initial would look like. Notice how the letter lines up with the ascenders of the first line of text and falls below the descender line. The first word is in all lower case.

THIS is an example of what a sunken initial would look like. Notice how the letter lines up with the ascenders of the first line of text. The first word is in all upper case.

THIS is an example of what a sunken initial would look like. Notice how the letter lines up with the ascenders of the first line of text and falls below the descender line. The first word is in small caps.

A drop cap like this is very hard to do. With InDesign we set up the paragraph for a drop cap, then created another text frame and matched the size. We converted the letter to an outline and then brought it in as a graphic and did a text wrap around the graphic, which just happens to be the letter.

A quick and dirty approach is to put the letter in a text frame with a text wrap of none—the first choice at far left in the Text Wrap dialog box under the Object menu. Then, position it and draw a diagonal rule along the edge of the A and make the rule white. The rule forces the type away from the A and creates the proper wrap. You can also put drop caps in color, modify their horizontal and vertical scale, shade them, or change the font.

Baseline Grid   The Baseline Grid icons on the Paragraph palette determine if the selected paragraph text aligns to the document's baseline grid. When you have multiple columns of type, the baselines should line up from column to column, and the baseline grid is the way to accomplish this.

When this option is toggled on (Figure 7–32), InDesign adjusts the leading for the paragraph to ensure that its baselines align to the page's underlying grid.

Baseline grid alignment is a problem for all programs if you have different point sizes, with space before and after heading and sub-headings. You may wish to set up a style sheet so that the text aligns and all the eccentricity in the heads and subheads is allowed to stand as the originator desires. See Figure 7–33.

Figure 7–32
Baseline Grid function in Paragraph palette. Top box sets value. Bottom left is off; right is on.

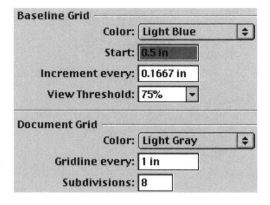

Figure 7–33
Baseline Grid preferences.

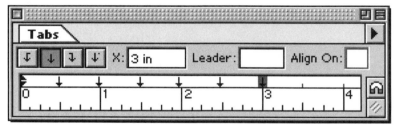

Figure 7–34
Tabs dialog box under Type menu.

Tabs   To align the tab ruler with the text frame containing the text cursor, click the magnet icon over on the right (Figure 7–34).

There are four types of tabs:

- left
- center
- right
- character-aligned

Character-aligned tabs align the tab to any character you specify in the *Align On* box—unlike decimal tabs, which always align to a period, or, in European use, to a comma. This is handy if you have a financial report with parentheses indicating a loss or you're creating a timetable and you want arrival and departure times to align to a colon. InDesign tabs are like QuarkXPress tabs, with improvements.

You can also specify leader tabs, which may contain up to eight characters and use character formatting independent of the text. You will certainly want to make the leader dots in a tab a smaller point size. This is one of those features we have wanted for a long time. Leader dots can also be spaced with tracking.

Small Caps Most of the characters we read are at the x-height. Small caps match the x-height of a particular type and size and are slightly expanded. There are two types of small caps, manufactured and true. Manufactured small caps can be created by some software programs. In InDesign, when you tell the program to use small caps, it is not a true form but is created by reducing the font size, and may also not be the same weight (Figure 7–35).

True small caps are the same x-height and are usually equal to the normal cap width. Some programs create their own, but true small caps are only found in expert typeface sets. Depending on the typeface, additional letter spacing may need to be added if the characters look too crowded or tight. Specify small caps from the side pop-out of the Character palette (Figure 7–36).

Figure 7–35
Small cap preferences in Text preferences for manufactured small caps.

Character Settings

	Size	Position
Superscript:	58.3%	33.3%
Subscript:	58.3%	33.3%
Small Cap:	70%	

Figure 7–36
Small caps are selected in the Character palette side pop-out.

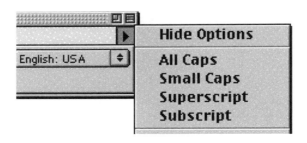

In the old days, small caps were used for awards, decorations, honors, titles, etc., following a person's name. Words that are specified as all caps may look better in small caps. Old-style figures also look best with small caps. Use all caps or small caps for the following:

- For the word "whereas."
- For the word "note" introducing an explanatory paragraph.
- For the words "section" and "article" in reference to part of a document by number.
- For the speaker in a dialogue or play.
- For ascription to the author of a direct, independent quotation.
- For words ordinarily in italics that appear in all-cap-and-small-cap or in an all-small-cap line.
- For the abbreviations "a.m." and "p.m." and "b.c." and "a.d.", there should be no space between the letters.

Small capitals are useful for section headings or chapter titles, to accent important words or phrases in mid-sentence, or at the beginning of a paragraph for a lead-in. [Our editor violently disagrees with this last comment.] True small caps are one sign of a truly professional job.

InDesign has small caps automation built-in. If you format text as small caps and the font you're using has a small caps typeface designed into it (only a few are now available), InDesign automatically maps to the small caps typeface, disregarding the small caps formatting options. Because the stroke weight, x-height, and other attributes are taken into consideration when small caps are designed, this approach yields much better looking results than simply scaling the uppercase characters a prespecified amount.

Keep Options Keep options allow you to control widows and orphans and the movement of paragraphs between text frames. Keep Options is in the side pop-out of the Paragraph palette (Figure 7–37).

The *Keep with next_lines* option (Figure 7–38) allows you to specify how many lines of the following paragraph must appear with the

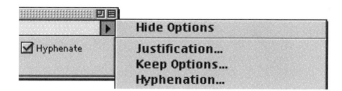

Figure 7–37
Keep Options from the Paragraph palette.

Figure 7–38
Keep Options dialog box.

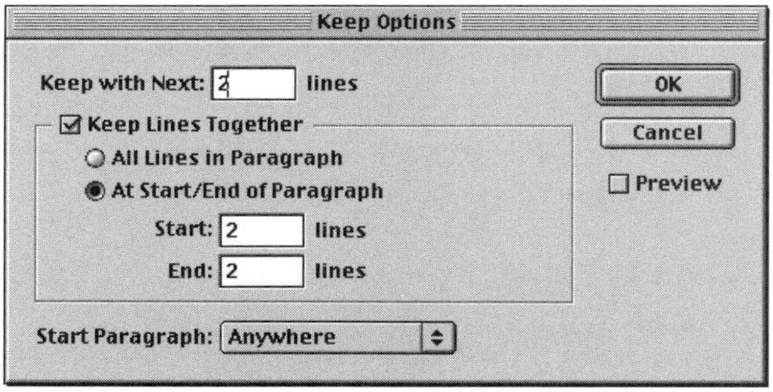

current paragraph to ensure that heads and subheads don't become isolated from the body text they introduce.

You can also choose *Start Paragraph* options to begin a paragraph in a new column or on a new page, which ensures that certain heading types always begin on a new page or at the top of a new column.

If you check *Keep Lines Together*, you can decide whether you want all the lines of a paragraph to move together or just the beginning and end lines. By entering a value greater than 1 for the *Start lines* option, you can eliminate any orphan lines by forcing those lines to new text frames. Entering a value greater than 1 for the *End lines* option eliminates widows by ensuring that at least two lines of its paragraph appear at the top of a new text frame.

InDesign defines a widow as the first line of a paragraph at the bottom of a page, and an orphan as the last line of a paragraph at the

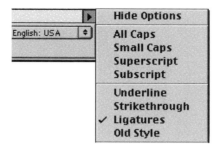

Figure 7–39
Select Ligatures in the Character palette side
pop-out.

top of a page. Traditionally, a widow has been any text line less than
one-third the width of the text line, usually the last line of a paragraph resulting from a word break. To fix that type of widow requires
re-writing the text in many cases.

Ligatures   Ligatures are multiple characters combined into a single
glyph. In English, the ligatures ff, fi, fl, ffi, and ffl are most common.
Most fonts include ligatures, finding them is difficult, and once
they've been inserted, they can't be edited easily. Because they
change the characters in a word, they cause spellcheckers to balk.
InDesign's automatic ligature substitution eliminates these problems. Just check *Ligatures* on the Character palette menu (Figure
7–39).

The ligatures included in the specified font display on-screen and
they print, but the text remains fully editable and the spelling of
words containing ligatures is unaffected. Many current fonts only
have fi and ff, so we expect more ligatures in more fonts soon.

Paragraph Rules   Paragraph rule controls are accessed from the
Paragraph palette side pop-out menu (Figure 7–40). You can set a
paragraph rule above or below (or both) any paragraph or line id type
to add emphasis to headings or to set text or paragraphs apart.

You can control the weight, color, position, width, and indent for
the rule (Figure 7–41). In addition, you can check Preview to see the
rule as you make adjustments to it.

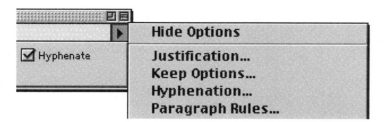

Figure 7-40
Find Paragraph Rules in the Paragraph
palette side pop-out.

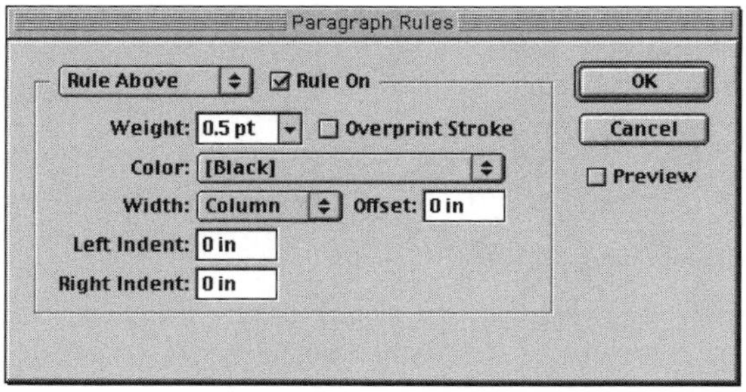

Figure 7-41
Paragraph Rules dialog box.

This function works very much like QuarkXPress and other programs. It links the rule or rules to the text so they all flow together as
text is edited. This is quite important as text reflows. The width can
either be based on the column or the text itself. For rule width we
still recommend .25 to .5 point—never hairline, which outputs one
row of pixels at printer resolution. This is okay at 600 dpi, but the line
will be invisible at 2540 dpi.

Character and Paragraph Style Sheets   Character and paragraph
styles are the best way to format your documents consistently—and
allow global changes to text formatting. Paragraph styles combine all
character-level and paragraph-level attributes so you can apply them
quickly to selected ranges of text.

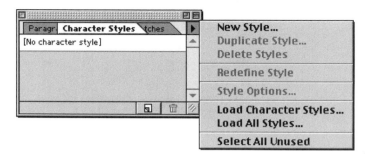

Figure 7–42
The Character and Paragraph style sheet palette with side
pop-out menu.

Go to Type ➠ Character or Paragraph to get the Character or
Paragraph style palette (Figure 7–42). Or, use Command/Control +
Shift + D for Character style sheets and Command/Control + Shift +
F for Paragraph Style sheets.

The side pop-out menu lets you select a New Style; the following
dialogs result (Figures 7–43 through 7–46).

You can define inheritance ("based on") relationships among paragraph styles and among character styles; if you change an attribute in
the parent style, it automatically applies to the child style as well. You
can also assign keyboard shortcuts to styles.

Menus for each palette provide options for importing styles from
other documents, duplicating styles, and selecting all unused styles.

You can specify a paragraph style for the paragraph that follows
what you've typed—a handy feature for heads and subheads.
Character styles isolate one or more character-level attributes, so you
can override a paragraph's formatting to create run-in heads, give
certain words extra emphasis, and more. Character styles can also be
edited, so you can quickly change the look of subheads or switch a
style from bold to italics.

Paragraph styles have more choices (Figure 7–47), and you can
pretty well control the look of an entire document.

When you import styles from another document, you can import only the paragraph styles, only the character styles, or both. If you apply local formatting that overrides an applied style, the style palette displays a plus sign; imported styles display a disk icon for easy identification.

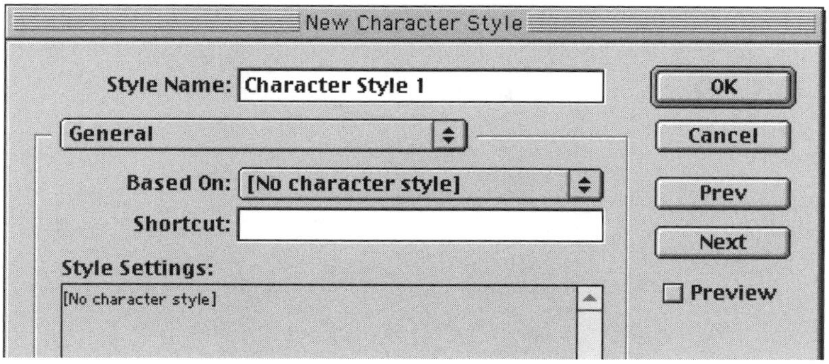

Figure 7–43
The General panel of New Character Style.

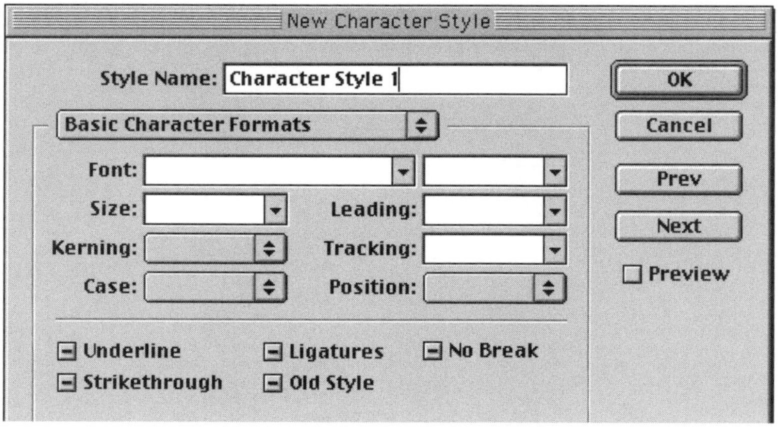

Figure 7–44
The Basic Character Formats panel of New Character Style.

Flush Space This one is not really a space but it is important. InDesign calls it the flush space. Available on the right-click menu on Windows (Control + Click on the Macintosh platform), this character adds a variable amount of space to a line and is designed to be used with justified text. The amount of space that the flush space adds to a line is determined first by whether the text is justified or not, and then by how much space is available on the line.

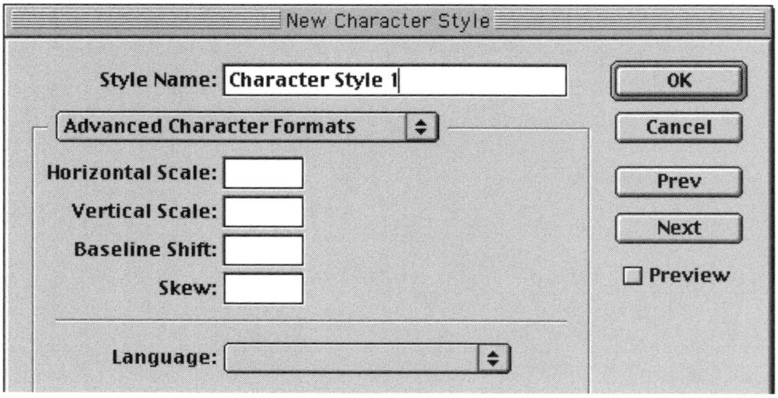

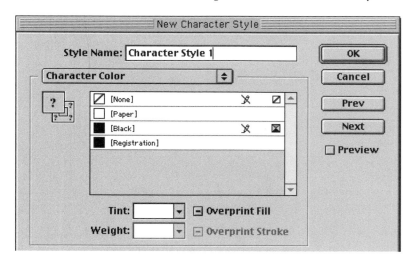

Figure 7–45
The Advanced Character Formats panel of New Character Style.

Figure 7–46
The Character Color panel of New Character Style.

In the old days, it was called Insert Space or Quad Middle and was a sort of super word space. It pushes text on the left to the left margin and text on the right to the right margin. In ragged text, the flush space acts just like a normal word space. In justified text, it expands to consume all available extra space on the line. Some magazines use an end-of-story character that is right-aligned. If the final paragraph

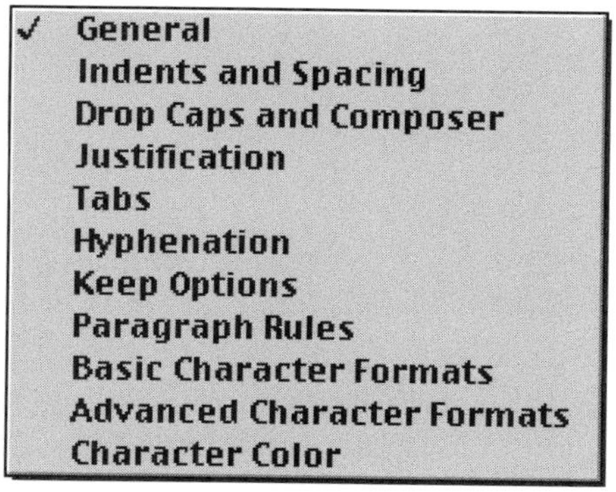

```
✓  General
   Indents and Spacing
   Drop Caps and Composer
   Justification
   Tabs
   Hyphenation
   Keep Options
   Paragraph Rules
   Basic Character Formats
   Advanced Character Formats
   Character Color
```

Figure 7–47
The panel choices for Paragraph
style sheets.

in a story is full-justified (meaning the last line must span the full width of the paragraph), you can insert a flush space, and the character will align properly.

Large Page and Spread Sizes   Yep, you can now set type on a bus. Not while sitting in the bus—imaging on the bus. InDesign supports custom page sizes as small as 1 pica (1/6 in., 0.421 cm.) square or as large as 1296 picas (18 ft., or 5.48 meters) square, so you can specify any "page" size you need up to extremely large signage. You can also select predefined page sizes, such as letter, A3, or B5.

Pages are organized into spreads, which can contain up to 10 pages. At the maximum page size, a 10-page spread reaches 180 square feet—now fold it. Every spread has its own pasteboard for storing spread-specific items (or you can save items in the Library palette to share assets across publications and platforms). The pasteboard allows an extra page of space at either end of a spread for a maximum length of 216 feet.

Kerning and Tracking

Kerning is the process of adding and subtracting space between specific letter pairs. InDesign offers four different kerning options:

- manual pair kerning
- optical pair kerning
- metrics pair kerning (kern pairs built into a font)
- tracking

Manual Pair Kerning   Typefaces are designed so that each character has a specific width and essentially lives in a little rectangle, even for characters with oval or diagonal shapes. When you combine these characters into words and sentences, obvious spacing inconsistencies appear between the letters. Kerning makes these irregular spaces more even. Kerning and tracking live on the Character and Paragraph palette (Figures 7–48 and 7–49).

With manual kerning, you fine-tune the space between two letters by eye. To kern manually, enter or select a kerning value from the Kerning menu on the Character palette (Figure 7–49).

Or, hold down Option or Alt as you press the left or right arrow key to increase or decrease letter spacing by the value specified in the Units & Increments preferences dialog box (to .001 of an em). Hold down Command/Control + Option/Alt as you press the left or right arrow key to increase or decrease the kerning space by five times that value.

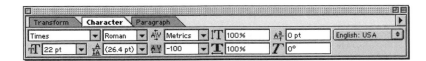

Figure 7–48
Kerning and tracking in the Paragraphs palette.

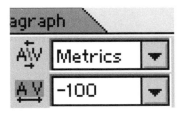

Figure 7–49
These two dialogs control kerning and tracking.

Manual kerning cannot be specified as part of either a paragraph or character style. It overrides both optical and metrics-based kerning.

Optical Pair Kerning   Optical kerning is a major innovation in desktop typography. By calculating the area between two adjacent character shapes, the ideal spacing between two characters is determined based on their optical appearance. Because the approach is visually based rather than metrics-based different point sizes or font changes are easily accommodated. Automatic optical kerning is essentially kerning on-the-fly, and it makes short work of what can be a tedious manual process. It is pretty good, but for very large point sizes, we prefer a trained eye controlling the process.

To apply optical kerning to selected text, choose *Optical* from the Kerning menu on the Character palette (Figure 7–50). The field displays the word *Optical*, but if you move your cursor between letter pairs, the calculated kern amount displays in parentheses.

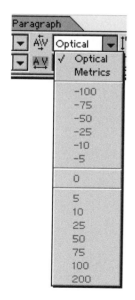

Figure 7–50
Kerning pop-up menu.

Metrics Pair Kerning   Using the pair kerning metrics in a font is an alternative, font-based solution to automated kerning. Many typefaces include a table of kern pairs, which contain instructions for adjusting the relative space between two characters wherever that pair occurs. Some fonts include extensive kern pair tables; if you specify these fonts, InDesign (by default) uses the kern pair metrics included in the font.

If a font includes only minimal kern pairs—or none at all—using its kern pair metrics won't have much effect. When you select a range of text, the manual kern field on the Character palette displays the word Metrics by default to indicate that kern pairs are being used. Moving your cursor between character pairs displays the actual kern amount in parentheses.

Tracking   Tracking affects spacing across a range of letters, three or more. Unlike manual kerning, it can be defined as part of a paragraph or character style. To apply tracking to a selected range of text, use the same option on the Character palette used for kerning. Tracking works cumulatively with manual, optical, and metrics kerning. Kerning is for two letters; tracking is for three or more.

Glyphs

Special characters are used in the course of almost any design project. You will use a variety of special characters, from ligatures and typographer's quotes to em dashes and copyright symbols. Most of these characters are accessed through keyboard shortcuts, which is handy as long as you can remember them.

Insert Character   There are 256 glyphs in a PostScript font. Many of these are the typewriter set, but there are hundreds or even thousands of glyphs that are used in typesetting, ranging from multiple versions of individual letters to typographically correct small caps, fractions, symbols, ornaments, and more. Until the release of InDesign, designers had no way to access many of these glyphs

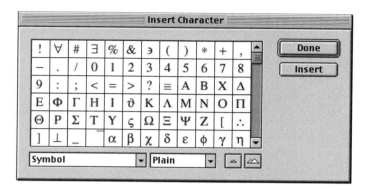

Figure 7–51
Insert Character dialog box.

except by investing in expert versions of fonts. Even then, expert fonts typically made only a portion of a font's glyphs available. With InDesign, you have access to every glyph in every font, including Japanese fonts, through the *Insert Character* dialog box, which lives under the Type menu (Figure 7–51).

Fonts such as Adobe's Galahad include multiple versions of certain characters for different language requirements. The Insert Character dialog box puts all of these characters, er, glyphs, at your fingertips for immediate insertion into your layouts.

To add more commonly used special characters, such as dashes, discretionary hyphens, and fixed spaces, right-click for Windows or Control + Click with MacOS at the text insertion point and choose *Insert Special Character*. The menu appears in Figure 7–52.

There is no other way to get at this menu. But what a menu it is. Here are all the problem characters that have plagued us for years—all in one place. No more crazy keyboard shortcuts or weird key cominations to remember. *In fact, to make you feel better, Table 7–2 reminds you of what it took to get at some of these characters. You can still use the old method in some cases if you are just a glutton for punishment.*

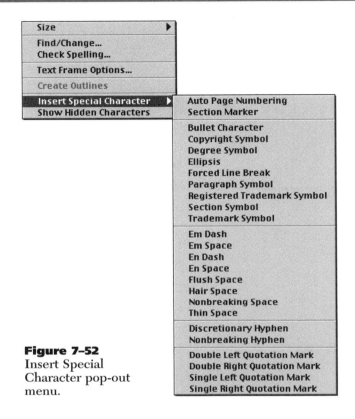

Figure 7–52
Insert Special
Character pop-out
menu.

Quote Conversion   When you select *Use Typographer's Quotes* in
the Text Preferences dialog box, InDesign automatically converts
single and double straight (inch) marks into typographer's (curly)
quotes for the language you've specified. French text will automatically use guillemets, whereas English will use curly quotes. You can
convert these marks into typographer's quotes when you import text
by choosing the *Convert Quotes* option in the Place A File dialog
box. We still have not figured out an easy way to just get an inch mark
for inches.

Table 7–2

Pre-InDesign combinations for special characters.

Character		Windows key combination
Ellipsis	…	Alt-0133
En dash	–	Alt-0150
Em dash	—	Alt-0151
Bullet	•	Alt-0149
Open Double Quote	"	Alt-0147
Closed Double Quote	"	Alt-0148
Open Single Quote	'	Alt-0145
Closed Single Quote	'	Alt-0146
Trademark Symbol	™	Alt-0153
Copyright Symbol	©	Alt-0169

Character		Macintosh key combination
Ellipsis	…	Option-;
En dash	–	Option-Hyphen
Em dash	—	Shift-Option-Hyphen
Hyphen	-	Hyphen
Bullet	•	Option-8
Open Double Quote	"	Option-[
Closed Double Quote	"	Shift-Option-[
Open Single Quote	'	Option-]
Closed Single Quote	'	Shift-Option-]
Trademark Symbol	™	Option-2
Copyright Symbol	©	Option-g

Design Effects with Type

InDesign special effects are possible because Adobe brought illustration tools to the page layout process.

- You can apply gradients to strokes and fill text with color.
- You can convert any text to editable compound paths and, using the Pen tool, modify the letterforms.
- Inline graphics let text and objects flow together in a text file.
- Text wrap lets you run text around any shape on all sides.

Text-to-Bézier-path Conversion   InDesign has the ability to convert any text to editable outlines. In conjunction with the new Pen tool, which is based on the one that is in Adobe Illustrator, you can create custom logotypes on-the-fly, as well as create other designs that are based on type. You could convert a character to a path, then use that path as a border.

In Figure 7–53, we have taken Times Bold and converted it to outlines using Type ➡ Convert Outlines. After that we could change the shape, add color, place a picture in the letters, or generally go wild—creatively speaking, that is. For those display fonts that cannot be embedded in PDF—convert them to outlines and fill with color.

Inline Graphics   Inline, or anchored, graphics (objects) act just like text characters, and can be used for images that accompany a particular paragraph. Any object can be an inline graphic, and inline

Figure 7–53
Text converted to outlines.

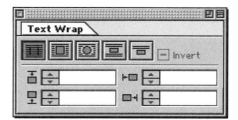

Figure 7–54
Text Wrap dialog box.

graphics can be selected and manipulated in the same way as other page elements.

As in QuarkXPress, if the width of the graphic frame hits the right-hand column, everything disappears, so keep these elements a few points away from the right margin guide. Inline graphics are especially useful in long-document work.

Text Wrap   Any page element can have text wrap applied. You can even invert a text wrap boundary to create a specially shaped text frame. Adobe Photoshop files with clipping paths can apply text wrap boundaries to those paths to wrap text along their shapes.

Object ➡ Text Wrap, or Command/Control + T to access the Text Wrap dialog box (Figure 7–54).

In addition to the standard rectangular, contoured, and jump-over offsets, you can set an element so text jumps over it to the next column, or you can set it to ignore text wrap altogether (a runaround of none). You can also control the spacing on all sides of the object. QuarkXPress introduced text wrap on both sides of an object in version 4.0.

Type Standards

Type is changing—again. InDesign supports both Unicode and the new OpenType font standard. The Unicode standard proposes a streamlined approach to the way fonts are stored and shared across computer platforms. The OpenType standard provides an exponentially larger set of possible characters in a font, making it easier for graphic designers to address publishing needs that are more and more global and multicultural in nature.

If you select a few letters and turn them to paths, then select the whole frame and turn the content to paths, InDesign asks if you want to delete the inlines created by turning selected letters into paths. Not a big deal. Text changed to paths uses the fill/stroke colors of the first character in the frame or selection to be converted.

Unicode Support   The Unicode standard was designed to provide:

- standard character encoding
- address character set limitations of the ASCII standard
- a solution for cross-platform character encoding

The 8-bit extended ASCII character set can store up to 256 characters. With 26 uppercase letters, 26 lowercase letters, 10 digits, and 20 or 30 punctuation symbols, this would seem to be sufficient. Not so. Accented characters, ligatures, spaces with specified widths, mathematical and scientific symbols, and characters used by non-English languages can easily add up to over 300 characters. As cultures become more inclusive, the ability to typeset names and words with special characters is increasing. Type is now global.

Japanese, Chinese, and Korean fonts each include thousands of characters (glyphs), which require a great deal of storage space. Unicode fonts, in a shift to 16-bit character storage, can represent up to 65,356 glyphs. This provides a common format for both Roman and Asian languages, as well as a standard for encoding fonts that work across multiple computing platforms. Unicode fonts are now available from Adobe as well as from other vendors.

OpenType Support   The OpenType font format was developed jointly by Microsoft and Adobe. It supports both PostScript and TrueType font data in a single format. OpenType fonts offer broad multiplatform support, standardized support for extended character sets through Unicode encoding, and more advanced typographic controls. This new technology provides both protection for font data and smaller file sizes to make font distribution more efficient. "Layout" tables contain information on glyph substitution, glyph positioning, justification, baseline positioning, and other controls to improve text layout. Because they support Unicode character encoding, OpenType fonts can contain glyphs for different alphabets. A single font can include Roman, Greek, and Cyrillic alphabets designed to work together visually.

OpenType fonts use the TrueType SFNT font file format. PostScript data included in OpenType fonts can be directly rasterized or converted to the TrueType outline format for rendering, depending on which rasterizers have been installed. OpenType fonts can contain digital signatures, which allow operating systems and web browsers to identify the source and integrity of font files, including embedded font files obtained in web documents, before using them.

Multiple Master Support   Multiple Master fonts are PostScript Type 1 font programs that include two or more master fonts within a single font file. These unique fonts have one or more axes, which represent the weight, width, or optical size of the font. Using Adobe Type Manager Deluxe to interpolate one or more axes, you can generate an "instance" of the font ideally suited for typographic needs. Multiple Master fonts with an optical size axis offer the potential of the highest-quality digital type available today.

In the days of metal type, designers and punchcutters (those who cut the punches for a font from metal) would subtly alter the design of each character to optimize its legibility for the exact size of the final printed letters.

Multiple Master fonts with an optical size axis provide a mapping between the optical size coordinates and the point size selected. Using the optical size axis in a Multiple Master font tweaks the font's lettershapes to look the way the designer intended. You can turn a global preference for using a font's optical size on or off by selecting the *Automatically Use Correct Optical Size* option in the Text section of the Preferences dialog box under the File menu (Figure 7–55).

Figure 7–55
Type Options in Text preferences.

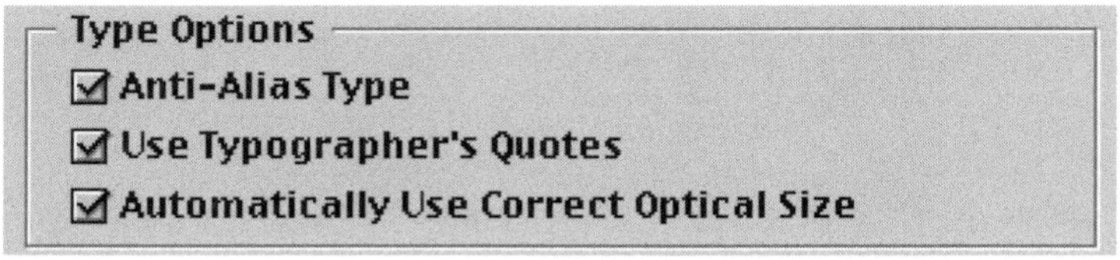

> Text cut or copied from Illustrator and pasted into InDesign cannot be reformatted in InDesign. If the text includes Multiple Master fonts, spacing and other aspects of the font appear (and output) incorrectly.

> If you apply a character style which specifies a font family variant (such as bold or italic) to text formatted with a Multiple Master font, the Character palette loses track of the available instances of the Multiple Master font. The instances are still listed, however, in the Type ➡ Font menu.

Intelligent Font Handling   Choosing a font is the most common design decision. InDesign is typographically pretty smart:

- Fonts added to your system are available immediately, so you don't have to quit the application and restart after you install a new typeface.
- Font families are grouped together on the Type menu instead of listed alphabetically. It's easier to see at a glance which families you have installed, as well as what faces are included in any given family—a big improvement over scrolling through font lists that are humongous.
- To choose a font in a dialog box or from the Character palette, simply type the first few letters of its family name rather than scrolling through the list.
- If your document contains a font that is missing from your system, InDesign highlights in pink any text with that font applied and displays a close approximation of the font instead. (To prevent InDesign from highlighting missing fonts, you can change the preference in the Composition panel of the Preferences dialog box under the File menu.)
- Missing fonts are grouped on the Font menu, so you can use them even if they aren't currently installed. You can use the Find/Change controls to locate any text that has the missing font applied and switch it for a font that is available.
- Compositional problems (keeps violations, as well as hyphenation and justification violations) are highlighted in yellow.

Multiple shades of yellow are used to highlight compositional problems, so you can see how serious the violation is.

8

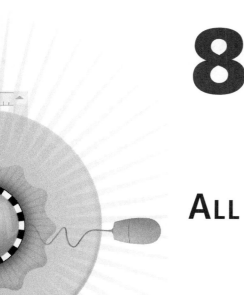

ALL ABOUT TEXT

Pages usually begin with text. InDesign starts with its *Master Text Frame* in the New Document dialog box (Figure 8–1). This is the equivalent of the QuarkXPress Auto Text box. When checked, it places a text frame on every page of the document. As we have said before, this begins the process of page and document assembly.

Figure 8–1
The New Document dialog box.

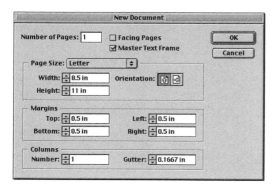

Text lives inside text frames that can be moved, resized, linked, and modified. The InDesign tool you use to select a text frame determines the kind of changes you can make to a text frame.

- The Type tool **T** lets you enter or edit text in a frame.
- The Selection tool ▶ lets you position and size the frame.
- The Direct Selection tool ▷ lets you alter the shape of the frame.

Text frames can be linked to other text frames so that text from one frame flows into another frame—this is called *threading*. The text that flows through threaded frames is called a *story*. This is exactly the way QuarkXPress does it, only InDesign does it without the "chain" link tools but does have alternative approaches. Text frames can have multiple columns (Figure 8–2).

Text frames can be placed on master pages and still receive text on document pages; they can be based on, yet independent of, page columns. A two-column text frame can sit on a four-column page, as an example. We used Object ➡ Text Frame Options to specify the number of columns in Figure 8–2.

Figure 8–2
A multicolumn text frame.

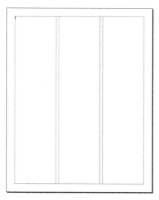

Text can be added to a document in several ways.

- You can place or paste text without creating a text frame. InDesign will create one automatically.
- You can add text to a text frame by typing, pasting, or placing text. If the word processing program supports drag-and-drop, you can drag text into InDesign. InDesign will then automatically create a new text frame. We tried this with a Word document and it worked very well.
  You can also drag a text file or word processing file directly from Windows Internet Explorer or MacOS Finder into your InDesign document. Neat.
- The *Place* command is the most useful way to add text to a document from a variety of word processing and spreadsheet files. Original formatting is preserved, based on the import filter applied.

To create a text frame:

- Click and drag the Type tool [T.] to establish a text frame. Hold Shift as you drag to constrain the frame to a perfect square. A text insertion cursor appears.
- Clicking the Type tool inside an empty graphic frame or path converts either to a text frame. You can also create a circle or other graphic shape and make it a text frame.

If there is a text frame on a master page (that is, you clicked "Master Text Frame" in the New Document dialog box, Figure 8–3)—hold down Control + Shift (Windows) or Command + Shift (MacOS) as you click in the frame on the document page, and use the Type tool to add text.

Figure 8–3
Master Text Frame checkbox.

☑ **Master Text Frame**

Most cursor icons in InDesign (for example, the drawing tool cursors and the "loaded" cursors that appear when you place text or graphic files) change appearance to indicate when InDesign's "snap to" features will determine the exact positioning of objects. These snap-to icons remove the guesswork of knowing when the cursor is within the snap-to zone relative to a guide or grid increment. (The snap-to zone distance is specified in the File ➠ Preferences ➠ Guides dialog box.)

If you did not select text or click an insertion point, the pasted text appears in a new text frame which InDesign automatically creates. If you have a text insertion point or text is selected in a text frame, the text appears at the insertion point or replaces the selected text.

- Using the Selection tool �, or the Direct Selection tool ▸, select an existing frame. The placed text will replace the contents of the frame. Make a mistake? Use the "Oops" function. Choose Edit ➠ Undo Replace.
- Choose File ➠ Place.
- Select a text file.
- To keep the formatting of the text file, select *Retain Format*. Deselect this option to strip all formatting from the text file upon importing. You get a plain vanilla file.
- To replace inch marks and other "typewriter" characters in the imported text, select *Convert Quotes*. InDesign converts inch marks (") and primes (') into typographic quotes (" ") and apostrophes (').
- To display options for importing the file you've selected, select *Show Import Options* or hold down Shift.
- Click *Open* (Windows) or *Choose* (MacOS). If you selected Show Import Options or held down Shift, InDesign displays a dialog box containing import options for the type of file you're placing. Select your options and click the ever-popular OK.

If you didn't already designate an existing frame to receive text, the pointer becomes a "loaded" text icon, ready to flow text wherever you click or drag.

Linking and Flowing Text   When your pointer becomes a loaded text icon ▦, you are ready to flow text onto your page or pages. When you position the loaded text icon over a text frame, parentheses enclose the icon.

The icon can display in one of three manifestations, corresponding to the method you choose to control the flow of text on your pages.

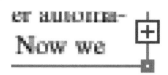

Figure 8–4.
Click outport to manually flow text.

- ⊞ Manual text flow adds text to one frame and stops flowing when it reaches the bottom of a text frame or the last of a linked set. Reload the text icon to continue flowing.
- ⊞ Semi-autoflow works like manual text flow, but different. The pointer reloads as a loaded text icon each time the end of a text frame is reached until all text is flowed.
- ⊞ Autoflow adds pages and frames until all the text is flowed.

To flow text manually one frame at a time: Use Place to select a file or click the *out* port of a text frame, at the lower right of text frames (Figure 8–4).

- Position the loaded text icon anywhere in an existing frame or path and click. Text flows into the frame and any other linked frames. Text fills the frame with the top of the leftmost column, even if you click a different column.
- Position the loaded text icon in a column to create a frame that's the width of that column. The top of the frame appears where you click.
- Drag the loaded text icon to create a text frame the width and height of the area you define. The loaded text icon becomes a pointer icon. If there is more text to be placed, a red plus sign (+) appears in the *out* port (see Figure 8–6 later in this chapter).
  If there is more text to be placed, click the *out* port and repeat until all text has been placed.

When you place text in a frame that is threaded to other frames, text always autoflows through the threaded frames, regardless of the text flow method you use. To flow text semiautomatically when you have a loaded text icon, Shift-click on a frame. The text flows one column at a time, as in manual flow, but the loaded text icon automatically reloads after each column is placed.

To flow a story automatically with the loaded text icon displayed, hold Alt (Windows) or Option (MacOS) as you do one of the following:

- Click the loaded text icon in a column to create a frame the width of that column. InDesign creates new text frames until all the text is added.
- Click inside a master text frame on a document page. The text autoflows into the frame and generates new pages as needed, using that text frame's attributes.

To cancel a loaded text icon without placing text, click any tool in the toolbox to cancel the loaded text icon. No text is deleted.

Text Frames on Master Pages   When you start a new document, you can select the *Master Text Frame* option to place an empty text frame on the document's default master page. This frame has the column and margin attributes specified in the New Document dialog box.

The appearance of the document window looks the same whether or not the Master Text Frame option is selected. As with QuarkXPress, you need to be aware whether you are in the document or in the master page. If you go to the master pages and click the page using a selection tool, you can see the selected text frame. With text frames on master pages:

- Set master text frames when you want each page in your document to contain one page-sized text frame into which you can flow or input text. If the document requires pages with multiple frames or frames of different sizes, leave the Master Text

Frame option deselected and set the frames and link them manually.

• You can add empty text frames to a master page as placeholders and thread them for a later flow even if you do not select the Master Text Frame option.

• You flow text into master text frames the same way you would with frames created on document pages.

• If you need to input text in a master text frame on a document page, hold down Command/Control + Shift as you click the text frame on the document page. Then, click in the frame with the Type tool and begin typing (and, eventually, voice inputting).

• Selecting the Master Text Frame option does not affect whether new pages are added when you autoflow text.

• If you place text into one of a series of master text frames on a document page, the text flows only into the frame you click with the loaded text icon, even if the frame is threaded to other frames on the master page. That's because clicking the icon in the frame overrides only that frame, allowing it to have text that is unique from other document pages.

• However, if you hold down Option/Alt as you click in a master text frame to autoflow text, InDesign overrides all of the threaded text frames, flowing text into each and creating new pages.

• If you add text to a master frame on a document page and then modify the frame's options on the master page (number of columns, insets, or others), those changes will be reflected on the document page. However, if the master frame contains text and you override the frame and edit the text on the document page, most changes you make to the original text or its frame on the master page will no longer be reflected on the document page. However, changes to the fill, stroke, or stroke width of the master text frame will still be reflected on the document page.

This last area is a little confusing. InDesign blurs the distinction between master pages and document pages. To see what is going on, go to View ➥ Display Master Items, or Command/Control + Y to see items coming from a master page. You can base a master page on another master page (this is called a parent-child relationship) so that changes to the parent affect all children.

Essentially, master pages in InDesign work the way they do in QuarkXPress. If you are coming from PageMaker, you will need to learn this area from scratch, as will users of illustration and image programs.

Threaded Text Frames   The text in a frame can be constrained to that frame, or it can flow between connected or linked frames. Linked frames can be on the same page or spread, or on any other page in the document. The process of connecting text among frames is called threading text. You cannot thread text between different documents, so don't even think about it.

Every text frame contains an *in* port and an *out* port.

- An empty *in* (Figure 8–5) or *out* port indicates the beginning or end of a story.
- An arrow in a port indicates that the frame is linked (threaded) to another frame.
- A red plus sign (+) in an *out* port (Figure 8–6) indicates that there is more text in the subbasement of the text frame—overset.

Figure 8–5
In port.

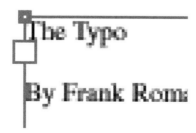

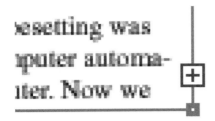

Figure 8–6
Out port indicating overset text.

Threading Text   You can thread text frames even if they do not contain text. Using the selection tool, click the *in* or *out* port of a frame. If you click the *out* port, InDesign loads a text icon ⌷.

- Position the loaded text icon ⌷ over the frame you want to connect to. The icon changes to the thread ⬭ icon.
- Position the loaded text icon where you want to create a new text frame.

Click inside the frame or drag to create a new text frame. InDesign threads the two frames. If you've started to thread two frames and change your mind, you can cancel the thread by clicking any tool in the toolbox.

To show text threads:

- Choose View ➡ Show Text Threads.
- Using the Selection tool, select any frame in the story.

If you want to see threads from different stories at the same time, Shift + Click to select a frame in each story. To turn off text thread viewing, choose View ➡ Hide Text Threads.

To unthread text frames:

- Use the Selection tool to click an *in* port or *out* port.
- Position the loaded text icon over the previous or next frame to display the unthread icon (a broken chain link).

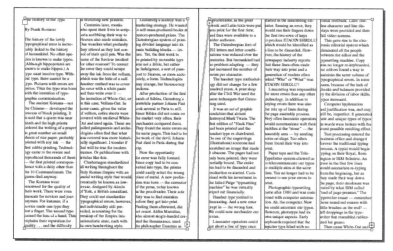

Figure 8–7
Linked p;ages.

A pasted frame includes a copy of any text it originally contained, but the frame is no longer threaded to the original story. Although the frame or frames were removed with a copy of the text, no text is removed from the original story. If you cut and paste a series of threaded text frames at once, the pasted frames maintain their connection to each other but lose connection to any other frames in the original story.

- Click in the frame. InDesign breaks the connection between the frames. You are unlinked.
  Double-click an *in* port or *out* port to break the connection between frames.

To add a frame inside a sequence of threaded frames:

- Use the Selection tool to click the *out* port at the point in the story where you want to add a frame.
- Drag to create a new frame, or select a different text frame. InDesign threads the frame into the set of linked text frames containing the story (Figure 8–7).

To disconnect or delete a frame from a thread:

- Using the Selection tool, select one or more frames (Shift-click to select multiple frames or objects).
- Choose Edit ➡ Cut.

The frame disappears, but any text contained in the frame flows to the next frame. If you delete the last frame in a story, the text is stored as overset text in the previous frame.

- If you want to use the disconnected frame elsewhere in your document, go to the page where you want the disconnected text to appear and choose Edit ➠ Paste.

Setting Text Frame Properties   You can use Text Frame Options (Figure 8–8) to specify formatting attributes.

You can specify the spacing inside the frame. This space is called the frame's inset, and InDesign lets you have a different value for all four insets. These insets are especially important if you will be stroking (framing) the frame with a border. Without the insets, type would butt against the border.

You can also make the text in a frame flow into the number of columns you specify.

To change properties for a text frame:

- Select a frame by using the Type tool; click a text insertion point or select text.
- Choose Object ➠ Text Frame Options.
- Select *Preview* to preview any options before accepting the changes and closing the dialog box.
- Go to the *Columns* section.
- Set the number of columns.
- Set the column width.

Figure 8–8
Text Frame Options dialog box.

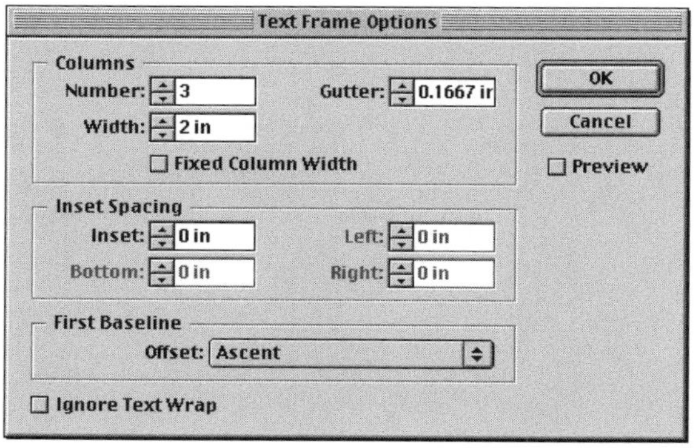

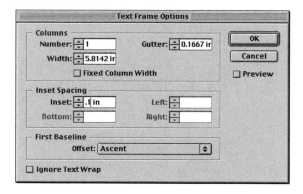

Figure 8–9
Inset options for a circular text box.

- Select *Fixed Column Width* to maintain the width of the columns when you resize the frame. When this option is selected, resizing the frame can change the number of columns, but not the width of the columns. Leave this option deselected if you want the column widths to change when you resize the text frame.
- Specify a *Gutter* value to set the distance between the columns in the frame. In the *Inset Spacing* section, enter the offset distances you want for *Top, Left, Bottom,* and *Right*. If the frame you've selected has a nonrectangular shape, the *Top, Left, Bottom,* and *Right* options are dimmed, and a single inset option is available instead, as shown in Figure 8–9.

Most columns do not need an inset, only those that will have borders around them.

For First Baseline Offset:

- Select *Ascent* so the distance between the baseline and the top of the frame is the value of the font's highest ascender (even if the highest ascender isn't on this line).
- Select *Cap Height* so the top of uppercase letters touch the top of the text frame, especially if it has a border.

- Select *Leading* to use the text's leading value as the distance between the baseline of the text and the top inset of the frame.

Ignore Text Wrap will make the text in the frame ignore text wraps.

Selecting Text   You can select single characters, single words, or ranges of words. Using the Type tool T , do one of the following:

- Hold down the mouse as you drag the cursor over a character, word, or range or words to select it.
- Double-click a word to select the word.
- Triple-click anywhere in a paragraph to select the entire paragraph.
- Click anywhere in a story and choose Edit ➡ Select All to select all the text in that story, or Command/Control + A.

> **To move through the story more quickly, you can use keyboard shortcuts for cursor movement similar to those in most word processors.**

Editing Text   InDesign includes many word processing features. As you move the insertion point through a story, InDesign scrolls and, if necessary, turns pages to display the current insertion point position.

Deselecting Text

- Click a blank area of your document window or pasteboard.
- Select a different tool in the toolbox.
- Choose Edit ➡ Deselect All.

Viewing Nonprinting (Iinvisible) Characters   When editing text, it's helpful to be able to see nonprinting (or invisible, as QuarkXPress calls them) characters such as spaces, tabs, and paragraph codes.

Choose Type ➡ Show Hidden Characters. A check mark appears next to the menu command. To hide the invisible characters, choose the command again to remove the check mark (Figure 8–10). Command/Control + I toggles them on and off.

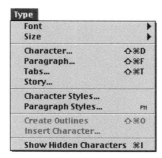

Figure 8–10
Showing the hidden
characters.

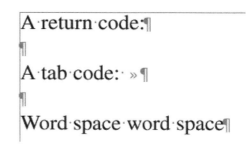

Inserting certain characters in your document may cause the spell checker to flag a properly spelled word.

Inserting Font Characters This material is also covered in Chapter 7 but is included here, briefly, to make this chapter more inclusive.

Inserting symbols, spaces, and hyphens: You can use the Context menu to insert common characters such as em dashes and en dashes, registered trademark symbols, em spaces and en spaces, and different types of quotation marks.

- Using the Type tool [T], click an insertion point where you want to insert a character.
- Choose Type ➡ Insert Character.
- Scroll through the display of characters until you see the character you want to insert. You can change the size of the display by clicking the zoom buttons.
- To display different characters, select a different font family (such as Symbol or Zapf Dingbats) and type style.
- Double-click the character you want to insert, or select the character and click Insert. InDesign inserts the character at the text insertion point. Click Done to close the dialog box.

To insert common symbols:

- Using the Type tool, position the insertion point where you want to insert a special character.
- Right-click (Windows) or Control-click (MacOS) on your page to display the context menu, select *Insert Special Character,* and then select one of the special characters from the Context menu.

Linked Files When you place text or images in a document, InDesign adds the text or image file to the Links palette (Figure 8–11), so it can be updated and managed. When you update a linked text file, any editing or formatting changes applied within InDesign are lost. Linked text files are not automatically updated when the original file is edited. However, you can update the linked file, using the Links palette.

To edit a linked text file in its original application:

- Choose File ⇒ Links to open the Links palette.
- Select the text file to be edited in the Links palette and choose Edit Original from the Links palette menu.

To update a linked text file:

- Choose File ⇒ Links to open the Links palette. Select the text file you want to update in the Links palette. If the original

Figure 8–11
The Links palette.

When you import text that has had bold or italics applied to it through an application's user interface (a keyboard shortcut), the font face may not convert properly. InDesign will report the bold or italics in the font face field, but other parts of the font face name may be missing as a result. Expert, Ornament, and Symbol fonts are the most likely to be affected. For example, if you applied bold to a symbol font like Mathematical Pi 2, InDesign will convert the font as Mathematical Pi [Bold] and consider it a missing font. If you applied italics to a font like Christiana Small Caps, the text will be converted as Christiana Italics. To resolve the problem, select the text and reapply the desired font from the Type menu.

has been edited since the file was placed, an exclamation mark appears to the right of the file name.

- From the Links palette menu, choose Update Link. If additional formatting was applied in InDesign, you are notified that all new formatting will be lost. Click OK to update the file.

Find/Change   You can search for and change specific occurrences of characters, a word, or a group of words, or text formatted a certain way. Searching for strings of text is pretty common, but the search for and changing of almost any character- or paragraph-level formatting sets InDesign apart. You can search for any character or paragraph style and replace it with any other style. Or you can search for a particular font, and replace it with a different style or another font altogether. See Figure 8–12.

You can find and change text across a selection, a story, a document, or multiple open documents.

Figure 8–12
Find/Change.

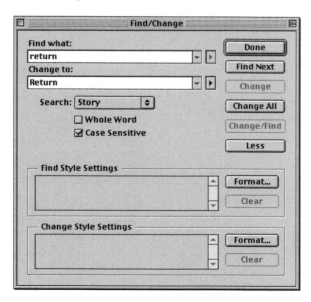

- To restrict a search to a specific frame, story, or selected text, click the Type tool ⊤ inside a frame or select text within a frame. To search more than one document, open the documents.
- Choose Edit ➧ Find/Change, or Command/Control + F.

For Search, specify the range of your search by selecting

- Document (searches entire document)
- All Documents (searches all open documents)
- Story (searches all text in the threaded text frames, including overset text)
- To End of Story (searches from the insertion point)
- Selection (searches only the selected text)

For *Find What*, type or paste the text you want to find.

- To change the text, type the new text in the *Change To* box.

To search for formatting only, leave the *Find What* and *Change To* boxes blank.

To search for tabs, spaces, and other special characters or for unspecified or wildcard characters, select InDesign's metacharacters from the pop-up menu to the right of the Find What text box.

Select *Whole Word* or *Case Sensitive* as desired.

- *Whole Word* disregards the search text if it is embedded within a larger word. For example, if you are searching for "can" as a whole word, InDesign disregards "can't."
- *Case Sensitive* searches for only the word or words that exactly match the capitalization of the text in the Find What text box. For example, a search for "InDesign" will not find "Indesign" or "INDESIGN."

Click *Find Next* to begin the search. To continue searching, click *Find Next, Change, Change All* (you are informed of the number of changes), or *Change/Find*. Click *Done* when changes are complete.

Find/Change will find and change text formatting such as styles, indents and spacing, and stroke and fill colors. However, you cannot find and change text formatting if the range of your search is set to *All Documents*. You can find; you cannot change.

When you have specified formatting for your search criteria, alert icons appear above the *Find What* or *Change To* boxes. These icons are a reminder that formatting attributes have been set and that the find or change operation will be limited.

To remove all formatting attributes in the *Find Style Settings* or *Change Style Settings*, click the *Clear* button.

Here are some basic tips to simplify finding and changing text within InDesign.

- You can include wildcard characters in your search. For example, typing "b^?rn" in the Find What box will search for "barn," "born," and "burn."

- Always clear formatting from a previous search. If you have pasted text into the *Find What* or *Change To* boxes, nonprinting characters such as tabs or returns are included as part of the text that is searched for or replaced.

- InDesign remembers as many as the last 15 entries in the *Find What* or *Change To* boxes. Click the down arrow next to these boxes to select one of your previous searches. These saved entries do not include formatting attributes, but the fact that you can go back to previous find/change entries is very useful.

- If *Change To* is empty and no formatting has been set, clicking *Change* or *Change All* will delete the occurrence of the text you found. This is the fastest way to remove unwanted text.

- You can use the Find/Change dialog box to replace missing fonts with fonts installed on your system. In the *Find Format Settings* dialog box under *Basic Character Formats*, missing fonts appear in brackets at the bottom of the Font list.

- To find the next occurrence of a previously searched for string without having to open the *Find/Change* dialog box, choose Edit ➠ Find Next.

Spellchecking   You can check the spelling of a selected range of text, in all of a story, in all stories in a document, or in all stories in all open documents. InDesign highlights misspelled words, unknown words, words typed twice (such as "the the"—bless you Adobe), and words with possible capitalization errors. When you check the spelling of the text, InDesign uses the dictionary for the language you assigned to the document.

- To narrow your spell check to a frame, story, or selected text, click an insertion point inside a frame or select text within a frame. Choose Edit ➟ Check Spelling (Figure 8–13).
- For Search, specify the range of the spell check.
    Document (checks the entire document)
    All Documents (checks all open documents)
    Story (checks all threaded frames, plus overset)
    To End of Story (checks from the insertion point)
    Selection (checks only selected text)
- Click Start to begin spellchecking.

As you can see in Figure 8–13, the InDesign spelling checker looks somewhat familiar. Unlike QuarkXPress, it does not include a word count.

Figure 8–13
Check Spelling dialog.

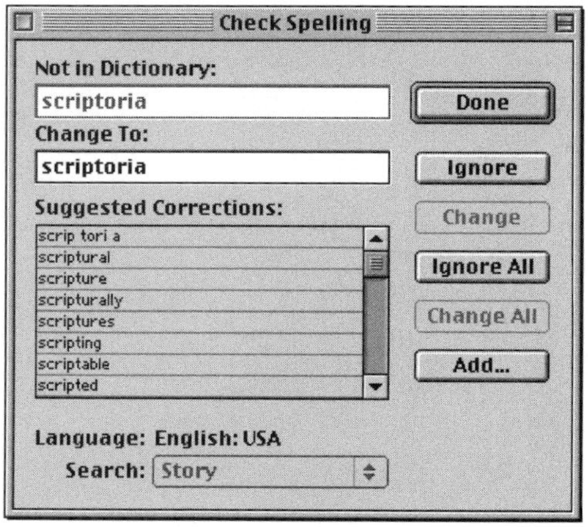

When InDesign displays flagged or misspelled words or other possible errors, choose an option.

- Click *Ignore* or *Ignore All* (the word will be ignored until you exit InDesign) to continue spellchecking without changing text.
- Select an entry from the Suggested Corrections list or type new text in the *Change To* box, and then click Change to change only that occurrence of the word.
  Or click *Change All* to change all occurrences.
- Click *Add* to store the unrecognized word in the dictionary so that subsequent occurrences are not considered misspellings.

Customized Dictionaries   If you use more than one language in a document, you can tell InDesign which language dictionary to use to check spelling and hyphenating words in a particular language. Use Edit ➧ Edit Dictionary to get the Dictionary dialog box (Figure 8–14).

By default, InDesign uses Proximity dictionaries to verify spelling and to hyphenate words. If you have installed hyphenation or spelling components from a different company, you can select a different vendor for each installed language.

Figure 8–14
Dictionary language dialog.

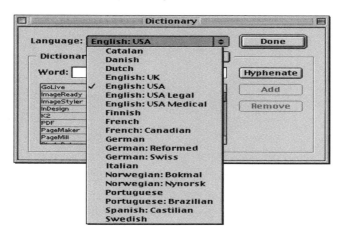

Make sure all other users have the same customized user dictionary so that a document uses the same spelling and hyphenation rules regardless of which system it is on. If you use the Proximity dictionaries installed by InDesign, you can recognize the user dictionary file for each language by its .udc filename extension (such as usa.udc).

You can use your system Find command to locate and copy user dictionary files from one workstation to another.

After you add a user dictionary, exit and restart InDesign, or use Command/Control + Option/Alt + / (slash) to recompose all text. To set Dictionary preferences:

- Choose File ➡ Preferences ➡ Dictionary and specify the language to be used (Figure 8–15).
- If you have installed a Hyphenation plug-in from a different company, you can select it in the *Hyphenation Vendor* menu.
- If you have installed a Spelling dictionary component from a different company, you can select it in the *Spelling Vendor* menu.
- Click the ever-popular OK.

To add a word to the user dictionary:

- When a spell check displays a word in the Check Spelling dialog box, click *Add* to add it to your dictionary.
- Choose Edit ➡ Edit Dictionary. If you previously selected a word, InDesign displays that word in the *Word* box. Or, type the word to be added.

Figure 8–15
Dictionary preferences.

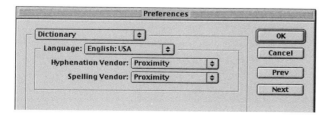

Hyphenation points interact with hyphenation settings in your documents. A word might not break where you expect it because of this. Monitor control settings by choosing Hyphenation from the Paragraph palette menu. U.S. hyphenation is based on syllables, or pronunciation.

- Click Hyphenate to see the word's default hyphenation. The tilde (~) indicates possible hyphenation points.

If you don't like the choice of hyphenation points, go to Edit Dictionary (Figure 8–16).

- Type one tilde (~) to indicate the best possible hyphenation point in the word. If the word has only one acceptable hyphenation point, type only one tilde.
- Type two tildes (sounds like Dr. Seuss) to indicate the second-best choice.
- Type three tildes to indicate a poor but acceptable hyphenation point.
- If you have no hyphenation preference, type the same number of tildes between each syllable.
- If you want the word never to be hyphenated, type a tilde before the first letter of the word. If you need to include an actual tilde in a word, type a backslash before the tilde (\~). Hyphenation breaks are ranked by tildes (~)
- Click *Add* and then click Done. InDesign adds the word to the user dictionary.

Figure 8–16
Edit Dictionary dialog.

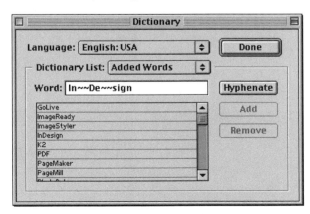

Attaching a Frame to Text (Inline or Anchored Frame) With the Type tool selected, you can paste or import a graphic or text frame into text. This frame is called an inline frame and behaves as if it were a text character, flowing as the text flows.

You can select an inline frame with the Type tool and then change its leading, baseline shift, and other attributes.

When the text reflows, the graphic moves accordingly. You can paste a text frame into another text frame. You can even paste an inline frame inside another inline text frame.

To create an inline frame by pasting a frame:

- Select the frame you want to paste as an inline frame.
- Choose Edit ➧ Cut or Edit ➧ Copy.
- Using the Type tool [T], click an insertion point in a text frame where you want the inline frame to be placed.
- Choose Edit ➧ Paste.

To create an inline frame by placing:

- Using the Type tool, click an insertion point in a text frame where you want the inline frame to be placed.
- Choose File ➧ Place.
- Select the graphics file you want to import.
- Click Open (Windows) or Choose (MacOS). InDesign places the graphic as an inline frame at the insertion point.

If autoleading is on, the inline frame may cause an increased amount of space above the line it is on. To remove the space, either resize the inline object or use a fixed leading value for the surrounding lines.

To adjust the position of an inline frame:

- Use the Type tool to select the inline frame, and specify a value for *Baseline Shift* in the Character palette.
- To move the inline frame aligned to the baseline, specify a value for *Kerning* and adjust the baseline shift distance using the Character palette.

- Use the Selection tool ![icon] or Direct Selection tool ![icon] to select the inline frame, and then drag the frame perpendicular to the baseline. You can't drag the frame parallel to the baseline, nor can you drag the bottom of the frame above the baseline or the top of the frame below the baseline. You can resize, rotate, or transform an inline frame.

Wrapping Text   You can make text wrap around any frame, including text frames. When you apply a text wrap to an object, InDesign creates a boundary around the object that repels text (it is anti-text).

- If you want to wrap text around the shape of an imported graphic, make sure you save the clipping path in the application where you created it. When you place the graphic in InDesign, make certain the *Create Frame* from *Clipping Path* option is selected in the Image Import Options dialog box.
- Text frames inside a group ignore any text wrap you have applied to the group.
- To prevent the text in a frame from wrapping around text wrap boundaries, use the Selection tool ![icon] to select the text frame and choose *Object Frame Options*. Select *Ignore Text Wrap,* and click OK.
- You can move the text wrap boundary anywhere on the current page or spread, and you can reshape the wrap boundary so that it totally different from the frame.

In Figure 8–17 we wrapped around a graphic frame that contains a screen shot of the Text Wrap dialog box. By making the frame larger than the image, we negated the need for space around the image to provide a cushion between the image and the text. However, if the frame had a border, it would need that cushion, which is specified in the Object ➠ Text Wrap, or Command/Control + T.

To set default text wrap options for all new objects, deselect all objects and then set the following options.

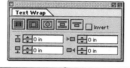

Figure 8–17
A text wrap.

To apply a text wrap to an object:

- Choose Object ➡ Text Wrap for the Text Wrap palette/dialog.
- Select a frame.
- In the Text Wrap palette/dialog box, click the desired wrap shape:
  - Wrap Around Bounding Box ▣ creates a rectangular wrap whose width and height are determined by the bounding box of the selected object.
  - Wrap Around Object Shape ▣, also known as contour wrapping, creates a text wrap boundary that is the same shape as the frame that has been selected (plus or minus any offset distances).

- Jump Object  keeps text from appearing in any available space to the right or left of the frame in the column containing the frame.
- Jump to Next Column forces the next paragraph to the top of the next text column or text frame.
- Enter offset amounts. Positive values move the wrap away from the edges of the frame; negative values position the wrap boundary inside the respective edges of the frame.

To apply text wrap to items on a master page, hold down Command/Control + Shift and click the item on a document page.

With the image selected on the document page, apply text wrap. To change the shape of a text wrap:

- Using the Direct Selection tool, select an object that has a text wrap applied to it. If the text wrap boundary is the same shape as the object, the boundary appears superimposed on the object.
- Use the Pen tool and Direct Selection tool to edit the text wrap boundary.

Text Import Filters   You can import text from other InDesign documents, from word processing applications such as Microsoft Word, text or table editors (or any application that can export text in the text-only, or ASCII, format), or Microsoft Excel. All file formats are listed in the Format menu in the File ➡ Place dialog box, or Command/Control + E.

All filters go in the Filters folder (Figure 8–18) in the InDesign Plug-ins folder.

SimpleText read-only files are not recognized by the InDesign Text-only filter. Open the file you want to place from within SimpleText, and save it with the default save format setting. InDesign can then recognize the file and let you place it.

Figure 8–18
Filters list.

9

Color

Color Models

Additive and Subtractive Color

There are just two basic methods for reproducing color:

- The additive model starts with the absence of light—adding light in the form of varying percentages of red, green, and blue (RGB) produces color. Adding more RGB increases the amount of light transmitted to the viewer.
- The subtractive model requires the presence of light, and describes light reflected through a transparent filter (a printing ink, a fabric dye, pigments in plastics, etc.) which presents varying amounts of RGB light back to the viewer. Adding more of a subtractive color to a filter reduces (subtracts) the amount of light reflected back.

RGB Color   Red, green, blue are the three additive colors used by your computer monitor and a television set to display millions of other colors. Additive color describes a color model where light is emitted from a luminous source, such as three spotlights with red, green, and blue gels over them. Where all three additive colors overlap, the color in the middle will form a neutral gray patch at 50% illumination (Figure 9–1). As the lights become brighter, the neutral patch eventually turns white. Where two additive colors overlap, they form a subtractive color.

White light is a combination of red, green, and blue light, and "white" includes sunlight, nasty fluorescent office light, candlelight, et cetera. These all look a little less than perfectly white because each method of producing the illuminant—nuclear fusion inside a star, excitation of noble gases by high voltages inside a glass tube, or rapid oxidation—generates differing levels of RGB. Consequently, things can look different under different types of light.

Process/CMYK Color   Process colors are created from varying tints of the three subtractive–color inks: cyan, magenta, and yellow. Black ink is also used in the printing of process color. These inks are abbreviated CMYK (K is used instead of B because of an old habit of some printers to call cyan blue). Process color operates on the following principle: white light passes through the ink and reflects back from the paper, through the ink again, to the viewer's eye.

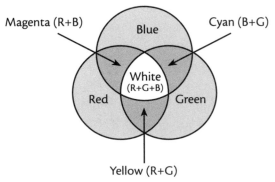

Figure 9–1
Additive color.

Process inks are transparent and will only pass certain wavelengths of light back through to your eye; if you print cyan and yellow over each other, you get what appears to be green, because cyan blocks red light and yellow blocks blue light, leaving just the green part of the white light to get back to your retinas (Figure 9–2).

Tints of process ink appear lighter because part of the white light is being reflected back to the viewer by the paper. Because of the reflection process, the color of the paper stock can have a significant impact on the final printed color. Some color proofing systems can use the final printed stock for this reason.

Process inks are usually printed as solids or as screen tints. As the dots of one ink get larger, they will begin to overprint dots of the other inks, creating a color shift. This applies to all four ink colors, each of which can be adjusted independently to achieve the desired color. The dot size can be controlled by the percentage of ink specified in the color panel.

If you print 50% cyan, magenta, and yellow inks on top of each other, the resulting patch on the paper will look pinkish-gray. As the percentage of each ink increases, adding more color-filtering ink to the paper, the neutral patch eventually turns into a brownish mess due to hue contamination in the inks, which is why genuine black ink is used for printing real old-fashioned black, rather than mixing the other three inks to produce a less-than-satisfactory (icky, in other words) black.

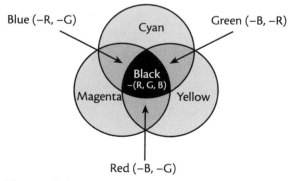

Figure 9–2
Subtractive color.

Hue contamination is a fancy term for the fact that due to manufacturing constraints, no process ink is ever 100% pure cyan, magenta, or yellow, and each of these contains a tiny bit of the other's spectral filtering abilities. Most modern color processing software can be set to account for hue contamination. It can also be monitored on press by using a 50% three-color overprint patch, which in ideal conditions will look just like a 50% tint of black ink. A neutral three-color gray indicates correct gray balance, which in turn makes printing accurate color a lot easier. In fact, to achieve gray balance, one must usually print more of cyan ink than of the other two inks, due to the presence of significant magenta and yellow hue contamination in most cyan inks.

The first step in color-correction of scanned CMYK images is neutralizing highlight and shadow areas in the image by adjusting the percentages of the process color channels. Once a press operator achieves gray balance of CMY inks on press and assuming the images were color-corrected properly, the job is usually ready to run. Color correction is outside the scope of this book, but it is a critical step in the prepress process.

Process color is largely generated within a process color-capable computer program; while a press operator has a certain amount of color adjustment latitude when printing a process color job, the overwhelming factor in process color is accurate prepress processing in your application programs, unlike the computer-independence of spot color. Color printing of photographs is different from color printing of tints and spot colors, as we will discuss.

InDesign will allow you to convert a spot color into a process color, but the printed result will not match the original color found in a spot color swatch book. Specialized swatch books are available that show a spot color and a sample of the closest process color match side by side. If you have access to such a book, you can easily see that many spot colors cannot be accurately duplicated with the four-color printing process. There are certain spot colors that cannot be reproduced at all with process color, especially bright blues. Most graphic designers are forced to buy those spot color swatch books.

High-fidelity Process Color There are several printing processes that use more than four subtractive inks, the most common of which is PANTONE's six-color Hexachrome process. The various types of 4+ color printing processes are known as high-fidelity process color. Hexachrome uses enhanced CMYK inks with less hue contamination than most others, plus additional orange and green inks to provide a wider range of color than is possible with just the four process inks.

However, it also requires specialized software for separating scanned images into a six-color process model, and it also requires the use of a printer who has a lot of experience with it.

Hexachrome also lets you reproduce a much higher percentage of spot colors—it's become very popular in label printing where previously a family of, for example, salad dressing labels, required multiple press runs because the labels required a specific spot color. With Hexachrome, a label printer can usually print the entire family of labels in one press run, which reduces production cost significantly.

Unfortunately, InDesign 1.0 does not support Hexachrome. You can incorporate six-color images into an InDesign layout and then separate them correctly—you just can't create six-color swatches for use within InDesign. Expect full Hexachrome support in either a plug-in or a future version of InDesign.

Note: Hexachrome swatches created in QuarkXPress 4.0 files will be converted to process swatches when imported into InDesign. Swatches created with the QuarkXPress 4.0 multi-ink feature will suffer the same fate, since inDesign doesn't support multi-ink colors. Hexachrome swatches created in PageMaker 6.5 files will be converted to spot color swatches.

Spot Color Spot colors are custom printing inks that are premixed to match a color specification. Typically, samples of these colors are printed and referenced in a swatch book such as those sold by PANTONE. Swatch books are usually part of a color matching system and are produced by many companies, but in North America the PANTONE Color Matching System is the most frequently used.

InDesign contains libraries for most of the color matching systems used throughout the world.

Probably the simplest difference between spot and process color is this: spot color is completely independent of a computer. If you specify PANTONE 186 as a spot color within a document, you'll see a representation of PANTONE 186 on the screen (bright red), but the actual printed color depends solely on the physical color of the ink a printer uses when you ask for PANTONE 186. There are many sources of premixed spot-color printing inks, but some spot inks must be custom-mixed by a printer.

Unlike process inks, spot color inks are opaque—when printed on a white sheet of paper, they absorb certain colors and reflect others. The reflected colors are what your eye sees. The color of the paper usually doesn't cause much of a shift in a spot color's tone. Spot inks are available in many colors and also in specialty forms like metallic inks, pastel inks, and many different types of varnishes and coatings. Your software doesn't know or care about the physical qualities of these inks and coatings; all a program can do is separate spot colors into multiple printing plates.

Spot color inks specified by a color matching system have been carefully mixed to match the system's specification. Most often, black ink and a second ink, a spot color ink, are used in many projects, although you can use any two spot color inks you like (black is considered to be both a spot color and a process color). You can add interest to a two-color job by using tints of both colors in your artwork. It's possible to use more than two inks, but printing additional inks costs more and can become quite expensive, so you will rarely have the opportunity to use three or more spot color inks.

Large printing presses capable of printing four or more colors (Figure 9–3) are typically set up to print process colors, and you'll pay lots of money for the time it would take to purge the press of process inks, run your job, then purge the press of spot inks for the next job. Printing presses exist that can print eight or ten spot colors in one shot, but chances are most jobs aren't intended for such an expensive process, and these presses are set up to print process colors on both sides of a sheet, which is flipped halfway through the press.

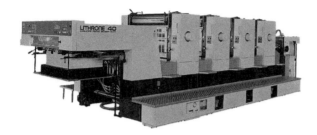

Figure 9–3
A four-color printing press. Count the units.

Most two-color jobs are printed on presses that only print one or two inks at a time (Figure 9–4).

Because each spot color in a layout requires a separate printing plate, it's very common for printers to receive incoming jobs with multiple spot ink specifications that cannot be printed as-is and must be reworked at significant cost to the client in order to make the job printable. This is why it's important for you to carefully monitor the use of spot colors in a layout.

L*a*b* Color   L°a°b° color (typically just called LAB) is a new color mode for page layout programs. Prior to InDesign, the only program that widely supported it was Photoshop 5.0, and a lot of people asked "what the heck is that?" and ignored it.

This color model is a 1976 refinement of a model developed in the 1930s by the Commission Internationale de l'Eclairage (CIE), an international standards organization devoted to color science. In the

Figure 9–4
One-color (left) and two-color (right) printing presses.

LAB model (Figure 9–5), a color is defined by its luminance (L*), and by two color component values, a* (red-green) and b* (blue-yellow).

The value of LAB color is that it encompasses a much wider gamut of possible colors than either RGB or CMYK, and in fact LAB is used by InDesign internally for color space conversions because of the large gamut. For this reason, LAB is being increasingly used for initial image acquisition, because it's becoming more frequent that an image will be used for both print and screen and it makes sense to capture an image with the largest possible color gamut.

Once in LAB space, an image can be converted to RGB or CMYK, which have smaller gamuts. Depending on how the conversion is done, it's possible to remap LAB color within the smaller spaces of the other two models while retaining image quality and faithfulness to the original.

You can also easily adjust the lightness of a LAB color by changing the L* value without introducing a shift in hue. In InDesign and

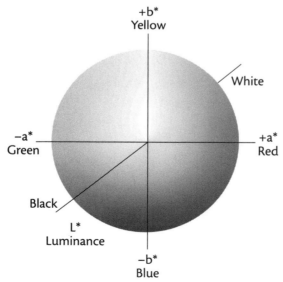

Figure 9–5
Color model.

Photoshop, L* values range from 0 (black) to 100 (white); a* and b* values range from –127 to +127.

Gamuts   Color gamuts are the theoretical "space" or range of colors within the visible spectrum that can be reproduced by a particular color mode. Of the entire range of color that the human eye can discern, LAB color has the widest gamut, RGB has a smaller gamut, and CMYK has the smallest overall gamut—for example, only about 60% of all PANTONE spot colors can be simulated with process inks, and even then the match will usually be less than perfect. The CMYK gamut can only reproduce a small portion of the RGB colors reproducible on a computer screen.

Out-of-Gamut Colors   An RGB or LAB color that cannot be reproduced by the CMYK printing process is said to be out-of-gamut. The methods for moving out of gamut colors into the CMYK gamut are a bit beyond the scope of this book, but, for example, if you perform an RGB ➠ CMYK conversion in Photoshop, you are remapping the RGB gamut, and some colors will be lost.

Careful application of color conversion settings can move some out-of-gamut colors within the CMYK gamut without noticeable hue shift. Software color management systems such as ColorSync and ICM perform gamut remapping in a different way. See "Color Management" later in this chapter for more information.

Which Should I Use?   Any color photographs in a for-print project will require the four-color printing process, so any artwork you create in InDesign for that project will also require the use of process color. However, the model you choose can also depend on your printer's requirements—some printers prefer to receive RGB originals and perform a conversion to CMYK based on their calibration and characterization of their equipment, while others will expect you to provide CMYK artwork. Find out before committing to a color model. The printing industry has long been preseparated CMYK, but RGB is the wave of the future.

You can convert color photos to gray-scale images and then use black or a spot color for a one-color print job. Most things like catalogs and magazines use process color, and things like newsletters, business cards, business forms, and the like typically use black and one spot color. Of course, it's possible to design pieces that will look great printed with only one ink, so adding additional color ultimately is a cost-based decision.

Projects destined for the World Wide Web or for a multimedia product should use the RGB color model, which is the native color space of a computer monitor or a TV set. If you plan to repurpose projects for both print and screen, you can use the LAB color model, and InDesign will automatically convert LAB colors to CMYK or RGB as needed during the color separation or HTML export process.

Color Separation   When a document containing one or more spot colors is color separated, each color is imaged either onto a separate piece of film, which can then be used to make a printing plate for the press, or directly to a printing plate. When a document containing process color is color separated, every object in the document, including any color photographs, is reduced to percentages of CMYK, and the separated process colors are imaged (either directly, with direct-to-plate technology, or indirectly, using film created on an imagesetter) to four separate printing plates.

If a document contains both spot and process colors, four process separations are generated, then any additional spot color pages are separated. If RGB or LAB colors or images are used in the document, InDesign can convert and separate those colors to CMYK.

What Is Registration?   "Registration" is a special color. While it looks like black, it is only useful in cases where you need to create crop and registration marks by hand instead of using InDesign's built-in crop and registration marks. You may need to do this when building artwork that has an unusual size, such as packaging, or building press forms. Coloring an object Registration will result in that object printing on every separation, whether it is spot or process. This gives a point of reference for each ink. Registration marks are placed outside the trim area of a printed piece and serve to provide press operators with accurate registration (or fitting) of the job's colors.

A press usually requires adjustment in the initial stage of printing, and a press operator will fine-tune the press's controls until the registration marks on the printed sheets line up precisely (Figure 9–6). A registered press will print marks that are solid black. A misregistered press will print marks that have a bit of color showing on the edges.

Crop or trim marks tell bindery operators where to cut the final piece. InDesign automatically creates crop marks if requested, but you can also make your own. Remember to fill/stroke any registration or crop marks you make with the Registration color. Do not use Registration for any other purpose. You can change how the Registration color appears in InDesign to help distinguish it from black where it is used.

Color in InDesign

InDesign and Illustrator treat color very similarly. If you know how color creation, application, and swatch management works in Illustrator, you already know how it will work in InDesign. There are a few differences, though—all colors are global in InDesign, and there's no support for pattern swatches.

Figure 9–6
Registration mark in register (left) and out of register (right).

Applying Color to Objects　　You can apply color to the following objects:

- Strokes of frames, paths, and characters
- Fills of frames, paths, and characters
- Imported gray-scale or 1-bit (line-art) images—only solid colors may be applied to images; no tints or gradients

To apply any color to an object's stroke or fill, select it with the desired selection tool, select the fill or stroke icon (Figure 9–7) in the toolbox (press X to flip between these), then select a swatch in the Swatches Panel, or mix up a new color in the color mixer. Use the Text tool to select characters for colorizing.

The Apply Color (,) and Apply Gradient (.) buttons will apply the last-used color or gradient to the selected object's stroke or fill. To remove a color or gradient from a stroke or fill, select the stroke or fill icon, then click the Clear Color (/) button. To reset the stroke and fill icons to the default of no fill, black stroke, click the Reset Stroke button (L). To swap the fill and stroke colors, press Shift + X or click the swap color icon.

Some colorizing actions will require multiple steps. Adding a stroke color to text will automatically give the text a 1-point stroke, which can seriously fatten the text and make it unreadable. Reset the stroke width for legibility after colorizing strokes on text.

Swatches and Unnamed Colors　　Unnamed colors in InDesign are those you create with the color mixer panel and apply to an object. Unnamed colors can also be created when you delete a

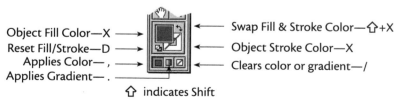

Object Fill Color—X ⟶　　⟵ Swap Fill & Stroke Color—⇧+X
Reset Fill/Stroke—D ⟶　　⟵ Object Stroke Color—X
Applies Color—, ⟶　　⟵ Clears color or gradient—/
Applies Gradient—.

⇧ indicates Shift

Figure 9–7
Applying color to objects in InDesign.

swatch and opt to leave the color intact in the document. Unnamed colors aren't listed in the Swatches panel. They can make things pretty miserable if you use lots of them and later have to make changes to any objects that use them, because you'll have to manually change every object that uses an unnamed color.

It's probably a good idea to avoid creating unnamed colors, unless you only want to use a color once or twice in a document and can remember where you applied it if it needs to be changed later. Swatches are very handy—you can create tints from them, you can change them and have the changes appear automatically throughout the document (including any tints derived from a swatch), and you can replace one swatch with another and have all objects that use the old color change to the new color.

The Swatches Panel   The Swatches panel (Figure 9–8) holds the default Black, Paper (white, of course), None, and Registration colors. You can add new colors at any time with the Swatches pop-up menu, or by adding them from an open swatch library, or by creating a new color in the color mixer panel and choosing the Add to Swatches command from the color mixer's pop-up menu.

You can't change the color for black, but you can change the on-screen colors for registration and paper. The "paper" color simply

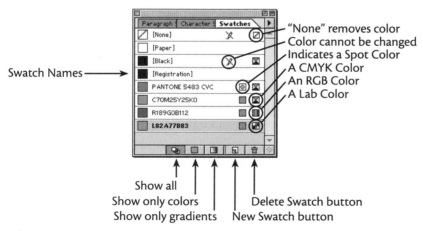

Figure 9–8
Swatches panel.

means that wherever it is used, no ink is applied. You can color the Paper swatch to simulate the appearance of a layout when printed on colored paper.

The buttons at the bottom of the panel control what swatches are shown and can be used to create and delete swatches. To create a swatch with the New Swatch button, an existing color must be selected; otherwise, the button is disabled. Clicking the button produces a copy of the selected swatch. To delete a swatch, click on it to select, then click the trash can icon. A dialog will appear to confirm the deletion and offer to replace the swatch with any other color in an existing swatch, or to remove the swatch and change any application of the swatch's color to an unnamed color.

The Swatches Menu　　The Swatches panel contains a pop-up menu (Figure 9–9) that offers some swatch management functions.

Choosing *New Color Swatch* or *Swatch Options* displays the swatch creator/editor dialog. Choosing *New Tint Swatch* displays the tint editor. Choosing *New Gradient Swatch* gives you the gradient editor. We'll talk about these editors in a bit. *Duplicate Swatch* makes a copy of the currently selected swatch. *Select All Unused* is a fast and easy way of cleaning up unused swatches when you finish a project, which is pretty handy especially if you've been working with spot colors.

Creating New Colors　　There are two ways of creating new colors: using the *New Swatch* command or using the color mixer panel. Using *New Swatch* always ensures that a color is named and saved in the Swatches panel, but using the color mixer will create unnamed colors unless you explicitly add the color to the Swatches panel.

Figure 9–9
Swatches pop-up menu.

To create a swatch, choose *New Swatch* from the Swatches panel's pop-up menu, or select an existing swatch and click the new swatch button, then double-click the copy that's created. Both methods present the New Color Swatch options dialog, shown in Figure 9–10.

Type a new name for the swatch, choose the type (spot or process), and the color mode. You can select CMYK, LAB, or RGB. In this example, we've selected RGB. Note that the color mode really does not matter for spot colors; the color mode only controls the appearance of the color on your screen. If you have CMYK equivalents for a spot color, you can enter them here. InDesign will use those values if you convert the color to a process color and also if you choose to separate all spot colors as process colors when printing.

Adjust the sliders to produce the color mix you want. If you have color management enabled for the document, InDesign will display a gamut warning: the little yellow screaming triangle with an ! in it means that the color can't be reproduced as CMYK when separated with the current settings.

You'll have to adjust the color until the warning goes away in order for the color to separate correctly. If you don't, the color will probably not look anything like what you wanted. Luckily, InDesign gives you a nifty tool for this situation. If you click once on the little color

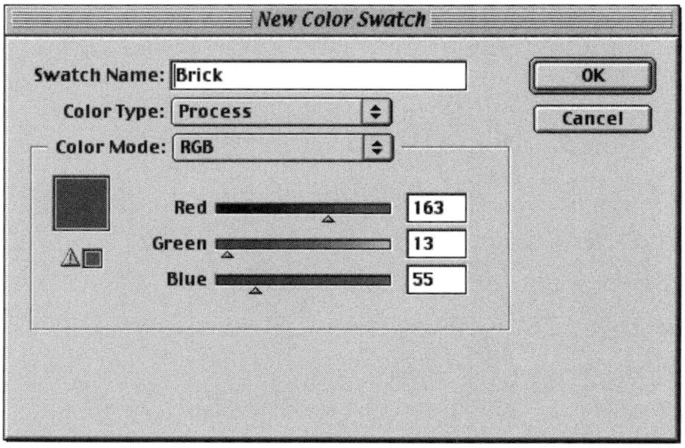

Figure 9–10
New Color Swatch panel.

patch next to the gamut warning, the color is adjusted to the closest match that can be printed in CMYK.

If you want to change the color of a swatch throughout a document, use the swatch options to change color values. All instances of that color, and any tints derived from it, will change to the new color.

You can also easily create colors (process only) with the color mixer panel (Figure 9–11). Choose Window ➟ Color or press F6 to show the panel. The mixer always shows the color of the current swatch and defaults to a tint adjustment; choose a color mode from the pop-up menu to show the color channel controls.

Set the new color by adjusting the sliders, by typing values into the color channel fields, or by clicking anywhere on the "rainbow" below the color fields to more or less randomly select a color. You can also quickly select black, white, or none from the ends of rainbow. Sorry, no pot of gold.

If you apply the new color to an object, the color becomes an unnamed color. To make an unnamed color into a swatch, either select an object tagged with the color or mix up a new color in the mixer.

Choosing *New Swatch* or clicking the *New Swatch* button in the Swatches panel will create a new swatch based on the current color's values that are shown in the mixer. If you click the *New Swatch* button, the new swatch is named *New Color Swatch*, which isn't very helpful, but you can double-click the swatch to change its name to something more meaningful.

The color mixer also features the gamut alarm and gamut remapping functions of the swatch editor. If the gamut alarm appears, click

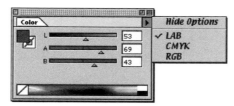

Figure 9–11
Color Mixer panel.

the alarm icon to remap the color to the closest process-reproducible color.

Creating Tints   Tints are simply screened versions of existing colors. You can create tints from both spot and process color swatches; tints of process colors will be created by multiplying the original swatch's CMYK percentages by the tint percentage to achieve a process tint.

To make a quick and dirty tint from an existing swatch, select an object that uses the swatch color, then open the color mixer where the swatch color is displayed.

You can't change a named color in the mixer, but you can easily tint an object that uses the named color by adjusting the tint slider in the color mixer. This creates an unnamed tint, though the unnamed tint will be changed if the parent color is altered later.

This is fine for onesy-twosy tinting, but it's a lot easier to manage tints by creating tint swatches. You can create a swatch from a tint made in the mixer by selecting the object that you tinted and choosing *New Tint Swatch* from the Swatches panel menu, or just choose *New Tint Swatch* in the first place to create a tint. Move the *Tint* slider to set the percentage, or type a value into the tint field (Figure 9–12).

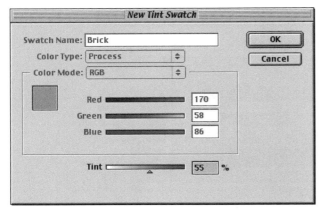

Figure 9–12
New Tint Swatch dialog box.

Tints are expressed as percentages, with the lightest having the lower values and the darkest having the higher values.

Tints of existing colors show up in the Swatches panel with the same attributes as the parent color, except a tint percentage value is displayed after the swatch name.

Creating Gradients   Gradients are transitional blends between two colors or between two tint levels of the same color. They're often called vignettes in the printing industry; they're often called many other things there, most of them unsuitable for repetition in this publication.

Use gradients with caution. These have probably caused as many reruns of print jobs as spot-color screwups—incorrect gradient setup causes lots of wasted film and rejected print runs, usually because the gradients appear banded when printed. Lots of older programs always convert gradients specified with spot color to process color when printed, which can really ruin your day if the job was only supposed to use two spot colors.

InDesign supports spot-color gradients as long as both colors are specified as spot colors. You can't mix spot and process colors in gradients—the spot color will be converted to a process color when printed.

A gradient will print with visible banding (Figure 9–13) if there aren't enough gray levels available between the start and the end points.

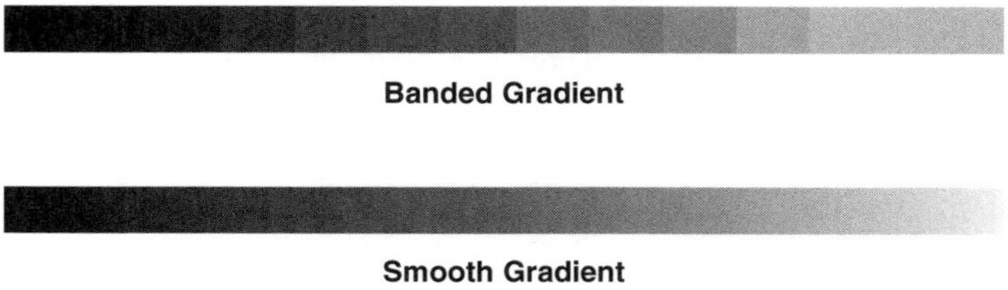

Banded Gradient

Smooth Gradient

Figure 9–13
Gradients.

Most high-resolution imaging devices, like an imagesetter, can create enough gray levels per color separation to reduce or eliminate banding, but the final result will depend on the resolution and line screen used for output, as well as the version of the PostScript interpreter used in the imaging device.

Many older devices still use PostScript Level 1 or Level II, which do not perform any sort of gradient optimization. A device that uses PostScript Level III will produce optimized gradients, but these devices are still fairly scarce in the printing industry. If you create gradients correctly, though, you shouldn't have to worry about things like the state of a random printer's imaging equipment.

You should always use the Swatches panel's menu to create new gradients. It's possible to create an unnamed gradient with the gradient panel, but we really suggest that you avoid using any unnamed colors or gradients.

If you want to use existing swatches for a gradient, you'll have to create them first. You can't specify spot colors or tints of a color in a gradient if they don't already exist in the document.

To make a gradient swatch, choose New Gradient Swatch from the Swatches panel pop-up menu, which produces the Gradient Editor in Figure 9–14.

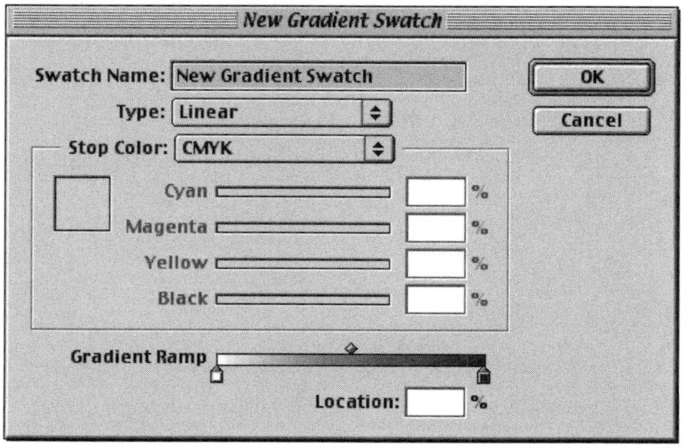

Figure 9–14
Gradient editor.

- Enter a name for the gradient in the Swatch Name field.
- Choose a Type, linear or radial—linear gradients start at the left side of an object, and radial ones start in the middle and spread outwards.
- Stop Color—very important. Here's where you choose the start and stop colors or tints for the gradient. You need to click on one of the end points before choosing the stop color from the menu. The very tip of the endpoint icon will turn black when it's selected.

While you can choose to create new (and unnamed) colors here, you should really choose *Named Color* from the *Stop Color* pop-up menu, especially if your job only uses spot colors—all unnamed colors exist as process colors, so you might get an unhappy surprise at the printer later. If you want the gradient to start or end with white, choose *Paper* as the stop color instead of using the color sliders.

Hint—If one of your stop colors is black and you're using process colors, make a new black stop color that contains 100% black and a high percentage of the predominant process color in the other stop color. This produces a nice rich transition.

- Gradient Ramp—this specifies where the stop color begins to blend ("ramp") with the other. Dragging an end point causes the stop color to remain solid up to the point where you drop the end point, where it will begin to blend with the other stop color.

The little diamond slider controls the midpoint of the gradient; that is, the area in the gradient that consists of a 50% tint of each color.

- You can add additional "stop" colors to the gradient by clicking under the gradient ramp between the two end stops. Choose a new color for the stop as before. Figure 9–15 shows a gradient with three stops, made from two spot colors plus white.

Figure 9–16 is an example of this gradient applied to an object.
How do you know when you've set up a gradient correctly? Well, consider a gradient to be made of thin slices of tint bands, which usu-

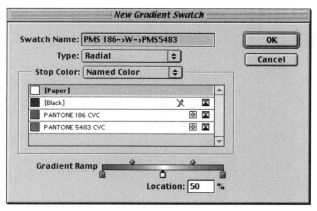

Figure 9–15
Gradient with three stops.

ally are skinny enough to appear without noticeable transitions. Bands become noticeable when the tint bands get too big. You need to make sure that the tint bands stay under 0.05 in. or else they begin to become visible.

General guidelines for gradient printing:

- Use colors or tint values with a fairly wide range, for example, 10% to 90%, in a gradient. Narrow ranges of color, such as a tint from 30% to 50%, force the use of larger bands of tint because fewer tints are available.
- Make your gradients of a reasonable size. A short distance between two colors in a gradient results in a smoother transition because the available number of tints is larger.
- Specify a higher print resolution and/or a lower line screen value. A higher resolution produces more tints, as does a lower

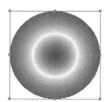

Figure 9–16
Gradient applied to an object.

line screen value. If your art shows banding at 150 lpi and 1800 dpi resolution, increase the resolution (the best option) or reduce the line screen value to 120 lpi or 133 lpi (not a good option, because this will make your screens a little coarser).

- Make sure the job is imaged on a PostScript Level III device.

You can use some basic math to calculate the available number of tints based upon the final output resolution and line screen ruling.

To determine the number of tints your final output device can image (N), divide the printer resolution (P) by the screen ruling (R), and square the result.

$$N= (P/R)^2$$

If your printer's imagesetter will be run at 1800 dpi and 150 lpi (a good compromise between speed and quality), the number of tints available will be 144.

To determine the actual number of tints you can use with your gradient's selected colors or tints, multiply N by the difference between the tint values expressed as a decimal (Z). For example, if your gradient starts with a 30% spot color tint and ends with a 60% tint of the same color, then the difference is 30%, or 0.30 in decimal.

$$T=(NZ)$$

Using our value for N, this will make 43 available tints in your gradient. If the gradient is small, it will not band.

Now, see if the tint bands between the start and the end of the gradient are big enough to be visible. Divide the distance between the start and end of the gradient (D) by the actual number of tints available (T). A tint band size (S) of 0.05 in. or less is required to eliminate visible banding. For a gradient size of three inches, we can calculate the tint band size and see if it's small enough.

$$S=(D/T)$$

Using our previous values, S=0.069 in., which makes a tint band that's too fat. Reducing the size of the gradient, or using a wider tint range, will help create smaller tint bands. Instead of using 60% for the end of the gradient, use 80%. This gives you 72 available tints and will result in a desirable tint band size of 0.041 in.

If you are using a gradient of two colors, determine the tint differences using both colors. For example, a gradient might go from 30% PANTONE 186 to 85% PANTONE 116. Subtract 30 from 85, and convert the result, 55, to a decimal, 0.55. Process color blends usually don't create significant banding problems, but you should be aware of tonal differences here. A process color blend that starts with 0c 75m 55y 0k and ends with 30c 25m 10y 0k may exhibit banding because of the tint difference between the darkest inks, in this case, cyan and magenta. Base your tint difference value on the difference between these two inks.

If you have no idea what the final output resolution and screen ruling will be, consider that 2400 dpi at 150 lpi is a very common output resolution and ruling for commercial printing. For newspapers, 1200 dpi at 85–100 lpi is pretty standard. Always ask your printer for this information as early as possible in the job's life. (See Chapter 11, Table 11-1, Available Gray Levels.)

Color Matching Systems   Color matching systems are color reference products from various companies, usually supplied as printed color swatchbooks in a variety of formats; some are fan-out books of printed color samples, and others include tear-out chips that can be attached to a job to communicate the color requirements to a printer.

The most common color matching systems in North America are those from Pantone, Inc. These include a range of spot colors, process colors, and specialty color systems such as those for process color simulation of PANTONE spot colors, others for specialty inks like metallics and pastels, and others that support PANTONE's Hexachrome system. You can buy printed PANTONE swatchbooks at most graphic arts supply stores. They're quite expensive, and since PANTONE recommends replacing them every year, you might be able to pick up used ones for free from an ad agency or print shop.

InDesign supports only PANTONE's coated and uncoated spot colors, and their basic process color swatchbooks. To use the metallics and pastels, you can reference the color's swatch number in a new spot color, since the on-screen appearance of a spot color really isn't very important—properly identifying the color and ink is. To use the PANTONE spot-to-process reference book, you need to decode the CMYK percentages used in the process equivalent to a spot color and then create a new CMYK swatch using those percentages. InDesign may support the PANTONE "ProSim" ("process simulation") and Hexachrome swatch libraries in a future version.

The DIC and Toyo libraries are spot color systems usually used in Japan. If you aren't preparing files for printing in Japan, it's probably not worth the trouble of specifying spot colors using these systems, but they can be useful in process color printing, because both of these systems use coding to indicate how well a spot color can be reproduced as a process color. If the swatch name has an asterisk after it, it means that the color won't reproduce well if converted to process color. Two asterisks mean the color can't be reproduced at all with process color, as is the case with a metallic ink.

Focoltone is a process color system usually used in Europe. Printed Focoltone swatchbooks might be difficult to find in North America, and the range of swatches it provides is pretty meager.

TRUMATCH is a process color system that was specifically developed for electronic publishing. Its swatches are arranged in the order that the colors appear in the visible spectrum, starting with reds, going through yellows, greens, blues, violets, and back to red. It's more intuitive than the PANTONE process color system, which isn't very logically arranged, especially if you're used to the HSB (hue, saturation, brightness) color model, which InDesign doesn't support directly. The first character in a TRUMATCH swatch is a number indicating its hue value, from 1 to 50.

The second character is a letter from a–h indicating the swatch's color strength; "a" means 100% saturation, and "h" means only 5% saturation. The third character indicates brightness in terms of the amount of black the swatch contains, which is added in 6% increments; this value ranges from 1, meaning 6% black, to 7, meaning 42% black, and if there isn't a third character, the swatch doesn't contain any black.

Swatchbook Libraries   InDesign includes numerous preset spot and process color swatches, and these are stored in swatch libraries. They are arranged by the type or by the maufacturer of the color matching system upon which they are based, and are selected by choosing Window ➠ Swatch Libraries (Figure 9–17).

You have to scroll through the colors to find the one you want, which is up there on the list of annoying things about InDesign.

Other swatch libraries are specific to computer displays. The web library contains the 216 so-called safe colors that will display properly on the lowest common denominator computer screen, an old standard based on the fairly elderly VGA display system, which had a pretty limited range of color that could be displayed without dithering; dithered colors looked terrible.

The system libraries are specific to each platform and contain the 256 default system colors.

Neither the Web nor System libraries are all that useful since nearly all modern desktop computers are capable of displaying more than 256 simultaneous colors, but they are provided if you need to preserve display compatibility with older computers.

Using Swatch Libraries in InDesign   To add swatches to the Swatches panel, choose Window ➠ Swatch Libraries, open the desired library, find the color you want (Figure 9–18), then double-click on it to add it to the Swatches panel, or choose the Add to

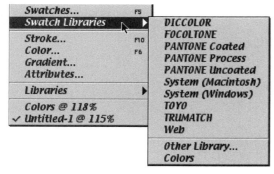

Figure 9–17
Swatchbook libraries.

Swatches pop-up menu on the Library panel. Unfortunately, you can't select a particular color quickly by typing its number as you can in QuarkXPress and PageMaker; you have to scroll through the whole list to find the one you want.

PANTONE spot colors with four-digit numbers are listed *after* all of the three-digit colors, another annoyance, since four-digit colors are listed in the correct numerical order in the printed swatchbooks.

InDesign includes two types of PANTONE spot color swatch libraries, coated, and uncoated. This reflects the fact that a full PANTONE swatchbook includes color samples printed on coated and uncoated paper. Because of the surface reflection differences between the two types of paper, the same color can look a little different on different papers. There's no difference in the on-screen appearance of these two libraries, but you should be consistent in choosing swatches from one or the other.

To import a set of colors as a swatch library from another InDesign document or from an Illustrator file, choose Window ➧ Swatch Libraries ➧ Other Library to browse for and locate the file. When the library panel appears, double-click the desired colors to add these to the Swatches panel. Imported libraries will appear in the Swatch Libraries menu until you quit InDesign. You can copy an InDesign or Illustrator file that contains the swatches to the InDesign Swatch Libraries folder for further reuse.

Hint for owners of both Freehand and Illustrator: Freehand includes swatch libraries for many other PANTONE matching sys-

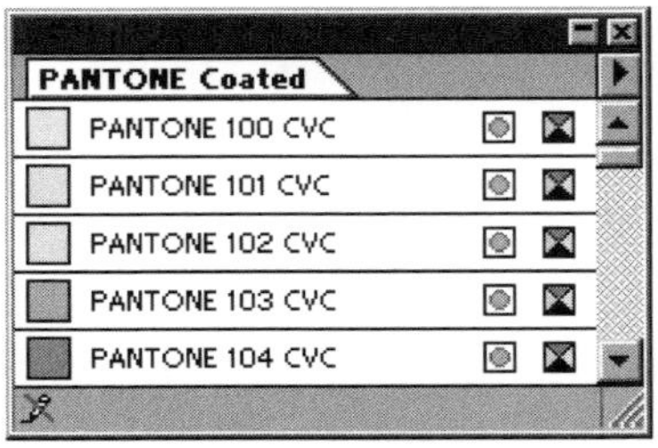

To select a PANTONE color by typing the number, open the swatch library, then Command + Option/Control + Alt + Click over the library list. This "focuses" the list. Type the numbers for your PANTONE color and it *should* select itself in the panel. However, this doesn't work with four-digit PANTONE numbers, it doesn't work if the number starts with a zero, nor does it work with named PANTONE colors like Rhodamine Red or Cool Gray 4. Oops.

Figure 9–18
A swatch library.

tems like metallics and process simulation of spot colors. You can load the desired swatches into a Freehand document (Shift + Click to select multiple swatches), export it as an Illustrator file, open it in Illustrator and then save it as a native Illustrator file, then open the resulting file's swatches in InDesign.

The Illustrator file exported by Freehand isn't entirely compatible with InDesign, which is why you need to open and save it from whatever version of Illustrator you have. Clumsy, but hey, it works.

You can drag and drop any global Illustrator swatch (except for pattern swatches) into an open InDesign document and they'll be added to the Swatches panel. You can also drag and drop swatches between open InDesign documents. If there's an identical spot color swatch in the destination document, you'll be asked if you want to make a copy and warned about making extra separation plates (Figure 9–19).

If there's any sort of mismatch, the swatch is added to the panel with "-2" appended to its name, for example, if you made a process swatch out of a spot swatch named PANTONE 186 CVC, then dragged it into another document that had a spot color with the same name, the new swatch is added as PANTONE 186 CVC-2.

Imported EPS Spot Colors   Be careful about how you name spot colors in other programs if you import art from them. InDesign will treat any spot color not exactly matching those it already contains as new ones, so if you create PANTONE 186 CVC, make sure you use the exact same name for that color in all programs like Illustrator, Freehand, Corel Draw, Canvas, or whatever.

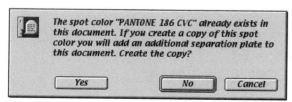

Figure 9–19
Separation warning.

If an EPS or Illustrator file contains spot colors, they will be added to the InDesign Swatches panel even if they aren't actually used in the imported file, and you can't edit or remove them from the Swatches panel until you delete the placed EPS file that contained them and then choose *Select All Unused* from the Swatches panel menu, which will make them editable or removable. Always remove unused spot colors from artwork files before importing them into InDesign.

If you already have spot colors defined in the Swatches panel with the same name, and the display color values differ from those in the InDesign document, you'll be asked if you want to replace the ones in your InDesign document with those from the placed file. As long as the actual spot color name is the same, replacing the swatch isn't a problem since the display color values only specify how the color is shown on your screen. If the swatches match for name and color value, the swatch becomes uneditable in InDesign without any sort of warning, since InDesign is replacing its swatch with the one from the placed file. Process color swatches from EPS and Illustrator files are not imported when such files are placed.

Converting from Spot to Process   To convert a spot color to a process color, simply double-click on its entry in the Swatches panel to display the swatch options (Figure 9–20). Choose *Process* from the Color Type pop-up menu—the color will derive its CMYK values from those shown in the Color Mode settings. You can't convert imported colors from spot to process, though you can specify conversion during printing of these colors.

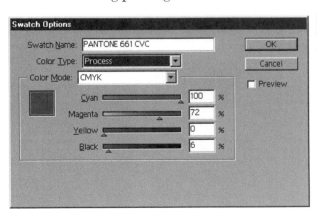

Figure 9–20
Converting from spot to process.

After conversion, the color appears in the Swatches panel as a process color. Process colors display a solid gray square in the color mode column of the Swatches panel (Figure 9–21).

You can convert any named swatch in InDesign to a spot color, but really, there's no reason to ever do this unless you make up a swatch intended to represent something like a spot varnish but forget to set it to spot when you first create it. There's no way for a printer to know what color of ink a spot color swatch named Lil' Green Bugs is supposed to represent.

Spot colors must have names that conform to a color matching system to prevent chaos and lots of screaming when the job is submitted for printing. You can name process colors anything you want since they're all combinations of CMYK, which a printer obviously understands.

Replacing or Deleting Swatches   Suppose your finished project is built with Black and PANTONE 186. Your client calls and tells you that she has decided to use PANTONE 5483 instead. There are a few ways of dealing with this: the easiest and most error-prone would be to instruct the printer to simply substitute PANTONE 5483 wherever the separations call for PANTONE 186.

Knockout—if two objects of different colors overlap, the object on top knocks out the object below; that is, the color underneath the foreground object is not printed.

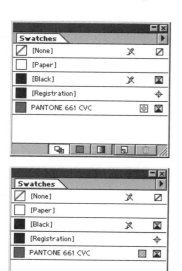

Figure 9–21
Spot PANTONE 661 (top) and Process PANTONE 661 (bottom).

But this isn't the most professional and reliable solution. Ideally, you should replace all occurrences of PANTONE 186 with PANTONE 5483, including any tints, to prevent miscommunication and the possibility of a ruined press run.

To do this in InDesign, create a new swatch for the new color, then delete the old one. InDesign will ask if you want to replace the swatch with another color or if you want to make it an unnamed color (Figure 9–22).

Choose the replacement color from the Named Swatch pop-up menu and click OK. The original swatch is replaced with the new one, and any tints or gradients that used the original color will now use the replacement color. This works the same regardless of the color model used in the swatches.

You could choose to just delete the swatch and convert it to an unnamed color if you like, but if you do this with a spot color and if there are any objects in the document that use the color, the resulting unnamed color will be a process color based on the CMYK conversion of the spot color. Make sure that this is really what you want to do before you do it!

Shift-click multiple swatches to delete them. You'll see the same *Delete Swatch* dialog shown in Figure 9–22, and you can replace multiple swatches with just one or make them unnamed. Choose *Select All Unused* from the Swatches panel menu to grab any extraneous swatches and get rid of them.

Figure 9–22
Deleting a swatch.

Other Types of Spot Colors

There are inks and coatings that are not in InDesign's Color Libraries. Examples include opaque white ink (typically used on dark-colored papers or transparent materials), fluorescent and metallic inks, and clear varnishes.

These cannot be reproduced with process color and must be created as spot colors. Varnishes really aren't inks, but they are applied to paper like ink and can be used for some really creative effects. They provide areas of gloss or matte over the artwork or can be used alone to make interesting glossy/matte patterns on the page.

As far as InDesign is concerned, they are just another spot color. The easiest way to create a "spot varnish" over an object is to clone the object and set its Fill and Stroke, if any, to the varnish color. You may wish to keep varnish objects on a separate layer.

Be sure to set all varnishes to overprint; we'll discuss overprints and knockouts in the next section.

Trapping

Recall our discussion of the registration color and of registration. In a perfect world, there are no taxes and all printing presses are in perfect registration, meaning that they will print all ink colors in exact relation. No printing press is ever in perfect registration because the sheet or web (roll) of paper will shift ever so slightly as it flies through the press. Some printing presses operate at fantastic speeds, and it's amazing that the level of control an operator has over these things exists at all. A big publication gravure press can be four meters wide and a few hundred feet long, and at top speed one of these could probably fill a football stadium with paper in a few hours.

Any printing press is subject to small variances and mechanical slop in its works that can result in minor misregistration no matter how carefully a press operator adjusts all of the knobs, mystery handles, electronic control systems, and the other fiddly bits of a press.

Misregistration can show up as gaps in knockouts, which can be quite apparent and are usually grounds for the rejection of the job, as shown in the example in Figure 9–23.

In register   **Out of register**

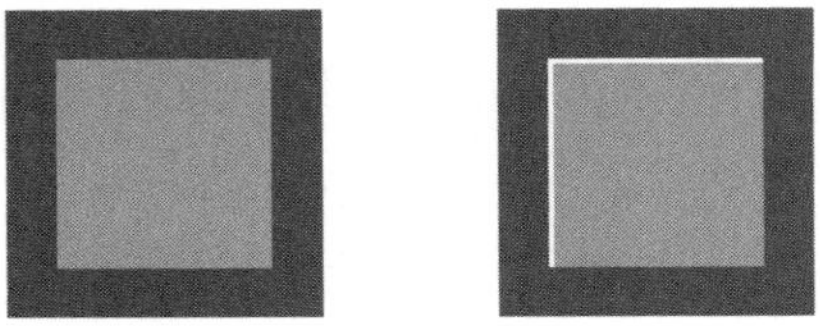

Figure 9–23
Registration.

There are actually two definitions of trapping: If you ask an electronic prepress operator, the response will be registration trapping, the type we're going to discuss here. Ask a press operator and you'll get a response that describes the process of printing inks over each other. Ink trapping is an entirely different topic, and for discussion purposes assume that we're discussing registration trapping.

Fundamentally, trapping is the process of deliberately introducing a bit of distortion into the artwork that visually corrects for minor (and typically unavoidable) press misregistration, although no amount of trapping can correct gross registration errors. Done properly, trapping is never noticeable even if the press is in perfect register, although close examination of a printed piece can sometimes detect applied traps. Bad trapping is usually worse than not trapping at all, and it's something you really ought to leave to a printer, but we're going to tell you how to create basic traps anyway. The process of trapping an object to another object of a different color can be a very technically complex process and in most cases it is beyond the scope of this book, but there are a few things you can do in InDesign to make sure that your project can be printed successfully. Complex trapping is best left to professional prepress technicians, as trapping specifications can vary quite a bit depending on the press, the paper stock, and the type of printing technology to be used for the job.

InDesign lacks the trapping features that are built into QuarkXPress and PageMaker. It does, however, include comprehensive trap specification settings that work with imaging devices that support Adobe's "in-RIP" trapping system; that is, no trapping occurs on your computer and the specifications set in the InDesign trapping dialog (located in the Print dialog) are sent to the imaging device, where they are used to perform trapping as the job is separated and imaged.

Typically, such devices can also perform color separation, which frees up your computer much sooner than if you had to create the separations as you printed the job. InDesign's in-RIP trapping is supported only on Adobe PostScript Level 3 RIPs (Raster Image Processors).

Software programs like ScenicSoft's TrapWise and DK&A Trapper perform this step on a standard desktop computer rather than at the imaging device. InDesign can export files that are designed to work with these programs, but unless you work in a print shop or service bureau, it's very unlikely that you'll own, much less need, these very expensive and complex programs.

We'll talk about in-RIP trapping in Chapter 11, but here we'll be talking about how to create your own simple traps without using any special equipment or extra software, and we'll discuss document construction tips that can help avoid trapping disasters if your printer does not have imaging equipment that performs in-RIP trapping.

Companies that offer Adobe Post-Script Level III in-RIP trapping systems:

Agfa
Autologic
ECRM
Fuji
PrepressSolutions
Xitron

Expect other companies to offer in-RIP trapping soon.

Trapping Tips

- You can avoid trapping issues completely by designing artwork that does not use abutting colors. This isn't always possible, but it is the one sure method of eliminating trapping problems.

- When using process colors, choose abutting colors that contain a high percentage of common process inks. For example, yellow type set over a green background will not show signs of misregistration because the green background is really an overprint of both cyan and yellow process inks, and thus won't show any gaps if registration is slightly off.

    The example in Figure 9–24 shows overprints of solid cyan and yellow, which make green when overprinted. The same idea applies to tints of process inks that are used to produce any process color.

- Images do not require trapping unless other objects are placed over then, like colored type or filled objects and, in this case, the overlying objects can be trapped to the image with overprinting strokes.
- Gradients can be very difficult to trap if one overlaps another.
- Black objects should always be set to overprint anything under them, rather than having them knock out underlying objects. The only time blacks should not overprint is if a black object has significant coverage over an object like an imported image, because the image may be slightly visible through the black ink. In this case, if your job is to be printed with process colors, you can create a "rich" black, which is 100% black with smaller percentages of the other three process colors. Rich black, when printed over an image, eliminates show-through of the image under the black.

The traditional formula for a rich black is 100% black, and 60% cyan. You can also add smaller percentages of magenta and yellow to obtain a very solid, saturated "super" black (Figure 9–25), but check with your printer for the recommended rich black formula.

- Never specify a rich black as 100% of all four inks. Some paper stocks cannot tolerate heavy ink coverage and they might delaminate or pick apart on press. This is a particularly messy problem and requires a complete washup of the printing press.

Cyan separation   Yellow separation   Final Print

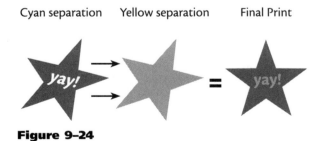

Figure 9–24
Overprinting.

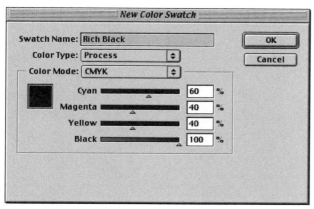

Figure 9–25
Specifying a "super" black.

- Do not color overprinting black text with rich black unless the type is very large. Typical body text covers a small percentage of a background, and any show-through will be negligible. Using rich black in text will make the slightest misregistration of the press very obvious.
- Using rich black in reverses requires the use of "keepaways," which is another fun printer's term for spreading reversed objects in the C, M, or Y separations of an object (type or whatever else) that's knocking out a rich black area. A keepaway also chokes the edges of a rich black area. QuarkXPress automatically creates keepaways in rich blacks, but InDesign doesn't, and creating these by hand would be a nightmare. You'll need to use in-RIP trapping or a trapping application to generate keepaways for InDesign documents.
- Avoid using light tints or process colors in type unless the type is set in a large size, usually over 14 points, or is set in a heavy, bold display typeface. For one thing, light tints can make type very hard to read. For similar reasons, type colored with process colors can also be difficult to read, especially at smaller sizes. Slight misregistration on press can be very apparent in process-colored type.

Manual Trapping in InDesign   The manual controls available to you in InDesign for trapping concern the overprinting of strokes and fills. You can specify object-level overprinting with the attributes panel, and you can specify in the InDesign Preferences that all blacks overprint. You have similar controls available to you in illustration programs like Illustrator, Freehand, and Corel Draw, and you can apply what you learn here to artwork created in those programs that will be placed into an InDesign layout.

You can't adjust any overprint settings for imported artwork, and the Overprint Black preference in InDesign does not have any effect on imported art. These illustration applications also have their own trap-creation tools, and any overprints or knockouts you create in them are honored in InDesign.

First, we need to explain the concept of chokes and spreads. Chokes are used with a light foreground color and a dark background color, and the lighter color is "choked under" the darker color. The portion that chokes under the darker color is overprinted, so if there's any misregistration, the choked portion will hide it (Figure 9–26).

Spreads are used with a light foreground color and a dark background color. The lighter color is "spread into" the darker one, which is set to overprint, so the darker object's edges overprint the spread lighter color, which again hides misregistration (Figure 9–27).

Creating Traps   You can control whether an object will overprint or knock out with the attributes panel. InDesign will always

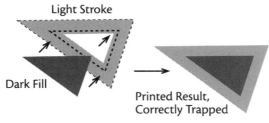

Figure 9–26
A choke.

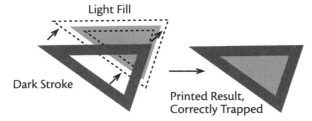

Figure 9–27
A spread.

overprint black if you check that option in the preferences, so there's no need to worry about it even if the Attributes panel doesn't signal that a black object is set to overprint. It will. If you've turned off the black overprint preferences, then follow along and treat black as any other dark color.

The simplest traps to create are spreads in stroked and filled objects that aren't overlapping anything else. If an object's stroke is dark and the fill is light and since InDesign measures strokes from the center out, setting the stroke to overprint will create a trap (Figure 9–28).

However, this only works if the stroke is darker than the fill. If it's lighter than the fill, then you have to do a little more work to make a choke because if you overprint a light stroke, it will end up looking half as wide because the inner half will seem to vanish, since you're essentially telling InDesign not to knock out the dark fill that's under the inner half of the stroke.

If that's OK with you, it will work, but if you don't want to change the stroke's apparent weight, you need to manually create a choke.

Here's how: clone the object, then scale the clone about 95%. Select both the original object and the clone, then use the Alignment panel to make sure that both are in exact center alignment. Set the clone's fill to white (paper). Send the clone behind the original, then set the fill of the original to overprint.

The amount that you scale the clone is approximate, but it should be enough to allow at least 0.25 point of overprinting to occur for

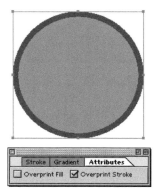

Figure 9–28
Creating a trap with light fill and a dark stroke.

trap. Because you set the clone's fill to white, which will knock out anything behind it, overprinting the original object's fill will not cause any color shifts (Figure 9–29).

You can use a similar strategy to trap paths, overlapping objects, and colored type. Just remember these rules:

- Light over dark spreads.
- Dark over light chokes.
- Chokes require cloning: scale the clone or adjust its stroke weight to accommodate the required trap width. If the clone

Figure 9–29
Creating a trap with dark fill and a light stroke.

is a line segment, set it to white; if it's a filled path or frame, set the fill to white but leave the stroke alone. Send the clone behind the original, and set the original to overprint.

- Objects that partially overlap each other may require you to create clones, then use the Scissors tool to separate and discard the portion of the clone that doesn't overlap and make your choke/spread operations on the portion that remains.
- Filled objects without strokes that overlap other objects may need a thin overprinting stroke that's the same color as the fill added to them to create a trap.
- InDesign allows you to create strokes that use gradients, but this won't help you trap a gradient to another gradient. You can use a solid overprinting stroke to trap an adjacent gradient.

A quarter-point trap width may not be large enough for some printing processes like flexography, newspaper (non-heatset web offset lithography), packaging gravure and lithography, or screen printing, so always check with your printer for the recommended trap widths.

Trap widths for commercial sheet-fed offset lithography, heatset web offset lithography, and publication gravure printing will typically be in the quarter-point range. If there's any doubt about trapping your documents, you really ought to let your printer handle the process.

These examples are geared to creating very simple traps, and anything much more elaborate is probably best left alone and put through a dedicated trapping system like Trapper, TrapWise, or an Adobe in-RIP system.

Color Management

Fundamentally, a software-based color management system (CMS) attempts to convert image color data from an input source to an output source with the smallest possible loss of color data as possible. With a CMS, it is possible to move a single image through several iterations of devices with no change in the original—all color conversion is done at the output or display stage. Such conversion leaves the original image in a wide-gamut, *device-independent* color state that allows for multiple versions of the image to be output to any number of devices, as long as those devices have been characterized within the CMS so that their reproduction characteristics are known to the CMS.

Practically speaking, the use of a CMS allows you to scan all images into RGB or LAB space, preserving a wide gamut, and to convert on output to accommodate gamut limitations of any RGB or CMYK device, which can be a monitor, an RGB film recorder, a color printer, or a color separation device like an imagesetter or platesetter. This is desirable because once an image is scanned as an RGB or LAB image, it has a much greater level of device independence and no permanent color space conversion of the image occurs—it is always converted on-the-fly during output, and the original remains untouched.

A CMS also helps maintain color consistency across different types of printing presses, printing technologies, and cross-media publishing, such as a magazine that is both printed on a press and also available on a web site as an HTML or PDF document. Many publications are printed at different sites across the world, and some are printed using different printing processes. For example, the North American edition of National Geographic is printed with gravure presses. Regional editions in other languages, which have smaller print runs, are printed with web offset presses. Using color management can help to ensure that all editions of a publication maintain consistent color, even if they are printed completely differently.

Color management is not "push button" color. It is no substitute for a thorough knowledge of color reproduction. It will not turn a bad scan into a printed masterpiece. It will not allow printers to hire minimum-wage high school kids to run the prepress operation.

Lots of high-end scanners (the ones in the $100,000 and up price range, not the flimsy things you can get for $79 at the CompuMegaSoftMart) perform RGB-to-CMYK conversion internally, since all scanners "see" in RGB, and in the not too distant past, high-end scanners scanned an image directly to separated film. More recently, they scanned to a CMYK TIFF file, which could be opened in Photoshop or placed into a page layout program.

Traditionally, CMYK images were scanned with very specific uses in mind, such as a particular printing press where the operators had, through experience, observed the press's characteristics for things like dot gain, gray balance, and so forth. When done right, these images reproduced very nicely, but if the image had to be used for another type of printing process, it often had to be scanned again with a different set of scanning parameters.

Scanning into RGB or LAB and then using a CMS to manage the output allows for device independence—the gamut and color range of such an image is wide enough to allow for conversion to many different color spaces and to very different separation parameters, all from one image, and the image need only be scanned once. Device-independent color is one of the advantages of color management; another is the potential to eliminate a lot of time- and money-intensive prepress activities.

Done right the use of a CMS will result in consistent color reproduction and can reduce the costs involved with color printing; for example, instead of creating expensive analog film-based proofs like Matchprint or ColorArt, you can print proofs directly to a relatively inexpensive inkjet or dye diffusion printer and get results that, while lacking actual halftone dots, will be a very close match to what will spew out of the delivery end of a printing press.

The presence or absence of halftone dots in proofs is still a topic of contention among prepress professionals and clients, but it's going to boil down to money; a digital halftone proofing system like the Kodak Approval costs over one hundred thousand dollars, while a high quality dotless proofer can be had for well under US$10,000. 'Nuff said.

Color Management, the Short Course Remember EFIColor? Well, that was one of the first attempts at automatic color management, and it didn't work very well. In fact, it probably introduced more problems than it ever solved.

In 1993, Apple Computer introduced an operating-system-based color management system called ColorSync. This first version was pretty limited and no applications supported it. It was an interesting idea, though—the first attempt at an operating-system-level color management system on any computer. The idea was to provide a system that not only provided consistent color reproduction, but one that reduced the amount of time spent manually tweaking images and adjusting them for various types of output devices, and also one that reduced the need for highly skilled scanner operators and color separation specialists.

It was a neat idea, but it took some time for it to catch on. The graphic arts industry has been slow to accept computerized color management and prefers to rely on good ol' human smarts to achieve consistent, high-quality color reproduction. Even in 1999, there aren't very many print shops that use any sort of color management system, probably because there's still no substitute for an experienced color pro, and because the implementation of a color management system is expensive, time-consuming, requires extensive training, and also requires that clients of printers and other graphic arts service providers be trained as well.

Given the fact that a large number of incoming jobs still require correction of many mistakes made by producers, it's not very likely that the average graphic designer will invest the time required to learn and implement a CMS, even though more and more designers or other producers are scanning their own artwork because it's cheaper and faster than using a professional scanning service.

Such a scenario is a perfect argument for the use of a CMS, since few end users really know very much about the intricacies of color and color correction. If producers had access to accurate device profiles and had a bit of training, many of the common production-halting problems that occur once a job is handed over to a printer could be reduced significantly.

The International Color Consortium (ICC) is a group of software and hardware developers that has developed a standard for current color management systems. The ICC-developed device profile is particular data that describes the input or output characteristics of a particular piece of equipment. The profile is embedded within an image and is interpreted by an application, such as Photoshop or InDesign, for display and printing purposes.

Color space conversions or image adjustments are performed with the operating-system-level color management engine, which is either ColorSync 2.6 on the Mac, or Image Color Matching 2.0 (ICM2) on Windows 98. By putting the core of the CMS at the operating system level, embedded device profiles can be used across platforms by any application that supports ColorSync or ICM2 color management. Nearly all professional prepress and graphic arts applications support both now, and profiles can be moved between Macs and Windows machines.

The components of a color management system are the input and output device profiles and the color management module (CMM), which acts as an interface between an application and the operating-system-level color management system. CMMs are numerous and have been developed by a number of companies, including Adobe, Kodak, Heidelberg (formerly Linotype-Hell), Agfa, and others. Each has its own merits, and we're not going to recommend one over another.

The Adobe CMM is automatically installed when you install InDesign or any other recent Adobe application. The Heidelberg CMM is the system default for ColorSync and ICM. It's really important that all of your CMS-capable applications use the same CMM, which can be chosen both at the operating system level and at the application level. Always use the same CMM throughout a workflow, even across platforms.

Color conversion occurs in a Profile Connection Space (PCS) which is the bridge between an input and an output profile. This space is typically the LAB color space, although other CIE-defined color space models can be used, such as the XYZ space.

Device profiles, when created properly, contain all of the specific color characteristics of a device. For input devices like a scanner or monitor, the profile typically contains an RGB ➟ PCS ➟ LAB color lookup table and a gamut range definition, and not much else. Since a monitor can be both an input and output device, its profile will also include a LAB ➟ PCS ➟ RGB lookup table.

Output profiles usually contain LAB ➟ PCS ➟ CMYK and CMYK ➟ PCS ➟ LAB color lookup tables, and they'll usually include specific instructions for color separation parameters such as dot gain, under-color removal (UCR), gray component replacement (GCR), under-color addition (UCA), and tone compression data.

Output profiles contain bidirectional color lookup tables because they can also be used as source profiles for CMYK images that do not contain an embedded profile (so-called legacy images) but which have been prepared and separated for a particular output device.

You can create your own profiles or use many "canned" profiles included with many devices and often included with many applications. Creating profiles yourself requires a serious commitment both in time and money if you want to do it right.

Each device (meaning *each and every* monitor and printer and proofer and scanner and printing press and digital camera and film recorder and video frame grabber and so on in your facility) must be *profiled* with specialized software and often with specialized equipment. The ICC profile created from a profiling application can then be used in production.

"Well, that doesn't sound so bad." You wish. For accurate profiling, expect to either A) hire an expensive consultant or B) spend up to US$15,000 in equipment and software. If you are trying to achieve accurate, consistent color, you cannot rely on any canned profiles for any equipment you have. You will need either a colorimeter or a spectrophotometer, and an application that can communicate with such instruments and interpret the data that they generate.

Profiling steps differ depending on the device in question. Scanners are probably the easiest to profile since you don't need any fancy colorimeters, and some scanners include the software necessary to generate the profile. First, a known color target is scanned.

These targets are typically a bunch of gray and colored patches reproduced onto transparencies or photographic prints that have been produced to very exacting tolerances, and the color reference values for these targets are known to the profiling application. A common target used in device profiling is the IT8.7 series of targets (Figure 9–30), which are available in numerous types and brands of photographic media.

You want to use the IT8 target that's going to represent the type of media that you scan; for example, if you always scan reflective photos printed from Agfa film on Agfa paper, you need an Agfa paper IT8, but if you also scan Kodak Ektachrome transparencies, you need an Ektachrome IT8 transparency target. These things are not cheap, and they're easily damaged. Each target you purchase should include a file containing its reference LAB color values against which measured values are referenced when generating a profile.

If you want to get really particular, you'll buy targets and recreate profiles annually. Film manufacturers are always changing their film dyes, emulsions, and processing chemistry, so, for example, a

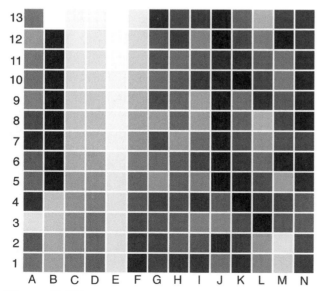

Figure 9–30
An IT8.7 target.

FujiChrome IT8 transparency from 1996 won't be the same as one from 1999, which means that any photographic prints or transparencies you scan will also exhibit variation in their color characteristics from year to year.

The variation is usually quite minimal, but you should be aware of it if you are involved in image scanning and reproduction.

Once scanned, the profiling software samples each color patch in the resulting digital image file, compares the scanned colorimetric values to the known values, and reflects the difference in the profile. Once the profile is generated, the scanner's quirks and operating characteristics are known quantities, and the profile can be used to adjust scanned images to known colorimetric parameters. Using a CMS and a scanner profile won't fix a terrible photo, but it ensures that what you get out of scanner is going to be a lot closer to the actual scanned artwork than without it.

You profile digital cameras by photographing a reflective IT8 target with the standard lighting and exposure settings you normally use, and the profile is created the same way as it is for a scanner after the image is downloaded from the camera.

You can make a rough profile of your monitor with the Adobe Gamma utility that was installed along with InDesign, but it's no substitute for a colorimeter and a profiling application. Instructions for using Adobe Gamma are in your InDesign manual, but if you're serious, you really need either a monitor that has its own calibration device (typically a suction-cup colorimeter) or a standalone colorimeter with a suction-cup attachment and a profiling application. Once the profile is created, you must always use that profile with that monitor, and since monitors go out of whack all the time, you need to recreate the profile every few weeks. Old monitors are bad candidates for use in a color-managed workflow because they're often too dim or the controls just aren't controlling much anymore.

Profiling of printers, proofers, and printing presses is expensive and takes a lot of time. Ideally, you should have an XY-scanning colorimeter or spectrophotometer, because you'll be reading gazillions of little color patches during this process and you will (not maybe) slip up eventually and create a bad profile. These things automatically sample each patch on a printed color target, which is usually the same one used for the profiling of a scanner.

One stumbling block to widespread adoption of color management is this: to really take advantage of the color consistency benefits, you need to not only profile every output device, but you must profile that device every time a variable changes. With some devices, like digital color proofers or analog proofing systems, the substrate and pigments don't change much, but think of a printing press. Not only are there thousands of different papers and other substrates, there's also a huge number of ink suppliers—if you sampled cyan inks from ten different ink manufacturers, you'd end up with ten different spectral curves.

Fortunately, you can usually get away with using a profile developed for a printing standard, such as those from SWOP, GRACoL, SNAP, FIRST, and GAA, instead of trying to profile every paper and ink ever. However, it's probably a good idea to create a press profile if you *always* run the exact same paper stock, always use ink from the same supplier, and always perform incoming inspection of paper and ink, or receive certification from suppliers that these materials are in conformance to your specifications. This way, you can achieve a much more accurate characterization of your particular press, printing conditions, papers, and inks than you could by using, for example, a SWOP profile, which is a pretty loose specification.

You could do better, but it's not worth the effort to generate custom press profiles if papers and inks keep changing. It can take from one to three days to perform a thorough press characterization, and most shops won't bother with that sort of time commitment. Instead, you can choose from one of the standard press profiles that closely matches your printer's recommendations for GCR/UCR, dot gain, paper stock, and ink set.

Creating a profile for a proofing device, color printer, or digital color press involves printing a target, typically an IT8 or other target, on the device, measuring the printed results with a colorimeter, then creating a profile from that data.

To create a profile for a conventional press, you separate and image the target, make plates, hang the plates on the press, ink up the fountains with your standard process inks, and do a complete make-ready on the press as if this test were any other print job. Too many printers, due to time and financial constraints, don't allow the press to come up to color completely and the result is a profile that's probably worse than a canned one. Only after standard ink densities and gray balance levels are achieved should the printed result be measured and profiled.

Some profiling applications require the use of proprietary color targets, some of which may contain over a thousand color patches. You must use the digital target included with or generated by the profiling application to get consistent results, not a scanned version of a target, because digital targets are created with known color values against which output color values are measured.

Applying Profiles, Generally Speaking   ICC profiles exist as individual files on your computer, but a profile is of little use until it is embedded within an image. You apply a scanner profile when you scan an image, and it is saved with the image. Scanner profiles are always input profiles.

A monitor profile might seem to be obviously an output profile, but most of the time it's really an input profile, because you'll be making adjustments and corrections to the image based on the monitor display and you want that monitor's characteristics to carry along with the image. For artwork created on the computer, your monitor profile is also the input profile. In fact, if your monitor is properly calibrated and profiled, you should substitute its profile for that of the scanner if you make any sort of adjustments or edits to the image.

You can leave the scanner profile embedded if the image is unchanged. Use the monitor profile for RGB images that lack embedded profiles.

More and more digital stock photography includes embedded profiles, which should always be used as the input profile for these images unless you modify or change the image, in which case you should embed the monitor profile.

Once the image is captured or created, you can edit it visually until it looks the way you want it to, then you can soft-proof the image on the monitor by setting the monitor profile as the source and the final output device as the, well, output device, or destination.

Proof the image on your printer by using these same settings, but choose your proofer as the device that will simulate the final output. You can change the output profile to simulate how the image might look when printed on a different type of press or other final output. Save the image with the monitor profile embedded in the image.

When you place the image into a page layout application that supports color management, select the correct profiles in the application's display, proofer/printer, and final output profile settings. Select default profiles for any artwork created within that application, which means choosing profiles for RGB, LAB, and CMYK color models. These last profiles can also be applied to images that lack embedded profiles.

To soft-proof the entire layout, use the monitor to simulate the final output device. Use the proofer or printer profile when you're ready to make a proof. If you need to make traditional analog proofs from film, such as a MatchPrint or WaterProof, use a profile created for that proofing system.

Once the proof looks okay, you can then send the entire job to the final imaging device or write it to a PostScript or PDF file. Choose the final output profile for your printing press or other final output as the output device. The choice of sending preseparated or composite data depends on your equipment or your printer's needs.

Rendering Intents   When you assign a profile to an image, you can also specify a *rendering intent*. A rendering intent is a set of instructions that tell the CMS how an image should be converted from one color space to another. Recall our discussion of color space gamuts—LAB has the largest gamut, RGB the next largest, and CMYK the smallest. If you have an image in LAB space and it is to be converted to CMYK for separation, you want to tell the CMS how to handle LAB colors that exist outside the CMYK output gamut. Because the CMYK gamut is so much smaller than the others and because CMYK is the color space of anything that gets printed in color, differing methods for handling the conversion were developed to accommodate the needs of different types of images.

The *perceptual* rendering intent is ideal for scanned color photographs. Choosing this intent causes the CMS to perform gamut compression, which preserves the visual relation between color spaces while compressing the tonal range and gamut of the source profile to map within that of the destination profile. Saturation of colors may decrease, but hue shifts are minimized. Colors are moved into gamut proportionally and are not overlapped or "clipped."

The *saturation* rendering intent is intended for typical office graphics like charts and such, where color accuracy is not critical. This intent attempts to preserve apparent color saturation at the expense of hue accuracy. The gamut is not compressed; rather, out-of-gamut colors are mapped to the closest in-gamut equivalent; this is called *clipping*. Different colors outside of the destination gamut may end up looking the same after gamut mapping

The two *colorimetric* intents, *relative* and *absolute*, behave like the saturation intent as they move out-of-gamut colors within the gamut of the destination device, where they may overlap. Similar but slightly different out-of-gamut colors may end up looking the same after being clipped. However, all clipping is performed with maximum hue accuracy in mind rather than saturation. The colorimetric intent is best used for solid-color images like corporate logos and process-color derivations of spot colors, where color matching accuracy is important. The absolute variant directly maps the source gamut to the destination gamut; the relative variant takes the white point of the source and destination into account when performing the conversion.

The white point is usually the colorimetric value of a paper stock or a monitor's brightest point. The relative variant is only useful if the profiles contain accurate white point information, which you really won't know unless you created them yourself. The absolute variant is really not recommended because it ignores the device's white point, which is important because the white point is used to define an image's appearance, especially in lighter areas. In general, use the relative colorimetric intent only for critical color matching. The colorimetric and saturation rendering intents should never be used for photographic images.

Will You Shut Up Now?!   But wait, there's more! In some cases, you might not even want to use a color management system. If your production process is completely under your control from start to end and you're very familiar with it and the nuances of a CMYK workflow, you probably don't need to bother. But, if you're preparing work for printing at multiple sites or if you want to repurpose stuff for cross-media publishing, you may benefit from a color management system.

If you're a designer or producer of content, the decision to use or not use a color management system will really depend on the capabilities of your production service. If they don't use a color-managed production workflow, then there's not much point in your using one either, but if they do, then you could really stand to gain from learning how to implement color management in your own production process.

Be aware that if you create your own profiles and supply profiled images to a print shop, and one of the profiles happens to be no good, you will probably be financially responsible at the prepress end for fixing the problem.

Color Management in InDesign

OK, here's how this all works in InDesign. We've tried to be brief (for some value of the word "brief") but thorough about color management because it is a complex subject on which billions of words have been written, most of them incomprehensible to anyone except their authors. You do need to know how and why to use color management before trying to use it in any application or workflow.

Currently, color management only works with bitmapped images; it won't do anything to vector EPS files, although bitmapped Photoshop EPS files can contain embedded profiles which InDesign will honor. Vector art from programs like Illustrator or Freehand must be converted to TIFF with an embedded profile for InDesign to color-manage it.

It's possible for EPS files to contain multiple bitmapped images, each of which can have its own embedded profile. PDF files created with Acrobat 4.0 can also contained embedded profiles and, like EPS files, a PDF file with multiple images in it can contain multiple profiles. You can't reassign a profile to any EPS or PDF art in InDesign as you can with a TIFF image.

If you convert QuarkXPress or PageMaker documents that contain color-managed images, the profiles embedded in those images are preserved. If the images' profiles are not ICC-compliant, they will be replaced with the default InDesign profiles you specify in the application color settings. This can happen if you have old QuarkXPress 3.3 files that have EFIColor profiles in them or PageMaker files that have profiles from the old Kodak color management system.

Setting Up the CMS   InDesign has two levels of color management settings: an application-wide set, and a document-specific set. To perform the inital setup of the CMS for InDesign, choose File ➠ Color Settings ➠ Application Color Setting (Figure 9–31).

- *Engine*—By default, Adobe's own color management system is chosen here, and it's the only choice in the Windows version of InDesign. On the Macintosh, you can leave the setting at Adobe CMS, or you can choose ColorSync to use the MacOS as the color management engine. If you choose the Heidelberg CMM, you'll be using ColorSync with the Heidelberg CMM, which isn't readily apparent from the dialog. However, you should probably leave the Engine setting at Adobe CMS, especially if you plan to share files across platforms, which will take advantage of the Adobe Rainbow Bridge system that's used in all recent Adobe applications for both platforms.
The Adobe CMS is built into Photoshop and Illustrator, and it's actually called "Built-In" in Photoshop. You can also change to a different engine in those programs. Be sure that all of your

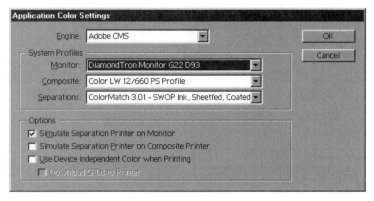

Figure 9–31
Application Color Settings dialog box.

applications are using the same CMS or CMM for consistent results.

- Choose the monitor profile you made with the Adobe Gamma utility or with your profiling application.
- *Composite* refers to a proofing device or color printer that is capable of printing RGB or CMYK data. Typically, this will be set to the proofer/printer device profile you created.
- *Separations* refers to the final output device, which can be a digital or conventional printing press or an analog proofing system.
- Choosing *Simulate Separations Printer on Monitor* will give you a pretty good idea of what your final printed piece will look like. This process is called "soft proofing," and while it's pretty close, it's no substitute for an actual printed proof unless your monitor is one of those $5,000 ultra-accurate proofing monitors from companies like Barco, and then only if the thing is calibrated regularly.
- *Simulate Separations Printer on Composite Printer* will produce the closest possible reproduction on a proofer of what you'll get on the final printed piece by compressing the gamut of the composite printer, which is almost always larger than

that of the separations printer or actual printing press, to fit within the gamut of the separations printer.

- *Use Device Independent Color when Printing* only works with imaging devices that support Adobe's PostScript color management, which is not the same thing as ICC color management. Choosing this option causes InDesign to send composite (unseparated) document data to the imager, which is where color separation will occur. InDesign converts all ICC profiles in the document to a format required by PostScript color management, called a color space array (CSA). The imager contains its own color rendering dictionary (CRD), which it uses along with the CSAs to convert all image gamuts to its own gamut. In general, unless you have experience with this type of equipment and are actually using it, leave this option off.

- *Download CRDs to Printer* should be off, unless you specifically want to override the CRD that's built into a PostScript color-management-capable device or if the device doesn't have its own built-in CRD. The new CRD is generated from the Separations profile specified in this dialog and then sent to the imager.

What the Heck is PostScript Color Management?   Well, it's a fancy term for the way a CMS works with Adobe RIPs that support in-RIP color separation.

Typically, CMYK color separation of RGB and LAB color images and art occurs on your computer as you print to a separations device like an imagesetter, but if you have in-RIPs seps, you send composite, unseparated data to the RIP or imager where it is separated internally, which frees up your computer a lot more quickly. Since PostScript has no clue about ICC profiles, these must be converted to the CSAs mentioned above, and the device's CRD is used to perform the gamut space conversion.

Few of us have such a device at our disposal, so very few people other than prepress technicians need to be concerned with these settings and you can probably ignore any reference to PostScript color management settings unless you're a prepress tech.

Further Setup of InDesign Color Management   After you've set your profiles in the Application Color Settings dialog, you set up the document color settings. If you do this with no document open, these settings will be applied to any new documents you create afterwards. If you apply these settings with a document open, they only apply to that document.

By default, color management is off in InDesign. You enable it in the document color settings. It's off because there wouldn't be much point in having it on unless your application color management settings were already set up, which is why you do that first.

To apply document color management settings, choose File ➡ Color Settings ➡ Document Color Settings (Figure 9–32).

- *Enable Color Management* is pretty obvious. You need to turn it on explicitly for each document.
- *Source Profiles*—These are the default profiles used to color-manage any artwork you create in InDesign. They are also used when an imported image lacks an embedded profile. Choose the profile that represents the most common source of your images.

  The CMYK profile should usually be set to the same profile as your separations device, which you set in the application color settings.

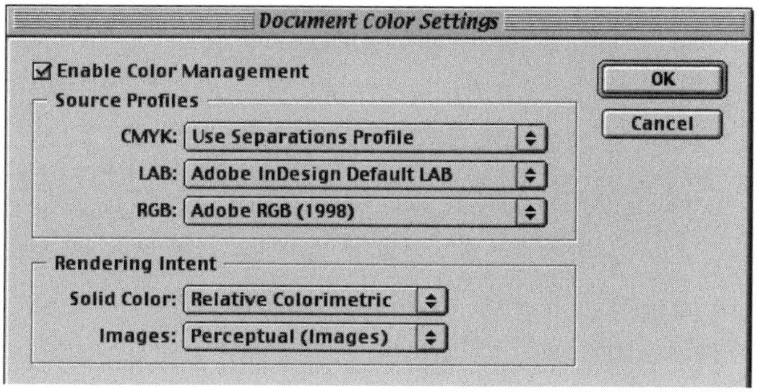

Figure 9–32
Document Color Settings dialog box.

The LAB profile choices are *Adobe InDesign Default LAB* or *Generic LAB Profile*. The *Adobe InDesign Default LAB* profile matches that used in Photoshop and is the better choice. The RGB source profile should be the one for your profiled monitor. You can also choose from several other RGB color space profiles that are used in Photoshop, but the monitor profile is the one you want.

Photoshop Notes—The Adobe RGB (1998) or the ColorMatch RGB spaces are the best choices because they offer the widest RGB gamut of all the choices. The basic difference is in the gamma and white point settings. Generally, the D50 white point and gamma of 1.8 in the ColorMatch space is preferred for print work. You can also choose your monitor's color space, which is derived from its profile. Never, ever, choose the sRGB space. sRGB is a lowest common denominator profile with a tiny gamut and was never intended for professional publishing. Even though RGB as a general color space offers a wide color gamut, compressed RGB color spaces have been defined for various outputs, such as television, photographic paper, motion picture film, a web page, and so forth. The Adobe RGB profile is derived from a wide-gamut RGB specification defined by the Society of Motion Picture and Television Engineers (SMPTE) known as SMPTE 240-M.

If you're going to use color management, you should set up Photoshop's Profile Setup to embed profiles in all images. In the RGB setup, choose the *Adobe RGB* (1998) space and check the *Display Using Monitor Compensation* checkbox. In the CMYK Setup, choose *ICC*, make sure the chosen profile matches that of your separations device, and choose the Built-in CMS, which is the same as the Adobe CMS in InDesign and Illustrator.

- You can choose a default rendering intent. In general, you should not change these settings for the reasons we discussed already about the various rendering intents. The only one you might want to change would be for solid colors, which you could set for saturation rendering for various types of business charts or if you are more concerned with saturation of solid colors (which, despite the name, includes tints) than with faithful reproduction of solid colors.

Once you've made your choices and have turned color management on, you're ready to start placing images. If you're working with a document that's open and already has color-managed images placed in it, InDesign will read the profiles and perform any visual adjustments needed, especially if you've chosen to simulate your final output on the monitor.

Colors will probably appear a lot less bright and vibrant after you do this, but that's just color management doing its job. You really do want to see as close a simulation as possible to your final output. Your display options must be set for *Full Resolution Display* in order for InDesign to color-manage image display. If you use Proxy Preview, the images are color managed when they are printed, but not on the screen.

Applying Profiles in InDesign   When you import/place an image, InDesign displays its usual file dialog box, but there's a checkbox there—usually off by default—called Show Import Options (Figure 9–33). We've already seen this in use when we discussed clipping paths. There's another part of the Show Import Options that deals with image profiles.

Here you can choose to either color-manage an image or not. If you choose not to, the image is never color managed. You might want to choose this option for preseparated CMYK images that don't require any further color changes. If document color management is turned off, you can still choose to enable it for an image and select a profile; it's just that nothing will happen with that image, color management-wise, until you turn document color management on.

If the image has an embedded profile, the Profile field will default to *Use Embedded Profile*. You can change the source profile, but you really ought not to unless you know that the embedded profile is

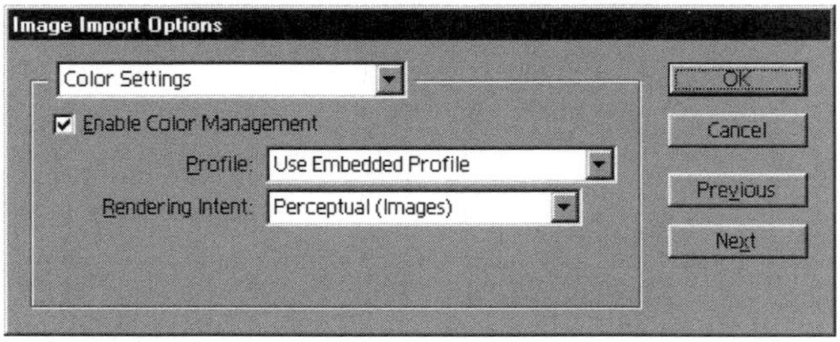

Figure 9–33
Show Import Options dialog box.

incorrect, or if it is out of date and a new profile has been generated
since the image was acquired or edited. You can also choose a rendering intent, but the default intent is usually correct.

If an image lacks an embedded profile, the Profile field in the dialog will read Use Document Default, which will assign the appropriate LAB, RGB, or CMYK profile as set in the document color settings, or you can specify a particular profile. If color management is
enabled, all placed images without profiles will have the defaults
assigned to them unless you specifically choose otherwise when placing the image or changing the image's color management settings
from the Image Color Settings dialog, coming up next.

You can change or assign profiles to images that have already been
placed in an InDesign document. Choose Object ➭ Image Color
Settings to display the image settings dialog (Figure 9–34), which
gives you the same level of control as is available in the Image Import
Options.

Sometimes profiles can have the same names yet have different
characteristics. If this happens, any embedded profile will take
precedence over any document-specific profiles.

Exporting Profiles We discuss all of the various means of
exporting an InDesign document in the next chapter, but basically, as
long as you have color management enabled, profiles are exported
along with an InDesign document. If it's turned off, profiles aren't
exported.

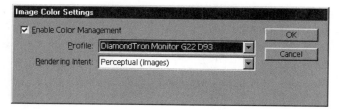

Figure 9–34
Image Color Settings dialog box.

Color Management for Nonprint Media   Long story, short: don't bother. Adobe Acrobat 4 supports color management for screen viewing, but chances are good that most people viewing PDF files on their computer screens have never calibrated their monitors. The same applies to web graphics—even though Microsoft's Internet Explorer supports ICC color management, the vast (and we mean vast) majority of web surfers have never calibrated their monitors or created profiles for them, so it's a rather specious feature except in tightly controlled web environments.

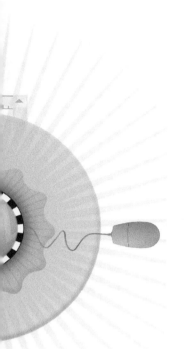

10

Import and Export

Image Import

Image Types   Images can be loosely divided into two types:

- bitmap (raster) images
- vector images

In professional publishing, bitmaps can be saved as TIFF or EPS files; vector images are always saved as EPS files. EPS files can contain either type of image or a combination of both. Other formats can be used if necessary, though converting these to either TIFF or EPS will decrease the likelihood of problems when the document is printed.

InDesign can import the following types of images, along with PDF files which may already contain them, as shown in Table 10–1.

Table 10-1   Image types that can be imported.

Vector	Bitmap	
EPS	TIFF	JPEG
Windows WMF	EPS	Scitex CT
	DCS EPS	Macintosh PICT
	BMP	PCX
	GIF	PNG

Vector EPS files usually come from illustration programs like Illustrator, Freehand, Canvas, and Corel Draw. TIFF and bitmapped EPS files usually come from image-editing programs like Photoshop. Scitex CT files are produced by high-end Scitex imaging workstations. DCS EPS files are similar to regular EPS files except that DCS (Desktop Color Separation) files are preseparated when they are exported from the originating application. Ask your printer if DCS files are preferred, since they usually process more quickly than plain EPS files. You cannot use DCS files for a composite PDF file; you'll only see the black separation of the file in the resulting PDF.

Table 10–2 summarizes key information about the major file formats. PDF/X is a proposed extension to PDF that is more attuned to high-end printing.

Table 10-2   Comparison of file formats.

	Vector	Raster	Composite	Separate CMYK	Embed Fonts	Editability	Preflight Capable
User Program	Yes	Some	Yes	Yes	No	Yes	Yes
PostScript	Yes	Yes	Yes	Yes	Yes	Some	Some
EPS	Yes	No (1)	Yes	Yes	Some	No	Some
DCS	Yes	Yes	No	Yes	Yes	No	No
PDF	Yes	Yes	Yes	Yes	Yes	Yes	Yes
PDF/X	Yes	Yes	Yes	Yes	Yes	Yes	Yes
TIFF/IT	No	Yes	Yes	No	Yes	No	No

(1) Sometimes raster, as in DCS.

Deciding whether to save a bitmapped image as a TIFF, EPS, or native Photoshop file depends on a few factors. If you have created a clipping path in Photoshop, you can use any of these formats because InDesign will recognize embedded clipping paths in them. However, if you need to regularly support older page layout applications, you'll need to save Photoshop files as either TIFF or, preferably, EPS. QuarkXPress 3.3 only supports clipping paths in EPS files, and many people still use QuarkXPress 3.3, so for maximum compatibility with the rest of the world, save images with clipping paths as EPS. QuarkXPress 4.0 and PageMaker 6.5 also support TIFF images with clipping paths, though the Windows version of PageMaker 6.5 won't display them properly.

Leaving images in the native Photoshop format has a few advantages: you don't have to keep saving out flattened TIFF or EPS copies of the image, and you only need to maintain one file. The downside is that complex images with many layers tend to create enormous files, and you'll have to send the whole file along with an InDesign document. A flattened TIFF or EPS version of the same file will usually be a lot smaller. InDesign is currently the only application that can place a native Photoshop file.

Photoshop monotones, duotones, tritones, and quadtones must be saved as EPS. Any native Photoshop files that have had spot-color channels defined must be saved as DCS EPS files because InDesign won't import spot color channels from these files.

DCS EPS is a special format for EPS invented years ago by Quark to support CMYK printing from QuarkXPress 2.0, which could not separate anything by itself. A DCS file consists of a master EPS image file and four or more preseparated CMYK files, plus files for any designated spot colors. Photoshop lets you export a CMYK image as single- or multiple-file DCS, and the choice of single- or multiple-file format is really up to you and your service provider. Single-file gets you one giant EPS with all of the separations embedded in it; multiple-file gets you a smaller EPS along with a separation file for each process and spot color. Some imaging equipment still requires multiple-file DCS, so always ask if in doubt. There's really no need to use DCS anymore for CMYK images, but you must use it for getting spot or Hexachrome color channels out of Photoshop and into anything else. CMYK images can be saved in TIFF, EPS, or DCS format with no difference in the final quality of the image. You cannot create a composite PDF, EPS, or SEP file from an InDesign document that contains placed DCS images—DCS is only intended for a preseparated workflow.

TIFF files have evolved quite a bit since the mid-80s when the format was introduced. TIFF files can contain monochrome (the so-called bitmap mode in Photoshop, which really should be called "line art"), gray-scale, RGB, CMYK, or LAB image data. They can be saved uncompressed, with JPEG "lossy" compression, or with LZW "lossless" compression. You usually don't see a huge compression factor with LZW compression except with monochrome line art. TIFF files can also contain clipping paths, OPI comments, and alpha channels, which are masks created in Photoshop. InDesign supports OPI comments in TIFF files, but it can't use alpha channels, so if you make masks in Photoshop, you'll need to create clipping paths from them. InDesign will place TIFFs regardless of any applied compression, though it may take longer to place compressed TIFFs and print documents containing them.

Scitex CT (for ConTone, or continuous tone) images are similar to bitmapped EPS files and are generated by very expensive and increasingly obsolete Scitex color imaging workstations. There are millions of archived images in the CT format. The other Scitex image format, LW (LineWork, which is the same as line art and rasterized type) is not supported by InDesign.

PICT, PCX, GIF, PNG, and BMP aren't well suited for quality printing. Files in these formats are typically low-resolution, low-color bitmap files that will print poorly. If you want to use them in a layout that will be printed, open them in Photoshop and convert them to TIFF before using them in an InDesign document. They're well suited for use in a web page, and InDesign will always convert these and any other images to GIF or JPEG when exporting a document to HTML.

Always convert WMF files to EPS before attempting to use them for professional publishing. Freehand can open and convert WMF to EPS on either platform; Illustrator can only do this on a Windows machine. InDesign supports only vector data in WMF files, even though they can contain bitmap data too. Unconverted WMFs will print poorly or not at all.

JPEG images can be used directly in an InDesign document. JPEG is a highly compressed image format that achieves its some-times-spectacular compression levels by discarding portions of the image that the compression routine considers to be expendable. This is called lossy compression. Lossless compression, such as an LZW-compressed TIFF, preserves all of the image data. People who use JPEG images for printed material are sometimes unpleas-antly surprised when compression artifacts (unacceptable mottling and patterning that appear especially across areas of flat color and around edges) appear in the printed piece. The higher the level of compression, the more data discarded from the image, and the arti-facts will become more and more pronounced. JPEG images can also cause problems at the print shop because not all prepress imag-ing systems can successfully color-separate them. The shop may have to convert all JPEGs into TIFF or EPS files, and you'll have to pay for their time.

Converting a JPEG image to another format does not eliminate compression artifacts; it merely makes the file more easily printed. You can use JPEG encoding within an EPS or DCS file, which isn't the same as saving a JPEG file right out of Photoshop. However, both types of JPEG files support RGB, CMYK, and gray scale and can include clipping paths. It's really up to you and your printer to evaluate whether JPEG can be used successfully in your workflow.

Color Issues   A lot of time and money is wasted when a job arrives at a printer and the prepress operator discovers that the job is essentially unprintable as-is because the images and colors are not set up properly. Expensive rework is required to get the job on the press.

Here are a few pointers on preparing your files before sending them to the printer.

- If your job is printed with just black (or any single ink), use gray-scale or line-art TIFFs and create vector art with only black and tints of black.
- If your job is printed with spot colors (including black), make sure that the spot color names in all programs used to create the project are identical. If not, InDesign will treat misnamed colors as separate spot colors. Your two-color job may suddenly become a four-color job because InDesign can't differentiate between PANTONE 116 CVC and PANTONE 116 CVU. Don't use PANTONE Process Black for black in an illustration program, because you can't edit black in InDesign and you'll have to change it back to plain old black in the originating program—to InDesign, it is just another spot color. TIFF images in spot color jobs should be saved as gray-scale or line art and then colored in InDesign, or you can create duotones of black and/or spot color inks in Photoshop. You can use up to four inks with Photoshop duotones. Watch the color names! Photoshop 5 allows the use of spot color in images without the need to create duotones.
- If your job is to be printed in four-color process, spot colors must be converted to process colors before printing; otherwise you'll end up with extra separations and a whopping bill. If you plan to use both spot and process colors in a job, convert all named colors to process except for the ones that will print as spot separations.
- InDesign imports any named spot colors in EPS files (including Photoshop duotone files). If you import EPS files and any colors appear in the Colors panel, and if you need to print the job in four-color process, you should convert the colors to process in the original application (or convert a Photoshop duotone to RGB or CMYK) and export it again. After you update the image in InDesign, you can delete the spot colors

from the Colors panel. InDesign can be set to convert all imported or native spot, LAB, and RGB colors to CMYK, but the results may not match what you expected.

- Be very wary of enlarging bitmapped images (TIFF or EPS) in InDesign. The image quality degrades, and it will become pixelated at enlargements much over 110%. Always try to scan or create bitmapped images at the actual size you plan to use. Alternatively, if you don't know what the final size will be, you can oversample an image when scanning or creating it; that is, use a higher resolution. Typically, images are scanned at twice the value of the lines per inch (lpi) screen ruling that will be used in the printed piece. If your job will be printed at 150 lpi, you should use a 300 dpi resolution. If you aren't sure about the final size or screen ruling, you can scan it at a higher resolution, and when you decide on the size, you can reduce or enlarge the image in Photoshop and then downsample it to the optimum resolution.

  Always try to use the optimum resolution. If you reduce a 300 dpi image to 50%, it becomes a 600 dpi image, and will take much longer to print than it would at 300 dpi without any increase in quality. Similarly, a 300 dpi image enlarged 200% becomes a 150 dpi image and will look terrible when printed.

  An exception to the dpi = 2 x lpi rule is scanned line art, which is always black-and-white. Because this type of artwork is usually very sharp and detailed and is not generally converted to a halftone when imaged, it should be scanned at a very high resolution of at least 1200 dpi. The same warnings about enlargement and reduction apply to high-resolution line art.

- InDesign can convert RGB images to CMYK when you print separations, but this will almost always result in a final image that may look quite different from the original RGB image. Unless you've implemented a color management system, you might always want to convert RGB images to CMYK (or gray scale or duotone, depending on your print process) before you import them. That way you can see for yourself how much the image's colors might change, and you can make any needed adjustments in the image's original application. The same applies to non-CMYK colors defined in illustration programs and in InDesign. Always define colors according to the printing process used:

- spot
- four-color process

A printer will charge you extra to make these conversions, and you may have little control over any necessary color correction.

Placing Images in InDesign

Place vs. Drag-and-Drop and Paste   InDesign lets you drag and drop, or paste in artwork in from Illustrator and Freehand. Such artwork does not show up in the Links panel (coming up real soon now) and can't be updated if it's changed in the original application. Once you drag and drop something in from Illustrator or Freehand, it becomes a native InDesign object. This can be useful if you need to edit the art to fit a particular layout or solve a design problem or if you want InDesign to color-manage the artwork. You can't drag and drop gradients from Illustrator; they'll show up as solid black objects. If the dragged-and-dropped art is complicated, it can take forever for InDesign to parse and evaluate the art, and you might even think your computer has crashed on you since it will seem to stall while InDesign digests the artwork. If you want to use this method, keep the artwork simple.

Placing   Placing artwork and images is a time-honored tradition, started in the heady Elysian days of PageMaker version 1.0 (way back in 1985) when about the only things available to place were awful low-quality MacPaint doodlings. Placed items can't be modified, which in most cases is desirable, and they can be updated automatically if you like whenever there's been a change.

You can place items two ways: by using the Place command (File ➧ Place, or Command/Control + D), or by dragging a file's icon from an open desktop window into an open InDesign document. You lose the Import Options settings if you fling an image onto a page in this manner. Placing an image is ridiculously easy. You don't need to select or create a frame before placing an image, but if you've already done so, selecting the frame prior to placing targets that frame to receive the image. If you just plop the image onto a page, a new frame is created that is defined by the object's boundaries.

To place, select (or don't select) a frame, then press Command/Control + D. A file dialog appears that's more or less the same on both Windows and Macintosh computers. On a Macintosh, all file types, whether text, art, or image, that InDesign knows how to import will be listed, and you can opt for a preview of the content (as much as InDesign can display, given a file's type)—Figure 10–1. On Windows, you can also choose to list only files of a particular type from the Files of Type pop-up menu in the Place dialog, but there's no preview option (Figure 10–2).

Figure 10–1
Macintosh Place dialog.

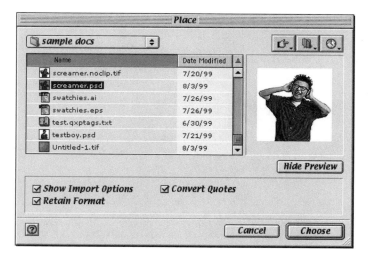

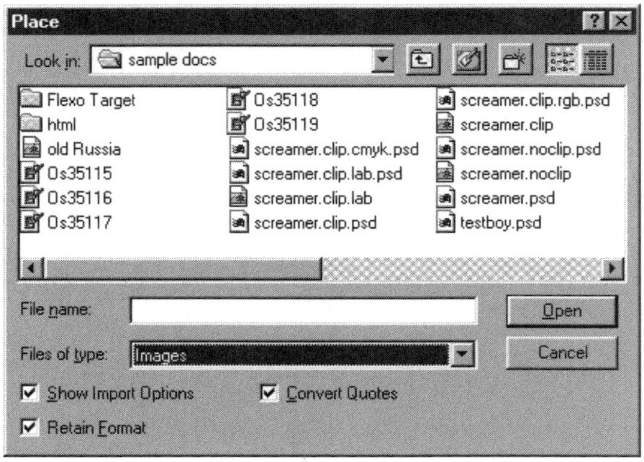

Figure 10–2
Windows Place dialog.

Both platforms show a checkbox for Show Import Options. This is an innocuous-seeming checkbox that presents assorted options depending on the type of image you're placing. You can also get to the Import Options by holding Shift while you choose a file. For a TIFF or other bitmap image, the Import Options are shown in two parts.

The first part shown in Figure 10–3, lets you set clipping path creation options and the resolution of the proxy image, shown if you have Display Proxy Images chosen in the Preferences. A lower resolution here provides faster screen updates, but it looks terrible.

Figure 10–3
Image Import Options—Image Settings.

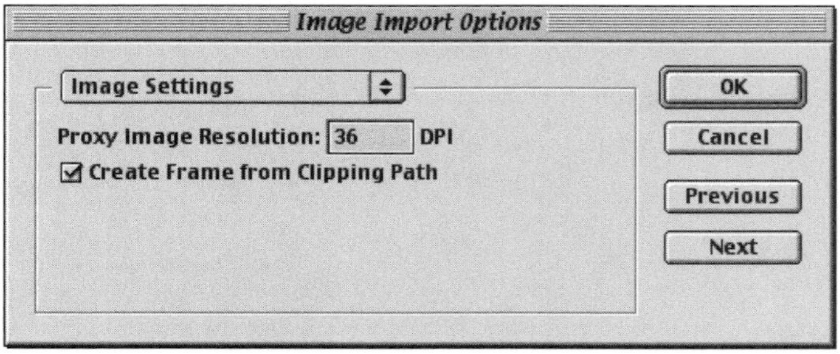

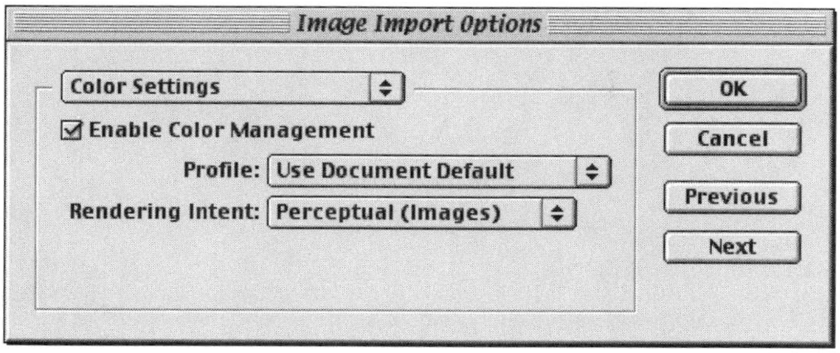

Figure 10–4
Page Image Import Options—Color Settings.

Remember that color-managed images are only shown in simulation of a separations device if you choose Full Resolution image preview.

Create Frame from Clipping Path was discussed in the Frames chapter, but recall that if an image contains a clipping path and you don't select this option, the clipping path is completely ignored.

The second part of the Import Options for bitmapped images, shown in Figure 10–4, is concerned with color management. Click Next or choose *Color Settings* from the pop-up menu to show this part of the Import Options.

Here's where you can set color management options for images as they are placed. You can of course change these later. EPS files, whether vector, bitmapped, or DCS, will present a different Import Options dialog. shown in Figure 10–5.

OPI (Open Prepress Interface, sometimes called APR, or Automatic Picture Replacement) links are instructions or comments in a file that tell another application to substitute high-resolution

Figure 10–5
EPS Import Options.

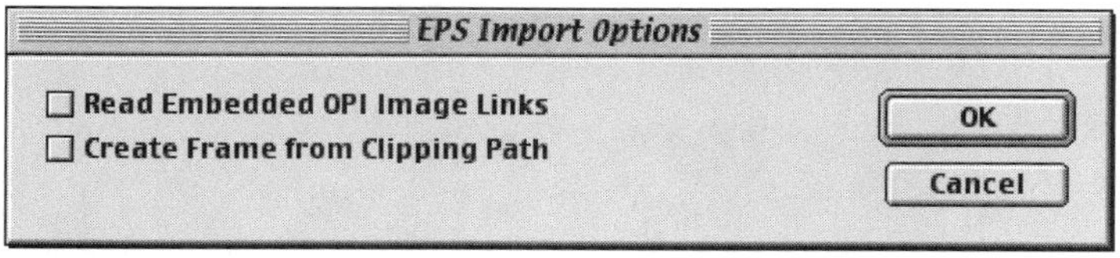

images for low-resolution proxies that are created from the high-resolution files. The proxies are given to the designer, and the large, high-resolution images are kept on a fast file server that is directly connected to an imaging device. This really speeds up printing of documents with large bitmapped images, but in most cases you won't be using this unless you are imaging documents to an imagesetter or platesetter. OPI requires the use of a file server and specialized software, which few end users will have.

If your service provider has given you low-resolution proxy images from scans they have made and you have placed any of these in an EPS file, then you should deselect this option because you want their server to manage any image replacement at imaging time. If you are doing your own OPI image replacement, choose this option to let InDesign manage this process, but leave it off to let the server handle it. Select it if the EPS file contains OPI comments but does not contain the proxy image, so InDesign can locate and replace the image at print time.

The Create Frame from Clipping Path option works only with bitmapped EPS images from Photoshop that contain clipping paths, even though it presents itself when placing vector EPS files from Illustrator or other programs. Choosing this option with a vector EPS has absolutely no effect.

InDesign parses all placed EPS files and scans for any missing fonts; if the file contains PostScript errors or missing fonts, you're told about this when you try to import the file, rather than at the end of the process when you or someone else is trying to get the document separated on an expensive piece of equipment. Load the missing fonts before trying to print the file. PostScript errors in EPS files can be very tedious and tiresome; sometimes regenerating the EPS file from the original application can fix the problem.

Placing, Part Deux   If you selected a frame prior to placing an image, the image is placed into it once you choose it in the Place dialog and make any needed settings to its options. If you didn't select a frame beforehand, once you choose a file for placement, your cursor will change to one of two "loaded" pointers. Do not point a loaded pointer at anyone. If your pointer is not over a frame, it looks like this

PDF Security Password

This document is password-protected.   [OK]

Enter password: [   ]   [Cancel]

Figure 10–6
Entering a security password.

📝 , and you can click anywhere to place the image in a new frame defined by the image's bounds. If you move the pointer over a frame, it changes to this 📝 , and clicking it over an empty frame places the image in that frame.

Placing PDF Files   This works a bit differently from placing images. Because PDF files can contain multiple pages and also can be password-protected, the steps involved differ quite a bit from the usual file placement. To place a PDF, choose the *Place* command and select the file from the Place dialog. You should usually choose the *Import Options* when placing a PDF because the default settings are to place the first page of a PDF with a Content crop.

If someone's put a password in the PDF file, you'll be asked to enter it first thing (Figure 10–6).

Passwords are displayed as you type them, so make sure there aren't any shifty characters looking over your shoulder when you enter a password.

The Import Options for PDF files are shown in Figure 10–7.

Figure 10–7
Place PDF dialog box.

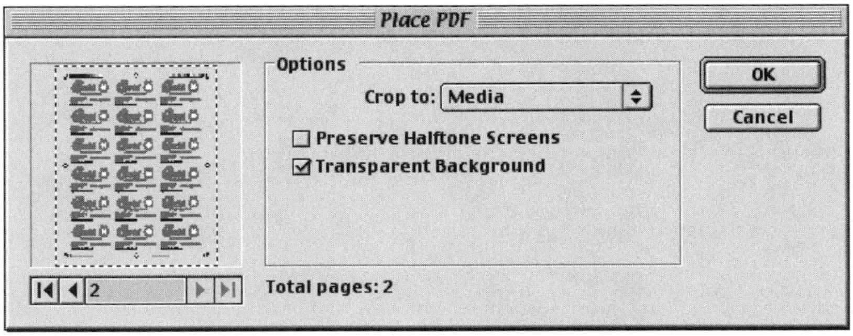

Place PDF

Options

Crop to: [Media   ▼]   [OK]
[Cancel]

☐ Preserve Halftone Screens
☑ Transparent Background

|◀ ◀ 2   ▶ ▶| Total pages: 2

First, select the appropriate page. Then choose what sort of crop you want. There are a few choices on the Crop pop-up menu (Figure 10–8).

Generally, if the PDF is saved with printer's marks, you want to choose the Media option. You can use the other choices to crop a PDF file in several ways.

- Content crop uses the actual image bounds.
- Art crop uses an author-defined image area.
- Crop, er, crop uses the area that would be displayed by Acrobat if you opened the document in Acrobat.
- Trim crop uses any printer's marks present in the file to crop the image to the page trim set in the original document.
- Bleed crop uses any bleed marks present in the file to crop the image to the bleed size specified in the original document. Not all programs include bleed marks in output, but InDesign can.
- Media crop throws everything into the crop if the page has printer's marks on it.

Then, set the remaining place options.

- Preserve Halftone Screens—You usually don't want to override halftone screens, but you can choose to do so. By preserving them, you will cause InDesign to use any predefined halftone screen rulings in the PDF and to ignore any that you set in the Print dialog.
- Transparent Background treats the PDF like an image with a clipping path. Anything behind the placed PDF will be visible in nonimage areas. Deselect this to make the background white, or you can add a fill to the containing frame of the PDF later on.

Figure 10–8
Crop pop-up menu.

The Crop settings are a little bit of overkill since you can always crop any image by adjusting its frame, but there they are. Once you've made your settings, you get a special PDF Placement Pointer (patent pending) which looks like this ⬚ if your pointer isn't over a frame, and like this ⬚ if it is. Place the file as you would any other image.

Linked Images

Once you place an image or a text file, it is listed in the InDesign Link panel. If the image changes or is missing, you'll see a warning to that effect in the Links panel, or you'll get a similar warning on opening a document that contains updated or missing images. Text files offer similar linking features.

The Links panel is analogous to the QuarkXPress Picture Usage dialog and to the PageMaker Link Info dialog, although, unlike either, you can have it open all the time.

Embedded Images   InDesign won't embed anything in a document file that's larger than 48K in size. You have the option, as you have in PageMaker, of embedding any image (up to 48K) in the document file, which is not really such a good idea. Link it rather than embed it.

Enormous PageMaker and InDesign documents with embedded images can and usually will cause all sorts of trouble when such a file is sent off for printing, especially if the images weren't prepared properly for color separation. Once a file is embedded into an InDesign document, you can't extract it for further alteration.

You can extract embedded images from PageMaker documents, but it's a pain. Just don't embed anything, and printers will remain your friend. The only way to alter an embedded image is to delete it and place it again from a file. Once a file is embedded, it is removed from the Links panel and you can't automatically update it.

The Links Panel   Press Command/Control + Shift + D to pop open the Links panel (Figure 10–9).

All linked images are shown here with their location ("PB" means it's on the pasteboard), status, and file name. If a link shows the "changed" icon, a little yellow triangle with an exclamation mark in it, that means the file's modification date has changed, which is how InDesign keeps track of such things. A broken link means that some devious person has moved the image from its original location or deleted it. If the image is up-to-date and in the right place, then there won't be any little mystery icons in the link entry.

OPI links within a placed EPS file will also be listed in the Links panel, but the Links entries don't discriminate between these and placed images within a document. Never mess around with OPI links. If you need to relink the EPS to another image, you need to do it in the originating application. Relinking or changing the link information within InDesign will probably cause problems when printing. OPI information is there to let you know that there are image links that you might otherwise not know about.

To display a linked image's information, just double-click on its entry in the Links panel to present the dialog shown in Figure 10–10.

Figure 10–9
Links panel.

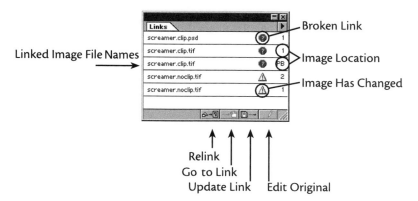

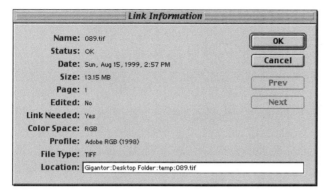

Figure 10–10
Link Information dialog box.

The Link Information box is pretty handy for checking an image's type, color space, and applied ICC profile, if any. The Link Needed bit will always be set to Yes if the image is over 48K in size.

The box also shows the directory path in which the image resides. Macintosh users might be surprised to see such a thing, but it's here, although you can't edit the path here. If you hold Option/Alt while double-clicking a link entry, InDesign zips right to the page where the image was placed, which is like the Show function in the QuarkXPress Picture Usage dialog. If an image needs to be updated, select it in the Links panel and click the Update button, or pick *Update Link* from the Links panel menu, shown in Figure 10–11.

If you update an image or, especially, relink to another, InDesign will preserve any modifications to the image and its frame, so if

Figure 10–11
Links panel menu.

you've scaled or rotated the original image, the replacement will retain the modifications, so you might get some ugly results if the replacement image is much different from the original.

You use the Relink button or the menu to reestablish a link to an image that has been moved to another location. Doing this presents the Relink dialog, shown in Figure 10–12.

You can type in a new path or click the Browse button to bring up a standard file selector dialog. It's unclear why Adobe put in this old DOS-like ability to directly edit a file's path, especially in the Mac version since no Mac application other than programming tools has ever allowed such intimacy with the operating system. But there it is, and if you know the exact path and file name, it might be faster to type it in rather than browsing about for it.

To relink or update everything Shift + Click on every link entry in the panel or deselect all entries by clicking around at the bottom of the panel where there aren't any entries. Choose either *Relink* or *Update*, and you're in business. If you choose Relink, you'll see a Relink dialog for each image that requires relinking, and you can click the Skip button to go to the next entry.

Links break easily if anything gets moved around, and this usually happens when you move an entire job from one computer to another. QuarkXPress offers the handy capability to relink everything as soon as you've located one image in a directory or folder that contains the rest of the missing images. PageMaker sorely lacked this ability. Unfortunately, the Windows version of InDesign won't do this for you, but the Mac version will. Relink one of the missing images manually, then Shift + Click the rest of the broken entries and choose *Relink*. All of the broken links will be magically restored. Linked

Figure 10–12
Relink dialog box.

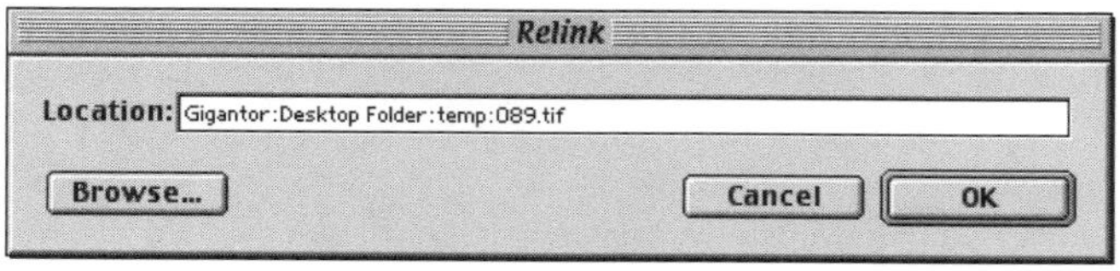

PDF files have their own special set of issues. If any of the following change in the original PDF file, the link can be broken and you'll have to place the file again:

- Pages are added, removed, or otherwise shuffled in the original PDF file.
- The original file's security settings are changed.

You can tell if a PDF link is broken because the placed page changes to a gray box in an InDesign document.

File Export

There are a number of ways of getting pages and documents out of InDesign and into a common format that can be read by just about anything. InDesign can export the following file formats directly.

- EPS—These can be placed into other applications and opened as editable art in Illustrator, but they probably can't be opened and edited in Freehand or other illustration applications. These files can also be rendered into bitmaps by Photoshop. EPS allows only one page at a time, but multiple pages can be exported as individual EPS files.
- PostScript .ps "dump"—Some service providers still prefer that clients give them a PostScript file that includes all fonts and images used in a document. This usually results in huge monolithic files that have a distinct disadvantage: they cannot be edited without some serious PostScript programming knowledge, and they are device-dependent because you must choose a destination device and its characteristics before saving as PostScript.
- The so-called Prepress .sep file—This is another PostScript file format that removes device dependencies and is usually intended for intake by another application for prepress functions like trapping and imposition.

- PDF—You don't need Acrobat Distiller to create PDF files from InDesign documents, but you need Acrobat to add any of the features supported in PDF but not in InDesign, such as annotations, multimedia objects, hyperlinks, and so forth.
- HTML—InDesign exports a single HTML file for each document and converts any images to web-friendly image formats. The results are surprisingly good if you use the Cascading Style Sheet format (CSS1) option, which is supported in most current web browsers. This is the only way, short of distributing on-line PDF, of preserving the basic layout of a page. Ordinary HTML without style sheets looks pretty plain, and CSS1 is designed such that older browsers that do not support it will not "break" or otherwise freak out, so it's probably advantageous to use CSS1 formatting.

PostScript Export This is performed in the Print dialog, so we'll cover it there.

EPS and Prepress Export This is probably the simplest export format for InDesign files. If you select multiple pages for EPS export, they'll have "_1, _2. . . . _n" appended to the file name, before the .eps extension.

To export one or more pages, open the document and choose File ➡ Export or press Command/Control + E. Name the file and add ".eps" or ".sep" to the end. InDesign will not automatically add the correct extension to the exported file, and in fact the wrong extension might be presented in the export dialog if the last export you performed used a different file format such as PDF.

The initial export dialog is shown in Figure 10–13.

Choose the file type from the Formats (Macintosh) or Save as Type (Windows) pop-up menu. The export dialog for these two formats is very similar, except that you don't get the option to add printer's marks in an EPS export, and you can't export as reader spreads (facing pages) with EPS, which only does one page at a time.

Figure 10–13
Export dialog box.

However, you will probably never export reader spreads for a pre-press file, because typically this is going to be processed by an imposition program and reader spreads will be the last thing you want in such a file.

Click Save to proceed to the Export Options dialog, which has two parts: one for page selection (and printer's marks, if exporting to .sep) and one for export settings. The example here will use the .sep prepress format.

Prepress or EPS options are shown first (Figure 10–14). There are a lot of choices to make here, and some of them can have a pretty profound effect on the results. These choices are the same for both prepress and EPS.

- Encoding—Your choices are ASCII or binary. In most cases, binary is the better choice because it produces smaller files. However, there are certain network setups and older printers that have trouble with binary files. You probably already know if this applies to you, but in most cases you can export with binary encoding. This issue is only a potential on Microsoft or Novell network setups, and ASCII encoding is not necessary for a Macintosh workflow. If your network is based on TCP/IP or AppleTalk, you can use binary encoding.

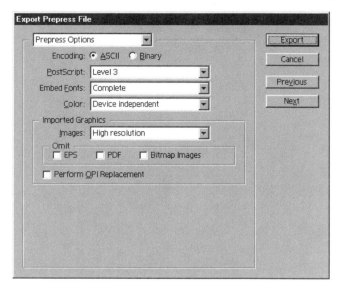

Figure 10-14
Prepress options dialog box.

Some companies won't allow you to embed their fonts into any type of file. Adobe lets you embed fonts into PDF and other formats without requiring that any recipients of the file purchase the font, but some others, like Emigré, don't unless everyone who reads or processes the file has purchased the font, which is pretty harsh. Read the license agreement that comes with the font to see if there are any restrictions on embedding.

Even though many prepress functions are being performed more and more with Windows computers, in a shop environment TCP/IP and AppleTalk are usually used if there are Macs networked. If in doubt, choose ASCII. It'll work on anything but makes bigger files.

- PostScript—Unless you know for certain that the final imaging device is running a specific PostScript level, you might want to leave this at the Level 1, 2, and 3 Compatible setting, which will ensure that the exported file will process correctly on almost any imaging equipment. Most current equipment, such as imagesetters and platesetters, uses Level 2, but some postprocessing applications that interpret PostScript data, such as TrapWise, are still only at Level 1. Using color management requires either a Level 2 or Level 3 imaging device.

- Embed Fonts—This should *always* be set to either Complete or Subset—don't set it to None unless you know in fact that the fonts will be available on the final imaging device. Complete will dump a copy of the entire font file into the exported file, even if there's only a single character in the document that uses that font. Subset only embeds the actual characters used in the document, which isn't all that big of a deal now. However, when OpenType fonts with multiple character sets become available, they're likely to be huge, so it makes sense to only include font data for characters that are actually needed. Embedding fonts is the one sure way of getting your document to someone else with all the fonts intact. The quickest way to halt production on a print job is to give someone all of your files but forget to include the fonts, sending the recipient on a mad chase to hunt down either you or the missing fonts. (See Chapter 11 "Preflight and Package," for another method of delivering documents to a printer or other service provider.)

- Color—Choose a destination color space for the exported file. All images will be converted to the specified space. Typically, you'll choose CMYK for printed work and RGB for display work, unless you are going to use an in-RIP separation system. RGB images are converted to CMYK with color management if you've enabled it in the document; otherwise, a generic RGB ➡ CMYK conversion is used. Any spot colors are preserved as such; if you want to convert spot colors to process, you need to do it before exporting the document. Device Independent color is only an option if you've enabled color management in the document and have chosen a Level 2 or Level 3 in the PostScript options. Color space changes can't be made to placed PDF files, so if you need to convert RGB images in a placed PDF, you need to do this in the original document from which the PDF was generated, unless you have enabled color management (correctly!) and have in-RIP separation capability.

- Images—In most cases, you'll want to have this set to High Resolution, which passes the image through unchanged. Low Resolution can be used if you are running an OPI system and don't want to use the Omit option, which results in gray boxes representing the omitted images. This is handy for files that require further editing.

Due to a bug in Macromedia's Fontographer program, used by many typeface designers, InDesign and Distiller may report that a TrueType font's embedding tag prohibits the embedding of the font in a PDF file. This is erroneous in most cases, but there's nothing you can do to change the fact except replace the font with a corrected version or manually alter the tag with a font editing program, such as the one Microsoft has made available on its web site, located at http://www.microsoft.com/typography/property/fpedit.htm. This program only works under Windows.

- Omit—Lets you omit any or all types of images for use in an OPI workflow. Nobody supports OPI replacement of PDF files, though the option is there should some enterprising programmer somewhere out there decide that the world really, really needs a PDF OPI replacement system. Hey, it could happen.
- Perform OPI Replacement—Use this if you want the resulting export file to contain complete, high-resolution images. If the file is to be processed through an OPI system, you probably don't want InDesign to do this, so turn it off. If the document contains small, basic TIFF and EPS files, then there's really no point in using OPI at all since the time savings will be minimal, so you can turn this option on for such documents with relatively little personal risk to your health or financial situation. If you do not use an OPI system, don't care, or aren't sure of where this exported file will end up, you should leave this option turned on to ensure that the entire job is exported at full resolution. If the placed images are low-resolution proxies with embedded OPI comments in them, you need to have all of the high-resolution images available to InDesign for this to work; otherwise, InDesign just maintains the OPI links and exports the proxy image.

Page Options (Figure 10–15) are accessed by clicking the Next button or choosing Pages from the pop-up menu at the top of the dialog.

You can choose all pages, a range of pages, or specific sections defined by section markers for export. To specify a range, use a hyphen for consecutive pages and a comma for nonconsecutive pages. For example, to export pages 2 through 14, and also 17, 19, and 22, you'd enter "2-14, 17, 19, 22" in the Page Range field. If you have defined sections in the document, they will be listed in the Sections field. To specify a bleed area, enter it in the Bleed field.

If you're exporting to EPS, the Reader Spreads and Page Marks options won't be available to you. A prepress export will include all of the specified pages in one file, but an EPS export will create one EPS file for each page specified.

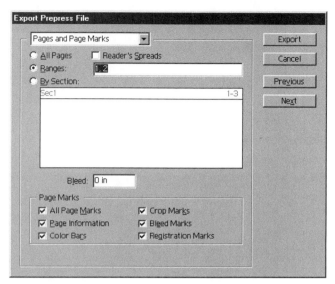

Figure 10–15
Page Options dialog box.

HTML Export   E-commerce is growing rapidly on the web, and prognosticators say HTML, and even XML, will be the great enabling approach that will spur the growth of the on-line world.

HTML Programming   Once the information is compiled, it has to be expressed as HTML documents so a web browser can interpret it. The Hypertext Markup Language is designed to specify the logical organization of a document, with important hypertext extensions. HTML allows you to mark titles or paragraphs and then leaves the interpretation of these marked elements up to the browser. One browser may indent the beginning of a paragraph, while another may leave a blank line instead.

HTML documents are made up of a hierarchy of elements. These can be divided into two broad categories—those that define the structure of the body of the document and those that define information about the document, such as the title or relationships to other documents. Elements are denoted by the tag <element_name>.

This is simply the element name surrounded by left and right angle brackets. Most elements mark blocks of document content for a particular purpose or for formatting: the <element_name> tag marks the beginning of such a section. HTML documents are structured into two parts, the head and the body. The head contains information about the document that is not generally displayed with the document, such as its title. The body contains the body of the text.

The Hypertext Markup Language (HTML) is a variant of the Standardized General Markup Language (SGML) developed to provide an application- and platform-independent means of creating, managing, and maintaining documents. HTML lacks many of the typographical features of InDesign, SGML, and more recent markup languages like Extensible Markup Language (XML).

There have been a number of iterations of HTML, all more or less downward compatible with earlier versions, but none begin to approach even the meanest word processor's text composition abilities. Hyphenation goes out the window, justification methods are crude, and so forth, so don't expect that your carefully designed InDesign document will ever look the same in HTML and viewed with a web browser.

In fact, the more you try to force HTML to behave like something it isn't, the greater the chances that it will not display correctly, or even at all, in every possible browser that a reader might choose to employ. While Microsoft and Netscape browsers are the most commonly used, they aren't the only ones.

If you must have your document appear to a reader exactly as designed, then you should not be using HTML. Export the document as a PDF file. Only then can you provide a format that nearly anyone can view and print. You can distribute PDF over the Internet easily enough, and anyone can download the Acrobat reader application for free from Adobe's web site.

This is not going to be an HTML tutorial, by the way, but the following is presented as a public service.

Broudy/Romano Basic Web Rules To Live By:

- Keep images to a minimum. Unless your pages are going on an intranet, you have no idea how fast or slow a reader's Internet connection is. Big images, lots of images = slow speed, even with some of the fancy new cable modems.

- Don't force text sizes and colors on readers. You don't know if a potential reader is color-blind, terribly nearsighted, or otherwise has trouble reading certain types of text. Some sites force such a small text size that even people with normal vision can't read it.

- For the same reasons, keep frames to a minimum, and make them user-adjustable.

- Don't force a specific screen size. It's annoying to see that the right margin of a page has disappeared off the screen, with no way to see it. Such pages can't be printed properly, either.

- Avoid heavy reliance on plug-ins. It's pretty frustrating to hit a site that requires you to locate, download, and install some bit of software that often behaves like it was coded by a squirrel with a bad methamphetamine habit.

- Likewise, if you're going to use the Java programming language, then use it effectively, and code it right. Half the sites out there that blare "Java-capable browser required!!" don't even offer anything that requires it, and there are far too many sites with badly-coded, amateurish applets that end up crashing the viewer's browser.

- Even though you can specify fonts with CSS1 and some special HTML tags, it's not a reader-friendly thing to do. It's a little rude, in fact. If a viewer has set his or her browser to use a specific font and font size that they like or that is the only one they can read comfortably, then you shouldn't mess around with it by specifying something else.

- With that last bit in mind, repeat this passage to yourself, over and over, until it sinks in: "The web is not print. I do not have complete control over another person's computer and browser, no matter how much I want to have it, so I might as well not force the issue, which would make other people mad at me." Of course, most people will ignore this. <shrug>. Can't blame them—CSS1 is pretty slick.

Once you export an InDesign document as HTML, you can't do anything further with it using InDesign except maybe export the original document again if you need to make changes. You'll need an HTML editor or a plain text editor to make any further changes to an exported InDesign HTML file.

To export a document as HTML, press Command/Control + E or choose File ➡ Export. As with the other export formats, you have to add the file extension. Use .html or .htm, depending on your web server's requirements. If the server is UNIX-based, and most are, file names become case sensitive, so if you reference a file by yaddayadda.html in another page and the file is really called BlaBla.html, your reader will get the old 404 Not Found server error message.

Keep file names short, but not so short that you'll forget what they mean. Most servers running UNIX can handle very long file names. Ask your server administrator for any special file-naming restrictions. You might want to create a new folder while you're here, because the export process can potentially generate hundreds of files, so it's easier if you keep them all together.

Click Save to continue to the HTML Export dialog (Figure 10–16).

The first dialog presented wants to know which pages of the document to export. You can choose to have it all mashed into one long HTML file or to have each page saved as a separate HTML file. InDesign will insert little spacer bars between pages if you choose single-file export.

The next dialog (Figure 10–17) asks how to present text.

You can force all colored text to be changed to black or to another predefined color in the color pop-up menu, or you can double-click on the color swatch to bring up a system color picker. If you choose Appearance for nonstandard text, the text will be converted to a bitmapped image.

Nonstandard text includes any text that has been rotated, sheared, scaled, filled with a gradient, or if the text's frame is not rectangular,

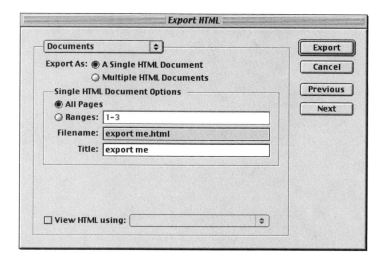

Figure 10–16
Export HTML dialog box.

has been altered, scaled, sheared, rotated, or otherwise is not a plain old rectangular frame with no fill and no stroke. If you choose Maintain Editability, the text is not converted to an image, but you lose all of the fancy attributes. You can also specify a background color

Figure 10–17
Export HTML formatting options.

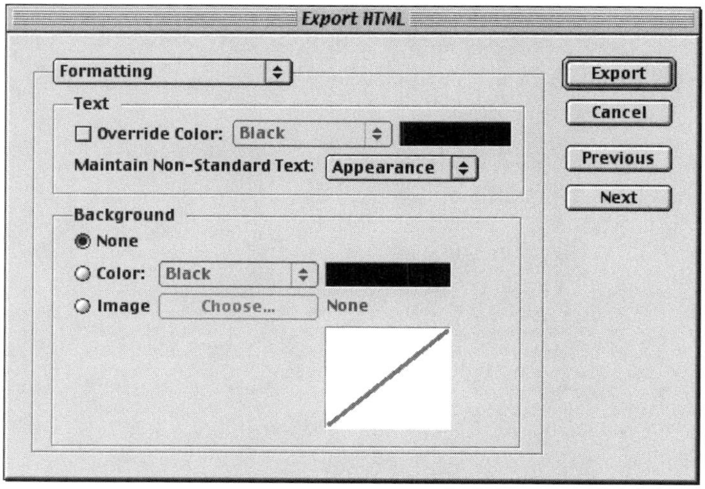

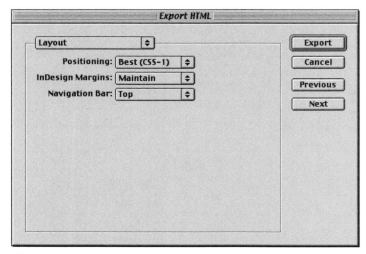

Figure 10–18
Export HTML layout option.

for the exported file, or specify a background image to use. Any background image you specify must already be in GIF or JPEG format.

The Layout options dialog is next (Figure 10–18).

Positioning asks what sort of formatting you want to use.

- Choosing CSS-1 will attempt to preserve as much as possible the layout of your document.

- Choosing None will not generate any CSS1 style sheets, which can be useful if you want to further edit the resulting HTML files with another program.

You have the option of maintaining the document margins, but in the interest of maximum flexibility for viewers, set this to None. Otherwise, you'll be faced with complaints about the right side of the text being cut off in the browser.

If you choose to export a document as multiple HTML files, you can have InDesign insert a very basic hyperlink that acts as a means of moving from one page to another. It's easier than coding this yourself, and you can always modify it later. Choose where you would like to have this appear with the options in the Navigation Bar pop-up menu.

"ppi" stands for "pixels per inch;" you will also see this represented as "dpi" or "dots per inch," which really isn't the same thing. See "Printing Basics" later in this chapter for more information about spots, dots, and pixels than you probably ever wanted to know.

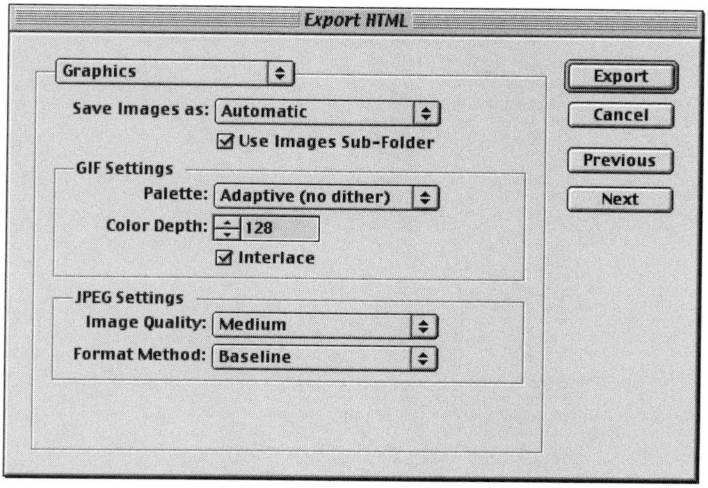

Figure 10–19
Export HTML—Graphics option.

The last dialog (Figure 10–19) asks for what to do with images.

You can either force GIF or JPEG format or trust InDesign to figure out the best format for document images. Typically, JPEG is best for photographs and other continuous-tone graphics and for complex illustrations. GIF is well suited to simple areas of flat colors or tints and for small logos and the like. You really ought to select the Use Images Sub-Folder because otherwise all converted images are dumped into the same directory as the HTML file, which can get pretty messy.

InDesign converts all placed images and illustrations, any artwork created in InDesign, or stuff that you might have dropped in from Illustrator or Freehand to either GIF or JPEG format, unless a placed image is already in GIF or JPEG format. All images are also downsampled to 72 ppi, since there's no benefit to using a higher image resolution on a web page. If an image is already sampled at 72 ppi, and is in GIF or JPEG format, it is passed through the process unchanged.

GIF is limited to 256 colors, making it rather unsuited to photographic images. You can specify a color palette for GIF as well as the color depth. The color palette choices are Adaptive, Exact, and Web.

The Adaptive palette will attempt to recreate as many colors as possible within the chosen color depth without dithering the image. The Exact palette will use the exact colors used in the image but only if it contains 256 colors or fewer, which won't work well for color photographs, and InDesign won't create an exact palette for images with more than 256 colors. Choosing Web will compress the image's color depth to fit within the tiny gamut of the so-called web-safe color space, which only allows 216 colors.

Choosing Interlace will display the image gradually in a browser as it is downloaded from the server.

None of these settings are necessary with JPEG images, which can contain millions of colors. All you need to choose for JPEG is the compression level and display method. For web images, choosing the *Low* setting makes sense since it will create the smallest files, though at the expense of image quality. Choose *Progressive* to have the image display gradually as it is downloaded, or *Baseline* to display the image only after it is loaded. Some older browsers will not display progressive JPEG images correctly.

PDF Export

InDesign exports PDF directly, without requiring the print-to-file then grind-through-Distiller shuffle you have to perform with any other program. The resulting PDF is the same as what you'd get from Distiller 4.0 using the same settings, with one exception: it's likely to be a lot smaller than what Distiller would generate. This is due to a bug in the first release of Distiller 4.0, and should be fixed by the time this book hits the stores. There is also a difference in the way InDesign performs image subsampling from that of Distiller, which we'll get to shortly.

Why Bother?   Well, because exporting to PDF is the easiest way to get your document to people 100 percent intact, even if they don't have InDesign on the other end. PDF has evolved greatly since its initial introduction, when it was intended as a sort of "paperless office" product that would allow people to share documents no matter what program was used to generate them. It's since become much more advanced and is now becoming a primary means of delivering press-ready files to printers.

Some magazines now require advertisers to deliver ads in PDF format because that way there are no loose images, fonts, and other debris floating around with the main layout document, and if pre-pared properly, a PDF will contain every image and font needed to print the job.

It has also become a very popular medium of electronic document distribution, to the point where many companies no longer include a printed manual with a software product but instead provide docu-mentation in the form of PDF files on the product's CD-ROM. Other uses are on-line distribution of documents, such as user guides for various products, and distribution of electronic books or other internal communication.

There are two basic export paths for PDF: on-line and for press. With an on-line PDF that will be distributed over the Internet or included on a CD-ROM, the main concern is with the resulting file size. If you want to make a PDF file from an InDesign document that contains high-resolution bitmapped images, and if you only want to use the PDF file for electronic distribution, on-screen read-ing, and for printout on basic office and home printers, there's no need to bloat the thing with large images. InDesign can *resample* high-resolution images intended for a printing press to a size more appropriate to screen display or for printing on a basic laser or inkjet printer.

A PDF file generated for press will generally not have image downsampling applied because you need the full resolution of the images for correct reproduction. The resulting file can be huge, but because compression can be applied to all images, the final PDF will usually be smaller than a PostScript version of the same document.

PDF files can be edited to some extent with the Acrobat program. While you cannot easily make major text changes in a PDF file, you can usually correct minor typographical errors. A PDF file also exhibits page independence, meaning you can rearrange the pages in Acrobat without worrying about text reflow. A PDF page is an island, so to speak, and can exist on its own.

Resampling of images can be specified in two ways when exporting from InDesign: by average downsampling or by subsampling. Distiller adds a third method, called bicubic downsampling, which is more accurate than the average downsampling method. Let's say you have a 300 ppi image in a document that you want to prepare for online viewing, so the ideal image resolution should be 72 ppi. Here's how resampling works.

- Average downsampling takes the average color level of all the colors in a group of 300 ppi pixels and replaces the group with a single big pixel of the average color. This usually produces pretty good results.
- Subsampling takes the one 300 ppi pixel at the center of a group that would occupy a single 72 ppi pixel, and replaces the entire group with a big version of that pixel. Subsampling will usually produce a more "jaggy" looking image than downsampling will, but it's a lot faster.
- The bicubic downsampling option available in Distiller takes a weighted average to determine the replacement pixel's color and can produce a better downsampled image than the average downsampling method, but to use it, you need to save a file as PostScript and run it through Distiller.

Since resampled images are usually intended for on-screen viewing, your choice of resampling method is probably not going to make a huge amount of difference in the end result. Experimentation is in order to find out which one works the best for your needs.

However, if you need to resample images that are intended for a printing press, you should always use the average downsampling method, or the bicubic method if you are going to use Distiller. This might occur if an image is scanned at a higher resolution than your output device can use effectively. For example, if you scanned an image at 400 ppi but are only printing it at 85 lpi, then the optimum resolution for that image would be 170 ppi.

By downsampling that image, you'll significantly decrease processing time at the imaging device because the excess data in the

400 ppi image is simply thrown away. Excess resolution will also result if you place an image into InDesign and then reduce it. Placing a 300 ppi image and then scaling it 50% will result in an effective resolution of 600 ppi. This will only slow things down at the imaging stage. You can specify a resampling resolution when exporting. This resolution should be at least 1.5 times the screen ruling of the final print job, and preferably two times. If a job is to be printed at a screen ruling of 150 lpi, then your image resolution should be 300 ppi. InDesign won't resample anything if the object's resolution is less than 1.5 times the specified resampling resolution. If these terms aren't familiar, see "Printing Basics" later in this chapter.

Font Issues   You can choose to embed a document's fonts for proper display and printing at another location, even if the recipient doesn't have the fonts. Some font vendors prohibit embedding. You can embed a *subset* of a document's fonts, which means that only the character outlines for those characters actually in the document will be embedded. This has a minor benefit of slightly reducing the final file size, but it has a major benefit because any subset font will have a new, custom name assigned to it, which means that even if the recipient has the same original font loaded, only *your* version will be used for display or printing. This is important because, like any other type of software, digital typefaces are revised on occasion and the metrics and kerning data may change.

If you set a document in an older version of Adobe Minion, then send it to a printer who has a newer version, and if you don't include your fonts with specific instructions to only use your version, then applying the new version might cause your document to reflow or to exhibit different kerning characteristics from those you set in your original document.

By embedding a subset of your font into a PDF file, you ensure that your version is the one used by anyone else. Setting the subset percentage to 100% is recommended. Setting it much below that might cause problems later if a particular character's outline is missing from the resulting PDF; then if it later turns out that you need it to fix a typo prior to printing, you can't do it. If you don't embed any fonts and the recipient doesn't have them, then the resulting PDF is displayed and printed with special Adobe substitution fonts. These are designed to emulate the spacing characteristics of any missing characters, but they are bland, generic typefaces that cannot reproduce a missing typeface exactly; if the missing typeface is a script or display face, the results will look nothing like the original. It's always a good idea to embed fonts. They don't add a lot to the final size of the PDF file, unless you are using Chinese, Japanese, or Korean fonts, which can take up an enormous amount of space. Even then, you'll need to embed these and other non-Roman typefaces if the final PDF is to be opened by someone who doesn't have those fonts or language systems installed.

PDF for Print   Adobe Systems dived into the competition in 1993, defining their Portable Document Format as a file format used to represent a document independently of the application software, fonts, hardware, and operating system used to create it. The software used to create this PDF was called Acrobat.

Adobe's PDF took the PostScript file of the document and RIPed it (called distilling) to a new format that saved every page as an individual item, compressed the type and images, and cut out almost all the variability of the programming language. What remained was a portable document file that could be viewed on almost any platform, Mac or PC, running DOS, Windows, MacOS, or UNIX. But the first version of Adobe Acrobat did not fully support high-end printing for color separations. The PostScript code needed for production printing was not included. This did not hinder the use of PDFs to view on monitors or to print to monochrome and color printers, but a composite CMYK file could not be output as four monochrome PostScript streams to be sent to an imagesetter or a platesetter.

Before preparing a PDF version of a document to be printed on a press, always ask your printer or service provider about any special needs they might have for the processing of PDF files, such as composite (RGB/LAB) vs. preseparated (CMYK), OPI or no OPI, color management or no color management, and the final screen ruling of the print run. While PDF is relatively device independent, the screen ruling will be used to determine the amount of resampling, if any, that you should apply. Once the images are resampled for a particular print run, the resulting PDF can't really be considered device independent.

PDF for On-line Use   The difference between PDF for print and PDF for on-line use is that you will resample your images to 72 ppi (Mac) or 96 ppi (Windows), and specify that all images be converted to RGB space if they aren't.

Exporting PDF   Open the file you wish to convert, then press Command/Control + E. Choose *Adobe PDF* (as if there were more than one type of PDF), name the file, append .pdf to the end, then click Save. You'll see the options shown in Figure 10–20,

Figure 10–20
Export—PDF options.

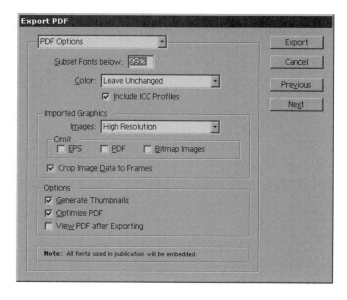

many of which are very similar to those we've already seen in the EPS and prepress export dialogs. The PDF Export process has four dialogs, though few people will probably use the fourth, which offers security options.

The first dialog wants to know about font, color, and some other options.

- Enter a percentage for the Subset Fonts field. Usually 99% is the preferred setting.
- Color lets you specify any color space conversion. These options are exactly the same as for the EPS and Prepress export methods.
- Include ICC Profiles is selectable if color management is enabled for the document. Choose this option if you are sending the PDF through an ICC-aware workflow and plan to use in-RIP separations. Otherwise, you really needn't bother.
- Images—Same as for EPS and Prepress.
- OPI—Same as for EPS and Prepress.
- Omit—Sorry, same as for EPS and Prepress.
- Crop Image Data to Frames—This eliminates image data that falls outside an image's frame. Some prepress applications, such as a trapping program, might use this information, so you need to experiment with this option.
- Generate Thumbnails—Acrobat can display a thumbnail view of a PDF page, but only if you create it when exporting a PDF file.
- Optimize PDF—This should always be on for on-line PDF. The option eliminates redundant data, resulting in smaller files, and allows one page at a time to be served up from a web server. This option really makes no difference when generating a PDF for print.
- View PDF after Exporting—Pretty easy to figure out. You can designate a specific application to view the resulting PDF, but your choices are pretty much limited to Acrobat or Acrobat Reader. InDesign always exports version 1.3 PDF, which can

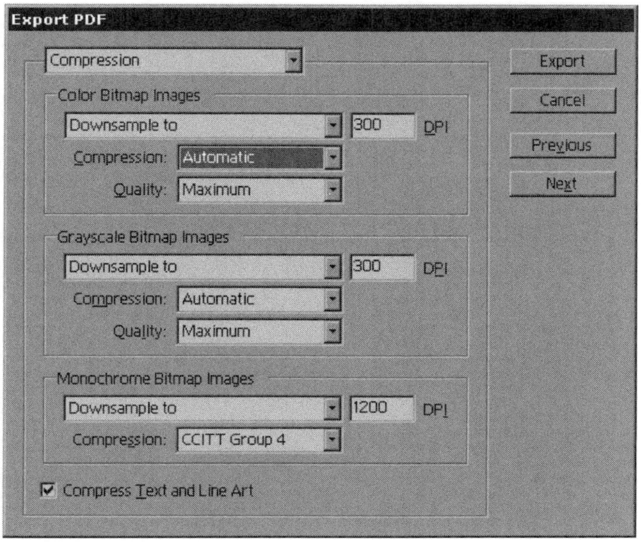

Figure 10–21
Export PDF—Compression.

only be read by Acrobat 4.0. You can't save a file for Acrobat
3.0 from InDesign.

The next dialog (Figure 10–21) lets you specify compression and
resampling.

For color and gray-scale images, you can choose JPEG or ZIP
compression. Recall that JPEG compression throws away data it considers to be redundant or unnecessary for proper display, but if you
choose the Maximum Quality level, the amount of data discarded by
JPEG compression is rarely noticeable.

ZIP compression doesn't work too well for continuous-tone
images like photographs, but it preserves all data in the image. Of
course, choosing None doesn't apply any image compression, which
is probably not really necessary for most PDF files destined for a
print shop or if you really don't care about the final file size.

For Monochrome Bitmap Images (line art and the like), the
CCITT Group 4 compression method works well and doesn't throw
anything away. CCITT Group 3 compression works the same way,

but it'll take longer to compress the image. Choosing Compress Text and Line Art will apply a default compression method to any text and InDesign-native artwork in the document. This type of compression doesn't throw anything away and there's no harm in applying it, since it'll help make the final PDF file a little smaller.

We've talked about resampling already, and here's where you can specify any resampling of images. Be sure to choose the correct resolution for the final printing specification. If you know your images are already at the optimum resolution for your reproduction needs, choose *None* in the Resampling pop-up menus for each image type.

Line art with a resolution much over 1200 ppi won't necessarily reproduce any better, and it'll take longer to process, so it won't hurt to enable resampling of line art images.

The next dialog (Figure 10–22) asks about which pages to export and whether to apply bleed and printer's marks. These are the same options available with the Prepress export function.

Figure 10–22
Export PDF—Pages and Page Marks option.

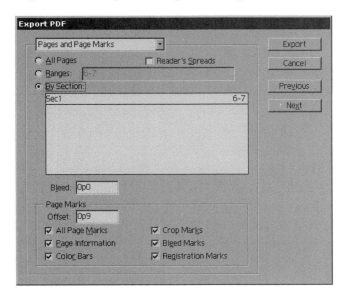

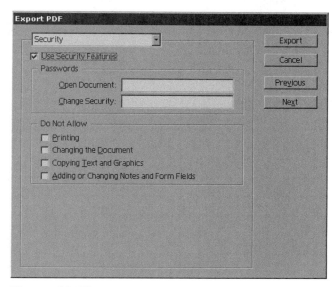

Figure 10–23
Export PDF—Security.

The final dialog (Figure 10–23) concerns PDF security. If you absolutely need to prevent any alteration of the resulting PDF, then you can enable security.

Entering a password in Change Security lets someone else alter the security settings as long as they have the right password. The other options concern specific activities that you can allow or prohibit.

However, once someone else gets the PDF file opened with Acrobat, they can always override your settings by choosing Save As and specifying None for Security in the Acrobat Save As dialog, so the security features of PDF files aren't all that secure. If you're really paranoid about interception of the contents of a PDF file, run it through some kind of encryption program before shipping it off.

11

Printing

Printing Basics

The printing industry accounts for $125 billion of business per year in the United States. Of that amount, $25 billion is waste—waste generated to produce the useful stuff and waste when the useful stuff does not get sold and waste when the useful stuff is discarded. Learning about the process will save you money and time, will earn you good will from print professionals, and will even cut some of the production waste. Printers don't like working with inexperienced people, even though they can charge a lot of money to repair novice mistakes. It's just another obstacle that must be dealt with before the job can be printed, and printers would rather keep their presses running full-time instead of having to spend unproductive time fixing problems.

Before preparing any jobs for printing, it's very helpful to understand the material in this section. Not only will you know a lot more about the printing process, you'll also save money on rework charges for corrections to your files by a printer before they can be printed.

Little Dotty Things

Images and words are put on paper in the digital process by means of spots, dots, and pixels. This applies regardless of whether the job is printed on a digital or conventional press, since both processes use similar imaging technologies up to a point. Learning about one gives you a head start on the other.

Spots   Spots are the most basic unit in a digital imaging system. A spot is the smallest mark that a digital output device can put on a piece of paper or film, a lithographic or flexographic printing plate, a rotogravure cylinder, or a display like your monitor. A spot is also the smallest unit that a digital input device like a scanner or digital camera can resolve. Spots vary widely in size, from 72 spots per inch on a typical monitor to 4,000+ spots per inch on some of the more modern film imagesetters.

Any digital device works fundamentally with the bit, the smallest representation of digital data. A bit is a single binary digit and is either 0 (zero) or 1 (one). A bit is used to tell a printer or other imaging device to print a spot in a specific location, or not. A spot is either on or off. A map of spots is commonly referred to as a bitmap.

Think of the potential imaging area of an imaging device as a piece of very finely ruled graph paper: each little square represents one printer spot (Figure 11–1). Each square can also be referenced easily by counting up, down, left, or right. So very simply, a computer

Figure 11–1
Spots.

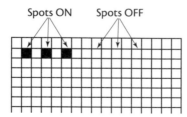

can tell a printer this: "put a single spot at location x, y" and the printer will oblige. It's sort of like playing the game "Battleship," which references the x,y coordinates. Thus, every location in the grid has an address. Each spot is said to be addressable.

When you print an entire page, your computer (or the RIP—raster image processor) is telling the printer exactly where to place each spot on the paper. If you print enough spots at the right locations, surprise, you end up with words and images on the page.

Dots   "Dots" is an old term, long used in the printing industry. In digital terms, a dot is made up of spots, and digitally, it is a grid of bits, some of which are turned on, and some of which are turned off—a bitmap. A dot on a page is used to create a halftone effect; that is, it is used to reproduce photographs or lighter tints of a solid color on paper. You can see these easily in newspaper photographs. A dot is made up of a group of spots, as illustrated in Figure 11–2.

Pixels   A pixel extends the idea of a dot to two dimensions. Now, not only do you have a grid of bits (a bitmap) that are either on or off, you also extend that to an eight-layer grid. A byte is a unit of digital information that is made up of eight bits. The grid can now be called a bytemap. With eight bits of information, you can create a multilayered dot, or a pixel, that contains up to 256 levels of gray. If you combine multiple pixels with others, you can create over 16 million colors on your computer display (in theory).

Figure 11–2
Dots.

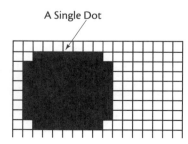

Page Description Languages   Many laser printers and all professional graphic arts equipment generate pages by interpreting a PostScript file. PostScript is a programming language invented by Adobe Systems; they designed it specifically for the needs of the graphic arts industry. PostScript printers include a computer (called the raster image processor) and memory, which is one reason they're often more expensive than a standard printer. An imagesetter or platesetter usually uses an external computer as its raster image processor (RIP).

When you send a file from a program like InDesign or Illustrator or whatever to the printer, several things occur before the page is printed. Your computer uses a program called a printer driver that receives the information that programs send to it and converts this information to PostScript. The driver then sends the PostScript data to the printer. The printer's internal computer interprets the stream of PostScript language information from your computer and generates a precise pattern of dots on the printer's imaging surface. When the imaging process is finished, the printer prints the page.

PostScript provides device- and resolution-independence. This means that the same file, printed on any kind of PostScript printer, will still look more or less the same. Other page description languages are used in inexpensive inkjet and laser printers. These printers are not used in professional applications, although they may be adequate for rough proofing.

Graphic Arts Imaging Equipment   Imagesetters can produce resolutions up to 5,000 dots per inch (dpi), resulting in the sharpest possible image. Usually, a film negative is imaged on an imagesetter and then developed chemically. Once a finished piece of film is processed and any necessary manual alterations made, a blank lithographic printing plate is exposed to high-intensity ultraviolet light through the piece of negative film.

Further chemical processing of the printing plate develops the image area of the plate. A positive-working film and plate system usually produces sharper plates than a negative system, but the negative-working system is used almost exclusively in North America.

The positive system is much more common in the rest of the world. Exposed imagesetter films can be used for imaging lithographic and flexographic printing plates and can also be used to image screens used in screen printing, although normally you can't use a set of films imaged for one printing process for another process.

Platesetters operate similarly to imagesetters, but with these devices, a blank lithographic plate is imaged directly to a light-sensitive metal or polyester lithographic printing plate, using a high-powered laser.

This bypasses the film step completely and even though current platesetters cannot achieve the ultrahigh resolutions of some imagesetters, they often produce sharper results because there is none of the optical gain or dot softening that can occur when a plate is conventionally exposed through a film negative. Platesetters require completed plate images, which means that all imposition and arrangement of pages must be performed prior to platemaking.

Platesetters for flexography are a fairly recent development, but they operate on the same principles as those for offset lithography: a laser is used to expose a light-sensitive flexible polymeric plate, which must then be processed with some pretty revolting and toxic chemicals. Some systems use the laser to physically burn away parts of the plate to create an image carrier. While this probably smells really bad, it's probably a lot more friendly to the environment than the giant baths of perchloroethane (commonly known as dry-cleaning fluid) used to process most flexographic plates.

Flexography is becoming much more popular for newspaper printing and has been traditionally used for printing low-end packaging and things like bread bags and other types of packaging that use plastic films.

Direct imaging devices for gravure printing have been around for quite some time; in fact, the low-profile gravure process was the first printing process that went all-digital due to the time and labor-intensive gravure cylinder preparation process, and this happened years before anyone ever heard of a platesetter or a company named Creo.

Digital gravure imagers drive electromechanical engraving machines that use one or more diamond stylii to bang tiny pits into a copper-plated steel cylinder.

These pits form the basis of the gravure image carrier. You really don't want to make any last-minute changes on a gravure job unless you have a budget similar to that of the U.S. Department of Defense, since changes mean reengraving another cylinder and sending the old one back for stripping and replating. Chances are that few readers will be involved in gravure printing, but you never know, as it is still the leading printing process for multipage jobs with runs much over one million finished pieces, and it is used to print everything from floor and wall coverings to putting the little Ms on your M&M candies.

Digital printing presses use a high-quality toner printing process. These devices are more akin to giant laser printers than to printing presses and range from black-only sheetfed devices like the Xerox Docutech, to sheetfed 6-color machines like the Indigo UltraStream, to large web (roll)-fed 4-color machines like the Xeikon DCP series of digital presses. These devices use electrostatically sensitive dry or liquid toners to image onto a charged cylinder, which is used to transfer the image to the paper or other substrate. Dry toner devices then use high heat to fuse the toner to the paper; liquid toner devices like the Indigo do not require a fusing process.

Screening   Screening is a basic graphic arts technique that has been around for over a century. The invention of screening followed that of photography, because photographs cannot be reproduced with ink and paper on a printing press. Screening allows the continuous tones of a photograph to be broken down into dots, which you can plainly see in newspaper photos.

Before computer-based screening was developed, a sheet of glass or plastic with a fine cross-hatch pattern etched into it was placed over a sheet of unexposed film and a high-contrast photograph was taken of the original, resulting in film showing only a fine series of dots. Screen dots vary in size to represent changes in tone: darker areas of a photo will produce bigger dots than will lighter areas of a photo. In the printing trade, a screened image is commonly called a halftone.

Screening is necessary to reproduce photographs with a printing press. The continuous tones of photographs are only possible because of special papers and chemical processes that are far too cumbersome and expensive for mass reproduction.

Screens are required to create tints of colors. A tint of 50% requires a screen that permits 50% of the light that strikes it to be reflected from the paper. A screen of 10% permits 90% of the light to be reflected. Photographs and tints are usually the only elements that require screening. Untinted type, fills, and artwork print at 100%.

Process color jobs, on the other hand, require that every element that is not 100% solid color (such as black type or process colors like red, which is formed from overprinting 100% yellow and 100% magenta) be screened. Process color requires screening. A process color made of 25% cyan, 55% magenta, 5% yellow, and 5% black will be reproduced on press, after separation, as screened tints of those four colors. Similarly, color photographs are screened after separation, and their tonal ranges are converted into varying screened tints of the four process colors.

In a PostScript RIP, screening is determined by the application or RIP settings. Typically, screening settings on a digital color press cannot be overridden by the application.

Screen Rulings   The number of lines of dots per inch on a screen determines the screen ruling. Screen rulings vary according to the press, the type of paper, and the intended use of the printed piece. They are measured in lines per inch (lpi), and you can specify the screen ruling when you set up the file for separation. Screen rulings apply to both spot and process color printing.

Fine screen rulings, typically above 150 lpi, are used for high-quality pieces like corporate reports, fine-art reproductions, sales literature for expensive products, and the like. Medium rulings from 120 to 150 lpi are usually used for weekly glossy magazines, menus, inexpensive brochures, and similar items. Low rulings, from 65 to 110 lpi, are generally used for newspapers, junk mail, color tabloid papers, and other things printed on cheap paper where permanence isn't an issue.

Digital color presses vary in their screen rulings. Because these presses don't have the same physical resolution as the imagesetter used to produce conventional printing jobs, they are designed to simulate the appearance of a fairly fine screen ruling. Typically, the screen ruling on a digital color press cannot be changed.

Screen Angles   Printing process color without changing the angles of the screens results in a big mess on the paper. All black-and-white halftones are printed at a 45 degree angle, which you can see on close examination of newspaper photos. At 45 degrees, the screening is not very noticeable, but if a black-and-white photo were printed in black ink at a 90 degree angle, you would definitely notice the screening.

As a result, black (or the darkest spot color) is always on a 45 degree angle, the next lightest color (for magenta or a second spot color) will be at a 75 degree angle, the third lightest will be at a 15 degree angle (cyan in process, or a third spot color), and yellow (or a light spot color), being very light, gets printed at a 90 (or 0) degree angle.

You won't notice the 90° angle of a yellow screen because of its lightness in comparison with the other process colors, although if an image has very heavy yellow coverage, the pattern of the screen might become a little noticeable. There's really not much you can do about that if it occurs.

You should never change screen angles except when you are separating spot color art that has overlapping tints, such as in a duotone or in spot-color gradients. The default screen angle values for process colors has been arrived at through years of refinement, so don't mess with them. Typically, the screen angles for duotones will be 45° for black, or the darkest spot color, and 75° for the lightest spot color. In most cases you don't need to worry about screen angles unless you are preparing your own preseparated files.

If that's the case, then always ask your printer for the recommended screen angles. These angles may change depending on the default dot shape generated by an imaging device. One that images elliptical dots may need different screen angles than one that images round dots. Most devices offer a range of dot shapes, and your printer will choose the one best suited to the equipment.

If you are working on a two-color project and feel that a third color would be useful but the budget won't allow it, in some cases you can overprint one spot color on top of another one. This works best when one spot color is quite a bit lighter than the other one.

Remember that spot inks are opaque and that the result of an overprint may just end up being a big old muddy mess. You might get better results from overprinting tints of spot colors rather than solids. Be sure to change the screen angle of any overprinted spot colors from the default of 45° if you are preparing your own preseparated files.

Resolution   Most imagesetters range from 1200 dpi to over 5000 dpi; the time needed to generate film increases greatly with higher resolutions, resulting in higher costs. Digital presses have much lower resolutions, from 600 to 800 dpi. Even though this sounds low, these presses are able to achieve fairly high quality levels through the use of screening algorithms that allow them to simulate the appearance of conventional printing.

In general, resolution is determined by the screen ruling chosen for the job.

A higher screen ruling requires higher resolution. If the screen ruling is too high for a given resolution, visible banding or other unwanted artifacts can become apparent. You always want to choose a resolution that provides the maximum number of gray levels at the chosen screen ruling in lines per inch. Table 11–1 provides a guide for the choice.

Table 11-1

Available gray levels.

Resolution	Maximum Screen Ruling
300	19
400	25
600	38
1200	75
1270	79
1693	106
1800	112
2400	150
2540	159
3000	188
3252	203
3600	225
4000	250
5000	313

Determine your final screen ruling, then request an output resolution that's higher than the resolution that will give you the minimum gray levels. For example, if you need an 85 lpi screen ruling, use 1693 dpi resolution or higher, since most imagesetters have fixed resolution levels and you can't set them to image at 1370 dpi, which is the theoretical optimum resolution for 85 lpi output.

Different machines have differing resolution settings; the ones listed in Table 11-1 are the most common.

The screen ruling you use will vary according to the type of printing process, paper or other substrate, and your own needs. For example, printing on corrugated cartons with a flexographic press will use a very coarse screen ruling around 65 lpi, whereas waterless offset lithography can reliably print rulings over 300 lpi on very high quality (and expensive) paper. Always consult with a printer to determine the optimum screen ruling for your substrate and printing process.

Printers that use nonstandard screening methods, as do many inkjet and other color printers, will have their own specifications for the maximum number of gray levels at a given resolution and screening method.

Digital printing presses like those based on the Xeikon digital color press (sold as the Agfa Chromapress 32 and 50, IBM Infocolor 70 and 100, Xerox Docucolor 70 and 100, and Xeikon DCP/32 and DCP/50) use a proprietary multi-bit-depth screening process that emulates either traditional amplitude-modulated (AM) screening or frequency-modulated (FM or "stochastic") screening, and each version of this press differs in its screening method because each vendor uses its own RIP for this press.

As usual, call first. FM screening doesn't use fixed screen rulings, but instead offers a choice of dot sizes, typically 21μ and 42μ. The smaller dot size will require a higher-resolution setting on any FM imaging equipment to achieve a higher number of gray levels.

Imaging equipment that is driven by an Adobe PostScript Level III RIP may be able to produce smooth, unbanded gradients even if the number of gray levels mathematically possible with a given screen ruling is lower than in the gray levels table (Table 11–1).

Dot Gain   When a halftone dot is printed with ink on paper, it may swell slightly, depending upon how absorbent the paper is. Newsprint will exhibit far more dot gain than will an expensive glossy stock. Your printer or prepress shop should handle compensating for dot gain, the degree of which will be known to them based on the paper stock and printing equipment used. Digital color presses exhibit a small amount of dot gain due to the propensity of dry toner to spread or scatter before it is fused to the paper.

Dot gain is typically controlled and adjusted when the final separations are created. If you preseparate RGB images to CMYK in Photoshop, compensation for dot gain is made in the CMYK Setup dialog. If you choose Built-in, you need to enter a dot gain percentage in this dialog.

Your printer can provide the correct dot gain percentage for his equipment. If you choose ICC in this dialog, then the dot gain specifications in a CMYK device profile will be applied to the image upon conversion from another color space. An imaging device that supports in-RIP separation will already be set up to compensate for dot gain.

Printing from InDesign

InDesign is very heavily dependent upon the print driver present on your computer. Other applications like PageMaker and QuarkXPress don't depend as much on the printer driver and write directly to the printer or to a PostScript file. Adobe provides the required print drivers on the InDesign distribution CD-ROM, and you must install the driver for your platform before you can print anything.

Adobe supplies the Adobe PS driver for both Macintosh and Windows computers on the CD. InDesign requires version 8.6 of the Adobe PS driver for the Mac, and version 5.1 (Windows NT) or 4.3 (Windows 98) for that other platform. You can choose a different print driver, but most of the print features offered by InDesign through the Adobe drivers will be absent if you choose another one.

Each type of printer, imaging device, or digital press needs to have its own PostScript Printer Description (PPD) file. This is a simple text-only file that contains specific information about an imaging device, such as its media sizes, different media inputs, color capabilities, separation and trapping capabilities, and so forth. Most PostScript printers include a disk with the correct PPD file, and you need to obtain PPDs for any printers or imaging devices for which you create PostScript files for imaging.

If your printer wants you to provide a PostScript file, then the printer needs to give you the PPD file to ensure that the PostScript file you provide is correctly set up for the imaging equipment. You can download PPD sets for most brands of imaging equipment from Adobe's web site—choose the Downloads link, then choose Printer Drivers for your platform. The PPD packages are listed below the Adobe PS drivers.

Preflight and Package

Preflighting is the process of verifying that all of a document's fonts, images, and ICC profiles are present and accounted for. There are commercial utilities for performing this process, such as FlightCheck from Markzware, and they do a more thorough check of a document than InDesign's built-in preflight function, but hey, the latter is free.

Packaging is Adobe's term for gathering all of the fonts, images, ICC profiles, and text files used in a document into a single location, usually a new folder, for delivery to a print provider. If your provider wants you to submit InDesign files rather than PostScript or PDF files, then this function will be very useful to you.

It's smarter than the QuarkXPress Collect for Output function, which only copies any placed images. PageMaker has an analogous function called Save for Service Provider, which is implemented as one of the few PageMaker plug-ins. The Preflight function is always performed before a document is packaged.

Preflight   To preflight an open document (Figure 11–3), choose File ➡ Preflight or press the finger-contorting keystroke of

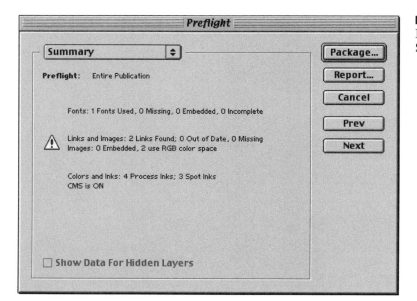

Figure 11–3
Preflight dialog box—
Summary.

Command/Control + Option/Alt + Shift + F. InDesign will grind and grunt for a minute or two, then produce a series of dialogs that display any problems found and the current state of the document.

After InDesign finishes its check of the document, a summary dialog appears, and from there you can inspect various components of a document's makeup or create a package.

The Show Data for Hidden Layers option is pretty obvious. Any warning triangles probably require further inspection. Click the Next/Prev buttons to cycle through the various dialogs.

InDesign will complain about missing fonts when you open a document, but if fonts used in placed EPS or PDF artwork are missing, the Preflight function will alert you to this fact (Figure 11–4).

The Preflight function reports on any missing images, or images that have been updated (Figure 11–5).

You can click the Relink/Update button to locate a missing image; the button's function depends on the state of the selected image link in the list. Click Repair All to relink or update all linked images.

Figure 11–4
Preflight dialog box—Fonts.

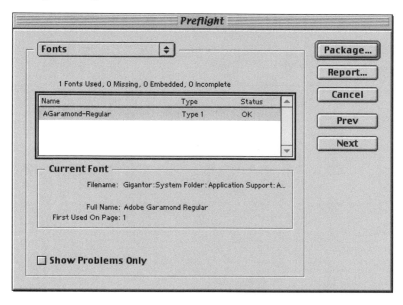

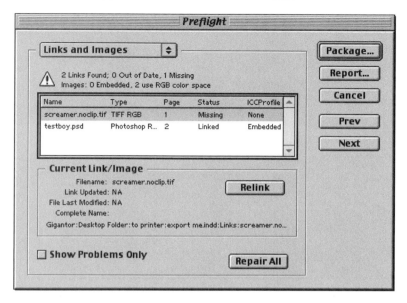

Figure 11–5
Preflight dialog box—Links and Images.

All linked images, including DCS and those linked through OPI comments, are displayed here.

InDesign will always warn you of RGB images, even if that's your intention, since it assumes that you won't be using an in-RIP separation system, which is sort of amusing since Adobe seems really keen on such things.

Images that lack embedded profiles will show a profile of None, even if you're using the default InDesign profile.

The next dialog (Figure 11–6) shows all of the color separations that the document's current color specifications will generate when it is separated.

Here's a great opportunity to catch any errant spot colors you might have created with the best of intentions but never actually used for anything or did use but maybe forgot to convert to a process color, or any spot color that was sneaked into the document with a placed EPS image, or something like that. It happens.

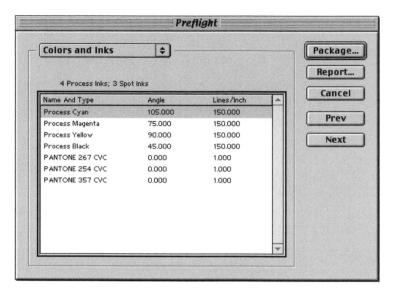

Figure 11–6
Preflight dialog box—Colors and Inks.

Now's your chance to fix it. Even if you don't, you can always force separation of spot colors into CMYK at print time, so it's not the end of the world.

Any missing ICC profiles will also be listed here, though this will only appear if you've removed any ICC profiles from your computer after placing into InDesign an image that lacks an embedded profile. Locate and reinstall the missing profile.

The screen angles and screen rulings shown are lifted from the currently selected PPD file. Spot colors show a rather bogus angle of 0 and a screen ruling of 1, but that's because this information is not present in the PPD and is set in the Print dialog when you print or export the document.

The last dialog here is the Print Settings, which really doesn't tell you very much unless you've gone and made changes to the default print settings for the document.

The next option in the Preflight operation is to prepare a Package. You can also click Report to generate a plain text file containing a listing of all of the fonts, images, and ICC settings used in the document.

Package   To package a document, click the Package button in the Preflight dialog, or choose File ➡ Package if you've skipped the Preflight operation. Not so fast, though, because the first thing InDesign does in the packaging operation, if anything has changed since the last preflight operation or if you've never done one, is a preflight check.

Once you've preflighted the document and fixed or chosen to ignore any problems presented, InDesign displays a Printing Instructions dialog (Figure 11–7). The information you enter here is saved, along with a full report of the document's characteristics, to a plain text file.

Of course, this step is purely optional, but it beats scribbling the information on a scrap of paper. After you click Continue, you'll probably be asked to save the document before proceeding, so click Save to continue.

The next dialog (Figure 11–8) asks where to save the package and gives you a few options as to what you want to copy to the package location. The document's file name is displayed in the dialog, but this will end up being the name of a containing folder,

Figure 11–7
Printing Instructions dialog box.

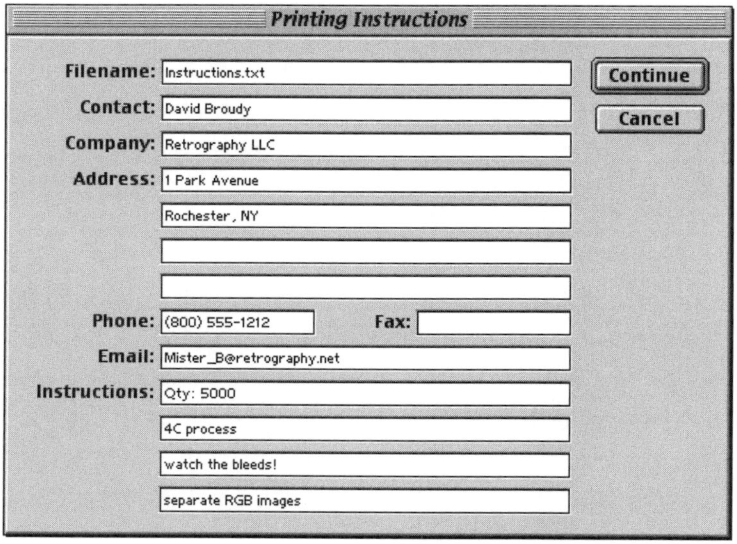

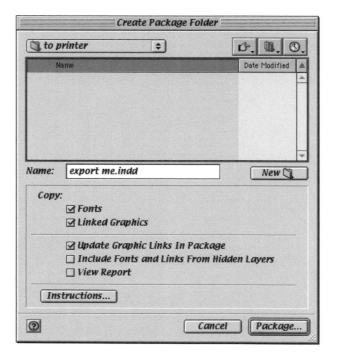

Figure 11–8
Create Package Folder dialog box.

so you can call it whatever you like. Your document will not be renamed.

In general, you'll want to use the defaults in this dialog. Choose to include fonts and images from hidden layers as you like; if these objects are hidden, there's probably a good reason for it, but this can be useful if a document contains multiple versions of a layout in the layers and you want to have your printer print all of the versions. Choosing View Report will send the report to either SimpleText (Mac) or Notepad (Windows) for your perusal.

After you click the Package button, InDesign will nag you about those pesky font licenses. While we agree with Adobe and others that font piracy is a big problem, there are limits to the lengths one should go to remind users of this fact. Nag screens are just that: naggy. The end result of a packaging operation is a folder with a fresh copy of the document, all of the fonts and linked images used in the document, and a plain text report. InDesign thoughtfully creates subfolders to

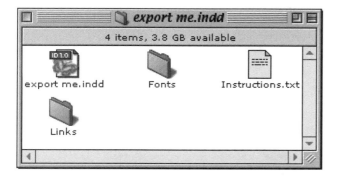

Figure 11–9
Package folder contents.

contain fonts and images, which is a nice little touch. Figure 11–9
shows it all tied up.

Macintosh vs. Windows Printing

There are a few platform-specific differences in the way things are
done in InDesign, mostly regarding printer setup and media size
selection, so we'll cover the Macintosh in detail and point out differences in Windows setup afterwards. This information assumes
you've already installed the required Adobe PS print driver for
your platform.

Virtual Printers   A virtual printer is really just a means of
specifying a printer's PPD, then printing a document to a
PostScript file that uses any printer-specific options. This is handy
for creating PostScript files for handing off to a print provider, or
for creating PostScript files that you need to run through another
program that enables PostScript printing on non-PostScript printers, such as most inkjets.

Print to PostScript   Follow the instructions for printing to a virtual printer if you want to make PostScript files from an InDesign document. Virtual Printer usually comes on the Adobe Acrobat Reader
CD-ROM. It is loaded when you load all of the PS Printer PPDs
(PostScript Printer Descriptions).

Macintosh Stuff   The Adobe PS 8.6 driver might look unlike any other printer interface you've seen before. There's a plethora of pop-ups, multiple specification panels, and all sorts of functions built into the InDesign print dialog, all enabled by this new driver. The Page Setup dialog may be new to you as well. Before you even think about trying to print an InDesign document, choose File ➠ Page Setup or press Command + Shift + P to show the Page Setup dialog. You won't be able to adjust critical Page Setup parameters, like selection of a PPD or of a page size, from the Print dialog.

Page Setup Dialog   After opening the Page Setup dialog, the very first thing you need to do is choose a PPD. We're showing an example of using a Virtual Printer (Figure 11–10), in this case, an Agfa SelectSet 5000 imagesetter, because neither of us actually has an imagesetter sitting around in our offices, and this machine is pretty common.

To select an actual plastic and metal printer, you need to go to the Chooser, select the AdobePS driver, then select and set up the printer or imaging device as a desktop printer. After you do this, the printer will be listed under the Printer pop-up menu. You can't change the PPD of a connected printer here; you can only do that from the Chooser.

To choose a virtual printer, select Virtual Printer from the Printer pop-up menu. This adds an option to the curiously unnamed menu directly under the Printer: menu called, unsurprisingly, Virtual Printer (Figure 11–12). Select this option, then click the Select PPD button to choose the proper PPD. The current PPD is always dis-

Figure 11–10
Virtual printer icon.

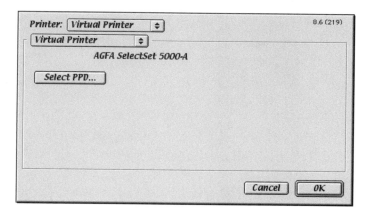

Figure 11–12
Select PPD.

played in this dialog. If for some reason InDesign doesn't point at the folder containing PPDs, it's in this path: Startup Disk ➡ System Folder ➡ Extensions ➡ Printer Descriptions.

Once you've selected a local or virtual printer, choose Page Attributes from the unnamed pop-up menu (Figure 11–13).

This dialog displays your current "paper" size, orientation, and scale. "Paper" in this case is really film; select a media size from one of the available imaging media sizes offered in the PPD from the Paper menu.

Figure 11–13
Page Attributes.

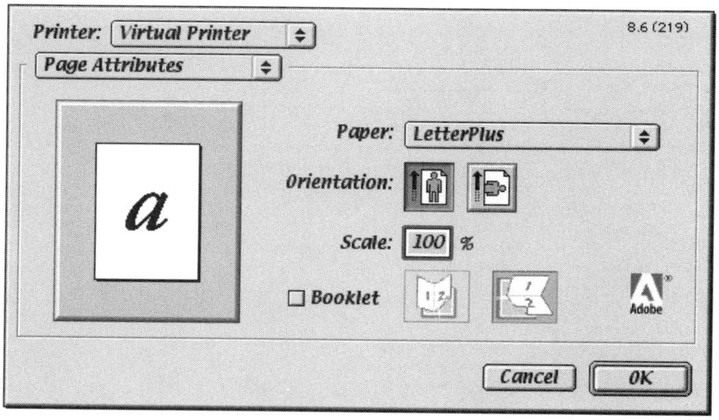

Here, LetterPlus is chosen to allow imaging of a letter-sized (8.5 x 11-inch) page, plus printer's marks. Orientation determines whether the page is imaged horizontally or vertically.

You should choose the orientation that matches your document, although in most cases, documents sent to an imagesetter will be turned 90° to conserve film.

If your Paper pop-up offers media sizes with the word "transverse" added to the end, the page will automatically be turned 90° when sent to the imager.

The Scale field should not be used here—you set scaling from the Print dialog if you need to scale a document's output.

The Booklet function is a MacOS-only feature. Don't get too excited, though, because it is not a substitute for an imposition package and is really only intended for printing to a laser printer a document that will later be folded and stapled.

We'll discuss booklet-building at the end of this chapter. It's sort of a tedious process, but you can use it to create simple impositions for documents that will be saddle-stitched.

You may wish to create a custom paper size, especially if you are sending the document to an imagesetter and the exact size you want isn't listed in the Paper Size menu.

Choose *Custom Page Default* from the mysteriously unnamed pop-up menu to create a custom paper size or to view the exact settings for an existing paper size (Figure 11–14).

Figure 11–14
Custom Page Default.

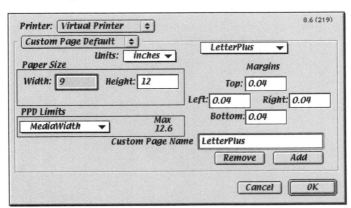

The measurements for the current media size are displayed here. The device's imaging limits are shown in the various entries in the PPD Limits pop-up menu. This tells you the maximum width, height, margins, and more, that the device can handle.

To create a new custom media size, enter the values for width, height, and margins. These, of course, have no bearing on the page width, height, and margins of your current document. You must enter a name for the new custom page and click the Add button to save the custom paper size. Once you create a custom page size, it will be listed at the bottom of the Paper menu in the Page Attributes dialog. It might take a little trial and error to get a custom page set up correctly.

The PostScript Options dialog offers some imaging controls. In most cases, you won't want to select any of the Flip (polarity) or Invert Image (negative) options unless you are sending to an imagesetter that is not automatically set up for the correct emulsion up/down or negative imaging, if any, required by your prepress process.

Most imagesetter film imaged in North America is negative, right-reading emulsion-down, the most common film imaging method for creating lithographic plates.

The example (Figure 11–15) shows the correct settings for negative, right-reading emulsion-down film imaging if your imagesetter

Figure 11-15
Virtual Printer—PostScript Options.

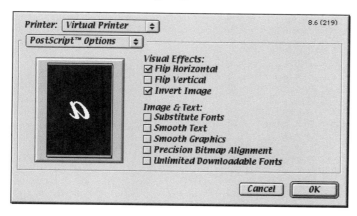

doesn't do this for you. If it *does*, then selecting any of these options will in effect reverse it; for example, films imaged for making flexographic plates need to be imaged negative, right-reading emulsion *up*, so if your imagesetter always converts everything to right-reading emulsion *down*, then you should check the Flip Horizontal option to get the right results.

The rest of the checkboxes should always be off. These are ancient leftovers from the early days of computer imaging, and there's really no need for them anymore. Click OK to save the Page Setup settings.

Windows Stuff   The steps and dialogs for printing may vary slightly depending on whether you are using Windows 98 or Windows NT. The only areas that are much different from printing with the Mac version are virtual printer setup and media size selection. The six control tabs in the Print dialogs correspond exactly to their counterparts on the Macintosh, so refer to the descriptions of these dialogs starting with Advanced Page Control. Some of the functions in the Mac dialog don't appear as tabs in the Windows dialog, and we've noted where these occur.

Setting Up a Virtual Printer   You have to run the Setup program for the Adobe PS driver every time you want to change a PPD for printing to a file. This program is located on the InDesign distribution CD-ROM, and it's supposed to install a link to itself on the Start menu after the first time you run it, but only for Windows NT.

To change PPDs, run the Setup program from the Start menu or the InDesign CD-ROM. Follow the usual steps, then, when the Select PPD dialog shows up, choose your PPD file. Select *FILE* from the Printer Port dialog and you're done. This creates a new "printer" in your Printers folder. The Print dialog in Windows 98 (Figure 11–16) is enormous, but it contains printer setup features similar to those found in the Page Setup dialog on the Mac, which is handy.

Choose your printer from the Name pop-up menu. Click Properties to select media size, then click the Paper (98) or Page

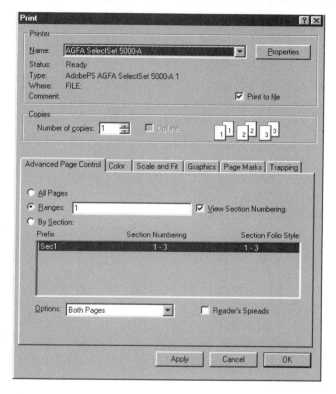

Figure 11–16
Print dialog box.

Setup (NT) tab. Scroll through the available choices and select a media size. If you create a custom page size, the PPD you chose must include support for custom page sizes.

To create a custom size, scroll in the list until you see the Custom Page selection, which should be at the end. This might appear as "Custom p+" in the scrolling list. The PPD you chose may offer a number of blank, generic custom sizes. Select one and click the Custom button towards the bottom of the dialog.

Enter a name for the new page size, along with the width and height (Figure 11–17). Click Transverse to turn the page 90° but be sure to verify the width and height settings against the limits indicated next to each field. You can specify an offset to move the image away from the side edge of the media.

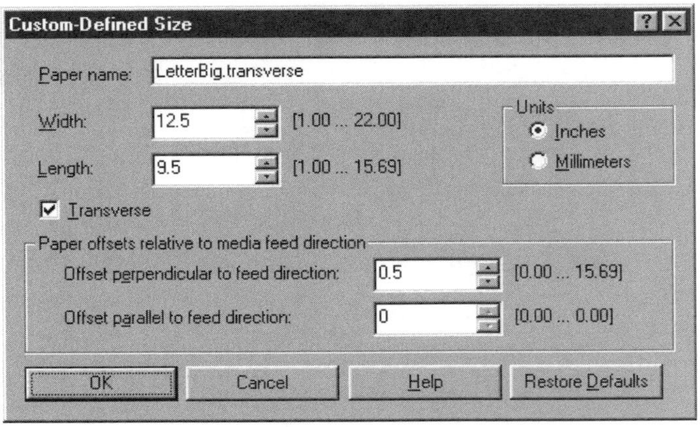

Figure 11-17
Custom-Defined Size dialog box.

Our PPD doesn't allow it, but you may be able to specify an offset from the top "edge" of imagesetter output. Click OK when finished. Custom page sizes are only stored once you complete a print job. Using the PPD for the Agfa SelectSet 5000, you can create up to three custom media sizes; other PPDs may allow fewer, or more.

To set negative output, click the Graphics tab and select *Print as Negative* image. Select *Print as Mirror Image* if you want right-reading, emulsion-down output. Of course, if your imaging equipment does this internally, then don't select these options. There is a scaling option here, but it is overridden in the Scale and Fit dialog in the main Print window. The rest of the tabs in the Properties dialog are ignored by InDesign.

Please refer to the Print Dialog settings for the Macintosh for information on the six tabbed dialogs in the Print dialog. The settings in these work exactly the same for Windows as they do for Macintosh.

Printing (Macintosh and Windows)

Once you've made your choices in the Page Setup dialog or are returning to us from WindowsLand, choose File ➡ Print or press Command/Control + P to show the Print dialog. It's big and messy and offers a huge number of choices in the unnamed mystery menu. Let's just call it the Function menu for now. (Windows people: we're talking about the Mac equivalent of the tabs in your Print dialog). Be sure to choose your printer from the Printer (Mac) or Name (Win) pop-up menu before doing anything else.

The Destination pop-up will change from Printer to File if you choose a virtual printer (Mac only). To print to a file with Windows, run the Adobe PS setup utility and change the printer's port to FILE, or click the Print to File checkbox in the Print dialog.

PPDs are stored in the Extensions Folder of the System Folder of the Macintosh. Here are a few of them at left.

Advanced Page Control   As shown in Figure 11–18, you specify which pages get printed, which can be consecutive or non-consecutive, only the odd-numbered or even-numbered pages, specific sections, or reader's spreads. If you want to print specific pages, specify them as ranges separated by dashes. Use commas to specify nonconsecutive pages. Choose *By Section* to print specific sections, if any are defined in the document. Checking the View Section Numbering box displays sections by their numbers; unchecking the box displays physical page numbers.

Choosing Even or Odd pages lets you print double-sided copies on a laser printer that only prints on one side—print the odd pages first, then place the printed pages face down in the input tray with the first page on the bottom of the stack, then print the Even pages. You'll probably have to choose Reverse Order from the next function dialog to get the even pages to print out correctly on the back of the corresponding odd-numbered pages.

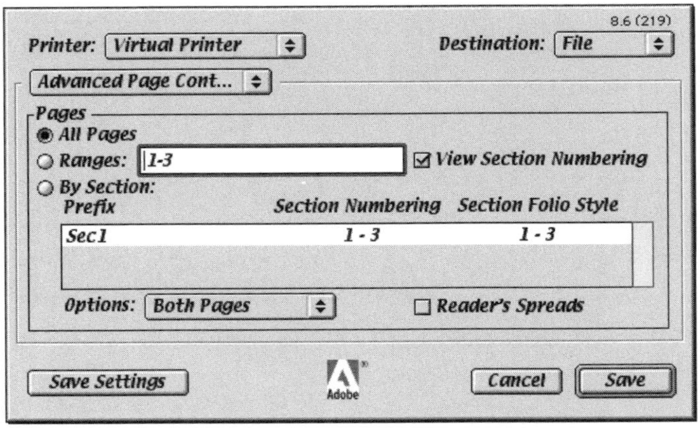

Figure 11–18
Virtual Printer—Advanced Page Control.

Selecting Reader's Spreads is only useful for printing two pages side-by-side on a sheet, and you'll need to specify a sheet size twice that of your document's page size, or scale the results to fit in order for Reader's Spreads to print out correctly. Reader's Spreads are useful for proofreading purposes, but nobody uses them in a production process unless the pages have been imposed manually.

General (Mac Only)   The next function dialog (Figure 11–19), prosaically called General, contains some duplicated settings from the Page Control dialog, namely the page range. Any settings here are overridden in the Advanced Page Control dialog. Windows people don't have a tab for this—use the Properties button to set up different paper sources.

You can specify the paper source if your printer's PPD indicates that multiple paper trays are available. Choosing Manual Feed means that you'll have to stand there and feed sheets to the printer. You'll have to do this to use the Booklet function, so be forewarned.

Most modern laser printers will sense when there's paper in the manual feed tray and load it from there, so you don't need to use the Manual Feed setting here to use the manual input tray as long as there's paper in the thing when you send the job. You can have the first page come from a different tray, which you might want if

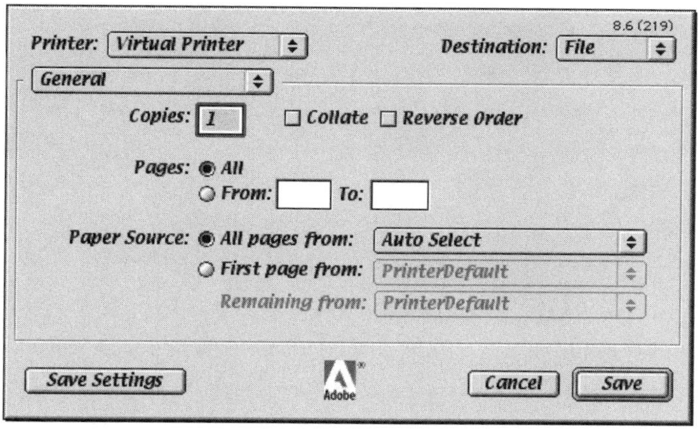

Figure 11–19
Virtual Printer—General.

the first page is to be printed on company letterhead, for example. These settings really have no meaning on imagesetters, though.

Color   To print color we must convert RGB to CMYK, but to view it on a monitor, we need to go back to RGB. To proof it, we go back to CMYK. Today we have an abundance of color management tools and color utilities but no one system stands out as the one that can do all that we want it to do. We try to capture color and print color by the numbers, converting and transforming from one device to another via look up tables (LUTs) or profiles or some other set of tables of equivalence.

Color separation was originally produced with graphic arts cameras. Then, the scanner came into use. That led to digital color and the ability to edit and manipulate color on computers. All three of those historical approaches were based on preseparated CMYK workflows. We think there is a fourth generation: digital color using RGB. We live in a multimedia world. The Internet browsers use GIF and JPEG. Interactive media use PICT or screen images. Print uses TIFF. Television uses NTSC. PhotoCD uses YCC. To switch among multiple image formats becomes more of a necessity every day. Print is only one form of communication and images are being repurposed routinely.

The Color function dialog controls color separation, choice of plates, screen angles, resolution and screen ruling, and the ability to force spot colors to separate into process colors. In the example in Figure 11–20, we have chosen 150 lpi for the screen ruling with a resolution of 2400 dpi. The Screening menu lists all available combinations of resolution and screen ruling that are available on a given device. In some cases, there will be only one choice for this option.

Choose *Composite* if you are sending the job to a device that does its own internal separations but doesn't use Adobe in-RIP separations. Some proofing devices find composite files more easily digestible. Choose *Separations* if you want InDesign to separate

Figure 11–20
Print dialog box—Color.

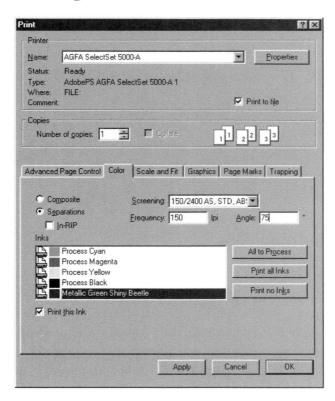

any non-CMYK images and colors. Clicking the In-RIP checkbox will perform separations on the RIP as long as the device's PPD indicates the availability of Adobe's in-RIP Separations capability. If you check the box and a message blares at you to the effect that the device does not support Adobe In-RIP separation, let InDesign do it for you.

InDesign will separate non-CMYK colors and images according to the ICC separations profile you've chosen, only if you have enabled color management for that document. If not, InDesign uses its default (and rather generic) internal separation tables. Preseparated images and CMYK colors are passed through unchanged if you have Separations turned on, even if you choose In-RIP Separations. All In-RIP Separations does, really, is send a composite stream of PostScript along with specific comments and instructions for the Adobe In-RIP system that aren't sent if you choose Composite in this dialog.

Don't change the Frequency and/or Angle settings for process colors. You can change the Angle for any spot colors present in the job, and then only if these are used in a duotone or tinted overprint with another color. Otherwise, the screen angle of any spot color tints can be pretty apparent. It's common for designers to define a spot color as one of the process colors, typically magenta—this eliminates any confusion in the output stage if it's understood that the magenta separation will be printed on press with the intended spot color instead of magenta—the screen angle for the spot color is always correct.

To omit specific ink colors, click on the name, then uncheck the Print This Ink checkbox. InDesign is smart enough to know when a document only contains one or two process colors and only prints separations for any present in the document, so you don't need to uncheck the box for unused process colors. Click the All to Process button to force the conversion of all spot colors to their process derivations. Remember that doing this will produce colors that are unlikely to match the actual spot colors.

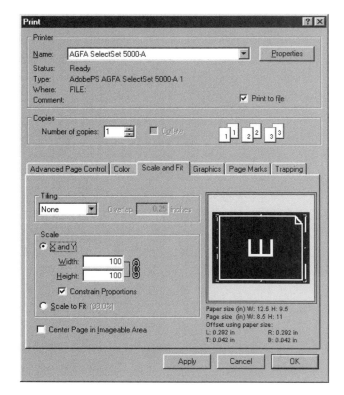

Figure 11–21
Print dialog box—Scale and fit.

Scale and Fit   For some reason, Adobe put the Scale and Fit dialog (Figure 11–21) *before* the Page Marks dialog, which seems a little silly. Here you can specify tiling, and scaling of a document, which is helpful only in the case where the document's page size is too big to fit on an output device's media size.

To tile a document page to multiple printer sheets, choose Automatic or Manual from the Tiling pop-up menu and enter an overlap value if you choose Automatic.

The overlap specifies how much of each tile will overlap with another, which is helpful when you have to align, cut, and tape the tiles together. Manual tiling lets you specify the upper-left origin of the first tile. To manually tile a document, reset the zero point of the page rulers to the desired origin, leaving enough room for page marks and overlap, then choose Manual in the Tiling pop-up. If you set tiling for proofing, turn it off for final output.

Scaling can be used to force a large page onto a small one. It can also be used to compensate, in the direction of plate rotation, for the slight elongation that occurs in a flexographic plate when it is mounted on the press's plate roller. To scale the output, enter a scaling value; to scale only in one direction, such as for flexo distortion compensation, uncheck the Constrain Proportions box and enter the amount of scaling in the long (presswise) direction.

This is really not used much, since most imagesetters used for producing flexographic plate films can be set up to automatically compensate for plate distortion. To fit everything onto the page, select Scale to Fit. This is handy for laser-proofing pages with printer's marks, which may fall off the page if the output isn't scaled.

Graphics   The Graphics function dialog (Figure 11–22) lets you choose OPI, proofing, and font options. The Send Image Data pop-up offers All, Optimized Subsampling, and Low Resolution. For high-resolution output to the final imaging device, always choose All.

Figure 11–22
Virtual Printer—Graphics.

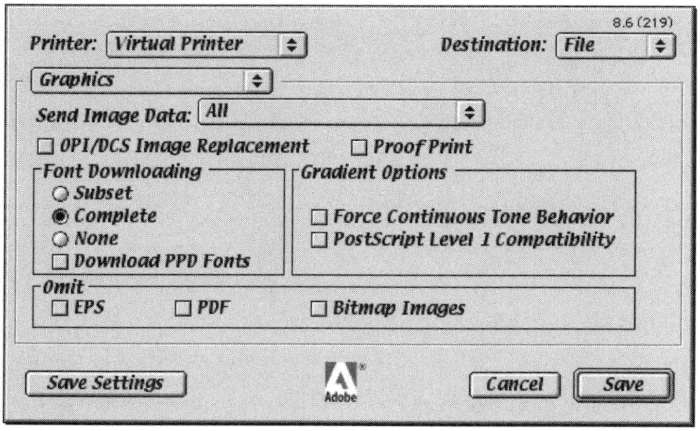

Optimized Subsampling is helpful when printing to a lower-resolution proofing device because it only sends the amount of image data necessary for optimum reproduction on that device. There's no benefit to sending a 300 ppi image to a 600 dpi laser printer, which only requires a small portion of the image data for best results, since it'll take a lot longer to image and the results won't be any better. Choose Low Resolution if you just want a rough proof that will print quickly.

OPI/DCS ImageReplacement works the same way here as it does in the Export to Prepress function described earlier. Use it if you are doing the final imaging steps or if your printer wants a PostScript file containing all of the high-resolution images. This only affects placed images with embedded OPI comments that contain links to the high-resolution images. Turn it off if you are performing the final imaging steps, are using an OPI/APR image replacement system, and have the high-resolution images stored on your server's disk.

Proof Print omits all images from the output and prints a frame with a big X through it instead. It's useful for printing review copies of documents for proofreading, since the images aren't really necessary for that purpose.

Fonts should always be downloaded unless the document uses fonts that are already resident in the printer and are listed correctly in the printer's PPD file. Even if the document is set in a resident font, such as Helvetica, the version of the font in the printer may differ from the version on your computer, and the results could be slightly different in terms of character shape and spacing. Choosing Subset only downloads the character outlines for characters present in the document. Choosing Complete downloads the entire font once per page, which seems a little silly. The time and file size difference between Subset and Complete isn't likely to be large, unless the document uses composite Japanese, Chinese, or Korean fonts.

Always use Subset for these types of fonts. Choose None if you're certain that the document only contains fonts that are resident on the printer; if they aren't, the result will be pages of Courier, the default font imaged if the specified font is missing. You can manually download fonts to printers and RIPs if they have nonvolatile disk storage, but if you do this, you should enter the fonts into the device's PPD file, save a copy of it, and use that PPD; otherwise, the resident fonts are ignored. Choose Download PPD fonts if you want to override any printer-resident fonts, which can happen if there's a version difference.

Enabling the Force Continuous Tone Behavior checkbox can be useful if you're trying to print gradients to a printing device, such as a dye-diffusion printer or some types of inkjets, that does not use standard halftone or FM screening and you're getting ugly banding in the results. Likewise, choose PostScript Level 1 Compatibility if your device only supports PostScript Level 1 (which would be a surprise) if the output is banded or if you keep getting errors when trying to print to the device.

Omitting objects will embed OPI comments for the objects into the resulting file for replacement by an OPI/APR server. You should not omit PDF files, since there isn't anything yet that can perform OPI replacement of them.

Page Marks   When printing in color or with bleed images, it is necessary to place marks to indicate the page size and trim area. These are also called crop marks, and they guide the finishing process in cutting paper to the proper size. They go hand-in-hand with registration marks or symbols that tell the press person if the colors are printed in registration.

Page Marks is pretty basic. Select any or all of InDesign's page marks in the function dialog (Figure 11–23).

The little proxy display will warn you if the selected media size isn't big enough to accommodate the marks, by showing the offset numbers in red.

They'll also show red in the Scale/Fit dialog. The Type menu will only contain the Default setting. It's possible that other language versions of InDesign may contain other options here, but we sure haven't seen any.

Figure 11–24 shows what these marks are.

Bleed and crop marks are placed at each corner of the page.

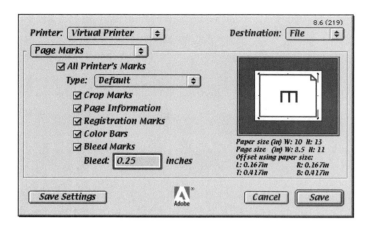

Figure 11–23
Virtual Printer—Page Marks.

Crops tell the cutter operator where to cut the finished pages. Bleed marks tend to be a bit of overkill, but you must specify a bleed in the Marks dialog or else InDesign will not image any area outside of the crop marks. Color bars can be helpful to a press operator when bringing the press up to color, but the majority of printers will ignore these and image their own color bars on the plates, especially if they are using any kind of scanning densitometers or spectrophotometers.

Registration marks (Figure 11–25) are placed at the top, bottom, and on both sides of the page. Ain't they cute?

Page information is imaged outside of the bleed at the bottom of each page (Figure 11–26). Also included are the date and time that the image was generated, useful perhaps for an alibi if someone screws up.

Trapping   In color printing and prepress, trapping is the adjusting of overlapping color areas to account for misregistration on the press. Typically, light colors are slightly spread or choked in relation to darker colors. For example, when printing light yellow letters on a dark blue background, you spread the yellow into the blue; the blue background maintains the sharp edge of the letter. However, when printing dark blue letters on a light yellow background, you choke

Bleed Mark

Crop Mark

Color/Gray Ramp Bar

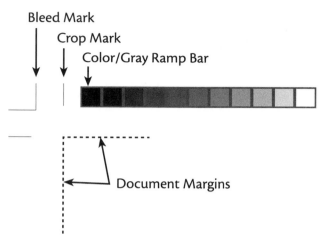

Document Margins

Figure 11–24
Page marks and color bar positions.

Registration Mark

Figure 11–25
Registration mark.

Figure 11–26
More crop mark positioning.

Page Information

Document File Name

Separation Name,
Document Page Number

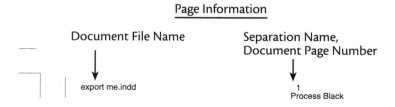

export me.indd

1
Process Black

the yellow background into the blue; the blue of the letter maintains the edge.

The Trapping dialog (Figure 11–27) does nothing for you unless you are sending the document to an imaging device that supports Adobe In-RIP Separations and In-RIP Trapping. If you happen to have such a device, you already know what needs to happen here. If you don't, don't waste your time messing with the settings, which look similar to those in ScenicSoft's TrapWise product.

Enter neutral density settings with the Inks button (Figure 11–28). Remember to fake a high ink density when trapping metallic or opaque inks, which will force the other inks to trap to the opaque ink. You can also alter the default ink-down sequence. Many

Figure 11–27
Trapping.

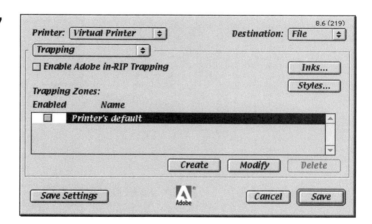

Figure 11–28
Edit Trapping Inks dialog box.

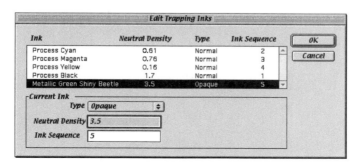

printers print KCMY and then any spot colors. Varnishes and coatings always go down last. Opaque inks need to be the last ink printed on the press. The RIP will take ink sequence into account when creating traps.

You can choose the ink type as well. Normal works well for all process inks and most spot inks. Use Transparent for clear varnishes, as this setting ensures that trapping occurs under the ink's overprint. Use Opaque for metallic inks, opaque white, and other opaque inks. The RIP will choke abutting inks under the opaque ink. Some opaque inks don't like associating with others and do bad things like stick to the press cylinders when they are trapped to other inks.

Choose *Opaque Ignore* for these boorish inks, which will not be trapped to any abutting inks. Certain UV-cured inks, specialty inks such as MICR, and rubber-based inks may exhibit this behavior.

You can create multiple trap setups with the Styles button (Figure 11–29). This will all look very familiar to TrapWise users. If you don't know what these do, then don't mess with them. If you are sending the document to an in-RIP trapping system, refer to the InDesign manual for more information.

Note, that is not a cop-out. So few people will actually use these options that it doesn't make sense to bloat this book more than it is.

Figure 11–29
New Trapping Style dialog box.

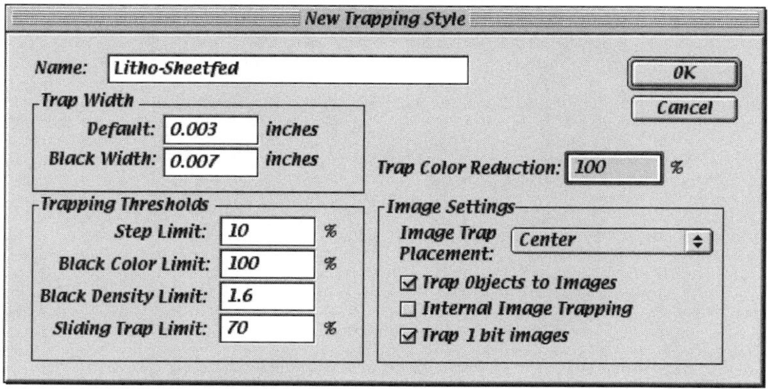

PostScript Settings (Mac only)   The PostScript Settings options (Figure 11–30) are exactly the same as they are for the Prepress export discussed previously. Any changes to the Font Inclusion menu here are overridden by the Graphics function dialog.

The Error Handling dialog isn't worthy of a screen shot. Choose either Summarize on Screen, or No Special Reporting. Never choose Print Detailed Report if your imaging device's media is something very expensive, like a platesetter, imagesetter, or color proofer. Choosing Print Detailed Report will waste an entire media sheet, printing plate, or section of film upon which a few lines of PostScript drivel will be written.

Layout   The Layout dialog (Figure 11–31) is pretty useless for anything besides forcing multiple document pages onto a laser printer page for a quick overview. Choose n-up pages per sheet, as you like. The pages per sheet function, well, as yet we've not been able to figure out just what anyone would ever use this for. It appears to be another way of tiling a document, but without any controls. Just ignore it, okay?

Windows 98 users can access the Layouts by clicking Properties, then clicking the Graphics tab. Choose a layout from the pop-up

Figure 11–30
PostScript Settings options.

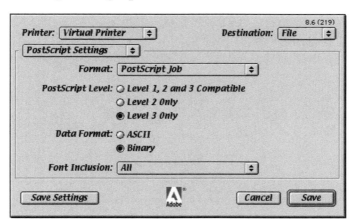

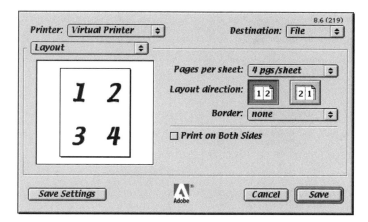

Figure 11–31
Layout dialog box.

The Mac version of the Adobe PS driver allows a very basic imposition for saddle-stitched booklets, where the pages are printed on sheets that are twice as big as the document pages, in landscape orientation, then folded and stapled through the fold. You can make these booklets on almost any office laser printer, and you could also use the feature for imposing simple booklets on an imagesetter, but only in 2-up format.

menu. Windows NT users will find these settings well buried in the Properties dialog, accessed by clicking the plus sign next to Document Options. Choose *Page Layout* and pick one from the list.

Other Options (Mac Only, Except for One)   The rest of the dialogs concern background printing, which you can turn on or off as your workflow system dictates, Cover Page, which nobody has ever used, and Printer-Specific Features, which are ignored and overridden by any imaging options you set in the Color dialog. You don't want cover pages on jobs sent to a platesetter, as you'll end up with a cover plate, and someone will be very cross with you over it.

Other dialogs may be listed in the Function menu, depending on the type of printer you're using, such as printer-specific things like resolution enhancement, extra gray levels, or things like the Watermark feature, a questionable feature if there ever was one. Windows users can find the Watermark option in the Properties dialog if they really want it. Once you've set all of your print options, just click Print (or Save, if printing to a virtual printer). Sit back, have a cocktail, and wait. Have two cocktails.

Booklet Printing   To use booklet printing, your document page size should be half as large as the final sheet size. You can get two 8.5 x 11-inch pages on each side of an 11 x 17-inch sheet, two 5.5 x 8.-inch pages on an 8.5 x 11-inch sheet, two A5 pages on an A4 sheet, and so forth. Ideally, your document should contain a number of pages that is a multiple of 4, since each final sheet will contain four document pages, two on each side.

If your pages aren't quite half the size of the final sheet, you can use the Scale and Fit function in the Print dialog to reduce or enlarge them to fit, but this might not give you a pleasing result.

To print the booklet, choose the correct PPD in the Chooser. Open the Page Setup dialog and select *Page Attributes* (Figure 11–32). Choose the correct sheet size—in this case, US Letter—and change the orientation from Portrait to Landscape. Click the Booklet checkbox, and choose the binding edge. The little picture in the dialog will give you an idea of the final appearance of the booklet. Choose any other options, then close the Page Setup dialog.

Here's where it gets fun. Once you're ready to print the booklet, open the Print dialog. Reset the Layout function dialog to 1 page per sheet. In the Scale and Fit dialog, make any necessary adjustments so the pages will fit on the sheets. In the General dialog, choose Manual Feed as the paper source. Click Print, then go sit by your printer with some paper ready for manual feeding.

Figure 11–32
Page Attributes dialog box.

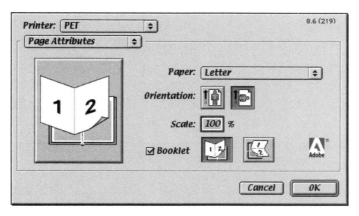

Put the first sheet in the manual feed tray, and when it prints, put it face-down in the manual feed tray, and the second side will be printed on it. Keep the sheet going in the same direction—the tail of the sheet as it comes out of the printer should go back in on the second pass. Most laser printers deliver printed sheets face down. Feed the rest of the sheets in the same manner, arrange the printed sheets into a booklet, then fold and staple it. Voilà! Instant booklet. If you plan to do this a lot, get one of those special long staplers from a graphic supply store.

12

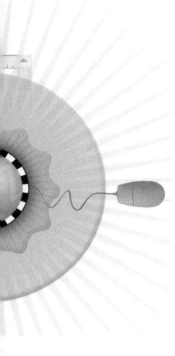

Odds and Ends

This is where everything we forgot to talk about ended up, because we had to submit chapters as they were finished and there was no way to go back and add stuff after the fact. Isn't the publishing business fun?

InDesign Libraries

Libraries are cool. Far too few people ever use them, and far too many people don't realize just how handy it can be to have commonly reused bits of digital flotsam and jetsam (just what the heck is that, anyway?) always at one's disposal in a panel. Libraries might not be a big deal if you're laying out a book, but if you're doing something that uses images or snippets of text repeatedly, such as a catalog, they're a huge time-saver. We use them constantly.

QuarkXPress and PageMaker both have libraries, so the fact that InDesign has them is neither surprising nor earthshaking. However, unlike those other programs, InDesign library files can be used across platforms, which in a mixed-platform environment is pretty handy, to put it mildly. A library file can sit on a file server where anyone with a PC or a Mac can open it and use the contents in a document.

Libraries don't contain files; they contain links to files, so when you put a library item into an InDesign document, a link is created to the file (image, text, whatever) as you'd expect if you placed the file directly. Native InDesign objects are, as you'd expect, copied wholly into a library file. Although you can swap libraries with other users, you can't have a library in use by more than one person at a time.

To create a new library, choose Windows ➡ Library ➡ New, name and save the file, and hey, up pops a new, empty library panel that will look like Figure 12–1.

To get a page object into an open library file, click on it, then either click the New Item button in the library panel or choose Add Item from the panel's pop-up menu. You can also add everything on the page, in one fell swoop, by choosing *Add All Items on Page*. You can add guides to a library by selecting them and choosing *Add Item*. Items that you've placed will be named by the linked file name associated with them; InDesign objects and grouped objects will be unnamed when they're added to a library.

The library feature has some cool things in it that almost, but not quite, turn it into a baby digital asset management system. You can

Figure 12–1
New Library dialog box.

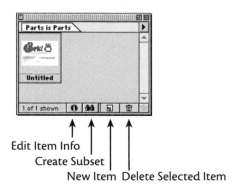

Edit Item Info
Create Subset
New Item   Delete Selected Item

search a library according to several criteria, and you can name and give a description to every object in the library and perform keyword searches on the description. You can also choose, for example, to show only those library items that are EPS or PDF files, or specify a before/after date, and you can combine these to come up with some pretty powerful filters for finding content.

To edit an item's description, double-click the item in the panel or click the Item Info button in the panel to show the dialog in Figure 12–2.

The Object Type pop-up rather foolishly will allow you to change the type from, say, Image to PDF, but apparently this pop-up seems to exist solely as a guide to library organization, and changing the object type will have no damaging consequences except possibly some future confusion. Enter a description or a few keywords in the Description field to help locate objects in the future.

The *Object type* will show as Geometry if you copy in any native InDesign objects, including guides. Pages will display, unsurprisingly, as Pages. Everything else will show as Image, EPS, PDF, or Text format.

Once you get a big ol' library going, it becomes a little messy to manage. You can keep multiple libraries open at once, and they'll all show up as tabbed panels in the main Library panel. Use the panel pop-up menu to add or close specific libraries.

However, if you do end up with a messy big ol' library, you can use the Subset feature to create a filtering mechanism for only display-

Figuare 12–2
Item Information dialog box.

Figuare 12–3
Subset dialog box.

ing objects that meet your search criteria. Click the little binoculars icon in the panel, or choose *Show Subset* from the pop-up menu.

The Subset dialog lets you choose a number of search options (Figure 12–3), and you can add more by clicking the More Choices button. The subset and search options are self-explanatory.

To add a library object to an open document, just drag it from the Library panel to the page. Easy. You can also choose *Place Item(s)* from the pop-up menu to plop one or more selected library objects onto the page. Any objects from a library, if linked, retain their links. Native objects are still native objects.

You lose the Import Options you normally get when placing an image or placing artwork, but the options that were set when the object was placed in the original document will carry through with the object when it is put into a library file.

Tagging Text

We already showed how you can import text that includes formatting tags, even if it came out of QuarkXPress or PageMaker files. To create tagged text in InDesign, select the desired text and choose File ➠ Export and choose *InDesign Tagged Text* from the pop-up menu. You'll see a few choices: Verbose vs. Abbreviated, and a choice of character encodings. Verbose tagging is mostly for your benefit, because with verbose tags you can see what they're really doing.

The abbreviated (should that not be "terse" instead?) tags are strange meaningless shorthand that you will not be able to understand. Files made with the verbose tags will be a little bigger than abbreviated ones, but it's probably not enough of a big deal to worry about unless you're exporting thousands and thousands of pages of text. If you want to see how these tags work, just export some tagged text, then open the results in a text editor or word processor. You will then see them in all their glory.

You can also choose a text encoding format when exporting tagged text. ASCII is, of course, the lowest common denominator format. Text exported as ASCII can be read by nearly any program ever created, but there are a few catches. ASCII accommodates up to 256 different characters, but only the first 127 are universally agreed upon.

The so-called high ASCII characters are used for a variety of things, such as accented and foreign characters or special characters like an em dash, but the actual ASCII codes used to represent them will vary according to the operating system.

InDesign codes nonstandard characters with a scheme that allows the characters to cross platforms successfully. For example, an em dash is represented as <0x2014> in a tagged-text export. There are other text encoding systems available when you export a file, such as ANSI, Unicode, Big 5, and Shift-JIS.

ANSI is a system used on MS-DOS and Windows systems, but it's not very well supported on the Mac.

Unicode is a fairly new standard that allows for thousands of characters, such as those used in non-Roman writing systems like Chinese or for non-Roman alphabets like Cyrillic or Hebrew.

InDesign supports Unicode internally and can import and export Unicode files, but there aren't too many other programs yet that support Unicode. It will become a very important interchange format within a few years, though.

Big 5 is an encoding system designed for Chinese characters, and Shift-JIS is a similar system for Japanese characters. These will eventually be supplanted by Unicode, but they exist for compatibility with current programs that support these encoding systems.

Why Is This Useful?   The biggest application of text tags is in database publishing. Any modern database management program like Filemaker Pro or Microsoft Access can insert formatting tags into an exported text file just about anywhere you like, resulting in, say, a seed catalog that's already formatted and just needs to have the images popped in.

You can just insert the most basic of formatting tags for things like bold or italic type, or you can go so far as to specify complete text styles in your tags, though this gets pretty tricky to set up as you can see from the example of tagged text shown in Figure 12–4.

As you can see, the complete definition of paragraph and character styles are exported for easy transfer to another document. You could also perform more advanced search and replace functions with a heavy-duty text editor, without messing up the tags, which will probably offer more powerful text mangling abilities beyond those that InDesign offers. Such an editor, for example, the MacOS-only

Figure 12–4
Tagged text.

```
<ASCII-MAC>
<DefineParaStyle:Body=<Nextstyle:Body><cSize:9.000000><p
BodyAlignment:Justify><cLeading:11.000000><pTabRuler:0.
000000,Left,.,0,;;0.000000,Left,.,0,;><cFont:MrsEaves>>
<ColorTable:=<Black:COLOR:CMYK:Process:0.000000,0.00000
0,0.000000,1.000000>>
<ParaStyle:Body><pDropCapCharacters:2><pDropCapLines:3>
<cSize:12.000000><cLeading:-1.000000><cFont:Adobe
Garamond>To the door of an inn in the provincial town
of N. there drew up a smart britchka<0x2014>a light
spring-carriage of the sort affected by bachelors,
retired lieutenant-colonels, staff-captains, land-own-
ers possessed of about a hundred souls, and, in short,
all persons who rank as gentlemen of the intermediate
category. In the britchka was seated such a gentle-
man<0x2014>a man who, though not handsome, was not
ill-favoured, not over-fat, and not over-thin. Also,
though not over-elderly, he was not over-young. His
arrival produced no stir in the town, and was accompa-
nied by no particular incident, beyond that a couple
```

BBEdit program, offers the ability to write UNIX *grep* expressions, which are impossibly obtuse directives allowing very powerful search and replace capabilities at the expense of a very steep learning curve.

Once you perform these functions, you can easily place the newly cleaned-up file back into an InDesign document. For example, you could replace all words in ALL CAPS with lowercase words that include tags for specifying that these words be set in italics. This is a common enough operation, especially with files that originate as plain ASCII files, like many online documents.

You could replace SGML or XML character attribute tags with InDesign tags, swapping

<cite>Bla bla bla</cite>

with

<cTypeface:Italic>Bla bla bla <cTypeface:>.

In the future, we expect that the ability to import files with markup tags like those used in SGML or XML will be available directly in InDesign, perhaps through a third-party plug-in, but for now, InDesign can't interpret any markup tags other than its own and those used in QuarkXPress and PageMaker.

When placing a tagged-text file, always click the Import Options checkbox in the Place File dialog (Figure 12–5). This will present the options for tagged text.

You can choose to override any styles defined in the tagged file as long as there's a style present in the InDesign document with the

InDesign has a few problems handling some tags out of QuarkXPress– character-level style tags appear to be the cause.

Figuare 12–5
Tags Import Options dialog box.

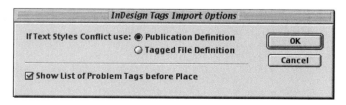

```
<ASCII-WIN>
<ParaStyle:><cTypeface:Italic>Bla bla bla, then some
more bla bla bla.<cTypeface:>
<ParaStyle:><cTypeface:Bold>Bla bla bla, then some
more bla bla bla.<cTypeface:>
<ParaStyle:><cTypeface:Regular>Bla bla bla, then some
more bla bla bla.<cTypeface:>
```

Figure 12–6.
Basic attributes.

same name, or you can choose to keep the style definitions in the tagged file. Styles imported from tagged files and preserved will have "copy" appended to the style name.

Clicking *Show List of Problem Tags before Place* will present any unrecognized tags in the file for your edification, and you have the option of ignoring these, saving the list of problematic tags to a log file, or canceling the import. This will probably only happen with files you've tagged by hand or tagged by text calculations in a database program.

There are some minimum required tags. For instance, if you aren't specifying styles and just want basic bold, italic, etc., text attributes, you only need to specify the text encoding method (and either MAC or WIN as a platform origin) and basic attributes, as in the example in Figure 12–6.

All formatting tags need to be preceded by an empty ParaStyle tag.

Plug-ins for InDesign

These plug-ins were shown or announced at the September 1999 Seybold Publishing Expo in San Francisco. Many others will become available by the time this tome is printed, bound, shipped, and shelved. Such is the nature of conventional publishing. These and others are available from The Power Xxchange, at 877-940-0600 or http://www.thepowerxchange.com

A2i, Inc., announced a plug-in that provides an active link to catalog data stored in A2i's xCat catalog publishing system, allowing users to manipulate and publish catalogs containing large, complex databases of product information. http://www.a2i.com

Advanced Firmware Development, the makers of Windows-based Graphics Publishing Workflow Series (GPS) software solutions, announced the general availability of Visual Capture for high-quality screen captures. http://www.advfirmware.com/dtp_tech.h

ALAP announced ShadowCaster to allow users to create soft drop shadows for any item directly within InDesign. ALAP's tool package, similar to XPert Tools, will provide additional features and enhancements to Adobe InDesign, allowing for increased user productivity. http://www.alap.com

American Computer Innovators, Inc., (ACI) will integrate the InDesign layout application as part of ACI's Dynamic Pagination solution and convert existing custom plug-ins, tool sets, and macros for use with InDesign, which will be integrated into the OpenPages Content Management database. http://www.aci-openpages.com

Baseview ProductionManagerPro has been designed to keep track of all the elements associated with an ad—graphics, fonts, logos, and more—and then flow them easily onto your pages.

Cascade Systems Inc. incorporated InDesign into the Cascade Merchant Publishing Solution, which enables merchants to plan and manage cross-media merchandising, advertising, and commerce activities in print and on the web. http://www.cascadenet.com

Cybergraphic announced that it will seamlessly integrate InDesign into its editorial product range, including such mainstream products as CyberPage and CyberNews.

Digital Zone International A/S announced support for InDesign in its media asset management and workflow software product, the Prelude Enterprise version 4.0.

Digital Technology International NewsSpeed 5.0 newspaper publishing system incorporates Adobe InDesign.

DK&A, Inc., announced development of a next generation imposition product, INposition ID to provide direct, integrated support to Adobe InDesign, the comprehensive new page layout and design application. http://www.dka.com

Em Software is porting its popular data and catalog automation plug-in products, to be called InData and InCatalog, to InDesign. www.emsoftware.com

These and others are available from The Power Xchange. 877-940-0600 or http://www.thepowerxchange.com/

Enfocus Software announced Enfocus PDF CheckUp plug-in for for automated preflighting of Adobe Portable Document Format (PDF) files saved in Adobe InDesign. http://www.enfocus.com

Harris Publishing Systems Corporation, a newspaper systems integrator, has integrated Adobe InDesign as part of their total publishing solution. http://www.harris.com/hpsc

HELIOS Software GmbH announced its network and prepress server software works with Adobe InDesign. HELIOS showed the integration of its EtherShare, PCShare, EtherShare OPI, PDF Handshake, and Print Preview servers. http://www.helios.com

LizardTech Inc. announced that it will offer a MrSID Portable Image Format plug-in for InDesign. http://www.lizardtech.com

Managing Editor Inc. (MEI) announced the MagForce magazine planning solution and its integration with InDesign—pagination planning and ad mapping software specially designed to streamline the book makeup process for magazine publishers. www.maned.com

MAPSOFT announced InForm, which enables the creation of Adobe Portable Document Format (PDF) links, bookmarks, articles, forms, action handlers and many other features in interactive PDF files.

Mediasystemen announced that the new generation of its current page make-up system, Olympus, is based on InDesign. Olympus will be part of the Forum News editorial system for publications. http://www.mediasys.triple-p.com

MVSPageInTools is an automatic layout product for the production of long, repetitive and complex documents.

North Atlantic Publishing Systems announced the NAPS Publishing System (NPS) with Adobe InDesign. www.napsys.com.

Pageflex, Inc., announced the availability of DesignOut, which exports InDesign files for use in Mpower variable data projects for customized marketing communications on demand. www.bitstream.com

PowrTools Software Inc., announced PowrTable 1.0, a table creation and editing plug-in for InDesign. This is actually the table program they give you with PageMaker. http://www.powrtools.com

Setanta Technology announced the incorporation of InDesign into its New World Workflow Manager for page production departments of newspaper publishers.

ShadeTree Marketing announced that it is shipping FRÆMZS for InDesign, a graphical plug-in that allows the user to generate custom borders directly within InDesign. http://www.Borderguys.com

Sii (System Integrators, Inc.) will integrate InDesign into its Insiight Editorial solution. http://www.sii.com

Ultimate Technographics announced InDesign in its prepress workflow, the On-Q Server, which includes imposition with Impostrip or IMPress, trapping with Trapeze, OPI and print serving with Ultimate Flow, and preflighting with Flight Simulator. www.ultimate-tech.com

Van Gennep-Media Automation Consulting BV announced that its PlanSystem production management software and DiHyph/InDesign, a hyphenation tool, will be available. www.vangennep.nl

Sonar Bookends InDex is an automated index and table of contents generator for automatic index generation. www.virginiasystems.com

WebWare announced its support of Adobe InDesign in its MAMBO (Media Asset Management by Objects) asset management software. http://www.WebWareCorp.com

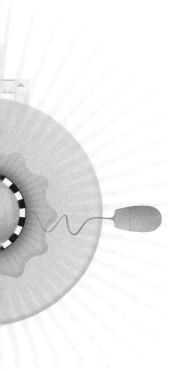

Appendix

Customizable Shortcuts

One of the most innovative—and most frightening—features of InDesign involves keyboard shortcuts. InDesign lets you use almost any feature without using the mouse—mouseless production, if you will. There is a humongous array of shortcuts to move through and modify documents. You can use the default InDesign shortcut set, the QuarkXPress 4 shortcut set, or—and here is the scary part—you can create your own shortcut set.

InDesign has a shortcut editor from that lets you view all shortcuts, generate a list of shortcuts, and edit or create your own shortcuts. The editor includes all commands that accept shortcuts but are undefined in the Default shortcut set. Using the shortcut editor, you can create shortcuts that suit your own workflow.

The Default or QuarkXPress shortcut sets cannot be edited. You can create a new set based on one of these sets and edit that new set.

Because of the complexity of the following list, please report any corrections to fxrppr@rit.edu

Shortcut Set: InDesign Default	**Shortcut Set: QuarkXPress 4.0**

EDIT MENU

Check Spelling

Mac: Command + I   Mac: Option + Command + L

PC: Control + I   PC: Alt + Control + W

Clear

[none defined]   [none defined]

Copy

Mac: Command + C   Mac: Command + C

PC: Control + C   PC: Control + C

Cut

Mac: Command + X   Mac: Command + X

PC: Control + X   PC: Control + X

Duplicate

Mac: Option + Command + D   Mac: Command + D

PC: Alt + Control + D   PC: Control + D

Edit Dictionary

[none defined]   [none defined]

Find Next

Mac: Option + Command + F   Mac: Option + Command + F

PC: Alt + Control + F   PC: Alt + Control + F

Find/Change

Mac: Command + F   Mac: Command + F

PC: Control + F   PC: Control + F

Paste

Mac: Command + V   Mac: Command + V

PC: Control + V   PC: Control + V

Shortcut Set: InDesign Default

Paste Into
Mac: Option + Command + V
PC: Alt + Control + V

Redo
Mac: Shift + Command + Z
PC: Shift + Control + Z

Select All
Mac: Command + A
PC: Control + A

Deselect All
Mac: Shift + Command + A
PC: Shift + Control + A

Step and Repeat
Mac: Shift + Command + V
PC: Shift + Control + V

Undo
Mac: Command + Z
PC: Control + Z

FILE MENU
Adobe Online
[none defined]

Close
Mac: Command + W
PC: Control + W

Color Settings
[none defined]

Shortcut Set: QuarkXPress 4.0

Paste Into
Mac: Option + Command + V
PC: [none defined]

Redo
Mac: Shift + Command + Z
PC: Shift + Control + Z

Select All
Mac: Command + A
PC: Control + A

Deselect All
Mac: Click
PC: Click

Step and Repeat
Mac: Option + Command + D
PC: Alt + Control + D

Undo
Mac: Command + Z
PC: Control + Z

FILE MENU
Adobe Online
[none defined]

Close
Mac: Command + W
PC: Control + W

Color Settings
[none defined]

Shortcut Set: InDesign Default

Document Setup
Mac: Option + Command + P
PC: Alt + Control + P

Edit Shortcuts
Mac: Shift + Option + Command + K
PC: Shift + Alt + Control + K

Export
Mac: Command + E
PC: Control + E

Links
Mac: Shift + Command + D
PC: Shift + Control + D

New Document
Mac: Command + N
PC: Control + N

Open Document
Mac: Command + O
PC: Control + O

Package
Mac: Shift + Option + Command + P
PC: Shift + Control + Atl + P

Page Setup
Mac: Shift + Command + P
PC: [none defined]

Shortcut Set: QuarkXPress 4.0

Document Setup
Mac: Shift + Option + Command + P
PC: Alt + Shift + Control + P

Edit Shortcuts
Mac: Shift + Option + Command + K
PC: Shift + Alt + Control + K

Export
Mac: Option + Command + E
PC: Alt + Control + E

Links
Mac: Option + F13
PC: Shift + F2

New Document
Mac: Command + N
PC: Control + N

Open Document
Mac: Command + O
PC: Control + O

Package
[none defined]

Page Setup
Mac: Option + Command + P
PC: [none defined]

Shortcut Set: InDesign Default

Place (Import)
Mac: Command + D
PC: Control + D

Preferences: Composition
[none defined]

Preferences: Dictionary
[none defined]

Preferences: General
Mac: Command + K
PC: Control + K

Preferences: Grids
[none defined]

Preferences: Guides
[none defined]

Preferences: Online Settings
[none defined]

Preferences: Text
[none defined]

Preferences: Units & Increments
[none defined]

Preflight
Mac: Shift + Option + Command + F
PC: Shift + Alt + Control + F

Shortcut Set: QuarkXPress 4.0

Place (Import)
Mac: Command + E
PC: Control + E

Preferences: Composition
[none defined]

Preferences: Dictionary
[none defined]

Preferences: General
Mac: Command + Y
PC: Control + Y

Preferences: Grids
[none defined]

Preferences: Guides
[none defined]

Preferences: Online Settings
[none defined]

Preferences: Text
[none defined]

Preferences: Units & Increments
[none defined]

Preflight
[none defined]

Shortcut Set: InDesign Default

Print
Mac: Command + P
PC: Control + P

Quit
Mac: Command + Q
PC: Control + Q

Revert
[none defined]

Save
Mac: Command + S
PC: Control + S

Save a Copy
Mac: Option + Command + S
PC: Alt + Control + S

Save As
Mac: Shift + Command + S
PC: Shift + Control + S

HELP MENU
Adobe Corporate News
[none defined]

Downloadables
[none defined]

Help Topics
Mac: Help
PC: F1

Shortcut Set: QuarkXPress 4.0

Print
Mac: Command + P
PC: Control + P

Quit
Mac: Command + Q
PC: Control + Q

Revert
[none defined]

Save
Mac: Command + S
PC: Control + S

Save a Copy
[none defined]

Save As
Mac: Option + Command + S
PC: Alt + Control + S

HELP MENU
Adobe Corporate News
[none defined]

Downloadables
[none defined]

Help Topics
Mac: Help
PC: F1

Shortcut Set: InDesign Default

How to Use Help
[none defined]

Online Registration
[none defined]

Top Issues
[none defined]

LAYOUT MENU
Create Guides
[none defined]

First Page
Mac: Shift + Command + Page Up
PC: Shift + Control + Page Up

Go Back
Mac: Command + Page Up
PC: Control + Page Up

Go Forward
Mac: Command + Page Down
PC: Control + Page Down

Insert Page Number
Mac: Option + Command + N
PC: Alt + Control + N

Last Page
Mac: Shift + Command + Page Down
PC: Shift + Control + Page Down

Shortcut Set: QuarkXPress 4.0

How to Use Help
[none defined]

Online Registration
[none defined]

Top Issues
[none defined]

LAYOUT MENU
Create Guides
[none defined]

First Page
Mac: Shift + Control + A
PC: Shift + Control + Page Up

Go Back
Mac: Command + Page Up
PC: Control + Page Up

Go Forward
Mac: Command + Page Down
PC: Control + Page Down

Insert Page Number
Mac: Command + 3
PC: Control + 3

Last Page
Mac: Shift + Control + D
PC: Shift + Control + Page Down

Shortcut Set: InDesign Default

Shortcut Set: QuarkXPress 4.0

Margins and Columns
[none defined]

Margins and Columns
[none defined]

Next Page
Mac: Shift + Page Down
PC: Shift + Page Down

Next Page
Mac: Control + Shift + L
PC: Shift + Page Down

Previous Page
Mac: Shift + Page Up
PC: Shift + Page Up

Previous Page
Mac: Control + Shift + K
PC: Shift + Page Up

Ruler Guides
[none defined]

Ruler Guides
[none defined]

OBJECT EDITING
Apply default fill and stroke colors
Mac: D
PC: D

OBJECT EDITING
Apply default fill and stroke colors
Mac: D
PC: D

Select 1 object down from selection
Mac: Option + Command + [
PC: Alt + Control + [

Select 1 object down from selection
Mac: Option + Command + [
PC: Alt + Control + [

Select 1 object up from selection
Mac: Option + Command +]
PC: Alt + Control +]

Select 1 object up from selection
Mac: Option + Command +]
PC: Alt + Control +]

Select all guides
Mac: Option + Command + G
PC: Alt + Control + G

Select all guides
Mac: Option + Command + G
PC: Alt + Control + G

Select through to bottom object
Mac: Shift + Option +Command + [
PC: Shift + Alt + Control + [

Select through to bottom object
Mac: Shift + Command + Option + Click
PC: Shift + Alt + Control + Click

Shortcut Set: InDesign Default

Select through to next object
Mac: Shift + Option + Command +]
PC: Shift + Alt +Control +]

Swap fill and stroke activation
Mac: X
PC: X

Swap fill and stroke colors
Mac: Shift + X
PC: Shift + X

OBJECT MENU
Arrange: Bring Forward
Mac: Command +]
PC: Control +]

Arrange: Bring To Front
Mac: Shift + Command +]
PC: Shift + Control +]

Arrange: Send Backward
Mac: Command + [
PC: Control + [

Arrange: Send To Back
Mac: Shift + Command + [
PC: Shift + Control + [

Clipping Path
[none defined]

Shortcut Set: QuarkXPress 4.0

Select through to next object
Mac: Shift + Option + Command + Click
PC: Shift + Alt + Control + Click

Swap fill and stroke activation
Mac: X
PC: X

Swap fill and stroke colors
Mac: Shift + X
PC: Shift + X

OBJECT MENU
Arrange: Bring Forward
Mac: Option + F5
PC: Control + F5

Arrange: Bring To Front
Mac: F5
PC: F5

Arrange: Send Backward
Mac: Shift + Option + F5
PC: Shift + Control + F5

Arrange: Send To Back
Mac: Shift + F5
PC: Shift + F5

Clipping Path
Mac: Option + Command + T
PC: Shift + Control + F10

Shortcut Set: InDesign Default

Compound Paths: Make
Mac: Command + 8
PC: Control + 8

Compound Paths: Release
Mac: Option + Command + 8
PC: Alt + Control + 8

Content: Graphic
[none defined]

Content: Text
[none defined]

Content: Unassigned
[none defined]

Corner Effects
Mac: Option + Command + R
PC: Alt + Control + R

Fitting: Center content
Mac: Shift + Command + E
PC: Shift + Control + E

Fitting: Fit content proportionally
Mac: Shift + Option + Command + E
PC: Shift + Alt + Control + E

Fitting: Fit content to frame
Mac: Option + Command + E
PC: Alt + Control + E

Shortcut Set: QuarkXPress 4.0

Compound Paths: Make
Mac: Command + 8
PC: Control + 8

Compound Paths: Release
Mac: Option + Command + 8
PC: Alt + Control + 8

Content: Graphic
[none defined]

Content: Text
[none defined]

Content: Unassigned
[none defined]

Corner Effects
Mac: Option + Command + R
PC: Alt + Control + R

Fitting: Center content
Mac: Shift + Command + M
PC: Shift + Control + M

Fitting: Fit content proportionally
Mac: Shift + Option + Command + F
PC: Shift + Alt + Control + M

Fitting: Fit content to frame
Mac: Shift + Command + F
PC: Shift + Control + M

Shortcut Set: InDesign Default

Fitting: Fit frame to content
Mac: Shift + Option + Command + V
PC: Shift + Alt + Control + V

Group
Mac: Command + G
PC: Control + G

Ungroup
Mac: Shift + Command + G
PC: Shift + Control + G

Image Color Settings
Mac: Shift + Option + Command + D
PC: Shift + Alt + Control + D

Lock Position
Mac: Command + L
PC: Control + L

Reverse Path
[none defined]

Text Frame Options
Mac: Command + B
PC: Control + B

Text Wrap
Mac: Option + Command + W
PC: Alt + Control + W

Unlock Position
Mac: Option + Command + L
PC: Alt + Control + L

Shortcut Set: QuarkXPress 4.0

Fitting: Fit frame to content
Mac: Shift + Option + Command + V
PC: Shift + Alt + Control + Alt + V

Group
Mac: Command + G
PC: Control + G

Ungroup
Mac: Command + U
PC: Control + U

Image Color Settings
Mac: Shift + Option + Command + D
PC: Shift + Alt + Control + D

Lock Position
Mac: F6
PC: F6

Reverse Path
[none defined]

Text Frame Options
[none defined]

Text Wrap
Mac: Command + T
PC: Control + T

Unlock Position
Mac: [none defined]
PC: Alt + Control + L

Shortcut Set: InDesign Default

OTHER
Close all
Mac: Shift + Option + Command + W
PC: Shift + Alt + Control + W

Close document
Mac: Shift + Command + W
PC: Shift + Control + W

Close document
Mac: [none defined]
PC: Control + F4

Create outlines without deleting text
Mac: Shift + Option + Command + O
PC: Shift + Alt + Control + O

New default document
Mac: Shift + Command + N
PC: Shift + Control +N

Next Window
Mac: [none defined]
PC: Control + F6

Previous Window
Mac: [none defined]
PC: Shift + Control + F6

Quit
Mac: [none defined]
PC: Alt + F4

Shortcut Set: QuarkXPress 4.0

OTHER
Close all
Mac: Option + Command + W
PC: Shift + Alt + Control + W

Close document
Mac: Shift + Command + W
PC: Shift + Control + W

Close document
Mac: [none defined]
PC: Control + F4

Create outlines without deleting text
Mac: Shift + Option + Command + O
PC: Shift + Alt + Control + O

New default document
Mac: Shift + Command + N
PC: [none defined]

Next Window
Mac: [none defined]
PC: Control + F6

Previous Window
Mac: [none defined]
PC: Shift + Control + F6

Quit
Mac: [none defined]
PC: Alt + F4

Shortcut Set: InDesign Default

Save all
Mac: Shift + Option + Command + S
PC: Shift + Control + Alt + S

Update missing font list
Mac: Shift + Option + Command + /
PC: Shift + Control + Alt + /

TEXT SELECTION
Find Next
Mac: Shift + F2
PC: Shift + F2

Load Find and Find Next instance
Mac: Shift + F1
PC: Shift + F1

Load Find with selected text
Mac: Command + F1
PC: Control + F1

Load Replace with selected text
Mac: Command + F2
PC: Control + F2

Move down one line
Mac: Down Arrow
PC: Down Arrow

Move to beginning of story
Mac: Command + Home
PC: Control + Home

Shortcut Set: QuarkXPress 4.0

Save all
Mac: Shift + Option + Command + S
PC: Shift + Alt + Control + O

Update missing font list
Mac: Shift + Option + Command + /
PC: Shift + Control + Alt + /

TEXT SELECTION
Find Next
Mac: Shift + F2
PC: [none defined]

Load Find and Find Next instance
Mac: Shift + F1
PC: Shift + F1

Load Find with selected text
Mac: Command + F1
PC: Control + F1

Load Replace with selected text
Mac: Command + F2
PC: Control + F2

Move down one line
Mac: Down Arrow
PC: Down Arrow

Move to beginning of story
Mac: Command + Home
PC: Control + Home

Shortcut Set: InDesign Default

Move to end of story
Mac: Command + End
PC: Control + End

Move to the end of the line
Mac: End
PC: End

Move to the left one character
Mac: Left Arrow
PC: Left Arrow

Move to the left one word
Mac: Command + Left Arrow
PC: Control + Left Arrow

Move to the next paragraph
Mac: Command + Down Arrow
PC: Control + Down Arrow

Move to the previous paragraph
Mac: Command + Up Arrow
PC: Control + Up Arrow

Move to the right one character
Mac: Right Arrow
PC: Right Arrow

Move to the right one word
Mac: Command + Right Arrow
PC: Control + Right Arrow

Shortcut Set: QuarkXPress 4.0

Move to end of story
Mac: Command + End
PC: Control + End

Move to the end of the line
Mac: End
PC: End

Move to the left one character
Mac: Left Arrow
PC: Left Arrow

Move to the left one word
Mac: Command + Left Arrow
PC: Control + Left Arrow

Move to the next paragraph
Mac: Command + Down Arrow
PC: Control + Down Arrow

Move to the previous paragraph
Mac: Command + Up Arrow
PC: Control + Up Arrow

Move to the right one character
Mac: Right Arrow
PC: Right Arrow

Move to the right one word
Mac: Command + Right Arrow
PC: Control + Right Arrow

Shortcut Set: InDesign Default

Move to the start of the line
Mac: Home
PC: Home

Move up one line
Mac: Up Arrow
PC: Up Arrow

Replace with Change To text
Mac: Command + F3
PC: Control + F3

**Replace with Change To text
   and Find Next**
Mac: Shift + F3
PC: Shift + F3

Select one character to the left
Mac: Shift + Left Arrow
PC: Shift + Left Arrow

Select one character to the right
Mac: Shift + Right Arrow
PC: Shift + Right Arrow

Select one line above
Mac: Shift + Up Arrow
PC: Shift + Up Arrow

Select one line below
Mac: Shift + Down Arrow
PC: Shift + Down Arrow

Shortcut Set: QuarkXPress 4.0

Move to the start of the line
Mac: Home
PC: Home

Move up one line
Mac: Up Arrow
PC: Up Arrow

Replace with Change To text
Mac: Command + F3
PC: Control + F3

**Replace with Change To text
   and Find Next**
Mac: Shift + F3
PC: Shift + F3

Select one character to the left
Mac: Shift + Left Arrow
PC: Shift + Left Arrow

Select one character to the right
Mac: Shift + Right Arrow
PC: Shift + Right Arrow

Select one line above
Mac: Shift + Up Arrow
PC: Shift + Up Arrow

Select one line below
Mac: Shift + Down Arrow
PC: Shift + Down Arrow

Shortcut Set: InDesign Default

Select one paragraph before
Mac: Shift + Command + Up Arrow
PC: Shift + Control + Up Arrow

Select one paragraph forward
Mac: Shift + Command + Down Arrow
PC: Shift + Control + Down Arrow

Select one word to the left
Mac: Shift + Command + Left Arrow
PC: Shift + Control + Left Arrow

Select one word to the right
Mac: Shift + Command + Right Arrow
PC: Shift + Control + Right Arrow

Select to beginning of story
Mac: Shift + Command + Home
PC: Shift + Control + Home

Select to end of story
Mac: Shift + Command + End
PC: Shift + Control + End

Select to the end of the line
Mac: Shift + End
PC: Shift + End

Select to the start of the line
Mac: Shift + Home
PC: Shift + Home

Shortcut Set: QuarkXPress 4.0

Select one paragraph before
Mac: Shift + Command + Up Arrow
PC: Shift + Control + Up Arrow

Select one paragraph forward
Mac: Shift + Command + Down Arrow
PC: Shift + Control + Down Arrow

Select one word to the left
Mac: Shift + Command + Left Arrow
PC: Shift + Control + Left Arrow

Select one word to the right
Mac: Shift + Command + Right Arrow
PC: Shift + Control + Right Arrow

Select to beginning of story
Mac: Shift + Command + Home
PC: Shift + Control + Home

Select to end of story
Mac: Shift + Command + End
PC: Shift + Control + End

Select to the end of the line
Mac: Shift + End
PC: Shift + End

Select to the start of the line
Mac: Shift + Home
PC: Shift + Home

Shortcut Set: InDesign Default

TOOLS, PALETTES
Activate last-used field in palette
Mac: Command + `
PC: Control + `

Apply color
Mac: , (comma)
PC: , (comma)

Apply gradient
Mac: . (period)
PC: . (period)

Apply none
Mac: / (slash)
PC: / (slash)

Direct Selection Tool
Mac: A
PC: A

Ellipse Tool
Mac: L
PC: L

Ellipse Tool (select hidden tools)
Mac: Shift + L
PC: Shift + L

Gradient Tool
Mac: G
PC: G

Shortcut Set: QuarkXPress 4.0

TOOLS, PALETTES
Activate last-used field in palette
Mac: Command + `
PC: Control + `

Apply color
Mac: , (comma)
PC: , (comma)

Apply gradient
Mac: . (period)
PC: . (period)

Apply none
Mac: / (slash)
PC: / (slash)

Direct Selection Tool
Mac: A
PC: A

Ellipse Tool
Mac: L
PC: L

Ellipse Tool (select hidden tools)
Mac: Shift + L
PC: Shift + L

Gradient Tool
Mac: G
PC: G

Shortcut Set: InDesign Default

Hand Tool
Mac: H
PC: H

Line Tool
Mac: E
PC: E

Pen Tool
Mac: P
PC: P

Pen Tool (select hidden tools)
Mac: Shift + P
PC: Shift + P

Polygon Tool
Mac: N
PC: N

Polygon Tool (select hidden tools)
Mac: Shift + N
PC: Shift + N

Rectangle Tool
Mac: M
PC: M

Rectangle Tool (select hidden tools)
Mac: Shift + M
PC: Shift + M

Shortcut Set: QuarkXPress 4.0

Hand Tool
Mac: H
PC: H

Line Tool
Mac: E
PC: E

Pen Tool
Mac: P
PC: P

Pen Tool (select hidden tools)
Mac: Shift + P
PC: Shift + P

Polygon Tool
Mac: N
PC: N

Polygon Tool (select hidden tools)
Mac: Shift + N
PC: Shift + N

Rectangle Tool
Mac: M
PC: M

Rectangle Tool (select hidden tools)
Mac: Shift + M
PC: Shift + M

Shortcut Set: InDesign Default

Rotate Tool
Mac: R
PC: R

Scale Tool
Mac: S
PC: S

Scale Tool (select hidden tools)
Mac: Shift + S
PC: Shift + S

Scissors Tool
Mac: C
PC: C

Selection Tool
Mac: V
PC: V

**Toggle between Selection
  and Direct Selection tool**
Mac: Command + Tab **or**
    Control + Command

Toggle to add anchor point tool
Mac: + **or** Num +
PC: + **or** Num +

Toggle to delete anchor point tool
Mac: - **or** Num -
PC: - **or** Num -

Shortcut Set: QuarkXPress 4.0

Rotate Tool
Mac: R
PC: R

Scale Tool
Mac: S
PC: S

Scale Tool (select hidden tools)
Mac: Shift + S
PC: Shift + S

Scissors Tool
Mac: C
PC: C

Selection Tool
Mac: V
PC: V

**Toggle between Selection
  and Direct Selection tool**
Mac: Command + Tab or
    Shift + Control + Command + F8

Toggle to add anchor point tool
Mac: + or Num +
PC: + or Num +

Toggle to delete anchor point tool
Mac: - or Num -
PC: - or Num -

Shortcut Set: InDesign Default	Shortcut Set: QuarkXPress 4.0

Type Tool
Mac: T
PC: T

Type Tool
Mac: T
PC: T

Zoom Tool
Mac: Z
PC: Z

Zoom Tool
Mac: Z
PC: Z

TYPE MENU
Character attributes
Mac: Command + T
PC: Control + T

TYPE MENU
Character attributes
Mac: Shift + Command + D
PC: Shift + Control + D

Character styles
Mac: Shift + F11
PC: Shift + F11

Character styles
Mac: Shift + F11
PC: Shift + F11

Create Outlines
Mac: Shift + Command + O
PC: Shift + Control + O

Create Outlines
Mac: Shift + Command + O
PC: Shift + Control + O

Insert Character
[none defined]

Insert Character
[none defined]

Paragraph (Formats)
Mac: Command + M
PC: Control + M

Paragraph (Formats)
Mac: Shift + Command + F
PC: Shift + Control + F

Paragraph Styles
Mac: F11
PC: F11

Paragraph Styles
Mac: F11
PC: F11

Shortcut Set: InDesign Default

Show Hidden Characters
Mac: Option + Command + I
PC: Alt + Control + I
        (toggles on/off)

Size: Other
[none defined]

Story
[none defined]

Tabs
Mac: Shift + Command + T
PC: Shift + Control + T

TYPOGRAPHY
Align center
Mac: Shift + Command + C
PC: Shift + Control + C

Align force justify
Mac: Shift + Command + F
PC: Shift + Control + F

Align justify
Mac: Shift + Command + J
PC: Shift + Control + J

Align left
Mac: Shift + Command + L
PC: Shift + Control + L

Shortcut Set: QuarkXPress 4.0

Show Hidden Characters
Mac: Command + I
PC: Control + I
        (toggles on/off)

Size: Other
[none defined]

Story
[none defined]

Tabs
Mac: Shift + Command + T
PC: Shift + Control + T

TYPOGRAPHY
Align center
Mac: Shift + Command + C
PC: Shift + Control + C

Align force justify
Mac: Shift + Option + Command + J
PC: Shift + Alt + Control + J

Align justify
Mac: Shift + Command + J
PC: Shift + Control + J

Align left
Mac: Shift + Command + L
PC: Shift + Control + L

Shortcut Set: InDesign Default

Decrease baseline shift x 5
Mac: Shift + Option + Command +
Down Arrow
PC: Shift + Control + Alt + Down
Arrow

Decrease kerning/tracking
Mac: Option + Left Arrow
PC: Alt + Left Arrow

Decrease kerning/tracking x 5
Mac: Option + Command + Left Arrow
PC: Alt + Control + Left Arrow

Decrease leading
Mac: Option + Up Arrow
PC: Alt + Up Arrow

Decrease leading x 5
Mac: Option + Command + Up Arrow
PC: Control + Alt + Up Arrow

Decrease point size
Mac: Shift + Command + , (comma)
PC: Shift + Control + , (comma)

Shortcut Set: QuarkXPress 4.0

Decrease baseline shift x 5
Mac: Shift + Option + Command +
Down Arrow
PC: Shift + Control + Alt + Down
Arrow

Decrease kerning/tracking
Mac: Shift + Option + Command + [or
Option + Left Arrow
PC: Alt + Left Arrow

Decrease kerning/tracking x 5
Mac: Shift + Command + [or
Option + Command + Left Arrow
PC: Alt + Control + Left Arrow

Decrease leading
Mac: Option + Shift + Command + ; or
Option + Up Arrow
PC: Alt + Up Arrow or
Shift + Alt +Control + ;

Decrease leading x 5
Mac: Shift + Command + ; or
Option + Command + Up Arrow
PC: Alt + Control + Up Arrow or
Shift + Control + ;

Decrease point size
Mac: Shift + Command + , (comma)
PC: Shift + Control + , (comma)

Shortcut Set: InDesign Default

Decrease point size x 5
Mac: Shift + Option + Command + ,
    (comma)
PC: Shift + Alt + Control +, (comma)

Define character style
[none defined]

Define paragraph style
[none defined]

Increase baseline shift
Mac: Shift + Option + Up Arrow
PC: Shift + Alt + Up Arrow

Increase baseline shift x 5
Mac: Option + Shift + Command + Up
    Arrow
PC: Shift + Alt + Control + Up Arrow

Increase kerning/tracking
Mac: Option + Right Arrow
PC: Alt + Right Arrow

Increase kerning/tracking x 5
Mac: Option + Command + Right Arrow
PC: Alt + Control + Right Arrow

Shortcut Set: QuarkXPress 4.0

Decrease point size x 5
Mac: Shift + Option + Command + ,
PC: Shift + Alt + Control + , (comma)

Define character style
[none defined]

Define paragraph style
[none defined]

Increase baseline shift
Mac: Shift + Option + Command + = or
    Shift + Option + Up Arrow
PC: Shift + Alt + Up Arrow or
    Shift + Alt + Control + D

Increase baseline shift x 5
Mac: Shift + Option + Command + Up
    Arrow
PC: Shift + Alt + Control + Up Arrow

Increase kerning/tracking
Mac: Shift + Option + Command +] or
    Option + Right Arrow
PC: Alt + Right Arrow or
    Shift + Alt + Control +]

Increase kerning/tracking x 5
Mac: Shift + Command +] or
    Option + Command +Right Arrow
PC: Alt + Control + Right Arrow or
    Shift + Control +]

Shortcut Set: InDesign Default

Increase leading
Mac: Option + Down Arrow
PC: Alt + Down Arrow

Increase leading x 5
Mac: Option + Command + Down Arrow
PC: Control + Alt + Down Arrow

Increase point size
Mac: Shift + Command + . (period)
PC: Shift + Control + . (period)

Increase point size x 5
Mac: Shift + Option + Command + .
      (period)
PC: Shift + Alt + Control . (period)

Insert bullet
Mac: [none defined]
PC: Alt + 8

Insert copyright symbol
Mac: Option + G
PC: Alt + G

Insert discretionary hyphen
Mac: Shift + Command + - (hyphen)
PC: Shift + Control + - (hyphen) **or**
      Shift + Command + Num + -

Shortcut Set: QuarkXPress 4.0

Increase leading
Mac: Option + Down Arrow or
      Shift + Option +Command + `
PC: Alt + Down Arrow

Increase leading x 5
Mac: Option + Command + Down Arrow
      or Shift + Command + `
PC: Alt + Control + Down Arrow **or**
      Shift + Control + `

Increase point size
Mac: Shift + Command + . (period)
PC: Shift + Control + . (period)

Increase point size x 5
Mac: Option + Shift + Command + .
PC: Shift + Alt + Control +. (period)

Insert bullet
Mac: [none defined]
PC: Alt + 8

Insert copyright symbol
Mac: Option + G
PC: Alt + G

Insert discretionary hyphen
Mac: Command + - (hyphen)
PC: Shift + Control + - (hyphen) **or**
      Shift + Control + Num + - **or**
      Control + - (hyphen)

Shortcut Set: InDesign Default

Insert ellipsis
Mac: Option + ;
PC: Alt + ;

Insert em space
Mac: Shift + Command + M
PC: Shift + Control + M

Insert em dash
Mac: Shift + Option + - (hyphen)
PC: Shift + Alt + - (hyphen)

Insert en dash
Mac: Option + - (hyphen)
PC: Alt + - (hyphen)

Insert en space
Mac: Option + Space
PC: [none defined]

Insert figure space
Mac: Shift + Option + Command + 8
PC: Shift + Control + Alt + 8

Insert flush space
Mac: Shift + Option + Command + 8
PC: Shift + Alt + Control + J

Insert hair space
Mac: Shift + Option + Command + I
PC: Shift + Alt + Control + I

Shortcut Set: QuarkXPress 4.0

Insert ellipsis
Mac: Option + ;
PC: Alt + ;

Insert em space
Mac: Shift + Option + Space
PC: Shift + Control + 5

Insert em dash
Mac: Shift + Option + - (hyphen)
PC: Shift + Alt + - (hyphen) **or**
         Shift + Control + =

Insert en dash
Mac: Option + - (hyphen)
PC: Alt + - (hyphen) or
         Shift + Alt + Control + - (hyphen)

Insert en space
Mac: Option + Space
PC: Shift + Control + 6

Insert figure space
Mac: [none defined]
PC: Shift + Control + Alt + 8

Insert flush space
Mac: Shift + Option + Command + J
PC: Shift + Alt + Control +J

Insert hair space
Mac: Shift + Option + Command + I
PC: Shift + Alt + Control + I

Shortcut Set: InDesign Default

Insert nonbreaking hyphen
Mac: Option + Command + - (hyphen)
PC: Alt + Control + - (hyphen)

Insert nonbreaking space
Mac: Option + Command + X
PC: Alt + Control + X

Insert paragraph symbol
Mac: [none defined]
PC: Alt + 7

Insert punctuation space
[none defined]

Insert registered trademark mark
Mac: [none defined]
PC: Alt + 2

Insert right double quote
Mac: [none defined]
PC: Alt + Shift + [

Insert right single quote
Mac: [none defined]
PC: Alt + Shift +]

Insert section name
Mac: Shift + Option + Command + N
PC: Shift + Alt + Control + N

Shortcut Set: QuarkXPress 4.0

Insert nonbreaking hyphen
Mac: Command + = **or**
        Option + Command + - (hyphen)
PC: Alt + Control + - (hyphen)

Insert nonbreaking space
Mac: Command + 5 or
        Option + Command + X - (hyphen)
PC: Alt + Control + X - (hyphen)

Insert paragraph symbol
Mac: [none defined]
PC: Alt + 7

Insert punctuation space
[none defined]

Insert registered trademark mark
Mac: [none defined]
PC: Alt + 2

Insert right double quote
Mac: Shift + Option + [
PC: Alt + Shift + [

Insert right single quote
Mac: Shift + Option +]
PC: Alt + Shift +]

Insert section name
Mac: Shift + Option + Command + N
PC: Shift + Alt + Control + N

Shortcut Set: InDesign Default

Insert thin space
Mac: Shift + Option + Space
PC: [none defined]

Insert trademark
Mac: Option + 2
PC: Alt + R

Keep options
Mac: Option + Command + K
PC: Alt + Control + K

Normal horizontal text scale
Mac: Shift + Command + X
PC: Shift + Control + X

Normal vertical text scale
Mac: Shift + Option + Command + X
PC: Shift + Alt + Control + X

Paragraph rules
Mac: Option + Command + J
PC: Alt + Control + J

Recompose all stories
Mac: Option + Command + /
PC: Alt + Control + /

Redefine character style
Mac: Shift + Option + Command + C
PC: Shift + Alt + Control + C

Shortcut Set: QuarkXPress 4.0

Insert thin space
Mac: Shift + Option + Space
PC: Shift + Alt + Space

Insert trademark
Mac: Option + 2
PC: Alt + R

Keep options
Mac: Option + Command + K
PC: Alt + Control + K

Normal horizontal text scale
Mac: Shift + Command + X
PC: Shift + Control + X or
      Control +]

Normal vertical text scale
Mac: Shift + Option + Command + X
PC: Shift + Alt + Control + X

Paragraph rules
Mac: Shift + Command + J
PC: Alt + Control + J or
      Shift + Control + N

Recompose all stories
Mac: Option + Command + /
PC: Alt + Control + /

Redefine character style
Mac: Shift + Option + Command + C
PC: Shift + Alt + Control + C

Shortcut Set: InDesign Default

Redefine paragraph style
Mac: Shift + Option + Command + R
PC: Shift + Alt + Control + R

Reset kerning and tracking
Mac: Shift + Command + Q
PC: Shift + Control + Q

Switch composer
Mac: Shift + Option + Command + T
PC: Shift + Alt + Control + T

**Toggle typographer's
  quotes preference**
Mac: Shift + Option + Command + '
PC: Shift + Alt + Control + '

VIEW MENU
Actual Size
Mac: Command + 1
PC: Control + 1

Display Master Items
Mac: Command + Y
PC: Control + Y

Entire Pasteboard
Mac: Shift + Option + Command + 0
PC: Shift + Alt + Control + 0

Fit Page In Window
Mac: Command + 0
PC: Control + 0

Shortcut Set: QuarkXPress 4.0

Redefine paragraph style
Mac: Shift + Option + Command + R
PC: Shift + Alt + Control + R

Reset kerning and tracking
Mac: Shift + Command + Q
PC: Shift + Control + Q

Switch composer
Mac: Shift + Option + Command + T
PC: Shift + Alt + Control + T

**Toggle typographer's
  quotes preference**
Mac: [none defined]
PC: Shift + Alt + Control + '

VIEW MENU
Actual Size
Mac: Command + 1
PC: Control + 1

Display Master Items
[none defined]

Entire Pasteboard
Mac: Option + Command + 0
PC: Alt + Control + 0

Fit Page In Window
Mac: Command + 0
PC: Control + 0

Shortcut Set: InDesign Default

Fit Spread In Window
Mac: Option + Command + 0
PC: Control + Alt + 0

Hide Guides
Mac: Command + ;
PC: Control + ;

Hide Rulers
Mac: Command + R
PC: Control + R
       (toggles on/off)

Lock Guides
Mac: Option + Command + ;
PC: Alt + Control + ;

Show Baseline Grid
Mac: Option + Command + ' (prime)
PC: Alt + Control + ' (prime)

Show Document Grid
Mac: Command + ' (prime)
PC: Control + ' (prime)

Show Frame edges
Mac: Command + H
PC: Control + H

Show Text Threads
Mac: Option + Command + Y
PC: Alt + Control + Y

Shortcut Set: QuarkXPress 4.0

Fit Spread In Window
[none defined]

Hide Guides
Mac: F7
PC: F7

Hide Rulers
Mac: Command + R
PC: Control + R
       (toggles on/off)

Lock Guides
Mac: Option + Command + ;
PC: Alt + Control + ;

Show Baseline Grid
Mac: Option + F7
PC: Control + F7

Show Document Grid
Mac: Command + ' (prime)
PC: Control + ' (prime)

Show Frame edges
Mac: [none defined]
PC: Control + H

Show Text Threads
Mac: Option + Command + Y
PC: Alt + Control + Y

Shortcut Set: InDesign Default	Shortcut Set: QuarkXPress 4.0

Snap to Document Grid

Mac: Shift + Command + ' (prime)

PC: Shift + Control + ' (prime)

Snap to Document Grid

[none defined]

Snap to Guides

Mac: Shift + Command + ;

PC: Shift + Control + ;

Snap to Guides

Mac: Shift + F7

PC: Shift + F7

Zoom In

Mac: Command + (plus)

PC: Control + =

Zoom In

Mac: Control + Click

PC: [none defined]

Zoom Out

Mac: Command + - (hyphen)

PC: Control + - (hyphen)

Zoom Out

Mac: Control + Shift + Click

VIEWS, NAVIGATION

100% size

[none defined]

VIEWS, NAVIGATION

100% size

Mac: Command + 1

PC: Control + 1

200% size

Mac: Command + 2

PC: Control + 2

200% size

[none defined]

400% size

Mac: Command + 4

PC: Control + 4

400% size

[none defined]

50% size

Mac: Command + 5

PC: Control + 5

50% size

[none defined]

Shortcut Set: InDesign Default

Access page number box
Mac: Command + J
PC: Control + J

Access zoom percentage box
Mac: Option + Command + 5
PC: Alt + Control + 5

Change Image Display preference
Mac: Shift + Command + F5
PC: Shift + Control + F5

First spread
Mac: Option + Shift + Page Up
PC: Shift + Alt + Page Up

Fit selection in window
Mac: Option + Command + 0
PC: Alt + Control + =

Force redraw
Mac: Shift + F5
PC: Shift + F5

Go to first frame
Mac: Shift + Option + Command + Page
      Up
PC: Shift + Alt + Control + Page Up

Go to last frame
Mac: Shift + Option + Command + Page
      Down
PC: Shift + Alt + Control + Page Down

Shortcut Set: QuarkXPress 4.0

Access page number box
Mac: Command + J
PC: Control + J

Access zoom percentage box
Mac: Control + V or
      Option + Command + S
PC: Alt + Control + 5 or
      Alt + Control + V

Change Image Display preference
Mac: Shift + Command + F5
PC: [none defined]

First spread
Mac: Shift + Option + Page Up
PC: Shift + Alt + Page Up

Fit selection in window
Mac: Option + Command + 0
PC: Alt + Control + =

Force redraw
Mac: Option + Command + . (period)
PC: Shift + Escape

Go to first frame
Mac: Shift + Option + Command + Page
      Up
PC: Shift + Alt + Control + Page Up

Go to last frame
Mac: Shift + Option + Command + Page
      Down
PC: Shift + Alt + Control + Page Down

Shortcut Set: InDesign Default

Go to next frame
Mac: Option + Command + Page Down
PC: Alt + Control + Page Down

Go to previous frame
Mac: Option + Command + Page Up
PC: Alt + Control + Page Up

Last spread
Mac: Shift + Option + Page Down
PC: Shift + Alt + Page Down

Next spread
Mac: Option + Page Down
PC: Alt + Page Down

Previous spread
Mac: Option + Page Up
PC: Alt + Page Up

Scroll down one screen
Mac: Page Down
PC: Page Down

Scroll up one screen
Mac: Page Up
PC: Page Up

**Toggle between current
and previous views**
Mac: Option + Command + 2
PC: Alt + Control + 2

Shortcut Set: QuarkXPress 4.0

Go to next frame
Mac: Option + Command + Page Down
PC: Alt + Control + Page Down

Go to previous frame
Mac: Option + Command + Page Up
PC: Alt + Control + Page Up

Last spread
Mac: Shift + Option + Page Down
PC: Shift + Alt + Page Down

Next spread
Mac: Option + Page Down
PC: Alt + Page Down

Previous spread
Mac: Option + Page Up
PC: Alt + Page Up

Scroll down one screen
Mac: Page Down
PC: Page Down

Scroll up one screen
Mac: Page Up
PC: Page Up

**Toggle between current
and previous views**
Mac: Option + Command + 2
PC: Alt + Control + 2

Shortcut Set: InDesign Default	**Shortcut Set: QuarkXPress 4.0**
WINDOW MENU	**WINDOW MENU**
Align	**Align**
Mac: F8	Mac: Command + , (comma)
PC: F8	PC: Control + , (comma)
Attributes	**Attributes**
[none defined]	[none defined]
Cascade	**Cascade**
[none defined]	[none defined]
Color	**Color**
Mac: F6	[none defined]
PC: F6	
Gradient	**Gradient**
[none defined]	[none defined]
Layers	**Layers**
Mac: F7	[none defined]
PC: F7	
Libraries: New	**Libraries: New**
[none defined]	Mac: Option + Command + N
	PC: Alt + Control + N
Libraries: Open	**Libraries: Open**
Mac: Shift + Option + Command + L	Mac: Shift + Option + Command + L
PC: Shift + Alt + Control + L	PC: Shift + Alt + Control + L
Navigator	**Navigator**
[none defined]	[none defined]

Shortcut Set: InDesign Default

New Window
[none defined]

Pages
Mac: F12
PC: F12

Stroke
Mac: F10
PC: F10

Swatch Libraries: Web
[none defined]

Swatches
Mac: F5
PC: F5

Tile
[none defined]

Tools
[none defined]

Transform
Mac: F9
PC: F9

Shortcut Set: QuarkXPress 4.0

New Window
[none defined]

Pages
Mac: F10
PC: F4

Stroke
Mac: Command + B
PC: Control + B

Swatch Libraries: Web
[none defined]

Swatches
Mac: F12
PC: F12

Tile
[none defined]

Tools
Mac: F8
PC: F8

Transform
Mac: F9
PC: F9

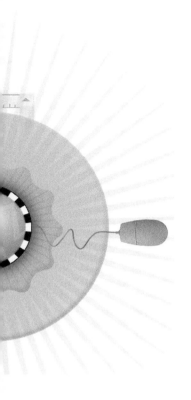

INDEX